❧ The Golden Riviera

also by Roderick Cameron

My Travel's History
Equator Farm
Shadows from India →
Time of the Mango Flowers
Shells
The Golden Haze
Viceroyalties of the West
Australia: History and Horizons

A Detail from the painting by Graham Sutherland is reproduced by kind permission of Olivetti and Mr Giorgio Soavi.

Cover design by John Alcorn.

The Golden Riviera

by Roderick Cameron

Editions Limited
Honolulu

First published by:
Weidenfeld and Nicolson
London 1975

Re-published in 1984 by:
Editions Limited
1123 Kapahulu Avenue
Honolulu, Hawaii 96816

ISBN 0-9607938-8-7

Printed in Singapore

Ce livre est dedié à Gilbert Occelli

Contents

Illustrations

The author and publishers are most grateful to the above copyright owners for permission to reproduce the pictures. All other photographs were taken by the author.

✋

Acknowledgements

I have spent several years in assembling the material for *The Golden Riviera* and would like to thank the people who have helped me. First comes my cousin, Douglas Cooper, for introducing me to M. Jean-Maurice Rouquette, Conservateur des Musées d'Arles, a lively, highly intelligent individual, a professional archaeologist with an all absorbing interest in his work. Accompanied by M. Rouquette I spent three fascinating days delving into Arles' Roman past, a past that listening to Rouquette appeared almost contemporary. Douglas Cooper also introduced me to M. Georges de Loÿe, the Conservateur en Chef of the Musée Calvet at Avignon who facilitated my photographing paintings in his care.

Nearer to home I would like to thank M.L. Thevenon of the Palais Lascaris at Nice for his kind cooperation, also Mlle Mouchot, Conservateur du Musée d'Archéologie at Cimiez. At the same time I would like to thank Monsieur Batier, Directeur des Musées de Nice who proved very patient in spite of all my demands, as did Jacques Bounin, a friend of long standing and Délégué aux Affaires Culturelles for the Alpes Maritimes. His humour and wisdom helped considerably in guiding me through the tortuous pages of Nice's history. Prince Louis de Polignac, another old friend and Director of Monte-Carlo's sbm also proved of assistance and with him Madame Merino the company's director of public relations. Mrs St George Saunders of Writer's and Speaker's Research has, as usual, saved me a great deal of spade work with her compiled lists of available works and her intuitive flair.

My gratitude is also due to Mr Gerald Yorke for allowing me to quote from Lady Polwarth, his ancestress's unpublished letters on Nice, and last but not least comes Mlle Yvonne Molinari who has sat uncomplainingly hour after hour taking down my dictation on her typewriter and once having produced the manuscript in legible form, suffered at least three re-writings.

It now only remains for me to express my gratitude to Graham Sutherland for allowing me to reproduce one of his water colours, painted originally for a private edition of his works printed by the house of Olivetti in Italy.

❧1

The South of France, a Bird's Eye View

The South of France, to most people, has come to mean the Riviera, but strictly speaking it should also include Provence. The Côte d'Azur of the poster extends from Marseilles to Menton and, geographically speaking, includes the departments of the Bouches-du-Rhône, the Var, and the Alpes Maritimes – is, in fact, the rocky, sea-washed base of a triangle, the other two sides of which encompass the hinterland, the Basses Alpes and the Vaucluse, two further departments without which the picture remains incomplete.

The south, whether arriving by train or driving down by car – one flies too high to include travelling by air – makes its appearance a little below Valence where the Rhône Valley suddenly widens out. Equally abrupt is the change in climate: the moisture begins to evaporate leaving the sky all but cloudless, and the air, crystalline clear, takes on a wonderful transparency. A luminous dust powders the horizon and buildings shine in the distance. Imperceptibly, almost, the dark, glossy green of the north has given way to the subtle, muted hues of the olive – 'smoke puffs' as Henry James refers to them when driving through Provence. It is a fascinating country, a part of France, yet so entirely different. Indeed Provence was an independent state up until the end of the fifteenth century and might, quite easily, have absorbed all the territory that eventually was to become France in much the same way that Saxony or Bavaria might have done in Germany when Prussia took over in 1871. There is a difference, also, amongst the people; they are Mediterranean and of very mixed blood, the Ligurians, the original inhabitants, having intermarried, first with the Phoenicians, then the Greeks, the Romans and even the Saracens. Each current of uniting blood naturally brought with it some new superstition or belief.

The coast was first colonised by the Greeks in about 600 BC, followed shortly thereafter by the Romans who liked it so well that they came to regard it as part of their own country rather than a colony the far side of the Alps. They preferred it to their own 'riviera' where the mountains pushed straight into the sea. Two of Rome's empresses are known to have pitched over the Via Aurelia in their litters to winter at Cimiez, the Roman settlement above the Greek port of Nice. Arles, during the first part of the fourth century, was so popular with the Emperor Constantine that for a while it became his chosen seat of power, his eldest son being born there, and the grandeur of this past has never really wholly died. Nor must one forget the popes in exile at Avignon. For nearly a century this city became the capital of Christendom.

Given time to reflect an endless list of names and events come to mind: St Louis at Aigues Mortes, embarking for the crusades; Petrarch at Avignon and his melancholy *Canzoniere* written for the beautiful Laura whom he met one spring morning when going to church. She had long golden hair and wore a green dress embroidered with violets. But Laura was already married and seems to have avoided the ardent advances of her impetuous admirer. Her circumspect behaviour only incited the poet's longing and for twenty-one years, until Laura died, he poured out his heart to her in, perhaps, the most beautiful love poems eyer written. Later one meets with the sympathetic Roi René, Duke of Bar and of Lorraine, Duke of Anjou and Count of Provence. He moves from kingdom to kingdom and was often at Angers but preferred Provence, travelling there by galley, sailing first up the Loire, then transferring to the Rhône, eventually coming to rest directly beneath the walls of his castle at Tarascon. His flotilla moves slowly from town to town, banners flying, the decks piled high with the royal furniture covered over with tarpaulins stitched in grey, black and white, the colours of the King's livery, the colours we are to find again in the beautiful primitive *Le Buisson Ardent* by Nicholas Froment hanging in the cathedral at Aix. René and his second wife, Jeanne de Laval, were the donors and their portraits form the pendants of the triptych.

But what of the coast itself – the base of our triangle? It was much slower to develop and the Riviera, as we know it now, is, in point of fact, a product of the last century, Nice having been little more than an overgrown village when Dr Smollett wintered there for his health in 1763. Monaco at the same period consisted of 'two or three streets upon a precipitous rock'; while Cannes, further down the coast, could be counted a mere settlement of fisherfolk hidden away among rushes and was so to remain until Lord Brougham, prevented from crossing the frontier to Nice by an outbreak of cholera, discovered it in 1834. Nice, it will be remembered, was Italian, the Var river, just short of the town, being the boundary between the two countries until it was definitely annexed to France by Napoleon III in 1860.

To the general traveller in the eighteenth century, south and south-eastern France appeared as little more than a rather uncomfortable corridor to Italy. Only a few of the better informed regarded towns such as Arles, Nîmes and Avignon as being of any interest other than staging places on the route to Genoa, Florence and Rome. Part of the trouble, of course, was the question of transport. Travel along the coast was mostly by small vessels known as *feluccas* and to get past Nice, by land, was impossible unless one was willing to travel by mule. In 1805 Napoleon ordered the construction of his famous road into Italy and this ribboned along the top of the Maritime Alps but, like them, on reaching the eastern extremity of the littoral plunged directly down to the sea. The traveller, in other words, got no further than Menton. There were also those who negotiated the mountain reaches to Genoa by carrying-chair, or on mule back, but it was not a form of locomotion that could be recommended to everybody. Indeed, the equitable climate appears to have been this region's only real asset, one that, prior to the habit of sporting oneself in the sea (a pastime indulged in by cranky old kings in the near-freezing waters of the English Channel) could really only appeal to the ailing and the decrepit. The ailing, during the eighteenth century, consisted, in large majority, of those suffering from lung ailments and these were generally treated, if treated at all, at Montpellier. It was pure chance that decided the tubercular Dr Tobias Smollett to pick on Nice. Smollett had been serving as surgeon's assistant in the British Navy, then engaged in the War of Austrian Succession. The English allied to the House of Savoy against France, the fleet had been ordered to defend the town against the French Navy based on Toulon. Smollett was to write a book on his year and a half's stay in Nice and reading his *Travels through France and Italy*, a vivid picture of the city emerges, though it must be admitted not always a very complimentary one. The municipality, however, ignoring his gibes have chosen to remember the irascible doctor as their benefactor and have named one of the streets in the old part of the town after him, but spelling it with only one 'l' and one 't'. Under the circumstances one wonders if this was not an intentional slight on the part of the city fathers, a way of recognising his services, but at the same time administering a slight reprimand.

The most exalted personages to follow in Smollett's footsteps were a couple of royal dukes, the Duke of York and, a year later, his brother the Duke of Gloucester. By December 1786 Nice and its neighbourhood were being described as 'presenting the air of an English watering place',[1] a watering place albeit recommended for invalids, especially for those suffering from tuberculosis. Later Menton was to take over from Nice and was much publicised by a distinguished lung specialist: Dr Henry Bennet, himself suffering from advanced pulmonary consumption and expecting to die any minute. Much to his astonishment he recovered almost completely and after one winter was able to consult again in London. Wishing to benefit his patients he published an account of his months spent on the shores of the Mediterranean, calling it *Winter in the South of Europe*: a fascinating work in which he explained why he singled out Menton, a question largely of climate. Like all good doctors Bennet is a sound psychologist and offers much wise advice to his readers, encouraging patients to exercise, and, above all, to take an interest in things. 'Happy are they if they can find pleasure in books, music, sketching, and the study of nature. . . .' He remarks that he has never known 'an unhappy misanthropical naturalist. As a class, I think they are truly the happiest and *most contented* of men'.[2] Moggridge, the horticulturist, was a patient of Bennet's and his book *The Flora of Mentone* is still one of the Riviera's classics.

Added, now, to the invalids came yet another class of visitors – the botanists, and more important still – the gardeners; men like Sir Thomas Hanbury, a retired merchant from Shanghai who, in 1867, bought himself an old palazzo known as La Mortola, situated in extensive grounds by the sea just over the border in Italy. He and his brother started collecting medicinal plants and plants that he believed would acclimatise. As Hanbury's interest in the place grew, he commissioned fellow naturalists to write books on the Riviera and the neighbouring mountain passes and in 1892 founded the Botanical Institute of the University of Genoa.

Invalids, naturalists and gardeners . . . and by degrees the invalids began to feel themselves *persona non grata*. It was becoming the fashion to winter abroad and those not themselves consumptive hesitated to stay in places which harboured contagious invalids. William Scott, writing in 1907, tells us, somewhat cynically, that if a hotel visitor is heard to cough the other visitors immediately complain and 'the unfortunate individual has to pack his trunk and seek accommodation elsewhere'.[3] Fortunately for the invalids new methods for the treatment of tuberculosis were being tried. It was felt that the evaporation of the sea was bad for the patient. Those suffering from lung complaints seemed to fare much better in the pure, crisp mountain air and consequently sanatoriums were being built in the Alps. This freed the hotels along the coast. No longer the haunt of a pale clientèle coughing its life away, they found themselves suddenly inundated by a far more remunerative milieu – the chilly aristocracy of the north, and with them, a large proportion of the crowned heads who ruled over them. Russia and Great Britain were particularly well represented; Russia by Alexander II and his Empress, their grand dukes and several hundred courtiers, and Great Britain, not so much by her Queen, who led a somewhat circumscribed existence tucked away with her suite in a large hotel at Cimiez, but by her son, the expansive, jovial Prince of Wales.

The railway, of course, was another important factor in the development of the Riviera. Starting at Marseilles in 1852 it had crept, kilometre by kilometre, along the coast, reaching Nice in 1864. The Nice to Monaco run had been opened in 1868 and the Italian frontier linked up four years later. Nice therefore was the first to benefit by the change, and throughout the winter months elegant crowds could be seen stepping down from the varnished carriages as the trains steamed into the station. Later they would meet, sunning themselves on the Promenade des Anglais that swept in a wide crescent along the shore of the Baie des Anges. Doris Langley Moore writes amusingly about the daily fashion parade in her book on Marie Bashkirtseff, an impressionable young Russian girl who had conceived a violent passion for the young Duke of Hamilton who, incidentally, she never met. The Russians and the British would appear to have been somewhat suspicious of each other. The Russians were a little too exotic for the British, or was it perhaps the other way around?

At any rate [writes Miss Moore] there was not much communication between them . . . but they knew about one another. The English knew which of the twenty Russian princes were Princes of the blood and which were newly landed gentry. The Russians knew which British noblemen were also millionaires – a matter requiring discernment since the Anglo-Saxons and the Celts seldom shared the slavonic taste for lavish display.[4]

Descriptions enough exist to illustrate this point and one account tells
of the grandeur in which the Russian empress travelled when abroad.
She is seen out driving, one day, by an English spinster who first met
with a splendid scarlet courier. Using authoritative gestures the courier
just waved the Englishwoman's unwilling coachman onto the pavement
while a smart barouche wheeled past them, followed by two outriders
in blue velvet jackets – 'silk velvet!' remarked the spinster's companion.
The empress, 'all veiled and bonnetted' remained unseen. There are
various palace-villas built by the Russians, especially in Les Baumettes
section of Nice. The Imperial court, however, seems to have preferred
renting villas and after one or two seasons they settled in a luxurious
house at Cap Martin which had belonged to Pierpoint Morgan. In no
time it became a veritable arsenal; sentinels were posted all around. 'A
special telegraph line with direct communication to the Russian capital
was laid down and an enormous retinue of servants was engaged, including corps of the Imperial Russian Ballet.'[5]

By the time the railway reached Monaco it had a newly built town
as its halting place – Monte-Carlo, or Mount Charles after the reigning
prince. Charles III, in a spirited effort to try and resuscitate the place's
dilapidated finances, had turned, or attempted to turn the Principality
into a gaming centre, modelled after those in Germany. His first ventures
failed but he soon found a backer to further his scheme; a rotund little
man called François Blanc, the principal shareholder of a very successful
gambling establishment in Homburg, capital of one of the many
miniature states into which the Germany of that time was then split.
Blanc, an astute man, foresaw trouble ahead for him with Prussia and
wanting to transfer his capital to a safer place, made the Prince an offer,
obtaining, in return, a fifty year concession. Immediately Blanc set
about building on the hilly promontory opposite the rock, a waste
stretch of land which, up till then, had been grown over with olives and
used as grazing land for goats and sheep. Garnier, the architect of the
Paris Opera House, was commissioned to design the theatre of the
Casino; the Casino itself was enlarged and the theatre and the Hôtel de
Paris built, all lavishly decorated. There followed a rash of villas,
balustraded in blue-glazing and hung with clashing bougainvillaea and
geraniums. Jostling each other for space, they are built out on stilts,
some of them with their foundations dynamited out of the very mountains themselves. Men in blue smocks laid out parterres of potted red
and white cyclamen, the Prince's colours. Cineraria and salvia followed.

Palms were grouped round a band-stand, and to this exotic new resort, living in a blaze of artificial light, duly flocked the glittering followers of fashion.

This, then, in very condensed form is the sequence of events we are to follow; a roughing out as it were of the terrain. The development of Cannes and of the other resort places along the coast will be dealt with in due course, also the details of the sudden change which occurred on the Riviera during the twenties when it first became popular as a summer resort. Again the change was brought about by foreigners, and this time, as it happens they were mostly American. It was a result of a post-war mood for a less restricted life, one that was immediately echoed in women's fashions: cropped hair, short dresses, freedom of movement and less attention to finicky detail. White powdered faces were no longer the fashion; everyone wanted to be sunburnt, to swim, drive and play golf. In 1921 the Cole Porters rented the Château de la Garoupe from the Normans, a large, pleasant house on the Cap d'Antibes. Cole Porter had a flair for doing things which other people had not yet thought of and he rented Garoupe for the summer, which, up till then people had considered impossible. Amongst the guests were Sara and Gerald Murphy. The Murphys were Scott Fitzgerald's first inspiration for Dick and Nicole Diver in *Tender is the Night*, a novel set partly in the South of France. Murphy, himself, describes his stay. 'At that time no one ever went near the Riviera in the summer. The English and Germans – there were no longer any Russians – who came down for the short spring season, closed their villas as soon as it began to get warm. None of them ever went into the water.' Murphy comments on the weather: the air was dry

> and it was cool in the evening, and the water was that wonderful jade and amethyst colour. Right out on the end of the Cap there was a tiny beach – the Garoupe – only about forty yards long and covered with a bed of seaweed that must have been four feet thick. We cut out a corner of the beach and bathed there and sat in the sun, and we decided that this was where we wanted to be. Oddly, Cole never came back, but from the beginning we knew we were going to.[6]

Indeed the Murphys took Villa America and round them gathered a talented and amusing crowd – Stravinsky, Léger, Picasso. Murphy, always an elegant man, set the fashion on the beach with his white linen shorts and a French sailor's striped jersey. Sara slung her pearls down her back 'because it was good for them to get the sun'. And this, more or less, is how people dress to this day. The trousers become shorts and change back again and the stripes vary from year to year according to the dictums of St Tropez.

This, then, brings us to a world with which I am familiar. I knew the Cole Porters, but met them much later, when they were out in Hollywood. I was a child of eight during their Garoupe period, but I remember old Lady Norman to whom the Garoupe belonged. My family also had a property on the Riviera, on Cap Ferrat, and Lady Norman would come over sometimes to swim. La Garoupe and our villa, La Fiorentina, were I suppose, and still are, what might be referred to as the show places of the Riviera.

❧2

La Fiorentina

These impressions of the South of France must, to a certain degree, be personal. I have been living down here, now, for the best part of thirty years and feel that any interpretation I undertake should stem, in part, from first-hand knowledge. For instance, it might be of some interest to describe the house in which we lived, as it typifies a certain way of life – the pleasures for which the south is famous. The making of a garden will, I hope, reveal yet another facet of the country. From here the circle widens, spreading like the ripples in a pool until the whole area is covered. If the reader will bear with me we should then, as I have already pointed out in the previous chapter, return for a while to the things with which I am familiar.

My earliest memories of the Riviera are of Monte-Carlo. I must have been about five years old, and I remember, very vividly, chasing the pigeons down the gravel paths of the immaculately manicured garden in front of the casino. Someone had told me that if I managed to sprinkle salt on their tails I would be able to catch them. It was Christmas time and I remember the warm sunlight and my governess's straw boater and her stiff grosgrain belt with a silver buckle. I cannot remember much about her as a character; she must, however, have been fairly indulgent with me about the pigeons for it was an amusement that never palled. Fortunately I was too young, or had been protected from the *tir aux pigeons*, a popular pastime which was indulged in only a few hundred yards away on a terrace the far side of the casino. The birds were specially prepared for the slaughter, had their tail and wing feathers carefully plucked in such fashion that they could barely fly and when let out of their cages fluttered erratically, to be blown to pieces by so-called sportsmen waiting with loaded guns. The standard of marksmanship must have been high if the clientèle could be judged by the people frequenting the casino; the poor wretched birds would, more likely than not, have been dropped by the first barrel. Should they escape an equally wretched fate awaited them on the beach below, where little boys were on the look-out to wring their necks should they flop exhausted on the shingle. I am told that my pigeons, plump and well fed, would often gather on a balustrade that gave onto this scene of destruction, and as far as could be ascertained were perfectly indifferent to the cruel treatment being meted out to their brothers.

Strange the things one remembers as a child. I remember being fascinated by anything spherical, especially the coloured postcards of oranges that were on sale at the kiosks. They appear to have dropped out of circulation but during my youth were immensely popular. It was always the same card; a sprig of dark, glossy leaves with wax-like pearls of blossom and nestling in the middle, two globular oranges. I remember also the blue bottle of orange flower water my grandmother used to keep beside her bed. She maintained that a little of this deliciously smelling concentration spilled over a lump of sugar and dissolved in water made one slip quietly into a peaceful slumber.

How well, too, I remember my mother in these first years immediately after the 1914 war. She was, quite rightly, considered to be amongst the great beauties of her period, and I remember one day standing in the hall of the Hôtel de Paris, with my governess, watching her walking down the central stairs. She moved beautifully and held herself very erect and had this extraordinary aura about her that made people stare. They would get up to watch her as she passed. On this particular occasion she was lunching at the palace. A *tricorne* hat dipped saucily to one side of her head, and she was dressed all in grey chiffon with a bunch of Parma violets at her slim waist. I can even remember her shoes; black and shiny with great steel buckles. Reaching the hall she stopped to talk to some friends, at the same time easing on her gloves. Seeing me she blew me a kiss and waved goodbye as she stepped into the waiting car. Naturally there followed the usual remarks, and I remember feeling immeasurably proud.

For me this picture of my mother epitomises the elegance of Monte-Carlo; an elegance, that, despite the changing times, seems, in some strange way, to linger.

I was an only child and never knew my father, who died shortly after I was born. I had a happy childhood but a lonely one, lonely, however, from my own choosing for I obstinately refused to play with other children. They terrified me. Thrown in upon myself I became all the more conscious of my surroundings, and being of an imaginative turn of mind, places and atmospheres meant a lot to me. Not all my holidays were spent in the south. I have vague memories of Dinard and Deauville and of the great expanse of beaches, further to the north, empty for most of the year, tenanted by the shrimp women with their big nets, lonely figures in black against the grey-green sky. It seemed to me then that the tide went out for ever and I remember walking over the sea-wet sand, walking so far that the ribbing with which it was patterned hurt my feet. I remember a great many things, England with its beautiful cloud-packed countryside and its great trees, but above all it is the memories of sun-filled days in the South of France that make the most vivid impact. I have only to shut my eyes and it comes flooding back to me. Light is everywhere, splashed on the floor, dancing across the ceiling, a brilliance that had to be kept out of my room by closed shutters. Childhood impressions are often remarkably accurate, and as an example I would cite those wonderful nights spent on the *Train Bleu,* an everlasting symbol, for me, of real luxury. Flying is so much easier these days and above all less time consuming, but with what pleasure one remembers those journeys by train; the varnished panelling in one's coach inlaid with motifs designed in the twenties, the thick carpet and the little cushioned plaque on the partition above one's head with a hook on which to hang one's watch. The solidity of everything; the heavy metal basin that folded into a corner, and the soothing, well-sprung clatter as the carriage slid over the points in the darkness; a luminous darkness stained a dark, vibrant blue by the night-light – and then the delicious surprise in the morning when one snapped up the blind exposing a sun-baked landscape of red rocks and blue sky, powdered with clouds of mimosa. Always impatient, my blind went up long before the scheduled time and I would sit, watching as the train bent in graceful curves round each gulf. It seldom quit the coast and tunnelled frequently to pierce the promontories. Reaching the chain of the Maures the railway turned away from the sea, joining it again at Fréjus. One kept with it as far as St Raphaël where it came up against the porphyry wall of the Esterel stained a fiery red in the morning light. Cuttings, tunnels and viaducts carry one through this violent upheaval; the cuttings reverberating like thunder to the noise of the train. This formidable defile passed, the horizon widens as one emerges suddenly on Cannes. Beyond stretches the Var valley; a flatness of green – the promised land! Behind are the great Alps capped in snow, flashing like tents against the sky. Olives clothe the hills rolling up to these giants, while cypress and pine seam the roads. The gardens are laden with oranges gleaming like small lanterns amongst their dark leaves. There are palms and dust green aloes, their asparagus-like blooms acting as points of exclamation in the landscape. Beyond the Baie des Anges lies Nice. One is carried through the back streets of the town with its tall houses and plunged again into a tunnel, emerging to skirt the Rade de Villefranche with beyond, Cap Ferrat, a rocky promontory reaching into the sea. More tunnels, a hurried glimpse of the Alps, advancing now, plunging abruptly into the water, then blackness and Monte-Carlo, usually reached just as one has finished breakfast served to one in Wagon-Lit's blue crested china. Little did I think then, and during subsequent visits to the south, that Cap Ferrat would one day be my home.

The scene now changes and I remember Christmas holidays during my teens spent in the Golf Hotel at Valescure, a resort some miles up in the hills behind St Raphaël. Lord Derby and some friends invested in what was a handsome forest of umbrella pines, carving a golf course out of their midst. The course was laid out in about 1911, the hotel being built after the war. I returned the other day after an absence of about forty years and the place has hardly changed. It was like reliving a dream, the coast so overdeveloped everywhere else seems, here, to be retreating into the past. We had drinks at the Golf Club, the echo of a cricket pavilion such as one might find in some English ducal estate, run by a retired French colonel. The hotel, as ungainly as I remembered it, remains a wonderful example of its period, like leafing through a back copy of *l'Illustration*, that once popular magazine depicting the twenties and thirties and, alas, no longer in circulation. What struck me were the carpets spread over a series of high-ceilinged halls. They were patterned all over with fantasy flowers, great kidney shaped petals in pale mauve, buffs and pinks. The remarkable thing about them was their quality for they had borne up to a generation of trampling by hob-nailed boots.

It is a curious fact but this time lapse found at Valescure occurs for a good part of the way in the vicinity of the neighbouring coast, say for a distance of about twenty miles between Agay and St Raphaël. The best way to see it is by motor-boat, spanking the waves past the rugged rock formations of the Esterel. An assortment of architectural styles are to be glimpsed among the pines to the east of St Raphaël ranging from solid stone houses, more or less Romanesque in appearance, to half timbered villas with steeply pitched gables, the kind of thing one might expect to find in a Chantilly racing establishment. This same nostalgic, vaguely depressing atmosphere is to be found in the resort towns along the Italian Riviera, in Menton and nearby Cap Martin. They have been left out of the swim of things, are no longer considered fashionable and somehow seem to have suffered from the neglect.

Quite some time elapsed before I again visited the South of France. My stepfather, General Cavendish, had died and my mother had since remarried, a Leicestershire hunting squire. Much in love, he had offered her a villa on the Riviera, and in order to look around she had rented La Léopolda. Situated on a hill above Beaulieu it has sweeping views out over the Mediterranean, and has always been considered one of the show places of the Riviera. Ogden Codman, its builder, a distinguished American architect of the twenties, had based his designs on a combination of two eighteenth-century villas, one the Villa Borelli near Marseilles, and the other the remains of a handsome house he found in Milan. There were few buildings to speak of on the coast at this period, and La Léopolda was Codman's interpretation if such a thing had existed. Formal gardens with *pièces d'eau* surrounded the house,while a long line of thirty-foot high cypresses framed the steps leading down to the view. It has been suggested that Edith Wharton helped with the garden, and this might well have been the case for the novelist was a friend of Codman's and had collaborated with him on a book dealing with decoration.

The Codman estate wanted to sell La Léopolda but my mother found the house too formal. Living in it would entail constant entertaining, and my mother, never fond of crowds, wanted something less spectacular and by preference a house with a garden down by the sea. The Agnellis subsequently bought La Léopolda and at the time they were exactly the right people for it. Young, handsome and extraordinarily elegant, they had both the taste and the means to live in it properly and it is a great pity they ever left.

Properties down here in the late thirties were easy to find and the prices comparatively reasonable. It was a question, really, of elimination and on what part of the coast one wanted to be. It took my mother about six weeks to find her ideal; a house right on the end of Point Saint Hospice with enough land round it to assure complete privacy. St Hospice is a small peninsula jutting out from Cap Ferrat and,

bending back like a thumb, faces out across Beaulieu Bay to the mainland, and is about as near to being an island as it is possible to be.
Angled east-west, the house faces due south and full out to sea on one
façade and to the shelter of a large, open bay on the other. The property
was known as La Fiorentina, and as its name suggests, was a Florentine
pastiche and was built just after the outbreak of the 1914 war by
Comtesse Robert de Beauchamp, and is illustrated, incidentally, in
Robert Doré's extremely useful *L'Art en Provence*. It was a typical
house of the period and remembering it as it used to look it is much to
my mother's credit that she saw its possibilities and understood what
could be made of it. I was not experienced enough in those days to
be consulted seriously and the whole responsibility rested with her.
It was a brave choice and, as it turned out, a very fortunate one.
Of course its whole *raison d'être* is the position, its gardens reaching
right down to the rocks and the heaving Mediterranean. The end of the
point was left wild and grown over with a tangle of stone pines tortured
by the wind into weird Rackham-like shapes, and it was for these
trees, I believe, that my mother really bought the place.

The Comtesse de Beauchamp had sold Fiorentina to Sir Edmund
Davis, a man who had made his fortune in South Africa, and it was from
him, or rather his widow, that my mother had bought it. The purchase
went through a few months before Chamberlain and his Cabinet declared
war on the Third Reich, and the family spent the first months at
Fiorentina, dispersing afterwards to their different duties; my mother
and sister to London, and myself, an American citizen, to a heavy
bomb group based in Nebraska. I was eventually transferred to the
Office of Strategic Services in Washington and from there moved to
London, on loan to MI5, England's Intelligence service. Fiorentina
stood empty for some time and was subsequently occupied by the
Germans when they moved over the demarcation line into unoccupied
France. Fearing an allied invasion they started fortifying what they
considered the strategic points along the coast, and our peninsula,
commanding the entrance to Beaulieu bay, was one of them. One
wonders, however, at their reasoning, for no invading force could
possibly have considered landing on a mountainous coastline that
dipped precipitously from the height of some thousand feet directly into
the sea. Fiorentina was made the local GHQ, the sea wall being fortified
with machine-gun posts while a vast cannon emplacement, able to
house some twenty men, was sunk into the gardens in a position com-

manding the bay. In addition to this they excavated an air-raid shelter nearer to the house, lining it with reinforced concrete. When the break-through came and the Germans retreated, they blew up their fortifications and it can be imagined what the place looked like. The house, bought fully furnished, was a shambles. Fortunately the contents were of no great worth, besides which it had always been our intention to rebuild the house and send everything to the local sale room, but despite this the first impression on returning was, as can be imagined, some-thing of a shock. ———

Again it is my mother who deserves the credit for the restoration. Alone, I would not have had the courage. Fortunately another house on the property known as Le Clos, the dower house as it were, had escaped completely untouched, and into this charming, late-eighteenth-century building we moved while work on the Fiorentina progressed.

Clearing the grounds appeared the first logical task to undertake and for this the government allowed us a contingent of German prisoners of war, silent, taciturn fellows as I remember them, who went about their work like automatons. I don't think I ever tried to talk to them, partly, I suppose, from embarrassment. Central Supply in Nice were unable to issue automatic drills, and day after day the poor wretches hacked away with their pickaxes. The conglomerate masses of concrete were not easy to move and the foundations went very deep, but they had to be cleared in order to replant. If roots come into contact with concrete, it usually kills the tree, and one twenty-foot cypress framing the broad avenue of steps leading down to the sea had to be changed three times because the clearing at this point had been superficial.

Once having decided what form the garden should take the planning of it was comparatively easy; the bones were already there – the lie of the land dictated the rest. It was to be a predominantly green and white garden, with its main accesses clearly laid out, and within this classical frame a series of separate compartments or rooms walled in behind clipped hedges. From the formal part one was to wander out into the different wild areas – the country's redolent *maquis*. Colours, other than the different blues, silvers and whites, and the dirty pink bloom of the round leafed *Bergenia delavayi*, massed in great carpets under the pines, were to be kept to the minimum. It was not to be the kind of garden in which annuals were bedded out, rather the accent was on shrubs, and not necessarily those which grow only in a temperate zone, but odoriferous ones such as choisya. Those parts of the garden exposed to the prevalent east wind were screened off by twenty-foot hedges of *Pittosporum tobira*, the only fragrant member of that large family; in the spring its small clusters of creamy-white flowers scent the whole garden. The pergola, framing the walk leading from a wild part of our point to the Clos, seemed an ideal place for the different jasmines, while the immediate approach to the house, a large empty rectangle, proved the perfect setting for a plantation of oranges. We bought mature trees to assure a uniformity of height, most of them over twenty years old – the kind of luxury one could indulge in before prices became so prohibitive. They were planted four rows deep in lines of ten and the drive swept up the middle. Under the trees we divided the ground up into a geometric pattern of triangles traced in low, clipped box hedges and further delineated, or relieved by alternate spacing of red sand in contrast to the earth; the sand being retained by an edging of tile set edgeways into the ground at the same height as the box. A further detail was the coating of lime with which we daubed the trunks and lower limbs. The citrus growers do this as a protection against parasites. We painted them for a purely decorative reason, to give luminosity to the dappled, subaqueous light filtering through the dark leaves. I had never seen this done before and we were rather proud of the result.

I hesitate to go into too much detail about the garden; amongst the more obvious sweet scented things that we planted were the handsome Carolina *Magnolia grandiflora* and Latin America's graceful trumpet flowered datura, also clumps of the white *Hedychium coronarium* from India. Amongst the less obvious odoriferous plants, and probably the strongest smelling of them all, comes the *Cestrum nocturnum*, the night blooming jasmine, known romantically in the Spanish speaking countries as *damas de noche*. An inconspicuous shrub with tiny clusters of yellow-green flowers, it is difficult to locate the first time one comes across it in someone else's garden; it is a question of degrees of smell. At the gates we massed a collection of Australian acacia – better known here, of course, as mimosa. At Christmas time they explode in a honey-scented, yellow cloud, to be followed later by the equally sweet-smelling *Coronilla glauca*, indigenous to several parts of southern Europe, and which we had naturalised in the *maquis* under the stone pines.

Another element in this combination of smells are the terraces of lavender below the loggia, where we always lunched in the summer time. The lavender, when not in flower, was kept clipped in tidy, clumped balls, treated in exactly the same way as the commercial lavender which one finds planted in great undulating fields in the stony fastnesses of the Var highlands. Clipped hedges of rosemary confined the lavender, the paths in between set, here and there, with flat circular pots of white pelargoniums. Large pots of lemon and bergamot, a species of rough-skinned orange, stood on the corners of the loggia terrace and against the wall behind. Detached from the house the Italianate loggia of honey-coloured tufa constituted one of the few original elements of the property that we kept, modifying it only by adding a terrace framed by curving stairs which lead into the lavender garden. The large terracotta pots were another legacy, imported from Tuscany where they have been firing them since the times of the Medicis.

The *pièce de résistance*, the focal point as it were of the garden – and the view most often reproduced in the different gardening books – are the great shallow grass steps leading down to the sea. Falconnet sphinxes frame the stairs and along the descent, on both sides, are planted tapering twenty-foot cypress. Below these tight, green columns grow dusty clumps of the Canary Islands blue flowering echium. They advance in waving lines onto the steps, and mixed in with them come a small white flowering convolvulus and the deep blue Corsican rosemary. The last, and seventh step is the pool spilling over into the glittering Mediterranean, and beyond, across Beaulieu Bay, comes the whole dramatic sweep of the mainland piled in a series of precipitous limestone cliffs rising to a height of nearly two thousand feet before collapsing, in folds of varying pastel shades, into Italy.

The garden quite obviously was a slow process and took several years to complete, and then there are all the amusing details: our pride, for instance, in our avocado pear trees, some of them given to us by Somerset Maugham, a near neighbour of ours on the Cap. His trees bore such quantities of fruit that he was reduced to hunting up new recipes in order not to waste them. As a rule, Maugham's food was delicious, but I took less kindly to his avocado ice-cream – a sweet green mush and quite tasteless, the cold killing the faint, subtle flavour of the pear. We had several varieties of avocado, one of which I had brought back with me from Guatemala in a shoe-bag – a young seedling given to me by Dr Wilson Popenoe, a distinguished botanical explorer who had spent a lifetime propagating the avocado, or *Persea Americana*, indigenous to the southern parts of Mexico and sections of Guatemala. But this is beside the point, particularly as nothing has been said as yet about the actual rebuilding of Fiorentina. A house is always quicker to achieve than a garden, but even so it proved a long undertaking. It was a question of feeling one's way and of having had enough training to know exactly what one wanted. No decorator was to be involved; however an accredited architect was needed to transcribe my ideas and to manage the technical side of things. It so happened that just the right man existed: M. Henri Delmotte from Nice. He was sensitive and quick to understand. Given an idea it was only a question of days before several versions of it appeared in blueprints. Maugham had used him when remodelling La Mauresque, his house on Cap Ferrat that had originally belonged to Monseigneur Charmeton, father confessor to King Leopold II of the Belgians, that rotund and bearded majesty who had amassed a fortune in the Congo and who had spent it with prodigality in Paris and on the Riviera, 'scandalising public opinion with his licentiousness'. The Cap in those days had been the King's personal property and he built extensively and, no doubt, finding it convenient to have his confessor close at hand, had persuaded the Monseigneur to follow suit. Charmeton, before entering Leopold's service, had been stationed in Morocco where he became interested in Islamic architecture, and the villa reflected his tastes – horseshoe doors and windows, even domes and minarets on the roof. It was this eastern flavour that Delmotte had been asked to eradicate, a task he accomplished by squaring off the openings and the roof, leaving only the villa's name as a reminder of its past. It was exactly the same problem, only on a more drastic scale, that we were faced with at Fiorentina. The principal walls of the house and the foundations were to remain, otherwise all was to go; the great loggia outside the drawing-room, which robbed it of light, the twin-towered entrance, even the roof, which had to be heightened a good two feet. The ground floor rooms had too much height and the bedrooms not enough. The drawing-room, with its ceiling dropped, was extended to open onto the cloister, facing south, while on the opposite wall five great windows gave onto the terrace where the loggia had been. The ceiling, incidentally, gold-starred and coffered, was cast in plaster and hung from chains attached to the rafters. This, and a false medieval fireplace were, perhaps, the worst features in the house. It was the entrance front, however, on account of its elevation, that proved the hardest problem to solve. The lie of the land necessitated a steep flight of steps which, owing to the overall scale, had to be imposing.

The house had been a poor pastiche of a Florentine villa, and after several false starts we finally decided that it should be rebuilt in the Palladian style, in what one hoped would be a much purer rendering. At least one felt it to be more appropriate to its position and to the sharp southern light. The other solution would have been to build something entirely contemporary which, if undertaken by an architect of Philip Johnson's calibre, could have been exciting. But it was a question, really, of our possessions, and with these in mind we decided on the former plan. It was, after all, in the English tradition to translate the ideas of Veneto's famous architect. They had been transferred to the dunes of Norfolk and the Yorkshire moors, why not to the shore of the Mediterranean? Having made up our minds on this score, I paid several visits to the beautiful, undulating countryside around Padua, once part of the Republic of Venice and the home of Palladio's architecture. Mark a circle on the map, Venice, Treviso, Vicenza and Padua; within it unfolds a magical landscape, there is a lyrical quality about it – it is touching, intimate, built over with columned houses, houses half temple, half farm, a mixture of grey lichenous statues and huge home-spun pots of white oleanders, chickens and hayfields, the grand and the homespun in just the right quantities. It was precisely on one of these expeditions that I came again on the Rotonda, a short distance outside Vicenza, and here of course was the solution to our problem. One had only to copy one of the four façades, in them were embodied all the elements; the stairs and the monumental portico, imposing, but at the same time open and not oppressive. All that remained was for Delmotte and myself to take the measurements and modify some of the details. One approaches the Rotonda up a fairly steep rise and the house when first seen stands outlined against the sky and further to dramatise the effect Palladio has placed statues at the corners and on the apex of his pediments. At Fiorentina the portico would be at eye level and this being the case we were afraid that statues might look out of place. We also elim-inated the two small *oeils-de-boeuf* flanking the inscription centred in the pediment; otherwise all is identical, except for the steps which, because of the terrain, needed to be less steep. The high walls framing them Palladio had dressed with figures of nymphs, and to substitute for these I eventually found a handsome pair of late-seventeenth-century terra-cotta griffons, which, judging from the bare shields they present, had probably once stood at the entrance to some town. A collection of potted plants, arranged in drifts, broke the austerity of the steps, and a further two great pots stood on each side of the doors planted with pittosporum. The doors were always left open and the pittosporum when it flowered in the spring filled the whole house with its scent.

Externally the house is faced with stucco and washed a pale buff, a colour commonly met with in the Veneto. It looks well with the green of the olives. Inside we kept to muted colours; pistachio green and dirty pinks marbleising in the hall and a blue ceiling with clouds, a popular conceit in most Latin countries bordering the Mediterranean. The second hall Martin Battersby painted for us in *trompe-l'oeil*, the theme being architectural drawings on simulated sheets of vellum attached to the walls and ceiling with thumb tacks, and so convincing is his work that one instinctively touches them to make sure they are not real. The ceiling represents the elevations of a dome drawn on a sheet of folded paper in sepia. Battersby had also kept one of my letters, and without my knowledge made a complete facsimile of it. It is not a product I would have chosen for public exposure and had been dashed off about some directives with one of those French post office pens. It is even grammatically incorrect, and there it hangs, tacked to the wall to confound me, I suppose, for at least my lifetime.

For the dining-room we had been fortunate enough to find a late-eighteenth-century Piedmontese fresco. Using advanced techniques it had been detached from its original wall and backed onto rolls of canvas, and in this state had spent the major part of the war in a London warehouse. The warehouse was eventually blitzed, but miraculously the cases containing the frescoes had escaped, and procuring the necessary permits we had them shipped to France. It was now a question of finding the men capable of transferring them onto the walls, no easy task considering the number of adjustments that had to be made. We were advised to use experts from Pisa. In due course they arrived and dressed in white linen overalls unrolled the thick canvases, and with perfect unconcern walked all over them in their stockinged feet, snipping away with large pairs of scissors. It made me nervous to watch, but they managed and with cool expertise made the joins. The painter is unknown but he must have specialised in rural landscapes and for our room had made a study of rocks and trees with, here and there, views of distant castles. Clipped hedges trained round white marble *putti* frame the doors, while birds flit from wall to wall, in company with a hawk who dominates the ceiling which, of course, is the sky.

It is not my intention to describe the house in detail; almost all the materials and most of the carpets came from Madame Lauer's *Tapis et Tissus de Cogolin*, the workshop responsible for the carpets recently woven for the Grand Trianon at Versailles which its curator, Gerald Van der Kemp, has so cleverly restored, rearranging it as it stood under the First Empire. Our carpets, I hurriedly point out, have nothing in common with those of Versailles, are only two-toned and worked in rough wool in a simple Sicilian design. The colours throughout the house are matt and quiet; umbers, olive-greens and faded blues and a great deal of white. For the walls of the big drawing-room the local painter mixed us a very faint green, matching exactly the silvery sheen to be found on the back of an olive leaf. It looked very well with the Chinese screens and black lacquer furniture. For the eight great windows Madame Lauer wove a small patterned *point de Hongerie*, white on white, so that the design is hardly noticeable.

The house when finished gave a wonderful impression of light. Indeed with such a setting it would have been all but impossible not to have made a success of it, and now that we have sold it and moved back to the Clos, my principal memory of Fiorentina is of this light, a kind of luminosity that flooded the downstairs drawing-room. Stretching enfilade the halls open one from the other giving into this large central room with its french windows facing north and south. The big double doors were always kept open, anchored with elongated stoppers of colourless Venetian glass and at certain times of the year the effect is quite extraordinary. The sun setting directly through the portico strikes right through the house, reflecting in the polished surface of the floors, touching the crystal chandeliers with points of fire. . . . At these moments the house takes on a special atmosphere, could be the precincts of some pagan temple at the auspicious hour of prayer, and in some strange way the Lunts have become associated with *this* memory. Lyn Fontanne and Alfred Lunt had been on a visit and were leaving. It happened to be one of those evenings of extraordinary – there is no other word for it – effulgence and Mrs Lunt had forgotten something in the library, at the far end of the house. We waited for her in the hall and on her return I watched her walk through the big room. She moved beautifully, with a kind of measured dignity; a rhythm she had acquired, no doubt, from her years on the stage. For a brief moment she was transformed, became a Tanagra figurine in floating draperies. It suddenly struck me, she was replaying the role she had interpreted in Giraudoux's *Amphitryon 38*. She was again the radiant Alkmena beloved by Jupiter, and was leaving the house, not for her car, but for Parnassus!

-᠍3

The Surroundings

Mornings on our point are magical. Mohammed brings me my breakfast out on the terrace shaded by great white awnings. The sea, a deep blue and shimmering, heaves noiselessly through the misty, grey foliage of the olives, moving in much the same way that water moves in stage scenery, and appears so close that one feels almost able to reach out and touch it.

How attached one becomes to routine, always the same china: Royal Worcester's 'Blue Dragon', a stylised pattern dating from the last century and one that is to be found in countless English houses. Mohammed, a Moroccan who has been with me for years, greets one with a flashing smile, produces the papers and pours the tea. Next to appear on the scene is Catherine. Catherine, of Italian extraction, was brought up in our village. She must have been very good-looking, and even at eighty-four is still handsome. Her face, lively and wrinkled, has changed very little in the thirty-odd years she has been working for us. Living in the village, she rides up every morning to the house on her *mobilette*, long *flûtes* of bread sticking out of the basket attached to the back of her bicycle. Unbeknown to her I was driving behind her one day as she mounted the hill from the village, and her progress was almost royal: *'Bonjour Madame Catherine.' 'Bonjour'*, she intoned with a dignified bow of the head, sitting very straight, averaging a pretty fast clip, too fast for me to overtake her. She is a remarkably good cook and loves being taught new dishes, working by instinct rather than measure. When we meet she stands, hands joined in front of her clean white pinafore, while we discuss the menu, a procedure we have reduced to a form of telepathy. I remember her, also, in the days when one used to attend the galas in Monte-Carlo. She would stand next to a great olive growing at the bottom of the entrance steps, waiting to see my mother, and this, also, would be discussed with next morning's menu.

She was crying, I noticed, the day we all drove off to Princess Grace's wedding.

Breakfast over I would do a tour of the garden, anything to put off the evil hour when I would be obliged to sit down at my desk and face that blank sheet of paper. More often than not, I would wander out to the point by the tortured pines and sit on the sea wall looking out towards the mainland. On still days the view is incredible, the bright mirror of the bay reflecting every object along the shore with a soft clearness, and far out the calm sea melting into the milky blue of the sky; a blurred horizon distinguished only where the sun catches a white sail in the distance.

Day after day, week after week, one will get these still clear days, and it is an accepted fact that the climate on our particular strip of coast is, apart from Menton, the most equable of any along the Riviera; a phenomenon explained by our position in respect to the mountains which rise directly in front of us across the bay. Facing due south and being practically devoid of vegetation, they act as reflectors to the sun, storing its heat, throwing it back along the shore line. They also attract the clouds and nearly always, and particularly in the afternoons, one can see great cumuli gathering behind Napoleon's mountain top road. They boil up into a variety of almost static forms but stay anchored to the heights, leaving the sky over us a clear, burning blue. It is with reason, then, that the environs of Beaulieu are known as *Petite Afrique*.

Surrounded as we are, one is, perforce, particularly conscious of the sea. The Mediterranean, a deep sea, is particularly deep along our part of the coast. This is always the case when mountains terminate abruptly in or near water, the abyss of the sea repeating the height of land which it reflects. As to the Mediterranean's proverbial blue, it is, in fact, bluer than most seas due to the transparency and clearness of its water; added to this is the density of salt, the more salt the bluer the colour; the less salt the greener it becomes. I have never seen it as the 'wine dark sea' of Homer's *Odyssey*, but how often, on still days, have I watched the sun setting in a path of molten gold. For a moment it blinds in its intensity, and then slowly fades, changing to silver in the luminous darkness, a boundless liquid plane that dances and glitters under the moon. During the summer, when the water is warm, it is shot with mysterious glintings of its own; a shoal of fish will send off a cloud of sparks, while a boat's course is traced by a shining furrow, each wave rippling past the prow bordered by a silver hem of phosphorescence. Plunge your hand into the water and little points will cling like wet diamonds. The reality is nowhere near as romantic – they are plankton, a lowly organism which live suspended in the upper layers of the sea and at night rise to the surface.

On still days currents are sometimes visible, seen as paths winding snake-like across the water, and according to Dr Bennet,[1] who has made a study of such things, they are the delight of marine zoologists, for the paths make wonderful hunting grounds for creatures not normally found except by dredging. The currents, it would seem, draw them to the surface. Muslin nets are trailed behind the boat and then drawn up and their contents emptied into glass jars. Hold the jar to the light and it is like looking at organisms through a microscope, a myriad of strange shapes darting about which had been quite invisible from above.

But what about the larger fish? Passing through the Straits of Gibraltar whales occasionally make their way into this land-enclosed sea, sharks also, not that I have ever seen one. They exist, however, for not so long ago our local newspaper reported a casualty on one of the beaches in which a boy lost a leg. No sharks, but I have actually met with a whale in what was nearly a head-on collision. It happened some time ago during the early part of the war. I had not yet left for America and was out in the middle of the bay goggling. I had a javelin with me, but was not fishing on account of the depth. Idling along the surface I was watching diagonal shafts of milky light as they splayed out, probing the depths – it was one of those moments when one feels grateful for being alive. Suddenly, not more than twenty feet away from me, glided a gigantic, greyish hulk. My first reaction was – submarine! There had been reports of German submarines in the Mediterranean, and the effect was electrifying. I can't remember accurately how long the episode lasted, a few seconds only I suppose; too long, anyhow, for it to have been a pleasant experience; and it was not until the horizontal flukes of its tail flashed by me that I recognised it as a whale and not an instrument of war! Both possibilities I found unnerving, especially as I learnt afterwards that it was a species of sperm-whale known as a cachalot, the largest of the toothed whales, measuring anything up to fifty feet – the animal, in fact, that had been responsible for swallowing Jonah!

Free of the polar currents the Mediterranean harbours not a few of the larger marine specimens; dolphins and tunny are quite often met with and can be seen about the middle of May. On rare occasions the monstrously ugly devil-fish, a ray of enormous dimensions, makes its appearance. Two were caught at Villefranche in 1807 and were the first specimens to be properly described. Risso, the well-known local naturalist, names them amusingly: *Cephaloptera Massena* after Napoleon's famous marshal, another compatriot of these parts! He also describes their end, and it makes a pathetic story. They were taken in a net and the female, weighing one thousand three hundred and twenty-eight pounds, moaned piteously when she was killed. The male managed to escape but hovered around for two days hoping to find his mate, and eventually suffered the same fate.

On Sundays, when the moon is full, fishermen come down onto our rocks, but I have never seen them catch anything except what they call *friture*, a form of whitebait. During the autumn evenings our gardeners can be seen hunting for octopi, which they bait with red rags bunched at the end of a long pole; the red is said to attract them in the same way it does a bull and must be seen, anyway, as something foreign and dark. The end of the cane is joggled over weed-grown cavities in the rocks and the octopus, if in hiding, makes a dart for the bait, impaling himself on the hook hidden amongst the rags. The largest octopus I have seen down here measured some five feet from the top of his hooded head to the tip of his dangling tentacles, and this is considered large for these parts. I have to admit that it is not a sport I find particularly appealing. I find octopi repulsive, and when caught they are far from docile. Fixing one with a malignant, cat-like eye, they will haul themselves up the cane, or then slither with a deploy of their muscular tentacles across the rocks. Charles, a head gardener of ours at one time, was a great expert at handling them; he would just make a grab at the repulsive, heaving mass and hurl it with all his force onto the rocks. Even this was not always enough to stun the animal, and the small ones he would pick up and bite between the eyes, or if too large for this summary treatment, he would incapacitate them by turning their hoods inside out.

In my youth I remember being much impressed by Prince Albert's Oceanographic Museum at Monaco. On one of the floors is the laboratory from Prince Albert's yacht, the 600-ton *Alice*, named after his second wife, the Duchess of Richelieu. Another yacht followed, the 1400-ton *Alice II* and it was in her that the Prince brought back his giant octopi, keeping them alive in a special tank. One of them now decorates the stairs of the museum and measures twenty feet across from tentacle tip to tentacle tip; the other, I understand, managed to make its escape and, slithering overboard during the night, disappeared into the darkness. It was a story, anyhow, that preoccupied me a good deal as a child, especially as I had the visual proof that such things really existed.

I have already extolled the view from our point; the way one overlooks the mainland as if seen from a ship. The mountains are thinly covered in brush, their shoulders, naked precipitous rock, stained rusty with age. Eze village perches in the very centre of the view and was built, as already mentioned, at a time when the population of the coast was being constantly harassed by pirates; first by the Saracens, then by the Turks and Moors of Tunis and Algiers. It was a notoriously poor coast, and one might well ask what the raiders were after: the answer is slaves. Though able-bodied enough to be abducted, the inhabitants, made up largely of labourers and fishermen, were no match for these surprise attacks and their only recourse was to retire inland, or, as is the case here, to the tops of their mountains. There are numbers of these mountain-top villages and to name the best known, Saint Paul, Cagnes, Roquebrune and La Turbie. Within sight of the sea, they are almost invisible from a distance; long years of buffeting by the weather having almost assimilated them to the rocks upon which they are perched. As with Eze, it is difficult to tell where the rocks end and the walls begin. Moving down the coast and above Eze comes La Turbie. Behind the village the Alps rise to nearly four thousand feet, attaining their highest peak at Mont Agel. From here one sees a gradual collapse, as they subside in varying degrees of colour and visibility into Italy. The view never palls; all the time the light changes, and it is quite remarkable the clarity with which things stand out when the mistral is blowing; every stone and tree on the distant hills is visible, while Ventimiglia and Bordighera in Italy look almost next door. At moments like this the sky is washed a cold steely blue, while the sea, flecked with foam, takes on a deeper hue. But this is only when the mistral is blowing, and more often than not the distances are smudged in an opaque veil of blue mist, giving the country the poetical quality of a Claude Lorrain landscape. Another feature down here that strikes one immediately is the terracing. The mountains rise far too abruptly from the sea for anything to grow without the terraces and they have thus become part of the landscape.

This now brings us to the climate, which is a mixture, as far as the temperature is concerned, of the tropics and the temperate zone. Spring registers around 56° fahrenheit and summer 72°, rising sometimes to about 90° but rarely going above it. The coldest I have ever experienced during the winter is 49°. About sixty-seven days of rain can be counted on during the year, and when it falls, usually does so in heavy showers. Thirty-two inches is the average over the whole period, a greater yearly rainfall than either Paris or London, a fact explained by the unevenness of the downpours. On the Riviera they occur in autumn and spring whereas in London they are distributed fairly evenly throughout the year. Thunderstorms, although not frequent, may occur at any season but are most usual in May and June. The dry period lasts about four months, from the first week in June to near the end of September. But it may be of much longer duration. This applies only to the coastal region. Droughts, however, are no longer a dreaded enemy since most properties, these days, are connected to the mains. One requests the amount of water thought necessary and anything in excess of this is paid for at a higher rate. But this is a comparatively recent innovation and no garden down here fifty years ago could have existed without its own supply, generally provided by large storage tanks disguised as ponds sunk on a level with the ground. There are, of course, freak storms that bring snow and hail, but snowfalls occur seldom and are of short duration, the snow seldom remaining on the ground for more than a few hours. Hail, however, does cause serious damage, and I have witnessed two devastating storms, both localised: one occurring in the spring of 1958 and the other in 1971. I watched the latter advance across the water from the direction of Monte-Carlo, cutting across the sea like a metallic curtain. Rapidly it came at us in a straight line and when it struck, thundered down in an icy deluge of stones about the size of greengages. The garden suffered considerably; all the large leafed plants were torn to shreds. Even the citrus trees, with their leathery foliage, had the appearance of having been peppered with shot. It took a whole year before the place really recovered. Of course, the ones really to suffer from these storms are the people with greenhouses. The carnation growers of Antibes were completely wiped out, and the hail in their region came down with such force that even their cars were dented. But these are freak storms. Fortunately I have never witnessed a frost. On the other hand, properties on Cap Ferrat, with scarcely a difference of more than two hundred feet elevation, have twice, in my memory, lost all their orange trees. Our proximity to the sea is what saves us from any unexpected drop in the temperature; retaining its heat longer than does the land it envelops the garden with a protective, moist atmosphere, acting as a form of open conservatory.

As to the winds, they are variable, sometimes changing several times in a day. April and May are the worst months. The winds all carry different names and at times it is difficult to tell which of them is blowing: the *gregaou*, or Greek wind, brings the rare hail, the *levante* the cold and the rain from the east. The *tramontana* blows from the north; the *sirocco*, hot and humid, sweeps up from the south-east bringing with it a muggy, enervating atmosphere, not to be confused with the *libeccio* from Libya which is also moist and warm. The *levante* is our dominant wind and blowing up from Italy brings with it most of our bad weather. Last, but certainly not least, is the splendid *mistral*, the wind that was deified by the Romans on account of its stringent qualities and, indeed, it is bracing and exhilarating for those who can stand it. *Magister* it was called in Latin: O masterly wind! *Vent magistral*, or *mistral*, and the name suits it well for without a doubt it dominates both Provence and its coast. It blows off the Massif Central, down the funnel of the Rhône valley and, spreading fan-wise, dies out eventually in the neighbourhood of Bordighera. However cloudy it always sweeps the sky clean, and brings with it a brilliantly dry atmosphere, singularly exhilarating at first, but liable eventually to produce a serious state of nerves. Local law, in fact, allows for its peculiarities and any offender accused of acts of violence committed while the mistral is blowing can count on a certain degree of clemency.

Most people seem to be enchanted with the weather on the Riviera, but there are, naturally, the exceptions. Georges Sand is one of them and in her letters[2] complains of the lack of contrast between the seasons – finds that the changes are not marked enough and misses the dramatic autumn colouring. True, the extremes are not as obvious as they are in the north, but how subtle the passing of time, the slow approach of autumn; the sadness when the last white flowers of the sweet smelling hedychium wilt and shrivel on their bulbous green heads; and when the persimmon start changing colour, growing from an opaque, burnt orange to an almost translucent amber. There is a dampness in the air in the evening and the lovely sunlit days of October are wreathed in thin veils of mist. Mildew turns the marrow's hairy, dentillated leaves to chaste silver, and the first fig leaf comes tumbling down with a dry, hollow clatter; the tang of hot grapes in the sun, and the rancid smell of over-ripe figs – and always the stillness. The sun, sinking behind Villefranche, catches some windows across the bay, touching them with icy pinnacles of light. I climb the terraces behind the house and pick the last of the *cols des dames*, so called on account of their fragile paleness. With the coming of winter their skins have become almost leathery; split a fig open and one discovers that the red seeds are reduced to the consistency of jam. Up where I stand the light is a copper pink and it is cold in the wells of the garden where the sun no longer reaches.

The spring is equally beautiful. I shall never forget a drive I took with a friend. We were on our way to Tarascon. Great, smooth-limbed planes vaulted the straight roads, mile after mile of them, and their tender growth, just beginning to burgeon, appeared as hovering, green clouds barely touching the branches giving them life. It was a tidy landscape gridded over in a geometric tracing of plaited cane screens and tall serried rows of dark cypress, windbreaks without which the *primeurs* – the asparagus, the tender peas and the delicious orange-fleshed Cavaillon melons – would never grow. Unless fenced in, the melons had no hope of attaining maturity and more likely than not would be met with hurtling along the ground in a frantic game of bowls played by the wind. The mistral is forever raging across these rich plains of lower Provence, tugging at the tops of the cypress, but on this particular morning all was miraculously still. For once, these tapering vegetable plumes were etched in, immovable against the pale sky. Not a breath stirred and the air was redolent with the sharp, pungent odour of the flowering apples espaliered on both sides of the road.

✄4

The Circle Widens

I think that those who really know the coast well will agree with me in thinking that the best moments down here are the spring and autumn months, and the lovely sparkling days of winter. This, however, does not mean that the summers are to be avoided. What they refer to as *les grandes chaleurs* generally comes towards the end of June and can last to the first days of September. The hottest days show on an average about 88° in the shade, and only occasionally does the thermometer go any higher: even then, for those living on the coast, the atmosphere is seldom too oppressive, cooled as it is by the fresh breezes from the Mediterranean. The nights also can be warm, but cool down generally towards dawn when a gentle wind rustles the curtains, bringing with it a lighter air from the mountains. It is this period of heat, once so studiously avoided, which is now considered the season. ⟶

I never tire of the warm, still evenings of late spring when the darkness is punctuated by the erratic wanderings of fireflies. On the far side of the house a colony of tree frogs have taken up residence among the lemons growing either side of the canal running through the Moorish garden. The French refer to them as *la rainette verte*, their correct name being *Hyla arborea meridionalis*. The locals say that they 'hymn the spring' – *cantano la primavera*, but this is an overly poetic way of referring to the almost deafening noise that they actually make, a croaking that Brangham, in his excellent book *The Naturalists' Riviera*[1] describes as 'a roar from a crowded stadium'. He hardly exaggerates and it is surprising that such a tiny creature should have the strength to produce so great a volume of sound. Clinging, almost invisible, to the smooth branches of a lemon tree, he looks like one of those jade animals made by Fabergé. About two inches long, he is so constituted as to appear all of one piece, his legs fitting perfectly in one flowing line with his body – a miniature Citroën! Our frogs were a tender leaf-green with pale yellow undersides. But I read in Brangham that they can adapt their colours to their surroundings, 'so that it is possible sometimes to see yellow, grey-violet, brown, and almost black specimens'. I have seen them turn an almost golden yellow in the sunshine, and staying with a friend in the Camargue have even met with a blue one, a real powder-blue with great staring, dark amber eyes. Comerford-Casey,[2] another naturalist, makes mention of the blue ones and writes of a potter at Menton who made a speciality of selling them at a handsome profit. People accused him of dyeing his specimens by making them swallow some pigment. But, poor man, they were perfectly genuine and, what is more, are a variety and *not* a tree frog camouflaging itself against a cloud of plumbago. Casey adds an amusing detail and tells us that this particular specimen of frog has a habit of feeding on fireflies. He watched it happening, and the victim continued to glow through the predator's translucent body, a phenomenon made possible by the creature's total absence of ribs.

Related to the *Hyla arborea* are the great toads that crawl heavily around the lily pond outside the library. They are known locally as the *bufo bufo*, a name as ponderous as their appearance, and they can be perfect pests during the mating season when they litter the paths, three or more of them glued together in a lewd squelchy ball. It happened to be the mating season the time we let Fiorentina to the Burtons who were working on a film at the Nice studios. Not sure of Elizabeth Taylor's reactions were she to meet with these monsters, I thought it wiser to get rid of them and had some two hundred of them carted off in dust-bins to be let loose in a neighbouring pond. I learnt afterwards that they migrate over considerable distances in order to return to a favourite spot, which left me in doubt as to the success of my good intentions. At least I had no complaints. I personally don't mind the toads since they feed on a variety of insects that are bad for the garden. I mightn't be quite so complacent, though, were I to come face to face with another of its kind that is said to inhabit these shores; so vast and pink, the Chamberlains[3] report that it could be taken for a new-born baby lying abandoned in the grounds.

Following the frogs come the nightingales. They arrive in April, perch in the olive trees, warble their hearts out, and leave for the north when the summer begins. Following them come the cicadas who take up a noisy tenancy in the pines. The glare of the sun makes the pines sweat, and it is on these sharp-smelling resins that the insects feed. It is a smell one grows to associate with summer, this and the clicking of the cones as they split open in the heat. Strangely enough, one becomes immune to the cicadas and it is only the newcomer who stands entranced listening to their 'shrilly tone', a see-sawing of noise that drowns out everything.

It is to this background of odoriferous, clicking heat that I remember our dinners out on the terrace, at a table made from a large slab of polished labradorite. The dark iridescent stone makes a fine foil for our china which in the evenings is always white. Along with the various sets we had collected some of the local faiences. Of these, Moustier, I think, is the most interesting but not all the potters working in the district produce the really top quality, and after much shopping around we found a woman at Riez in the Haute Provence. Riez lies some fifteen miles to the west of Moustier itself, and here, in an abandoned monastery, Madame Simone Favier has installed her kilns. She employs some twenty people and between them they turn out classical reproductions of the original faience as produced in the seventeenth and eighteenth centuries. Her milk-white glaze is nearer to the original than that of the other potters, and when she improvises with the designs, she does so with flair. She has made several services for us, one with a scalloped edge sprigged with blue, and another along more severe lines worked with initials. She also uses the traditional Moustier colours, mostly yellows and greens which are traced in an arabesque of gargoyles and grotesques. Madame Garnier in Moustier itself is another potter and specialises in beautiful script, while further afield, at Apt, Joseph Bernard produces (or rather, used to produce, before his recent demise) the classical yellow and brown marbleised wares named after the town with pale, buttercup-yellow trimmings, again based on an eighteenth-century formula.

Both Moustier and Apt are situated in the Vaucluse and entail a day's drive, but through very beautiful country, especially the road to Moustier which winds along the precipitous banks of a canyon, a spectacular sight at all times of the year, and probably at its best in the autumn.

Nearer to home is the Potterie Provençale at Biot, another of my favourite haunts. There the Auge Laribe family go on making the traditional Provençal services in green, yellow and black. There is also Madura, Picasso's potter at Vallauris, but alas the town is being rapidly ruined by the grizzly efforts of third-rate artisan .

To return to the house, when the weather was bad we would eat at one of the three round tables in the dining-room. Having three tables was a way of dividing the guests. Lunches we nearly always had in the loggia at a long table spread with a coarse linen cloth, and set with the local Biot pottery and glass and bamboo-handled knives and forks. White canvas curtains tied back onto the columns shaded us from the glare, and we sat on black Danish plywood chairs – a very successful combination.

Catherine, as I have said, is an excellent cook, but I can't think of any particular dish to single out, other than her *beignets* of marrow flowers. The flowers must be picked early and placed face downwards, preferably on a slab of marble to keep them from closing. At the last moment they are dipped in batter and then dropped into boiling oil. They must be served very crisp and eaten with a tomato sauce made with onions and different herbs. Another speciality are her water-ices, especially one made from the small Cavaillon melons.

We now come, inevitably, to the question of restaurants, an endless topic of conversation since everyone has his own list, and restaurants, in France, have a way of becoming an important part of one's life. Obviously I cannot do justice to the dozens of sympathetic small bistros such as the *Oursin* at Antibes that caters in sea food caught by relations in the neighbourhood. Some of the better known restaurants I have not mentioned at all for the simple reason that I find them depressing. They are what the French call *chiquet*. It is interesting to note that few of the Michelin's starred restaurants will serve typical Provençal food. '*La Cuisine Provençale*' as Paul Bocuse will tell you, '*est amusante mais ça ne sera jamais la grande cuisine*' [is amusing but can never be considered *la grand cuisine*]. Bocuse owns *L'Oasis* at La Napoule and was a pupil of the famous Point at Vienne's *La Pyramide*. *Ratatouille* is probably the best known of the local dishes and consists of a mixture of tomatoes, peppers, onions and eggplant fried in oil and heavily flavoured with garlic. *Pissaladière* is another popular plate – an onion tart laid over with black olives and strips of pickled anchovy. There are, also, all the different stuffed vegetables, always seasoned with garlic. *Salade Niçoise* needs no explaining and has many variants. The one concession that most good chefs are willing to make to the *cuisine Provençale* is Marseille's famous bouillabaisse. But how seldom is this soup what it should be. It takes hours to prepare and its ingredients consist of some twenty-one different kinds of fish.

Some restaurants, of course, depend more on their charm than their food. Such is the *Colombe d'Or* situated on the walls of the fortified village of St Paul up in the foothills behind Cagnes. It was started by a Sunday painter called Paul Roux, and out of nothing he created a small hotel and restaurant of undeniable charm. Roux had a flair for attracting people and made a great success out of his father's café and with the money he earned bought a tumbledown château in the Pyrénées and reassembled it incorporating his father's *guinguette*. It is a pastiche but done with great taste, the kind of place that thirty years ago was fairly new. Picasso working at Vallauris used to dine there. Braque, Léger, Vlaminck, Maurice Chevalier and Mistinguette were also amongst the habitués. Matisse, crippled, would appear in his wheelchair. Roux, a painter of sorts himself, was attracted to this milieu. He would tell one how Picasso with that extraordinary enthusiasm of his would scribble over any blank space at hand, especially on paper napkins, sketches that he tore up when he left. One day, Roux tantalised by seeing so much going to waste, rescued the latest débris and painstakingly stuck the pieces together, out of it assembling the face of a starry-eyed girl which he persuaded Picasso to sign. As time passed Roux added to his collection and by degrees assembled the paintings one now sees on the walls. After Roux's death in 1953 his widow took over, a charming, sensible woman who for some years presided in a simple black cotton dress. Of late her son and her English daughter-in-law have been doing most of the running, and Francis Roux goes on adding to his father's collection. There are few hotels that can offer its clients a Calder mobile by a heated swimming pool. In 1962 thieves broke into the place and made off with most of the contents, holding the family up for ransom for the repurchase of their collection. Twenty canvases were taken and one hears that Chagall pulled a wry face when he learnt that his painting was not included.

The French cinema world has now replaced that of the painters and the food is all right, but has no pretensions and gets no mention in the *Guide Michelin* other than a few polite words about its atmosphere which the guide categorises as '*vieille Provence*'.

Hostellerie Jérôme at La Turbie is another restaurant of considerable charm, but of quite a different nature; a painted ceiling and pleated pink silk lampshades on the tables. Jérôme comes from Lorraine and his food is rich. His *morilles à la creme* are delicious, so also are his crayfish, the latter being flown in from Poland and kept alive in an

aquarium – a ton and a half of them every year! *Michelin* gives the
Jérôme a fairly high rating, the same that they give the Bec Rouge in
Monte-Carlo; to my mind a better restaurant. Like *Jérôme* it is im-
maculate but offers a more varied menu and an atmosphere of quiet
prosperity. But to really appreciate Monte-Carlo, one should dine on
the terrace of the Hôtel de Paris overlooking Garnier's elaborate,
plaster casino. For an hotel the food is remarkably good and its
splendidly elaborate dining-room wears an air about it that can only
be found in places that have catered to the great of this world for over
a century. —

The *Réserve* at Beaulieu must come very high on anyone's rating,
and above Beaulieu, dominating the heights, sits the strange neo-
Gothic *Château de Madrid**, built originally by a Canadian woman as a
private house. Views from its terraces are vertiginous and very splendid,
so also is the bill, high enough to make even Barbara Hutton, who was
staying with us, notice the figure, usually the last person in the world
to be affected by such considerations. The *Chèvre d'Or* at Eze is another
restaurant that had once been a private house, and this, too, provides
a spectacular bird's-eye view of the coast, and, incidentally, delicious
oignons à la grecque. In this same area comes *La Chaumière* situated on
the Grande Corniche. Monsieur Piéri, who owns the place, comes from
Ajaccio, and true to form has hung garlic and dried herbs from the
ceiling. The menu is limited and of the barbecue variety; whole shoulders
of lamb and slabs of beef are thrown onto the hot coals, banked with
dried branches of rosemary. Baskets of raw vegetables and ten-litre
sized aluminium tins of fresh cream are brought to the red and white
checkered tables. The vegetables one dips into an anchovy sauce, and
the cream one dollops onto fresh raspberries. For some time now,
La Chaumière has been the fashion, but I prefer the more democratic
L'Haçienda in the Gorbio Valley, behind Menton. Run by a retired
Strasbourgeois merchant marine, his calling is reflected in the Robinson
Crusoe-like collection of buildings he has thrown up against the side of
the mountain. Australian sulphur-crested cockatoos scream at one as
one parts the hide curtains at the door, and inside the flames from a
roaring fire dance over the ceiling, the whole accompanied by nostalgic
Mexican songs executed on a guitar. I have seen the place grow from a
small, one-roomed shelter to what amounts to a whole settlement of
thatching. The home-made pâtés are delicious, so also is the baby
sucking pig served only on Sundays. In Nice there is *Le Petit Brouant*

*The Château de Madrid no longer exists as a restaurant having reverted again to its original use.

and *Don Camillo* where they prepare *fettuccini* that equals those of the famous *Alfredo* in Rome. They also produce delicious *mille feuilles*, but what a pity someone can't influence the owner regarding the decor. Much more sympathetic is *La Trappa* in the old part of the town. I have invariably been the only foreigner in the place, its clientèle being largely made up of employees from the *préfecture*, or horticulturists from the nearby flower market. The little eating places along the front at Villefranche have their charm but are much too expensive for the quality of food they produce. Far superior is *Les Mouscardins* at St Tropez, built into the old fortifications. It specialises in Mediterranean fish: *mostelle, pageot, dorade* and *loup* and produces a delicious *langouste à la crème*. I always order the *dorade*, a much finer fish to my way of thinking than the much vaunted *loup*. It is carefully steamed with a *bouquet garni* and served with rice and a delectably creamy *sauce mousseline*. Monsieur Lions has the reputation of being one of the best chefs on the coast, and several times I have tried to coax him into giving me the correct recipe for the sauce. He explains, adding how easy it is, but the result makes it painfully obvious that something is missing, no doubt a small detail but of vital importance to the finished product.

Much further afield is the *Oustau de Baumanière* at Les Baux, the restaurant that fed Queen Elizabeth on her tour of Provence. *Michelin* accords it the full quota of stars and forks, signifying both an agreeable setting and the fact that it sets one of the best tables in France. It deserves this accolade, but *Michelin* seems to have slipped up as far as concerns *Hiely* at Avignon. Its two stars are a gross injustice when one compares the two restaurants. Monsieur Hiely, its founder, was alas killed the other day in a motor-car accident, but his son carries on the tradition. They refuse to cater for two services; when the tables are all occupied there is no point in waiting. 'How', Monsieur Hiely père used to explain, 'can I keep up my standards if the place is overcrowded?' Even more remarkable than this admirable display of principles are the prices, for they compare very favourably with any less ambitious establishment. Indeed so unusual is the quality of the food that I have driven three and a half hours to Avignon for the pleasure of introducing a friend: a long drive and one that on this occasion was undertaken in the pouring rain.

While on the subject of gastronomy, it would seem appropriate to make mention of the Auguste Escoffier Museum at Villeneuve-Loubet

on the Nice to Grasse road. It is not mentioned in *Michelin*, and I have
passed it a number of times without ever suspecting its existence.
Escoffier was an important man: a master chef and the father of what
might be termed contemporary cooking. It was Escoffier who dealt the
death-blow to the tasteless, lukewarm *plat monté* so popular up until
the beginning of the Second Empire. ——

The son of a blacksmith, he was born in October 1846. As a boy he
showed a talent for drawing, but discouraged by his father, was packed
off to work for his uncle who ran a restaurant in Nice. He enjoyed being
in a kitchen, and at twenty was already chef of the *Petit Moulin Rouge*
in Paris. The Franco-Prussian war followed and then came a series of
engagements involving some of the best restaurants in Paris, including
the role of head chef for an hotel in Nice. In early middle-age he married
a Monégasque; they had no children and one hears little about his wife.
He was the perfect example of a dedicated man, and the best part of
his life was spent concentrating on his profession. The museum photographs show Escoffier when already famous, wearing his Légion
d'Honneur ribbon. He stands white-haired, in a frock coat, with
moustache and beard, the prototype of a distinguished diplomat and
the chef's cap which he is wearing appears as a whimsy rather than a
proud badge of trade. It does not show in the photographs, but it
seems he was almost abnormally small, and to counteract this was
obliged to wear platform shoes to give him more height when working
over his stoves. Despite his imposing appearance, he had an unassuming personality but was very meticulous about his work, not
allowing smoking or anything alcoholic in his kitchen. If his aides were
thirsty they could drink barley water, and anyone shouting was severely
told off. It goes without saying that he was a stickler for quality;
only the best would do and no question either of substitution: the
saucepans must be of copper, not aluminium, and the same applied to
the fuel since Escoffier maintained coal and wood to be far superior for
cooking than either electricity or gas. So meticulous was he in his work
that when an order came down to the kitchen the head waiter was
asked to note the name of the client so that Escoffier, if he knew him,
could give the order his special attention. He was also the first to serve
à la carte meals, and not only was he an inventive and brilliant cook,
but also an excellent organiser. It was while working in Monte-Carlo
that Escoffier met Cézar Ritz who at the time was managing the
Grand Hotel, and so began, as Page and Kingsford put it, 'the most

famous and successful partnership that the profession has ever seen'.[4] Between them Escoffier and Ritz launched the Carlton Hotel in London and the Paris Ritz, and 'they set the London Savoy on the road to being probably the greatest hotel there has ever been'.[5] Ritz Hotels were opening up in most of the great capitals, and it would be Escoffier's business to organise their kitchens. The Hamburg-America Line, then building a fleet of big transatlantic liners, commissioned him in the same capacity. In 1912 he set sail on one of their ships and on board, as a guest of honour on her maiden voyage, was the German Emperor. Escoffier even dined with Kaiser Wilhelm during the voyage and indeed throughout his life seems to have had meals with the majority of his famous clients, particularly the ladies. He had a great regard for them, and attributes his best dishes to the admiration they inspired – his *Fraises Sarah Bernhardt, Poularde Adelina Patti* and *Pêche Eugénie* for the Empress. The more famous *Pêche Melba* he named after the great Australian singer. Melba always stayed at the Savoy when singing at Covent Garden, one of her famous roles being Elsa in Lohengrin. Escoffier happened to be at one of the performances and was so moved by the diva that he experimented again with his peaches. His *Pêche Eugénie* consisted of chilled peaches mixed with wild strawberries sprinkled with sugar and flavoured with kirsch and maraschino. Just before serving, a chilled champagne-flavoured *sabayon* should be poured over the dish. For Melba he poached the fruit in a light syrup, placing them over a bed of vanilla ice-cream. Remembering the great swan in the second act of Wagner's opera, he had the dish served in a silver bowl sunk in between the wings of a bird carved in ice. Melba gave a dinner the night following her first performance and this was the occasion for the presentation. Delicious as everyone found it, Escoffier felt that there was an ingredient missing, and several years later added a purée of fresh raspberries for sweetness.

Escoffier died in Monte-Carlo in 1935 aged almost ninety, and at his death the town where he was born took over his parents' house and turned it into a museum; in its small rooms are displayed a collection of old menus and a fairly complete record of engravings and photographs of well-known chefs. Among them one finds Lully, the founder of French opera and chef to Madame de Montpensier during the reign of Louis XIV; also Laguipière who froze to death in the retreat from Moscow, and Carême his great admirer who worked for Talleyrand. There is an amusing daguerreotype of Louis Cubat and his brother Pierre who

turned La Paiva's house in the Champs Elysées into a restaurant. The
brothers had quite a career; Pierre became head chef to the Czar
Nicholas II, and later left for the court of Siam with Louis. Alexandre
Dumas and Léon Daudet are both represented, two men of letters, both
impassioned gourmets. Unexpected are the arrangements of wax flowers,
but it would seem that modelling them was a pastime of Escoffier's; an
art he practised as efficiently as his cuisine. Presiding over all is a small
effigy of St Fortunat, one-time Bishop of Poitiers. The good man spent
his time composing verses in praise of the table, and Escoffier, touched
by the Bishop's interest, adopted him as his patron saint and the
protector of all those who toil in the kitchen. ⌣

🍂5

To People the Landscape

Fifty years ago the phrase 'going abroad for the winter' clearly suggested the popular notion of the 'season' on the Riviera, and no one living in a certain world ever questioned which Riviera. It is a term which still evokes the South of France but with the broadened frontiers brought about by flying 'going abroad' has become a loose term that applies to dozens of places where the sun shines. The world can count resorts by the legion, and one can argue in favour of any number of them. None to my mind, however, can quite equal the charm of this coast. To look at it from a practical point of view, it has been in the business longer than any major holiday area and no place can provide a greater variety offering every conceivable combination of luxury or informality. For some years already, it has ceased being exclusively the haunt of the rich, and caters these days to any pocket, and yet, despite these democratic leanings, manages in some strange way to keep its prestige. It is partly, of course – despite the rash of uncontrolled building – the spectacular beauty of the country and something yet more subtle than this – the mystique of the Riviera, an aura lent it by the people who haunt its shores: the renowned of this world whose names in the papers still have the power to attract. They lend the place a certain air of distinction, and I, for one, who could almost be accused of being a recluse, find it impossible to disassociate the place from the people, for they are a definite part of the Côte d'Azur.

I was lucky enough to live down here between the wars, perhaps the last of the Riviera as our parents knew it, and in the following pages I will try and give a series of quick vignettes, for, as I say, without the inhabitants or at least their imprint, the place loses something of its savour.

Before his death we saw a lot of Maugham. A great deal has been written about him lately, and I hesitate to add to the accumulation. It

might be worth while, though, to enlarge on some of the details. So
often with well-known people it is the small unimportant things in their
lives that one wants to hear about most. Lunching at the Mauresque
was a pleasure that never palled. On arrival, the first thing one noticed
was Fatima's stylised hand picked out in red on the white plaster gate-
post. Being Mohammed's daughter, this cabalistic sign was supposed to
ward off the evil eye. 'My father adopted it', Maugham would explain,
'and later I followed suit.' Since then it has appeared on the cover of
some sixty million books, which to date represents his total published
works.

From the gate the drive curved up between built-up rocks planted
with clumps of agapanthi. Climbing sharply, one arrived at tall green
doors, and again the red hand confronted one, carved on the lintel above
the entrance. A single flowering red hibiscus grew over the trellis covering the entrance front, and, as I remember it now, it seemed to be
perpetually in bloom. There was no need of a bell, for with the noise of
the wheels on the gravel one of the doors would swing silently open,
attended by a white-gloved footman. During the summer months the
invitation generally included a swim before lunch, or then one was
expected punctually at one, and punctuality was of prime importance
to one's own enjoyment. The garden mounted in terraces behind the
house, and on the uppermost terrace lay the pool, framed by four lead
pine cones from Italy, and at one end the noise of trickling water dripping from the marble lips of a faun carved by Bernini. The view was
magnificent and looked out over the pines to Villefranche bay and the
hazy form of Cap d'Antibes beyond. A little to the back of the pool
curved a platform buttressed by reddish rock, and on one of the
mattresses with which it was set would be lying one's host. If not
swimming, one would find him under the orange trees shading the
terrace in front of the house, or in winter in the long drawing-room
seated on a stool before the fire. Alan Searle, his secretary, would meet
the guests in the hall and precede them into the drawing-room, and
there Maugham would be, legs and arms crossed, chin up, exactly as
Graham Sutherland painted him. He had great charm and a certain
kindly warmth for those he liked, and as one approached would spring
up, come forward, arms outstretched. The arms would drop back again
to the sides without contact, but it was meant as a welcoming gesture.
Alan always made the cocktails – very dry martinis, or, when it was
hot, 'white ladies' made from gin, lemon juice, white of egg and coin-

treau. Maugham more often than not was informally dressed in baggy white linen trousers and an open-necked shirt.

La Mauresque was a pleasant house and Maugham always pretended that it annoyed Syrie, his one-time wife and famous decorator, that he had made such a success of it. It had a restrained baroque flavour lent it by its Spanish furniture, its blackamoors and *savonnerie* carpets. Two large comfortable sofas framed the fireplace in the drawing-room, over which was enthroned a fierce eagle in gilded wood with outspanned wings. I remember also a round table piled high with the latest books sent by the different publishers.

Generous, austere stairs mounted from the hall which rose the height of the house. White and yellow were the colours, and I remember an over life-sized female figure in monochrome greys dating from Picasso's classical period, a highly-coloured Matisse, Chinese carpets on a black slate floor, and dolphin tables flanked by Spanish chairs. On the left, as one came in, sat a Kuan-Yin, the goddess of mercy found in Peking. Handsome twelfth- and thirteenth-century Siamese bronze heads decorated the landings. I think it worth mentioning that the hall was the setting for what must have been a traumatic experience for one of the guests. A young man, dead now, had been staying with Willie and was on the point of leaving. His host was saying goodbye to him when the butler appeared on the stairs with his luggage. Reaching the last step, he gave the largest of the cases a smart tap against the iron banisters thus forcing the lock, and out tumbled a first edition of Willie's collected works. The young man had apparently packed his own bag, and the butler, suspicious by nature, had given it the once-over, and discovering the contents had decided on this drastic course of action.

The dining-room was on the small side, with a very high ceiling. All the ceilings were high and the proportions in this particular room were not very happy. The table was round and could seat eight, though our lunches were seldom more than six, usually five, and in old age when Maugham had grown very deaf it tired him to entertain. The last time I saw him, a few weeks before he died, he came to lunch, alone, with Alan at the Fiorentina. His memory had almost entirely gone and it was difficult for Alan who was sincerely devoted to him. *La Mort d'Arlequin*, an early Picasso dating from 1905 hung in the dining-room, a lovely thing painted with light washes of oil on a brown composite board, which Picasso had not even bothered to cover. There was also a nude figure of an athlete by Toulouse Lautrec, not a typical work, and it would amuse Maugham to make people guess, especially as they invariably attributed it wrongly. Surprising, too, was a portrait of himself by Marie Laurençin, surprising because one does not associate her with paintings of men. She had apparently expressly asked to paint Maugham and he had accepted, and tells an amusing story in connection with his sitting. Gregarious by nature, Laurençin kept up a lively conversation and on one occasion happened to question him on the correct English translation of the expression *je m'en fous*. Maugham was afflicted with a bad stammer which had the effect of accentuating whatever he said. 'Wee . . . eell,' he stuttered, clicking his fingers trying to get the word out, 'I told her that if she really wanted to know iii . . . t meant I . . . doooo . . . nt give a fuck.' It would appear to be a trifle strong for the context in which the French use it, but I suppose he was right.

The two other rooms in the house that might be of special interest were Maugham's own bedroom and his study on the roof, where he worked. Both had a certain austerity about them. In the bedroom he slept crosswise, the bed jutting out from a corner near the window. Behind it stood a Spanish baroque effigy, and next to it, ranged in a bookcase built into the thickness of the wall, were gathered his favourite authors; the complete works of William Hazlitt, Samuel Butler, and Henry James; Grimm's *Fairy Tales*, the letters of Edward Lear and André Gide's diaries; poems by W.B. Yeats and Laurence Sterne and Shakespeare's sonnets. Opposite the bed hung Maugham's last purchase, a large Lepine representing the quays of Paris. In the room there was also a Rouault and a small Renoir of a seated nude representing the model he so often painted towards the end of his life. On the mantel shelf stood a charming Bonnard of a child with its fat and jovial nurse, a small self-portrait of Gauguin, and a photograph of his mother. She died when Willie was eight years old, and it shows her to have been a delicate, dark-haired woman with large eyes and a pretty mouth. A black velvet ribbon circles her throat, and she is wearing a décolleté dress that exposes her shoulders. Maugham makes mention of the photograph in *Of Human Bondage*, his autobiographical novel, the book he considered to be his finest work, believing that it was the one thing of his that might possibly live.

The Mauresque is a two-storeyed house, and Maugham's study sits on the flat roof – a fairly large oblong room reached by a small green wooden staircase. I remember the room in detail since I was commissioned by *L'Oeil* to do an article on it. The roof had been spread with white gravel and on one side of the white parapet walls stood a bronze reproduction of a Pompeian faun. All round were the tops of the pines, and beyond a view of the sea. Long french windows ran the length of one wall through which one entered, the wall to the left being solid with books. A plain, dark wood table of Spanish origin, acting as desk, faced the library shelves, the light coming from a small window in a raised recess at the back, invisible from where Maugham sat. At the time of this particular visit Maugham was eighty-five and working on what he thought was to be his last book, a collection of essays. 'With age, you know the inspiration dries up. It's a long time now since I felt the irresistible urge to write a novel.' He wrote his manuscripts in longhand, in a neat, tightly packed script. Some pages he had just been working on lay on the desk, and on top of them a pair of gold-rimmed spectacles, also a pair of pink elastic mittens with zip fasteners, an arm against poor circulation. At the far end of the room, opposite the french windows, stood what must have been the gilded top of an altar-piece, circular in shape and about six feet high, possibly Spanish-Mexican. But, of course, by far the most arresting piece of decoration was the famous Gauguin window. Not immediately apparent, one discovered it only after passing the desk and stepping up into the raised recess already mentioned. A small fireplace and a sofa covered in a blue batik con-stituted the furnishings with the Gauguin, set in the wall between them, forming the middle panel of a diagonal, three-paned window. Originally the Gauguin had been the glassed-in top of a door which Maugham discovered in 1916 while visiting a Chiefesse who lived twenty-five miles out of Papeete, an episode described by him in his *Writer's Notebook*. The painting represents a black-haired Tahitian girl with a yellow and white sarong gathered at her waist. She is carrying what looks like a breadfruit while a white rabbit squats at her feet. A kind of nimbus frames her head, while glimpses of the sea can be seen through the white flowering branches of some imaginary tree – the sea flecked with the sails of three canoes. The silhouettes are picked out in thin black lines, and the colours are flat, milky-blue, pale ochre and almond-green.

People have described the feeling of tension they experienced at La Mauresque, but I can't say I was ever aware of it. Admittedly one had to tread warily at times, for fundamentally Maugham was a formal man and not given to confidences. A certain amount of tact was needed, and Alan having lived with him so long knew exactly how to handle things;

knew Maugham's moods and was adept at steering the conversation. The subtleties of his manipulation became evident as Maugham grew deafer. No longer bothering to disguise his tactics, he just noted aloud that such and such was not a particularly happy topic at the moment, or that so and so was definitely out of favour. Maugham was not one to suffer fools or bores gladly, and could at times be very caustic, but this for the onlooker gave a certain spice to the gathering – providing, of course, that one was not on the receiving end.

At Maugham's death, the villa went to Lady Glendevon, his daughter, and not wanting to live in it herself it was put on the market and bought by an American real estate dealer.

Another house I always enjoyed going to was Madame Balsan's Lou Sueil.* It stands on the next hill to Eze and belongs now to the Balconies. One can perhaps question the Balsans' taste when they chose the eleventh-century Cistercian monastery of Le Thoronet, near Draguignan, as an inspiration for Lou Sueil, but then Madame Balsan had immense flair for making anything she lived in attractive, and no doubt her background precluded her from settling for anything less imposing. For years the châtelaine of Blenheim, she had perhaps become more accustomed than she realised to its splendidly pompous architecture. Whatever the reason, Lou Sueil had great charm when she was in it. I have memories of handsome Jacobean panelling, Clouet paintings, and comfortable chairs slip-covered in chintz, and outside, drifts of spring bulbs; carpets of hyacinths and bluebells mixed in with the grass under the olives.

Madame Balsan must have been in her fifties when I first knew her, and she was still a very handsome woman: tall and thin with an uptilted nose, amused eyes and a wonderfully slender neck. She wore her greying hair swirled forwards over dark arching eyebrows, and watching her it needed no great effort of the imagination to see her again as the provocative young woman etched by Helleu. There is also that splendid Boldini of her, now in the Metropolitan Museum in New York. Boldini always painted his women in exaggerated poses, sheathing their slim figures in tulle dresses that swirled out in boldly slashed blurrings of the brush. One sees Madame Balsan as the young and beautiful Duchess, seated, half-turned on a chaise-longue, her weight all on one arm, and with her Lord Ivor, her youngest son, who sprawls restlessly across her knees. Boldini, in common with Augustus John, had the reputation of

* *Lou sueil* in provençal means 'the hearth'.

seldom allowing the more seductive of his sitters to escape unmolested, and to protect herself from the attentions of this stocky Silenus the Duchess had dragged along Master Ivor, obviously the most reluctant of chaperons.

Madame Balsan had a remarkable memory and would often reminisce in a high clear voice. She would tell of the days when Horowitz, young and unknown, appeared from Russia to perform in Garnier's little theatre in Monte-Carlo. Toscanini conducts and Diaghilev takes up residence for the winter with his troupe. Passages from new ballets such as *Aurora's Wedding* and Stravinsky's *Night People* echo through the gold and white hall. Much later Lord Berners' ballet *Britannia* is joined to the list. Madame Balsan recounts how the English colony turned out with patriotic fervour to applaud and the following day she entertained him at Lou Sueil. 'What really impressed me,' Madame Balsan pipes in her little girl voice, 'was Lord Berners' Rolls.' A small harmonium had been installed facing his seat and at the back, on the felt lining, he had pinned a collection of butterflies. 'You can imagine,' she laughs, 'the effect this had on the French.' Madame Balsan was amusing also on the subject of her honeymoon with the Duke in Monte-Carlo in 1895. They were staying at the Hôtel de Paris and she describes their meals amongst a lively crowd

of beautiful women and elegant men, many of whom were acquaintances of my husband. When I asked him who they all were I was surprised by his evasive answers and still more startled when informed that I must not look at the women whose beauty I admired. It was only after repeated questioning that I learned that these were ladies of easy virtue whose beauty and charm had a price. It became increasingly complicated when I heard that I must not recognize the men who accompanied them, even though some of them had been my suitors a few months before.[1]

These first meetings with Madame Balsan take me back to the early thirties when tennis had become a great new attraction. One remembers Jean Borota and the ugly Suzanne Lenglen who moved about the court with the grace and agility of a ballet dancer; there was Tilden and von Cramm and the wiry old Gustave v of Sweden, who, in common with fellow royalty, 'appreciated' when playing a game to be allowed to win. Tall and cadaverous, he made quite a spectacle on the centre court. But what really struck me about him was the strange habit he had of spitting into a little silver box which he carried stowed away somewhere on the royal skeleton. It would appear that he had a chronic catarrhal condition and found the ordinary handkerchief totally inadequate.

Simultaneously with the tennis came years of burning summers, another dimension for the coast that had been helped along by men like Frank Jay Gould who had bought up most of Juan-les-Pins and had stakes in Cap d'Antibes. I think we must have passed through a cycle of more clement weather, for it seems to me that the summers were very much hotter during the years of my youth. Vividly it comes back to me – pictures of fashionable crowds bronzed by the sun and dressed by Chanel in trousers and beads. Chanel herself lived in an attractive house built by the architect Schwitzen. It sits in an old olive orchard on the side of a hill above Cap Martin. La Pausa, she called it, and it still goes under that name but is owned now by Mr Reves, Churchill's one-time agent and publisher. Reves has assembled a very personal and brilliantly chosen collection of Impressionists, but it is under Chanel's aegis that I like to remember the house: large low-ceilinged rooms, sparsely furnished, with handsome pieces of Spanish and Provençal furniture. Along with Syrie Maugham, she was one of the first to start the no-colour habit, only in Chanel's case the gamut ran in the beiges: quilted Provençal cottons and huge sofas covered, I think, in chamois leather. The garden was equally simple, planted only with lavender and rose-mary, and all round the smoky light filtering through the centuries-old olives. Chanel had a wonderful sense of luxury and great taste. I can't say that I was one of her intimate friends, rather I observed from a distance and listened; indeed this silence was a condition she imposed on most of those around her, induced by the fact that she seldom stopped talking. I remember her at La Pausa sitting on the floor of her terrace hugging her knees. Our conversation escapes me, but not her presence, which was tomboyish but alluringly feminine – the nose slightly tilted, the eyes dark and lively, and the mouth mobile and curled up at the corners. With the years the eyes were to grow more and more simian. She wore trousers and a sweater and a great deal of jewellery, wide ivory bracelets encrusted with a Maltese cross of rubies, and rows of pearls strung with seed pearls instead of knots in between each bead. Wound in with these were blobs of emeralds joined together with heavy gold links. Clip earrings hid her over-large ears. I think the secret of Chanel's great success as a couturier was the fact that she never designed anything that she could not wear herself, and which suited her piquant, boyish charm. Added to this was an unerring eye for colour and an innate sense of quality. Much of her jewellery was identical to that which she sold in her mirrored boutique on the Rue Cambon in Paris, the only difference being that hers was real! '*Le vrai imite le faux*'* as Sem the satirist once described her glitter.

Chanel was the innovator of many fashions, but the one which had the most effect on our lives down here was her penchant for buffet lunches. It made her nervous having servants around all the time, so banishing the footmen to the pantry she made us fend for ourselves, an unusual procedure in the thirties, particularly in that kind of a house.

The Hon. Mrs Reginald Fellowes was yet another of our neighbours who left their mark. A subtle one it must be admitted, for her dominance was of the most ephemeral kind and went no deeper than the social scene. But the fact remains that it is difficult to write about the Riviera without mention of her. She has coloured one's impressions of the coast for at least the length of time that any of us who knew her still lives. In all probability death will dispel the lingering reflections of the charm and the elegance with which she, and people like her, lived their lives. Like the faint odour of a long closed trunk, all will evaporate past recall. Perhaps not? It all depends on how many people will have remembered her in yet unpublished letters or will have made her live in unsuspected memoirs.

Mrs Fellowes had a house on Cap Martin, but spent most of her summers on board her yacht, *Sister Anne*, and the *Sister Anne*, like everything about its owner, was immaculately elegant. I forget the tonnage, but she was large enough to cross the Atlantic. Invited to lunch, Daisy Fellowes would appear in her yacht and drop anchor off our point. Leaving the ship, she would step into a spotless dinghy manned by one of her crew, and be rowed ashore, half hidden, more likely than not, beneath the shade of a parasol. How does one describe Mrs Fellowes? – quiet, composed, remarkably handsome, and *very* distinguished. Her father was the Duc Decazes and her mother an American, one of the Singers of sewing-machine fame. Those who knew her as a young girl say that she was rather a plain child and that the metamorphosis of later years was achieved by sheer effort of will. She was one of the first women in the fashionable world to have her nose changed, shaved down to the classical proportions one knows. The rest was just a question of intelligence and concentration. She had that

* 'The real thing is an imitation of the artificial.'

irresistible quality of making one feel the only person in the room whom she wanted to see. One has to admit, however, that not many women were subjected to this particular intimacy. Her stare was very direct and her voice pitched a little too high, but even this failing, which would have been unattractive in most people, she somehow managed to turn to effect. I have a very clear memory of her at a concert given in the Villa Kerylos at Beaulieu, a nineteenth-century interpretation of a Greek dwelling built by the archaeologist, Théodore Reinach. It was at night and the concert was given in the atrium and, whether by chance or not is hard to say, Daisy Fellowes had seated herself so that her profile stood outlined against the hard Doric fluting of a white marble column, and the impact, by candle-light, was quite remarkable. Mrs Fellowes would also attend the concerts given in the Place de l'Eglise high up on the mountain-side in the old town of Menton, an enchanting square paved in a mosaic of black and white pebbles. To reach the square ordinary mortals would have to leave their cars on the sea front and negotiate the climb by a double flight of stairs that compose a decorative ladder escalating the steep incline on which the town is built. It is an attractive approach, but somewhat of an ordeal – not however for Daisy. She had managed to ensnare the director of the festival and was allowed, as a special favour, to appear from behind the scenes, having been driven up to a point of vantage by her chauffeur. The different air companies were equally docile and Daisy's approach across the runways was invariably under escort; a progress led by her wheel-chair, a form of locomotion that she conjured up long before the symptoms of heart trouble really bothered her.

Indeed one had to pay court to Daisy; it was expected of one, and like all enchantresses she knew very well how best to ensnare – her nets, in her case, being her houses: Strawberry Hill Gothic in England, and a charming late eighteenth-century house on the Left Bank in Paris arranged in the 1960s by herself and Georges Geffroy, at that time certainly one of France's most talented decorators, a difficult character with a wonderful eye for unusual pieces. I remember one time he happened to be down on the Riviera with Arturo Lopez. We had just moved into Fiorentina and were given to understand that he would like to see it. A meeting was arranged, and he arrived and in total silence moved from room to room. Only on reaching the library at the back of the house did he enthuse over a basket of ostrich eggs. 'Ah that!' he exclaimed in French, emphasising the 'that', 'is very pretty.'

It was the one thing, of course, that I could lay no claim to, except for the fact of having assembled them!

Mrs Fellowes also had a villa on Cap Martin, and of the three, Les Zoraides was perhaps the most personal to her. Basically it was rather an ugly house, but one was never given a chance to become aware of its failings. Here she reigned supreme in her exoticism – simulated leopard-skin carpets put down long before the decorating world had become conscious of Africa's fauna, mirrored balls hung in clusters filling the stairwell – one passed from surprise to surpise. Great comfort, delicious food, and always the unexpected, the contraption for instance in which coffee was sometimes served, an object brought back from the Bosphorus in the holds of the *Sister Anne*: a kind of suspended glass beaker with an iron stopper at one end up against which one had to press one's cup in order to have it filled. 'So amusing', Daisy Fellowes would pipe. It was, in point of fact, hideously ugly, decorated with vine tendrils hammered out in black iron, but that it was seen in Mrs Fellowes's possession somehow exonerated it. The same applies to the enormous glass globe in the library. Triple-tailed Japanese goldfish sported themselves round its perimeter, whilst inside these double walls sat a warbling canary. I do not intend to give the impression that Mrs Fellowes was without taste; on the contrary she had great flair and courage, but was bored by the conventional. She dressed beautifully, was among the first to patronise Schiaparelli when under the influence of the Surrealists and a photograph of her exists wearing one of her most exaggerated creations – a black felt hat resembling a shoe. For a period of her life Daisy became managing editress of the Paris *Harper's Bazaar*. I did not know her in those days, but she must certainly have been as outré as that highly talented Diana Vreeland, the woman largely responsible for turning American *Vogue* into the most luxurious and imaginative product of the magazine world.

Dining with Mrs Fellowes in the summer was an enchantment. One sat outside on her terrace screened over with an awning of *canisse*, the split reed fences which the farmers down here use to protect their crops. From the terrace shallow brick steps carried one down to a distant pool backed by a colonnade of ancient columns. The scale was impressive, the steps vast and the pool huge. Imperial Rome could have conceived no better. Handled by anyone else the setting could easily have been pompous. One was constantly aware of Daisy's courage, and nowhere better than in her painting by Sutherland; it is not every

ageing beauty who would sit to Graham Sutherland for her portrait.
Sutherland, certainly the most perspicacious portraitist of his day, does
not exactly spare his sitter. Take, for example, his remarkable painting
of Helena Rubinstein – a great middle-European peasant standing
firmly in profile armoured by her own astuteness and hard work in a
carapace of glitter, enamelled in beads and jewels, looking like some
formidable twentieth-century Byzantine empress. I met her on several
occasions, and for me she always remained Sutherland's portrait,
monosyllabic, sometimes uttering no more than a grunt the whole way
through dinner. His painting of Mrs Fellowes is no less remarkable.
Painted in her *palazzo* in Venice, he shows her reclining on a chaise-
longue, elegant, handsome, with that direct enigmatic stare that was
hers, in this case fixed on some object out of the picture. He has even
suggested a slight thickening of her figure but without destroying the
image. Her hands are wrinkled but long and aristocratic, with manicured
nails, nails that some have felt as claws.

I first met the Sutherlands during the war in London with Kenneth
Clark and at gatherings at the Churchill Club, run as a cultural centre
for the Armed Forces. I took to them both immediately and, like most
of my friends, was a great admirer of his paintings, then largely concentrated on the ravages of war, for he was painting in an official
capacity as one of the war artists.

My impression then was that Sutherland had never been to the
Riviera, and I remember trying to describe it to him. One felt it was a
country he would be attracted to and would want to interpret – and
how remarkably well he has succeeded. He seems to express the very
bones of a landscape, at the same time charging it with a feeling of
suppressed excitement, a magic all of his own. An extraordinary
sympathy seems to exist between himself and the thing he is painting,
whether it be a palm-frond fence, a datura or a tangerine, split open
and lying in the sun. His tangerine, in some strange way, becomes
more tangerine than the fruit itself. The outcome of it all was that we
lent Sutherland the Clos Fiorentina, the dower house as it were on the
property, and the house I now live in. Later he rented another villa and
worked in a studio he found on the port of St Jean. Eventually the
inevitable happened, as it has happened to so many of us; Sutherland
was so taken with the country that he decided to move here and started
to look for a house, and eventually found La Maison Blanche behind
Menton. It is a contemporary building designed by a woman architect

who claims Le Corbusier as a pupil. At any rate, the style is recognisable and the Sutherlands very soon added their stamp to it, that touch of luxury all contemporary buildings seem to need to make them habitable. Additions were made and the garden enlarged and sitting on the new terrace one looks out over a sweeping view of mountains collapsing in misty folds to the sea, a sheet of blue some ten miles below. The room behind, shut off by sliding plate-glass windows, is handsome and airy and hung with a series of Sutherland's Welsh landscapes. The furniture, much of it, is also designed by him, and mixed in with it are a set of chairs coming from some eighteenth-century folly, composed of interlaced vine roots. As it happens, many of the guests are convinced that Sutherland is also responsible for the chairs, and they could, in fact, have been a product of his inventive mind.

The Countess Jean de Polignac, Madame Lanvin's daughter, was another of our neighbours who played an important part in our lives. She had a large property called La Bastide du Roy in the neighbourhood of Biot. It was a place of mellowed charm and one of the few houses that made me wonder sometimes whether it was a mistake to live on the coast. Once a royal hunting lodge, it stood on a hill dominating the surrounding countryside which one glimpsed through the cypress that framed its walks. Steps banked with yellow banksia roses lead up to the front door, and on the far side of the house formal beds of heliotrope and pale-green zinnias formed a parterre round a great tank, or pool. There were other *pièces d'eau* and balustraded views while the house itself rose in an austere oblong, its old walls blotched over in faded ochre and pierced by a quantity of shuttered windows. Another feature of the garden was the circular theatre cut and clipped in the manner of the *settecento* Italian gardens round Florence.

Very often, as one wound up the driveway to the Bastide, a metallic click would drift through the hedges. It was the châtelaine playing *pétanque*, a form of bowls. Despite a slight infirmity she was an impassioned player, the infirmity manifesting itself as an unsteady walk due to some derangement of the middle ear. On another occasion Francis Poulenc, seated at the piano, was playing the waltz out of his ballet *Les Biches*. I can hear it now if I close my eyes, and see Marie-Blanche standing by the piano, holding onto the edge, swaying slightly. Her tottering was really an added endearment, for she would rest her hand on one's arm when walking into a room. She had a sweet smile and lovely eyes, and despite the sophistication of her life remained in

G.R.—3

some funny way completely untouched. It was quite impossible to resist her, and few people did.

It was Marie-Blanche who taught me how to use my eyes. One would be going somewhere with her in her old Packard Cabriolet with its whitened wheels, driven by Jean who aged with the car but appeared, like his charge, indestructible. I knew Marie-Blanche for some twenty years, and neither chauffeur nor car ever changed. It was high off the ground, and I would sit in the back with her. 'But look, Rory, *look* at the colour of the sea against the pale sky', and when she talked she had the habit of gently patting her chest, a mere brushing of her fingers against a jabot. She wore little jewellery; two diamond bows in her hair, which attached the net that she affected instead of a hat. She was dressed, of course, by the Maison Lanvin which she owned, but I can't say I was ever conscious of her clothes. She herself appeared supremely indifferent to them and seemed detached about the business; or would it be more accurate to say that she gave the appearance of being so. Underneath this appealing helplessness of hers lurked a will of steel harnessed to a biting intelligence. One of her roles was that of playing Egeria to France's talented musicians, she herself being an accomplished singer trained under Nadia Boulanger. There was also her world of painting; the remarkable collection of the Impressionists she had formed with her mother. She had known Renoir and Monet and was herself like the dappling of light on his ponds – mercurial, quick, and yet with an almost oriental calm. Her own collection of paintings, inherited in part from her mother, she kept in Paris, amongst them a portrait of herself by Vuillard.

When we moved into the big house we decided to keep a strict eye on the visitors' book: signatures and dates, no comments, only professionals would be encouraged to perform. There were the exceptions, Claudette Colbert for one. Not a painter, she nevertheless did a likeness of herself, substituting her head for that of one of the sphinxes guarding the walk down to the sea.

The visitors' book starts off with a fine flourish, with the Graham Sutherlands and on the opposite page a gouache by the master, dated May 1947. Turning the pages brings back fond memories. One is reminded of incidents long since forgotten; the night, for instance, that Irving Penn, a well-known photographer, and his wife came to dinner. I was alone, it was spring and the garden was heady with jasmin and Fiorentina was looking its best; for houses, like people, have their good days. When the guests left I escorted them to their car and turned to walk the dogs, and was surprised when a few minutes later they drove back. I hardly knew them, and embarrassed at finding me there, they apologised 'but we had to have one last look'.

I find a page of George Auric's; he has written his initials, composing the letters with the opening bars of his *Matelos*. Louise de Vilmorin's four-leafed clover appears quite often, and Romain Gary has copied out a passage from his *Racines du Ciel*. Lesley Blanch, his wife at that period, was an even more frequent visitor, and from her I begged a paragraph or two from the *Sabres of Paradise*, an engrossing study of Shamyl. Maugham inscribed a page with worldly advice from his *Writer's Notebook* and Sacheverell Sitwell evokes the heat with the opening paragraph of *Southern Baroque Art* and how wonderfully evocative he can be. 'Six o'clock in the morning,' he writes, 'and already the heat of Naples was such that it required confidence to believe in any hours of darkness ...' Freya Stark is another contributor on the occasions she would drive over when staying on the Italian Riviera. Small, compact, her feet barely reaching the ground when sitting down – coiffed in the latest Reboux hat from Paris, a large blob of a jewel on one finger, she is the last person in the world one would suspect of being an intrepid traveller.

Of all the pages, the one that gives me the most pleasure is Peter Quennell's inscription copied from *Sign of the Fish*, what he is pleased to call an autobiographical fragment. The passage describes a flight of flamingoes viewed from our point during a period of migration:

Up the Gulf of Beaulieu, arriving from Italy, came a column of slowly travelling birds – not in extended order as wild geese fly, when they travel at night above the Scottish lowlands, but linked one by one in a gently undulating chain like the floating tail of a vast celestial kite, the drifting streamer that might follow an archangel or a loose ribbon attached to the Chariot of Venus. They were flamingoes making for the marshes of the Camargues, where, amid the lagoons and the reed-beds and the salt pastures of wandering black cattle, they are still permitted, even in the twentieth century, to lead their harmless unnecessary lives, and brighten the mudbanks on which they descend with a scattering of delicate rosy feathers. . . . They were flying in unison; and every rhythmic pulse of their wings momentarily revealed the rosy under-surface; so that the celestial streamer not only changed its shape – an exquisite arabesque forming and reforming through a variety of beautifully broken curves – but, at the same time, was constantly changing its time as it traversed the brilliant background of the heavens, now greyish, faintly flushed with rose, now the vivid rose of an unclouded summer dawn. –

Quennell has copied out this passage indicating 'the gently undulating chain' by a dipping and rising script. It is a beautiful page, and opposite to it Gerald Van der Kemp, the Curator-in-Chief of Versailles, has done a sensitive study of shells in gouache – a pink strombus and half of a greyish-yellow clam.

Quennell is an ideal guest and as good a conversationalist as he is a writer. With his acute sense of observation and an elegant and precise use of words, he can enlarge on the most trivial occurrences and give one a pungent rendering of some luncheon or dinner that before his interpretation had appeared indifferent, even boring. Sit him next to an attractive woman and he can be relied on to immediately gain her confidence, and such are his powers of persuasion that by the end of the meal she will have divulged her innermost secrets. It never fails.

Raymond Mortimer is another excellent talker, erudite, has great warmth and, above all, is immensely curious about a wide variety of subjects.

Cyril Connolly used also to be a frequent visitor in the days before we moved into the big house, and Cyril was another of those rare creatures able to weave a web of enchantment round the mundanities of everyday life. He would give a whole dissertation on the quality of a Charenton melon: its flavour, the consistency of its flesh, even the intricacies of its veinings. The same for a particular wine, or the virtues of such and such a place for swimming. But he was at his best on the sensuous appeal of objects. He would touch them, hold them, and his passionate concern was such that it gave an added appeal to the object in question.

Another page in the book is entirely taken up by Sir Frederick Mutesa's signature. It sprawls in secure English fashion proclaiming the hand of a gentleman. His Highness Mutesa II was the thirty-sixth Kabaka of Uganda, and had been almost exclusively educated by the British, with two years at Magdalen College, Cambridge, followed by an honorary commission in the Grenadier Guards. His stay at Fiorentina was a question of reciprocity. He had been our host at Kampala on *Mengo*, the royal hill.

The Kabaka, or King Freddie as he was affectionately termed by the press in London, was a young man of thirty when we visited him in 1954. Slight, elegant and of medium height, he had a pleasant easy manner and a dry sense of humour, and had proved an excellent host; he delegated Prince Harry, his younger brother, to show us the royal tombs, and that same evening had driven us out to his hunting lodge situated about an hour out of town over a dusty road through acres of sugarcane. He told us that he would have liked to take us swimming, he had his own private lake. 'But you know, I asked the gamekeeper about the crocodiles and he answered that it was perfectly all right – that there was only one that he knew of. One too many for me!' laughed the Kabaka. He had a charming, soft spoken voice, so soft at times that it was difficult to hear him. It was on taking our leave that we had invited him to Fiorentina, promising him, so we thought, a weekend of carefree bathing.

It was full summer when he arrived with his suite consisting of his brother, a young sister, an aide and several attendants. We all trooped down to the pool. King Freddie was enjoying himself and was in very good form. The ramp of the diving-board was about the height of a chair and if used as such dominated the scene. Instinctively the Kabaka installed himself and held court, while the drinks were passed round. The young Princess, in the meantime, had joined my brother and sister down by the sea. My brother dived in, to be followed promptly by the royal guest, her immersion taking the form of a wild jump. There ensued a terrible flaying of arms, followed by gasps and the Kabaka, had it not been for my brother, might have lost a possible heir. It appears the Princess had never been swimming before and had been ashamed to admit it. 'You see,' the Kabaka laughed, 'your bathing is not much safer than mine.'

One name that should have been in the visitors' book, only I never dared ask her to sign, was Garbo's. I knew of the occasion when she had been staying with Grace Moore in Connecticut and Miss Moore, to pay her a compliment, had walked up to Garbo after dinner, before they all left for New York, and asked her to be the first to sign. Miss Moore was holding the book open, at the same time offering Garbo a pen. There was a terrible moment of silence and Garbo, in real consternation,

like a trapped animal, had looked at the book and then up at her
hostess and in almost a whisper said, 'oh, no, Grace, I . . . can't'. Grace
Moore, not known for concealing her reactions, was clearly astonished
and vexed; Garbo burst into tears. The hesitation on Garbo's part was
not affectation; she has a real phobia about signing her name, is shy, in
fact, about a great many things; refuses, for example, to discuss anything to do with her work and has never been known to pass an opinion
on any of her own films – is what the press claims her to be, 'the most
enchantingly mysterious woman of her time'. Had I not known about
her before we met, I doubt very much whether I should have noticed
anything so different about her, except, of course, for her extraordinary
beauty. When down here in the South, Garbo always stayed with
George Schlee, a Russian-born American. Schlee was her accepted
chevalier gallant; a pleasant, amusing man, older than Garbo and clever,
one heard, on the stock market. I never saw Garbo without him, and
it appears that with him she lost much of the timidity that at times
turns her into a recluse.

I went on several occasions to Villa Le Roc, Schlee's house at Cap
d'Ail. Built by a Russian some time in the early nineteen-hundreds, it
had the air of a small *garçonnière*. It had no garden to speak of and sat
on a rocky promontory into which Schlee had sunk a pool, surrounding
it with a hedge of pittisporum, a precaution to ward off prying photog-
raphers. I remember very little about the house; it gave one a feeling of
sober solidity, very impersonal. Garbo's own room was even austere, no
signs of make-up, no bottles, no books; it looked like a suite in an hotel
when somebody is ready to leave. Garbo herself was (I use the past tense
since she seldom accepts invitations now that Schlee is dead) as un-
obtrusive as her face allowed her to be, quietly dressed, generally in a
pair of shantung trousers with a tunic top, a ring on the finger of her
young boy's hands, a small wrist-watch and a cigarette holder. She
loved Fiorentina, felt relaxed there, and laughed a great deal, throwing
her head back. It is difficult to describe the effect she had on one:
apart from the extraordinary beauty she wore an aura about her that,
like royalty, makes one a little shy. She seldom refers to people by their
Christian names, but with that wonderfully resonant voice of hers, with
a slight accent, she makes one's surname sound like a caress. Slowly she
pronounces it, teasing, with a slow smile.

I occasionally still run into Garbo – at St Tropez shopping, or in
Florence where she had gone with friends to see the Henry Moore show.

She has changed very little; a few lines more or less make little difference to the extraordinary presence. As to the legend, it seems to be growing. Periodically the different cinemas give Garbo festivals, and through these revivals she has become a star to a whole new generation – young people who had hardly heard her name.

✤6

Menton Man, Ligurian Tribesmen and the Greeks

The preceding chapters have dealt with some of the facets of Riviera life and have, I hope, managed to give an impression of the general atmosphere, and even the feel of the country. But the picture is a conventional one and deals mostly with the charm of the coast as a fashionable resort, a place to which one escapes to bask in the sunshine and forget – a delicious no-man's-land. Things, however, take on an entirely different aspect if one happens to live down there; the horizon widens and the land, in some strange way, imposes itself on one, awakens one's curiosity, makes one want to know something of its history.

The Riviera as we know it dates from comparatively recent times, going back no further than some hundred years. What, then, of its past? One starts delving, and the obvious place to begin is the archaeological museum at Cimiez, installed in the ground floor of a handsome eighteenth-century house known as the Villa des Arènes, situated, as its name suggests, on the precincts of an old Roman town. It is here that one will find the fine, life-size statue of Antonia, Mark Antony's daughter by Octavia and thus the great Augustus's niece. Armless and crowned by a diadem, she gazes out serenely to some point beyond the hall. The head is of a remarkable quality and one wonders what the statue is doing in a small provincial museum. The answer, of course, is that Cimiez was once a place of some importance, and the statue was found amongst the debris of a temple situated within a stone's throw of the villa. Any relation of Rome's first emperor would have been considered sacrosanct and thus treated with adulation, especially by those stationed the far side of the Alps. Julius Caesar had conquered Gaul and Augustus, his son by adoption, was the man to finally subjugate the troublesome tribes inhabiting the Ligurian shores and thus the real coloniser of the coast. The tribes he conquered were numerous, and one finds their names cut into the base of the great Trophée des Alpes which rises, an impressive ruin dwarfing La Turbie. The precise Roman script covers a space some hundred feet long by fifty wide and spells out a litany of strange sounding names. Here again one's curiosity is aroused, for not much is known about the Ligurians. Some of their sculpture has come down to us, and this is displayed in both the Musée Borély at Marseilles and the Musée Grannet at Aix. At Aix they have a whole series of heads with great, wide, staring eyes – sightless eyes, focused, one is told, on the beyond – staring with 'the eternity of heroes'. The heads date from about the second century BC and come from the Salluvii, or Salyens stronghold of Intremont, situated on the brow of a hill a few kilometres outside the town. The place is hard to find and even the local inhabitants are unable to point out the way.

Before the Romans came the Greeks, their passing commemorated in some of the sea-bound towns, names such as Antibes, or Antiopolis, indicating that it was over against Nice, the city of Nicaea, or Nike, itself recalling some long forgotten victory. But to start at the beginning one must dip back to geological times. Figures mean nothing when years are counted by the hundred million. As for the coast it would have presented a frightening aspect. The world was in a state of constant change as it formed and reformed beneath great ice sheets and crushing glaciers that came snarling down from the poles. Cycles of glaciations alternate with warm periods, and at times the hot climates advance high to north, their progress announced by volcanic eruptions of steaming rock which rise, only to sink again beneath a bubbling sea. Going back to the earliest times, Provence was the bed of just such a sea; a great inland ocean that gradually shrunk to the proportions of the Mediterranean as we know it today. Before the final shrinking one of its arms extended up the Rhône Valley and the surprising crag to be found rising abruptly behind the village of St Jeannet, above Grasse, is an inland height of coral left high and dry during one of these violent foldings, or changes. The Alps themselves with their precipitous limestone heights date back about fifty million years to what is known as the mid-tertiary times; a period during which the last of the great volcanic eruptions occurred.

The Rochers Rouges, or 'bone caves' of Menton are the most interesting prehistoric remains on the coast. Standing nine in a row, they form a small troglodyte village that, seen from a distance, looks like black flames licking into the reddish flanks of the mountain. At the present

time the caves are Italian property and for the moment are hard to
visit since further diggings are being carried out by a team of specialists
based at Bordighera. Originally, a century or two ago, the caves belonged to a farmer, and reports have it that he used the rich dark loam
he found spread over the floors to cultivate his vegetables. The top soil
could not have been very deep, and after a year or two of digging he
came to a deposit of animal bones and flints, and, eventually, human
remains. Not understanding the importance of his find, he nevertheless
hesitated digging any further, and, reflecting on the matter, decided to
open his caves to the public, arguing that he would make more this way
than by cultivating cabbages! His instinct was right. Up until 1846 the
caves came within the jurisdiction of Monaco, and on hearing of the
bones, Florestan I, the ruler at that time, immediately acquired the
property and organised proper scientific investigations. His successor
carried on the work and 'the peasants', as the reigning prince will tell
you, 'thought we were digging for our ancestors' – ancestors that the
authorities date back to about 100,000 BC!

Various archaeological teams have worked in the caves, and over the
years a quantity of different bones have been found; the femur of a
sabre-toothed tiger, parts of a gigantic stag and various bits and pieces
of other mammals, now extinct. In 1872 they brought to light the
fossilised skeleton of a man wearing an immovable necklace of incised
shells. Children's bones followed and, in 1884, another man whose well-
formed skull is to be found in the museum at Menton. Eight years later
three more skeletons came to light – two young men and a woman, and
the interesting thing about them was their height: they were almost
giants. Again the skulls are well formed and there appears to have been
nothing simian about their faces. Indeed the careful burial preparations
show that a considerable degree of civilisation had been reached. The
men had been powdered with red ochre and the woman literally
bedizened with *parures* of fish vertebrae. Another exciting find was the
so-called Grimaldi Venus, one of the earliest examples of figurative art
in existence. Several little statuettes came to light. Pot-bellied and
heavy breasted, they are not very beautiful but there is little doubt
that they were lovingly worked on to portray what were then regarded
as proud symbols of femininity.

Norman Douglas, in his book on this part of the world, describes a
visit to the little museum of pre-history at Menton and writes amusingly
about a young honeymoon couple he found there. They are being

shown round by the guard and he follows them, listening to the new bride's mounting suspicions 'concerning the habits of these remote people':

'And this', the guard waves a hand at one of the sadly neglected cases, 'is the jaw-bone of a cave-bear, the competitor, one might say, in a matter of lodging houses with the gentleman whose anatomy we have just inspected,' [the remains of hippopotami and rhinoceros hunted by the same individuals are pointed out] 'and the object on which your arm is reposing, madam, is the tooth of an elephant'. 'Elephant?' the bride queried. 'Did elephants scramble about these precipices and ravines? I should like to have seen that.' 'Pardon me, madam. He probably killed them down there', [and the guard's arm swept out over the blue Mediterranean lying at their feet.] 'Do you mean to say that elephants paddled across from Algiers in order to be assassinated by your old skeleton? I should like to have seen that.' 'Pardon me, madam, the Mediterranean did not exist in those days.' The suggestion that the boundless sea should ever have been dry land in the time of her own ancestors, was too much for the young lady. She smiled politely, and soon I heard her whispering to her husband: 'I had him there, eh? *Quel farceur!*'[1]

So much then for these time-misted beginnings, and from here we swing right into the pre-Christian era, the birth of our European civilisation in neolithic times, a period of some fifteen hundred years taking us up to about 2500 BC. But even at this comparatively recent date the traces left us are somewhat slim and concern a series of rock engravings to be found on a high plateau six thousand feet above sea level, a place shrouded in mystery, known as the Val des Merveilles. To reach it one takes the old road to Italy zig-zagging upwards through the Alps in a series of hairpin bends. At St Dalmas de Tende a new road branches off and is well sign-posted. The drive should take a little over two hours and offers some breathtaking views which, at times, seem to plunge directly into the sea shimmering in the haze twenty-five miles away. The climb is very abrupt and so is the change in the atmosphere, the air quickly becoming sharper. At this altitude June is late spring and is the best time of year to make the expedition. The snows are just melting and the wealth of alpine flora is amazing. At about two thousand feet the ground is carpeted with a succession of primroses, violets, little

white crocuses, blue hepatica and cowslips. In places one finds drifts of
gentians, in others anemones.

Arriving at the end of the road, one leaves the car at a refuge known
as Les Mesches. From here a rough trail winds to the westwards
towards a fjord-like lake, and it is this stretch of about ten miles that
constitutes the Val des Merveilles. Graffiti are everywhere, hacked with
little incisions across every rock face. Some forty thousand graffiti have
been discovered and many keep turning up, but despite their quantity
they are not easy to find. Age has weathered the rock facings, turning
them a greenish-orange, while the actual scratchings are lined with a
paler patina with the result that they have become almost invisible.
Fortunately, an official guide exists with detailed maps showing where
the principal engravings are to be found, many of them having been
tabulated by Clarence Bicknell, an English naturalist who had devoted
more than half of his life to the valley. Making Bordighera his headquarters he and his wife spent thirty years taking rubbings and
photographs of the graffiti.*

At first sight the signs are somewhat confusing. Horned figures seem
to predominate, and quite obviously represent heads of cattle or oxen.
The cattle are shown as if seen from above, the body is square and
another small cube represents the head from which branch the horns.
Legs and tail are traced by thin lines attached to the square and until
one knows about this somewhat unusual representation they could
easily be taken for beetles. At times the cattle are shown harnessed to
a plough which is incised as a cross. A small insect of a man, whip in
hand, follows behind. Very often the cattle are just indicated by a
mere scratching of horns, or a horned square. Lines enclosing a collection of dots Bicknell interpreted as a herd of cattle, while detached
squares with scratches at the top and the bottom represent hides drying
in the sun. Some rock surfaces are entirely given over to a collection of
different weapons: various forms of axes, bronze daggers and a long
implement that looks like a halberd. Using the most up-to-date equipment modern researchers have proved that the graffiti are not all of the
same period, some being considerably earlier than others. The colour
and texture of the patina in the lines is also another indication of their
age, so is the actual implement used in the scratching. Those picked out

---

* Bicknell died in 1915, and this material is to be seen in the Museo Bicknell at
Bordighera. The rock engravings were in Italy until Tende was handed over to France
as a result of the plebiscite in 1947.

with bronze are thought to date from about 2500 BC, while those hammered with an iron point are considered much later. A trained eye, the experts explain, can easily distinguish which of the two methods was used.

One knows, then, how to read the graffiti, but what of their actual purpose? Why are they there, and who are the people responsible for these scratchings? Here again Bicknell, by a process of elimination, comes to our rescue. Crops will not grow at this altitude, nor has any sign of human habitation ever been found. The engravings, therefore, must have been made by a migratory people, probably shepherds, who would come up from the lower valleys towards the end of June to graze their cattle on the rich mountain herbage. So far so good, but what force urged these Stone Age herdsmen to take with such diligence to their chisels? Here lies the real mystery. The main features of the valley have been explained, but no mention has been made of the great mountain that dominates the whole region. Pyramidal in shape, Mount Bégo rises to a height of just under nine thousand feet and looms over one in an awesome manner. Some maintain that Bégo in the Celtic-Ligurian tongue can be translated as 'Lord Divine', thus indicating a sacred connotation for the mountain. Admitting this one can very well suppose that the tribesmen inhabiting the coast believed this rocky fastness to be the throne from which their fierce deity reigned. Icy winds whistle down the valley, whipping thin sheathings of cloud across its cold rock walls and, standing there, facing towards Bégo, it takes little effort of the imagination to believe oneself in a presence of some kind, and not always a benevolent one. The Val des Merveilles can be regarded as a form of open temple and, if this is the case, it is more than reasonable to suppose that the graffiti were ritual engravings executed during the summer months, a form of silent prayer which the tribesmen hoped would assure fertility for their cattle and a plentiful winter for themselves when the snows drove them back again to the low-lying lands by the sea.

Of course other theories exist, and not long ago an article in the local Nice paper suggested that the graffiti are of African origin, the work of dark-skinned slaves imported by one of the Mediterranean civilisations to dig the mines on Mount Bégo which, the article claims, is nothing more than an enormous mass of zinc sulphate, information vouchsafed by a man called Rainaudo whose family has lived for generations within sight of the mountain. Rainaudo spends all his spare

time researching in the valley and has some strange things to say
about the region. As a boy, he remembers spending the night with his
grandfather on the mountain and being caught in a storm. 'It was no
ordinary storm.' The lightning sounded like a rushing stream and in
some extraordinary way seemed to emanate from the ground, followed
by a hideous crash. What really surprised Rainaudo was both his
father's and grandfather's calm acceptance of this unusual manifesta-
tion. 'It was always like this they told me. Something to do with
magnetism. The mountain being a highly concentrated amalgam of
metals the laws of nature are reversed and the lightning strikes upwards,
rather than down.' Rainaudo also claims that the 'sacred mountain'
once had certain phosphorescent qualities and that in ancient times it
glowed to the extent of being visible from the sea. This is a possible
explanation for the presence of the black slaves but why, one wonders,
should Bégo have lost its phosphorescence, if indeed it ever possessed
it. One is perfectly willing to believe in the strange effects of lightning
during a storm, a phenomenon that could possibly have some scientific
explanation; but that Bégo once flashed out, a vast lighthouse, would
appear a little farfetched. At least Rainaudo's experiences show that
the region can still exert a certain mysterious hold over people's
imagination.

Though interesting, one is really not much the wiser for a visit to
the Val des Merveilles and the coast offers up an equally tenuous
picture of these early peoples. Remains have been found but mostly
near the estuaries of rivers which suggests encampments on the actual
beaches – lean-tos of poles through which smoke seeped in lazy coils to
the sky. Given the character of the country, however, it is safe to suppose
that these wandering tribes became sedentary at a fairly early date.
Certainly they had established colonies by the time the Greeks arrived
in 600 BC. The Greeks named them the Lygiens but give no further
information. They must certainly have migrated from Asia and were
probably a fusion of more local elements, part Etruscan with a later
admixture of Berber blood from Spain. According to the Romans, they
were two distinct types – the highlanders and the lowlanders, the former
wild and uncivilised, the latter comparatively advanced in agriculture.
The wild ones were designated as *Ligures capillati*, or long haired, while
the coastal tribes were referred to as *tonsi* – the shorn ones. Dominated
by the *tonsi* the *capillati* had been driven back to take refuge in the
stony ridges of the Alps and thus cut off from arable land and unable

to produce enough to keep alive, they had turned to a form of brigand-age, making periodic descents on their neighbours, pilfering whatever came to hand, retreating afterwards to their walled camps occupying strategically placed mountain tops, referred to by the Romans as *castro*. It was these *capillati* who were to prove the most troublesome of the tribes to dislodge in Augustus's final subjugation of the coast.

Tradition has it that the Phoenicians, in the tenth century BC, were the first contact the Ligurians had with the outside world. The Phoenicians were remarkable navigators and amongst the early civilisations were the only ones to have passed out of the Mediterranean. Coasting northwards past the Scilly Isles they had established a tin trade with Cornwall, possibly penetrating as far north as the Baltic. In the western Mediterranean they had settlements on all the main islands and had managed to establish a rich trade in silver with south-west Spain, so rich 'that it was said that even the anchors of ships returning from there were cast in this metal'. The Ligurian shores must have appeared very poor in comparison, but being primarily merchants, rather than colonists, their main concern lay in finding convenient ports for their ships to trade from. Monaco, Eze and Villefranche are reputedly amongst the places they founded while another important port existed in the vicinity of the present Marseilles. No substantial proof exists to prove these contentions. The bulk of the Phoenician trade was far too ephemeral to leave any traces. Ivory, silks and amber, coral, and the purple dyes of Tyre and Sidon are not commodities that can be of much help to the archaeologist. The exceptions were the metals, and these we know the Ligurians used.

As it happens, the Greek occupation is as poorly documented as that of the sea-going confederacy from Tyre and Sidon, but fortunately for us one can fall back on the Roman historians. The Greeks in question were Ionians from Phocaea in Asia Minor, and they first sighted the Ligurian coast in about 600 BC. Like the Phoenicians, they were a sea-faring people and built large galleys manned by fifty oars, sturdy ships that raced across the waters and were capable of undertaking longer voyages than hitherto embarked on by any other of the Greeks. Over-crowded in their own city state, they pushed further and further to the west in the hopes of finding a suitable place to settle, and it was while on one of these expeditions that they discovered the mouth of the Rhône. Reports were so favourable that immediately a number of Phocaens decided to emigrate, setting up an expedition under the

aegis of their titular goddess, Diana of Ephesus. Her oracle blessed
those departing and stipulated that one of her statues, suitably attended,
should accompany them. An adventurer called Eumenes was put in
charge of the expedition, and their arrival in the flat delta country of
the Rhône is told in true heroic form; 'wrapped', as Charles Lenthéric,
the eminent nineteenth-century historian, puts it, 'in an aura of poetry'.
Lenthéric is sceptical as to the actual facts, but it makes charming
reading and like most chroniclers' tales is more than likely a symbolic
interpretation of the truth.

We know that the Phoenicians had a depot somewhere in the
vicinity of the Rhône delta, added to which the coast was already
extensively settled by the Salyes, one of the most important of the
Ligurian tribes. The Greeks, then, were not landing on a desert shore
and their first concern, very sensibly, was to ingratiate themselves with
the local inhabitants. Eumenes chose a handsome young Greek called
Protis as his emissary and, as luck would have it, he arrived at the
nearest Salyan village in the middle of an important betrothal
ceremony being held by the local chief for his daughter, a pretty girl
called Gyptis. According to custom the young maiden was to choose
her husband by offering up a libation to the man who pleased her the
most. As can be imagined, the arrival of the young Protis did not go
unnoticed. His Greek beauty, his graceful form and polished manners,
so different from the ruggedness and uncouthness of the Ligurians, had
an immediate effect. Gyptis lost her heart to him and Protis, putting
the proffered drink to his lips, the alliance was concluded. As her
dowry Gyptis brought Mes-Salia, the village in which they had met.

The story is no doubt a myth but the Ionian settlers must certainly
have contracted marriages with the natives, and the above tale must
be regarded in the light of an interpretation of what actually happened.

The little colony prospered and grew and when, fifty years later, in
542 BC, Cyrus's Persian armies marched against the Ionian cities of the
Aegean, Massilia was in a position to welcome its fellow citizens, who,
choosing to migrate rather than to submit to the Persians, escaped
westward in a large fleet of ships. Understandably the Ligurians were
opposed to this new migration. A handful of foreigners they could
accept but not a mass exodus. Being no match, however, for the
Greeks who were infinitely more advanced in technical matters than
themselves, the Ligurians realised that their only hope of success in a
planned uprising lay in cunning. Biding their time, they waited for a

public holiday, choosing the Greek harvest festival to put their plan to effect – a repetition, in another guise, of the famous Horse of Troy. Hiding their weapons under piles of offerings which they had loaded onto rumbling carts, they presented themselves at the gates of Massilia, requesting permission to attend the celebrations. But as already stated, Gyptis was not the only Ligurian girl to have married amongst the Greeks, and one of these wives betrayed the plot. The Greeks pretending ignorance surreptitiously gathered up the smuggled weapons and turning suddenly on the Ligurians slaughtered them with their own arms.

With security came further developments. The Greeks started moving eastwards along the coast, and Ptolemy lists their colonies. Their names transposed, they are: La Ciotat, Bandol, Sanary, Bréganson and Cavalaire. St Tropez follows, then Agay, Cannes and Antibes, Nice, Eze, Villefranche and Monaco. Tauroentum is the only port not to have survived and this disappeared some time ago, buried beneath the sand.

By and large the Ligurians benefited by their contact with the Greeks. Only the most rudimentary form of agriculture existed prior to their coming, added to which they brought with them the invaluable addition of corn, olive and vine. They are credited also with having imported cherry-tree cuttings, hazel nuts and the all-important fig. As to Marseilles itself it was soon to acquire an enviable reputation for learning, and in time came to be known as 'the Athens of Gaul'. Several august characters were born within her walls; geographers and astronomers and, the most renowned, the notable navigator Pytheas, the first explorer of the British Isles – 'the Humboldt', as he has been called, 'of antiquity'. Fortunately Pytheas kept a diary, much quoted by subsequent historians, and although somewhat fragmentary, enough remains for us to follow him on his course.

The main reason for the voyage was the discovery of the Phoenicians' source of tin. Tin is an important component of bronze and bronze was much prized in the ancient world, and the Phoenicians, jealous already of the Greeks who were fast encroaching on their trade, were determined, if possible, to keep the whereabouts of this mysterious land a dark secret. There were, however, some clues for the merchants of Marseilles to work on. They knew that this essential metal came from the north, from a land washed by cold seas, and that it arrived by an overland route through Gaul to the Rhône. They also knew that it was sometimes shipped through the Straits of Gibraltar. It was really a question of exploring, and Pytheas was the man chosen for the discovery. Leaving Marseilles in 330 BC, Pytheas sailed round Spain to Brittany and, crossing the Channel, beached on the shores of Kent. He made several other stops in Britain, and apart from discovering the home of tin, also charted the Thames. He next turns up at the mouth of the Rhine, then Jutland and so into the Baltic and the Vistula. From the Baltic he sails up the Norwegian coast to the Arctic circle, eventually swinging home via the Shetlands and Northern Scotland, ending up in the estuary of the Garonne and so on to Marseilles, overland.

As an independent venture, the Greek occupation of the coast lasted close onto five hundred years, and under the circumstances it comes as a surprise that, apart from the flora imported, so little of a tangible nature remains: no Paestum, not even a tumbled column of Pyrian marble. The best Provence can produce are a few inscriptions and a rude image of fertility to be found in the basement of the Grimaldi Museum at Antibes. The stone appears to have been shaped by the waves and was probably found by some fishermen on the beach. Vaguely phallic in appearance, one supposes that they carted it off to the nearest temple and there the priest had it inscribed with his name. 'I am Terpon', it reads, 'the servant and minister of the august goddess Aphrodite.' Other vestiges have come to light but seem to have been completely ignored, an example of this being the ruins of the Greco-Roman town of Pomponiana in the Bay of Giens, near Hyères. As crown prince, King Frederick VII of Denmark instigated some excavations, but his labours have long since been obliterated by the sands. Gone, too, are the potsherds found in the district during the last century. The ground round about was so thickly strewn with pottery that the peasants used the pieces to construct the walls dividing their fields. In his book on the Riviera,[2] Charles Lenthéric has a whole chapter devoted to the buried town of Tauroentum, already mentioned. Though engulfed by the elements, its disintegration, according to Lenthéric, was vastly helped by local customs officials. Lodged nearby, and for lack of something better to do, they appear to have scrambled away the ruins of an entire temple by playing ducks and drakes with the stones!

Time passes; there are migrations and a constant shifting of power. Already by the fourth century BC blond invaders from beyond the Rhine were beginning to spread southwards. They came in successive waves, intermingling with the Ligurians, though never occupying

Provence. Instead they swept eastwards, down into the Lombardy plains, and in 390 BC defeated the Romans at the battle of Allia, afterwards sacking and burning the Eternal City. It was a rude beginning to relations between Rome and the Germanic tribes. For two centuries intermittent wars were waged against the barbarians until finally, in 191 BC, the Romans had a decisive victory. But Allia was a defeat never to be forgotten, and for as long as the empire lasted, men feared the possibility of another Germanic invasion.

Recovering from Allia, the Romans wasted no time in gathering their forces, forging a remarkable fighting force that became the suzerain and protector of all of Italy. By 265 BC we see them embarking on the Punic Wars to forestall Carthage's intended occupation of Sicily. Forty-six years later, Hannibal, to counteract their thrust, invaded Europe. Marching at lightning speed across Provence, he forded the Rhône in the vicinity of Orange and, scaling the Alps, carried the war to the very borders of Italy. Those witnessing the arrival of his army in Provence must have found it an awe-inspiring sight. Added to the legionnaires were a contingent of five hundred Numidian horsemen in burnouses and thirty-seven elephants. One can only regret that Giovanni Bellini, the first of Venice's great painters, did not attempt to recreate the scene for us. Remembering his *Preaching of St Mark* in the Brea, one can imagine what fun he would have had with this medley of orientalism.

In the meantime, Rome, unaware of this forced march, believed Hannibal to be in Spain which the Carthaginians were in the process of occupying in compensation for having lost Sicily. On learning of the great general's movements, and frightened of dissension at home if Hannibal ever reached Italy, the Senate decided to try to intercept him. Accordingly, a large force under Scipio was embarked at Pisa. The Romans, never very good sailors, were unable to make the voyage direct to the Iberian Peninsula, and after five days the great lumbering *quinquiremes* appeared off Marseilles, the Greeks being allied to the Romans in this venture against what they considered a common enemy. Indeed it was while at anchor at the mouth of the Rhône that Scipio learned of Hannibal's presence not more than a hundred miles away. Immediately the Roman general dispatched a cavalry reconnaissance numbering three hundred legionnaire horsemen and some friendly Ligurians in the pay of the Massiliots, who acted as guides. Hannibal, on hearing of the Roman landing, in turn dispatched a body of five hundred Numidian horsemen. A battle ensued in which both sides lost heavily, but eventually the Romans got the upper hand and Scipio, hoping desperately to come to grips with Hannibal, pressed on to the Carthaginian camp. His wily opponent, however, proved too quick for him, and by the time Scipio arrived at the site on the banks of the Rhône opposite Rochemaure, the enemy had already been gone three days.

History recounts Hannibal's eventual fate; how, having lost half of his army in crossing the Alps, he was driven out of Italy. In 149 BC the third Punic War put an end to Carthage as a political power, the city itself being razed to the ground following the defeat. What is perhaps less well known is a small but nevertheless interesting detail concerning Hannibal's passage through Provence. In 1788 some workmen digging near Maillane in the St Rémy district came across the skeleton of an African elephant. Too early to have belonged to a travelling circus, the remains must certainly have been those of an animal which had died at the time of the famous passage to the Alps.

Returning to the Greeks, we find ourselves in the middle years of the second century BC. Though prospering, they were having increasing trouble with the tribes in the hinterland who kept up an incessant guerrilla warfare aimed at their lines of communication. As time went by these petty pilferings became more and more insistent. Modelling themselves on their neighbours, the Ligurians had acquired some useful knowledge regarding the tactics of war and now, unsettled by the invasion of the Germanic tribes from the north, they had decided to make a concentrated effort to rid themselves altogether of these prolific settlers. They chose their time well, for the Greeks had contributed generously to the Roman effort during the Punic Wars and they must have been feeling the strain. Whatever the reason, by 155 BC the Massiliots were obliged to send envoys to Rome begging for assistance against the Ligurians who were beleaguering, not only the mother city, but all the other Greek towns along the coast. It was important for Rome to keep her lines of communication open to her newly acquired colonies, wrenched from the Carthaginians in Spain, besides which one imagines they had a genuine feeling of loyalty towards the Greeks. Not only had they stood by them through the Punic Wars, but had also passed round the plate, as it were, at the time of the burning of Rome by the Germans. The Romans had never forgotten this, and as Bullock

Hall points out in his book on the Riviera,[3] they had rewarded the Massiliots' generosity by a permanent set of seats reserved for them at all public games held in the capital.

Rome thus lent a sympathetic ear to the Greeks and three commissioners were sent in a peaceful attempt to bring the Ligurians to reason. They landed somewhere in the vicinity of present-day Cannes, and unfortunately one of the commissioners was wounded in a skirmish with the Oxybii, the tribe occupying that particular stretch of coast. Immediately the Senate gave orders to fit out another expedition, an armed one this time. A battle ensued in which the Oxybii were soundly trounced, their head men being taken prisoners and sent in chains to Rome.

The coast was divided up between three tribes, the Salyes round Marseilles, the Oxybii in the Cannes area, while the Deciates occupied the rest of the Alpes Maritimes. To keep the peace, it was agreed that each tribe should send hostages to the Greeks at stated intervals, the Oxybii territory being occupied, but not annexed, by a contingent of Roman troops. For a time no more was heard of the Ligurians and then, in 125 BC, the Salyes embarked again on their raids. Again the Greeks sent envoys to Rome, and again Rome responded by mounting another expedition, this time commanded by the Consul Fulvius Flaccus.

The Salyes were a far better organised fighting force than the other Ligurian tribes the Romans had hitherto encountered along the Italian and French Rivieras. Occupying the open country between the Rhône and the Durance, they were the only ones to have proper pasture land for breeding horses, and could consequently put a formidable force of cavalry into the field, 'always a weak arm with the Roman armies before Caesar's conquest of Transalpine Gaul'.* Indeed, unable to match the enemy cavalry, Fulvius Flaccus was only partially successful in subjugating the Salyes, a second campaign being required to overcome their stubborn resistance.

By 121 BC the Romans had reached as far west as Toulouse, and the following year founded Transalpine Gaul. They had, in point of fact, annexed the whole of the coast from the Alps to the Pyrénées, and in 114 after the last of the fighting under Caius Sextus Calvinus, founded a

---

* The Bouches du Rhône and the other departments further north were to furnish an inexhaustible supply of horses during the Civil War, and subsequently during the empire.

new colony – *provincia Romana*, our Provence. *Aquae Sextiae*, the
present-day Aix, was made its capital, being so named on account of
the waters, and, not unnaturally, after the general. At the extremity
of the coast, not far from Nice, the Romans built Cimiez. They had
thus occupied the hinterland without interfering with the Greeks. It
was unfortunate for the Massiliots that, at the outbreak of the Civil
War in Italy nearly sixty years later, her statesmen should have voted
to side with Pompey rather than Caesar. Though it must be said that
they had done everything in their power to remain neutral and were, as
it happens, goaded into siding with Pompey by the sudden arrival of
seven swift galleys from the Etrurian coast commanded by one of
Pompey's generals. But the Civil War is not our concern here, other
than Caesar's isolated siege of Marseilles which the great man himself
describes in his *De Bello Civili*. For strategic reasons, it was essential
for him to obtain possession of Marseilles and its fort. Pompey's swift
action, however, had sealed its gates to him, and this meant an arduous
siege, for not only was the city one of the best furnished ports in the
entire Mediterranean basin, but, confined to a peninsula, also commanded an all but impregnable position. Three sides were washed by the
sea, and the land side, low-lying and rocky, was impossible to approach
by tunnelling. Great embankments had to be thrown up to provide
access to the walls, and this necessitated complicated shelters to protect
the Roman soldiers from the showers of missiles and rocks that would
be discharged by great catapults as they approached. If this failed to
smash up their mobile shelters, casks filled with burning pitch would be
hurled down onto their roofs. Obviously Marseilles was not to be taken
by storm. A lengthy siege was the only answer, and here again there
were difficulties. The Greeks and Pompey's general, Domitius, had
managed to scrape together a fleet of seventeen galleys and it was
quite obvious that if the Romans were to make any headway at all in
starving out the city, they must be in a position to seal off all the
approaches by sea. They had no ships, but nothing daunted, Caesar
ordered a fleet to be constructed at Arles, hewn, so the story goes, from
oaks cut down in a sacred wood where mysterious rites were performed.
At first the soldiers were superstitious about touching the trees.
Caesar, however, prevailed, and twelve ships were ready to put to sea
in exactly a month from the date of the order – a remarkable achievement which one feels was only made possible by Caesar's force of will.
One admires also the ingenuity and stamina he displayed in an

emergency. Ignoring the fact that there were no sailors to man the ships, he filled them with the pick of his legionnaires.

The ensuing naval engagement is vividly described in Marcius Lucan's historical epic, the *Pharsalia*, written some hundred years after the event. He describes Massilia's navy as 'nimble, clear and light!' It manoeuvres with ease and 'with best advantage can seek or shun a fight'. Not so the Romans: 'cumbersome hulks they lay, and slow and heavy hung upon the sea'. They acted, however, as battering rams, and once amongst the enemy ships the legionnaires threw out grappling-irons and treated the engagement as they would have done a skirmish on land, the Greeks thus losing all the advantage they might have had from the manoeuvrability of their ships.

> The rolling surge is stained around with blood
> And foamy purple swells the rising flood.

In the end, the city admits defeat. Caesar, called off to direct operations in Spain, misses the last stages of the siege but returns in time to accept the enemy's unconditional surrender and acting with his usual clemency spares all lives. No longer an independent republic, Marseilles is permitted, however, to enjoy the privileges of self-government and later on, under the empire, regained her position as an important centre of learning.

✸7

Marius and the Battle of Pourrières

Caesar's conquest of Gaul was a speedy affair – a question of three years. The strange, almost hypnotic effect he seemed to have exerted over his enemies plus his common sense and wide grasp of things must have helped considerably. He put it to the Gauls quite bluntly: they must either choose to be Romans or be overrun by savages. Hordes of half-starved barbarians were piling up behind the Danube and the Rhine, only too anxious for the opportunity to spill over and occupy the fertile plains to the south of them, and as a warning he could cite the recent chaotic experiences in connection with the migratory tribes from Jutland; the war-like Cimbri and the Teutons had literally hacked their way through several Roman armies to the very borders of Italy, eventually to be defeated by Caesar's uncle, Caius Marius, at Pourrières near Aix in 102 BC.

In concentrating almost exclusively on the Greeks, we have by-passed what was to prove the greatest Roman victory on Provençal soil – more than that even, an engagement that can well be considered amongst one of the world's most decisive battles. We must go back, then, some half a century and try and recapitulate, for Pourrières was of vital importance to the future of Provence, besides which its protagonists were the perfect example of Caesar's land-hungry giants from the north. Together, the Cimbri and the Teutons represented a mass migration of some half a million men, women and children. Lumbering forwards in great ox-drawn wagons, they were followed by their cattle, an ever-increasing herd that swelled with their plunder as they were pushed further and further southwards by those refusing to accommodate them; a tidal wave that had already annihilated five Roman armies as it disgorged, fanning out across the Rhône valley; a cataclysm that would have doomed Rome to premature extinction had it not been for Marius.

It is unfortunate that Livy's exhaustive history, a work of over a hundred volumes, should be incomplete, the books dealing with Provence being amongst the many missing. Others, however, come to our rescue, amongst them Plutarch, who gives us a vivid account of Marius's campaigns in his *Lives*. The Greek explorer Pytheas from Marseilles gives us first-hand information about the Cimbri and Teutons. Both tribes were of Germanic stock, the Cimbri being the inhabitants of what is now Jutland, the Teutons, their neighbours, living somewhat to the east of them. It would seem that the Cimbri started their wanderings in about 120 BC and according to Strabo, the Greek geographer, were set moving by a gradual but insistent encroachment of the sea. Dykes and embankments were still a thing of the future and at certain tides, when a strong inshore wind was blowing, their settlements were completely inundated. 'A mounted horseman', Pytheas writes, 'could barely escape by galloping from the rush and force of the sea,' and furious 'would shake his sword threateningly at the God of the deep, but to no effect for they lost more men in a year by water than in all their wars.' Small wonder, given the conditions under which they lived, that when they finally decided to migrate they should have proved such an implacable enemy. The Teutons, who joined up with the Cimbri as they made their way south, were an equally bellicose lot, and together they must have presented a frightening appearance. Plutarch tells of their fierce blue eyes and unruly red hair, and depicts them kilted in leather and clanking with amber beads. Ably seconding them in their ferociousness came the priestesses clad in long white robes with great glinting sacrificial knives slung at their waists – sharp blades that were only too ready to slit any alien throat that might come their way.

It has been surmised that their migration led them down the Elbe valley and as far to the eastwards as Yugoslavia. It was a hunt for land on which they were never allowed to settle. Doubling back again they came face to face with the Roman soldiers policing the passes down from the Alps, what today marks the frontier between Austria and Italy. It was their first encounter with Rome's armies and a parley ensued in which the invaders made their usual request for land. Cnaeus Carbo, the consul in command, proposed a truce and then treacherously fell on the tribes in the middle of the night. The plan misfired and the legions were driven back in disorder and, but for the timely intervention of a thunderstorm, would surely have been completely annihilated. Return-

ing to Rome Carbo committed suicide, or was possibly murdered for his
ineptitude. Suffering from a lack of inspired leadership, further setbacks
awaited the Roman armies. They were fortunate, however, in one thing
– the wandering tribes, apart from their brute force, were completely
lacking in any over-all strategy and time and time again wasted golden
opportunities of attacking directly. Carbo's defeat, for instance, left the
road to Italy wide open, and instead of marching on Rome they spent
three years wandering aimlessly around the northern foothills of the
Alps. Not until iii BC did they recross the Rhine and, following the
Jura, appear on the right bank of the Rhône. However, their time had
not been entirely wasted, for with them were the Ambrones from the
Bernese Oberland who had decided to join them. It must have been in
an almost threatening mood that they sent a deputation to Junius
Silanus, the Roman governor of the province they were about to enter.
Again they asked for land on which to settle, offering in return to place
their arms at the service of Rome. Silanus referred their proposal to the
Senate and the reply was an insolent refusal. A battle ensued and,
crossing the Rhône, the Germans fell on Silanus's troops, wiping out
every one man of them. Still the invaders failed to take advantage of
the situation. Again Rome put another army into the field, and yet
another, with equally disastrous results. Eighty thousand Roman
soldiers lost their lives trying to defend the Rhône valley. Not only were
the transalpine provinces without any defence, but the mother country
itself was in imminent danger. In desperation Rome called upon the
only general who inspired any confidence – Caius Marius, the hero of
North Africa's Jugurtine wars. Just back from his triumphal campaigns, he was immediately put in command with orders to stem the
threatened invasion. It was a dubious assignment considering the size
of his army as matched against the torrent of war-like humanity who
by now had every reason to believe in its invincibility.

Plutarch gives us a short sketch of this unusual man. Born of country
folk, he was a rough lad with little learning. Much of his youth had been
spent in army camps, with the result that he knew nothing of city life
or of politics. He was small, nervous and very brave, and later was to
develop a fierce temper. A rigid disciplinarian, he was nevertheless
scrupulously fair with his soldiers, ate with them when out campaigning
and they appreciated his rough severity. When his nephew tried to
seduce a young soldier and got killed in the act, Marius summoned the
boy in question and warmly congratulated him. Obviously Plutarch

considers this somewhat cruel side of his nature as a high commendation. More sympathetic is the story he tells to illustrate the man's bravery. His thighs and legs were netted with varicose veins, and caring about his appearance, he decided to put himself in the hands of a surgeon. They operated on one leg and not the flicker of a frown showed on the general's face, but the agony was such that he couldn't go through with it again for the other leg.

So much for Plutarch; for the rest one must read in between the lines. Like all good leaders, Marius seems to have been something of a psychologist. Before embarking for Marseilles, he enlisted the services of a Syrian soothsayer who had been intriguing Rome. He no doubt realised what an important weapon superstition could be, and having probably heard about the barefooted German priestesses and being solicitous of his men's morale, had engaged the Syrian woman to act as a foil. He was too good a tactician for one to believe that he could be dependent on auguries himself. It must have been a question of courting every possible advantage, an understandable precaution when one considers the forces arrayed against him: some three hundred thousand strong as opposed to his own army which numbered not even a quarter as many.

Martha was the oracle's name, and Marius saw to it that she travelled in suitable state, reclining in a litter attended by slaves. She was at Marius's side when he offered up sacrifices, dressed, so Plutarch tells us, in purple robes 'clasped and hung around with gold chains, holding a flowered javelin'. One can picture the black hair hanging in long snakes framing her remarkable eyes – clear, all-seeing eyes rimmed with dark circles that, following the Egyptian fashion, would be carried way beyond their natural confines by carefully drawn lines. Quite obviously Marius had a sense of the theatre and an ability to capture popular imagination. Plutarch assigns him two eagles that were said to follow him around in his wars, their presence being particularly noticeable when he was about to win a great battle.

And now to the terrain on which the drama was to unfold. After an arduous crossing, Marius disembarked his troops at the mouth of the Rhône, encamping at Fos,* a rocky promontory on the eastern edge of the delta. A second camp was pitched at the extreme western end of the Alps, at Glanum, from where he could keep an eye on the enemy. For

---

* Fos was to become an important harbour comparable to Ostia and parts of the old port were found under the sea not so many years ago.

some inexplicable reason, the Cimbri had just marched off across the Pyrénées into Spain leaving their allies to wander around until they returned. What Marius needed desperately was time, and this insouciant behaviour on the part of the enemy gave him exactly what he was looking for – a chance to spy out the land and recruit more men.

Astute administrators, the Romans had been careful not to antagonise the coastal tribes when helping the Greeks, and though forced to intervene, had left them very much on their own, allowing them their own organisations. The only radical changes made were those necessitated by the administration of Roman law and consequently an amicable relationship existed between the two sides. Marius had little trouble in finding the men, it was simply a question of knocking them into shape. A hard taskmaster, but at the same time reasonable in his demands, he got the best out of them. They were subjected to an intense course of physical training, cross-country runs, forced marches and herculean feats of manual labour which included the enlarging of the fort at Glanum, strengthening it with an outcropping of palisades and earthworks and the digging of a canal that ran some thirty miles from the sea meeting with the Durance not far from Glanum. It was a question of assuring his supplies.

Two whole years Marius waited, a delay that in all probability saved Rome, for by the time the Cimbri recrossed the Pyrénées, Marius's legions were ready for them.

Finally deciding to descend on Italy, the tribes divided up into two separate armies. The Cimbri were to take the mountain passes while the Teutons and the Ambrones were to keep to the coast, and the Ambrones, as a first offensive, were given the job of drawing Marius out into the open. Bivouacked in their wagons opposite the camp at Glanum, they did everything in their power to provoke the Romans. But Marius had his plans and nothing was going to make him alter them. In the meantime, to calm the men Martha was asked to consult her oracle. The answer came back – the men must be patient and wait. The enemy, baffled by these tactics and impatient of inaction, and, perhaps, as Bullock Hall suggests, compelled to move on to fresh ground having exhausted their supplies, broke camp and moved off in the direction of Italy. They moved so slowly in their unwieldy caravans that it took them a week to defile past the Roman fortifications, and as they passed, Plutarch tells us, 'they called mockingly to the soldiers, asking if they would write or send home anything to their wives, for they would be with them ere long'. This was precisely the chance Marius had been waiting for. Raising camp himself, he followed closely behind, as closely as he dared without being detected, ready to seize on the first opportunity of attacking them at a disadvantage.

Sir Theodore Cook, journalist and art critic, and one-time editor-in-chief of the *Field*, made a detailed study of the Battle of Pourrières in his excellent book *Old Provence*,[1] and following his text and with the aid of a map, one can follow the exact route taken by the Ambrones. They marched round the northern slopes of Les Alpilles to Orgon, down to Lambesc and Equilles, and then moving in a slanting line about ten kilometres to the west of Aix, encamped on the right bank of the river Arc, close by the present village of Les Milles. After months of reconnoitering Marius was thoroughly acquainted with the terrain, and using his knowledge dug himself in on sloping ground above the river some way back from the banks. Plutarch assumes that this was a calculated move on Marius's part to give his men that extra spurt of courage. Thirsty and tired after a long march, he presumed it would madden them to see an enemy that had so long eluded them floundering about swimming in the river. Whether correct in his assumptions, one doesn't know, but when the men asked for water, Marius pointed down to the Arc and suggested they go down and fetch it. A charge ensued headed by slaves and the newly recruited Ligurians. Backing them moved a living wall of legionnaires. The Ambrones were still at their midday meal, and according to Plutarch 'in their cups and over fed and in no state to do battle'. The Romans soon cleared the banks of the river and wading across attacked a hurriedly formed line of Ambrones drawn up between them and the enemy camp. The casualties were heavy and the Ambrones panicked, making hurriedly for the shelter of their wagons; an illusionary shelter, for here the poor devils met with an even worse enemy than the Romans close on their tails – their women, who enraged by the incompetence and lack of bravery, 'came out against them with axes and swords . . .'. Fortunately for the Ambrones, it was already late in the day and the Romans, wary of an ambush, retreated back to their camp where they spent a watchful night listening to the hideous noises 'like wild beasts bellowing and roaring' coming from across the river. The next morning the Ambrones, instead of counter-attacking, decided to retreat beyond Aix, to the plains where their allies the Teutons were already encamped. A good half of the invader's army was now gathered on the very spot which Marius had hoped might be one of the battle-fields: those fateful plains on which the terrible slaughter to come was to bestow so depressing a name.*

A quick look at the map will give us some idea of the lie of the land, and with Cook's painstaking research, one is able to plot out the battlefield. The wandering tribes, with their weighty army of chariots and wagons, were drawn up in a line measuring roughly five miles. Stretching across the river Arc, it ran southward to just above Trets and as far north as Pourrières. The Romans, having marched via Tholonet and Beaurecueil to Châteauneuf – practically the exact route followed by cars leaving from Aix for the coast – came to a halt about a mile and a half west of La Grande Pegière and occupied a line running at a thirty degree angle from that of the enemy, pivoting, like them, on Trets and reaching as far north as Puyloubier. By careful planning, Marius had managed to manoeuvre his troops onto hilly ground above the enemy. He had done the same thing in the previous battle. It obliged his adversary to fight an uphill engagement and put them at a disadvantage, since they were unable to wield their swords in those terrible down cuts so dreaded by the Romans. Bullock Hall, in his account of the battle, has Marius's army drawn up in front of his camp, on one of those natural terraces which stand out at various levels from the slopes of Mont St Victoire. This acted as a safeguard against possible encirclement by the enemy and at the same time gave Marius a chance to detach a part of his troops in a flanking movement round to the back of enemy lines, with orders to attack as soon as the battle was joined. Led by Claudius Marcellus, the detachment marched from Puyloubier north to Le Puits de Rians, and so down onto the plains, screened the whole way by outcroppings that hid them from the enemy below. One might wonder how Marius, knowing the fate of the armies that had gone before him and, above all, faced with such a vast preponderance of men, could even contemplate carrying the day. The numbers were literally ten to one, but to offset this absurd superiority of force it must be remembered that, man for man, the tribes were no match for their opponents, if intelligently led. Their discipline was poor and compared to the Romans they were wretchedly armed, depending only on shields for their defence, while the legionnaires glinted from head to foot in protective plating.

One presumes that a few days went by before the battle was actually engaged; then finally, on the morning of 24 April, when all was in

* Pourrières, a derivation from the Roman *campi putridi*.

readiness, Marius swung into action. Marcellus, with his orders to out-
flank the enemy, was well on his way by the time the first charge of
Roman cavalry came clattering down the hill, a feint to draw out the
enemy and so force them into a disadvantageous uphill engagemnet.
The tribes were impatient as always of awaiting attack; the trick worked.
The Ambrones, with the Teutons behind them, swarmed forward, the
Ambrones beating their shields in rhythm to wild cries of their own
name; a form of self-hypnosis, the word meaning the valiant, or brave.
It was a hot day and a strong mistral was blowing and great dust-
clouds mercifully obscured the onrushing men from the Romans. The
first onslaught dented their lines, but pressing forwards the Romans
gradually forced their assailants down onto the plains, and there,
before they could reform on the level, they were struck by Marcellus
in the rear. He had passed straight through the enemy camp, and the
women's cries caused the Teutons to wheel in counter-attack. As they
turned, Marius hurled his legions against them. Panic ensued, and their
overwhelming numbers only helped to intensify the chaos. Plutarch
spares us none of the details regarding the ensuing holocaust; there
were over a hundred thousand killed, and twice that number taken
prisoner. Those of the women who had the courage took their own
lives, and Plutarch depicts them, tall, Nordic harridans dressed in
black, dashing their children to death against the wheels of their carts.
The men who escaped capture strangled themselves with slip-halters
which they fastened to the oxen, sticking the animals with their swords,
thus maddening them into a headlong stampede. Small wonder that
the place became known as *campi Putridi* and that for years to come
the peasantry 'made pale hedges from men's bones' and boasted of the
fertility of their crops.

Following a battle it was the Roman habit to share out the booty
amongst the men. On this occasion there was a large surplus which
Marius is said to have burnt in an enormous bonfire to celebrate his
victory and, indeed, archaeologists digging on the site have unearthed
deep layers of burnt earth amalgamated with a mixture of ashes,
melted lead and calcinated pieces of pottery. I went to explore for
myself, and not far from the spot where they dug are the foundations
of a stone monument erected by Marius's men. It stands in a stony
field vaguely protected by a dilapidated wire fence. An equally broken-
down sign announces the spot and unless one knows more or less where
to look, it would be almost impossible to find. I learnt subsequently

that what remained of the monument was dismantled during the last century and reassembled in the form of a pyramid on the outskirts of the village of Pourrières. Here again the authorities have been impossibly vague, for in this case no sign of any kind attends it.

—Another monument that is thought to be connected with the battle is the beautiful so-called mausoleum at St Rémy. It stands next to the small triumphal arch which experts are agreed was erected by Julius Caesar after 49 BC to commemorate the taking of Marseilles. The workmanship in both monuments shows strong Greek influence and both are richly carved with beautifully executed architectural detail. As it happens, no book seems to agree as to the actual date of the arch or the mausoleum. A puzzling inscription runs along the north side of the mausoleum, ascribing the monument to Gaius and Lucius Caesar, Augustus's grandsons and supposed heirs who never inherited since they both died before him. Cook, the only authority really to stick his neck out, is categorical about his beliefs and insists that the monument is a century earlier than the inscription pointing out that the two figures* standing side by side under the dome are dressed in a simple toga, the kind that would have been worn by consuls on active service, and therefore could not possibly represent royal princes at the beginning of the empire. Even the official guide is careful not to commit itself as to the identity of the wearers. Cook, at any rate, is quite certain that this perfectly preserved, three-storied monument is not a mausoleum but a monument to commemorate the battle of Pourrières. In this case the second figure would represent Catulus, the general who, with Marius, decimated the Cimbri as they descended the Alps into the Po Valley, an action, of course, that took place after the battle of Pourrières. His argument appears to be sound. Caesar, proud of his uncle, would in all probability have wanted to perpetuate his memory, and here was a chance to exercise his cultivated taste by the erection of a sophisticated monument on the exact spot where Marius built his camp and first came face to face with the enemy as they filed past its palisades – the place from which he dictated the strategy of his victorious campaign. —

There is no arguing, anyway, with the people of the region; for them the monument is quite definitely that of their local hero, and French troops, when passing by, invariably salute as a mark of respect.

* They are now headless, decapitated during the revolution. Bad restorations were made during the empire, but so clumsily modelled that they had to be removed.

Should any further proof be wanted of the esteem in which Marius's memory is held, one has only to remember how many boys in Provence owe their name to him. The same can be said for his Syrian prophetess, for Marthe is an equally common girl's name.

Doubt there might be about the St Rémy monument, but there is none regarding the *Venus Victrix* found on the site of the battle and now in the Musée Lapidaire of Avignon – and then, of course, the most enduring memory of all: the flat-topped Mont St Victoire which dominates the whole countryside, the mountain that so appealed to Cézanne who had a retreat at its base in a wood of chestnut trees.

For those really interested, I recommend the climb. On the very summit, on a crag to the north, commanding the actual battlefield, a shrine of victory was built which in Christian times became a Cassianite convent and eventually a chapel dedicated to St Victoire, a Christian personification of the great event; the Saint's feast day, the 24th of April, falling on the same date as that of the battle. Sir Walter Scott used the chapel for one of the settings in his novel *Anne of Geierstein.* He describes a visit of the Earl of Oxford's son to Queen Margaret, and at the same time evokes an awesome picture of Lou Garagoul, a nearby rocky cleft down which Marius, at Martha's bidding, hurled a hundred prisoners; a gory human sacrifice to the god of war.

Until the revolution the villagers round about used to celebrate the 24th of April with dancing and bonfires lighted on a plateau next to the church. Joining hands, they would circle round the flames shouting 'Victory! Victory!', but whether in honour of their saint or to celebrate Marius's battle must have been a moot point in their minds.

It was a clear spring morning when I climbed the mountain with my camera. Resting after the climb, I looked up and saw what I believed to be a great tawny eagle wheeling, outlined in a taut silhouette against the pale sky. Alone, I felt a sudden tingling down my spine. Could this be one of the harbingers that Plutarch claimed haunted Marius in all his campaigns? With all of Provence spread out before me, veiled in the gold of a misty sunshine, it was a moment to indulge oneself in dreams.

✧8

The Coast and Provence
under the Empire

Octavian, the future Augustus, was a young man of nineteen when his great-uncle, and father by adoption, Julius Caesar, was murdered in 44 BC. Serving abroad at the time, he hurried back to Rome and by a series of clever political moves gradually took over command. A fine portrait bust of him was found recently at Arles when the vast substructure of the forum was discovered in 1951. It shows him wearing a beard, a beard at that period being considered by the Romans as a sign of mourning. It was therefore contemporary with the death of his uncle, and looking at it one sees that it is the face of an intelligent and unusually sensitive person. Suetonius, the historian, describes him of average height, 'but having an excellent presence', with clear shining eyes, curly fair hair and a bronzed complexion. He is 'most lovable and amiable but negligent about his person'. Later in life he developed a slight limp, while a bad case of frostbite affected the forefinger of his right hand making it difficult for him to write – a handicap he overcame by the use of a tortoiseshell finger-stall. An unassuming character he preferred his private house on the Palatine to the Imperial palace which he used only for official business. The house sounds attractive; doors wide open with pools or fountains in the private apartments. There is another likeness of Octavian in Arles' Musée Lapidère, but of a later date, taken when he had already become Emperor. He is portrayed naked to the thighs, which are thought to have been covered originally by stone draperies dyed the Imperial purple. The statue was over life-size and comes from a niche in the great stage wall of the theatre. The expression is pensive, even sad, but strangely enough neither of the heads are those of a man with exceptional force of character: rather they show us a compassionate dreamer, and not the energetic man of action that history proves him to have been.

With Caesar's death, a period of anarchy and bloodshed ensued.

Mark Antony, Caesar's self-appointed representative, believed in the restoration of republican government, but under the old order of things, that is, within the framework of Caesar's dictatorship but with the power delegated to the Senate rather than centralised under one figure. The nobles, suspicious of Mark Antony's real intentions, refused to support him, resulting in a serious rift between the two parties. Already on Octavian's return his uncle's partisans were in arms under Mark Antony, and Mark Antony, quick to realise Octavian's popularity with the troops, as Caesar's adopted son wasted no time in making an alliance with him.

But the reader will be familiar with the events leading up to the famous naval engagement of Actium, to be followed by the much dramatised double suicide. With Antony's and Cleopatra's death, Octavian's victory was complete, and on his return to Rome he was loaded with honours, amongst them the title of *princeps*. *Princeps* was simply a title of courtesy, but shortly thereafter the Senate decreed the additional cognomen of 'Augustus' and declared Octavian commander-in-chief of the army. This meant that the affairs of state were entirely in his hands, and it needed wisdom and restraint for one so young to manoeuvre adroitly and still keep the goodwill of the Senate. His task was a formidable one; in Egypt he was the successor of the Ptolemies; Numidia was under his sway, while in Spain the hill tribes to the north-west remained to be subdued in order to secure the entire peninsula. In Gaul, in addition to the *provincia Romana*, Augustus inherited the territory conquered by Caesar, thus carrying Roman rule up to the natural frontier lines of the Rhine and the Danube. Roads, like a great web, had to be kept open to connect these distant outposts with the seat of government in Italy, and up them would trudge an imposing mass of troops while flotillas of galleys cruised up and down the rivers. He was ruler absolute, and it was difficult, indeed impossible, for someone wielding such power abroad to maintain even the pretence of republican government at home. Augustus, in point of fact, had become Emperor in all but name; a semi-divine head of state and worshipped as such by the general public.

One looks again at the head of Arles and reads more into the handsome face than one might have done in the first place. Perhaps the secret was a deep humility, thus enabling him to assimilate the role thrust upon him without undermining his character. The question of playing godhead would have been an easy role for him to accept, for like every member of the Julian house, Augustus prided himself on his descent, through Aeneas, from the goddess Aphrodite. There was as yet no 'divine right of kings', but the East had always deified its rulers and Augustus no doubt felt it to be an additional token of loyalty and a convenient weapon to wield in the provinces. In any event he was to prove a highly capable administrator. For the first time the provinces were treated as departments of a single state, while their governors, from being independent and often irresponsible rulers, became the subordinate officials under the direct control of the Emperor. According to Suetonius, Augustus paid several visits to Provence, some of fairly long duration; expeditions no doubt to oversee the subjugation of the Ligurian *capellati*, the last of the rebellious tribes to take refuge in the Alps. Livy describes one of the many campaigns, and knowing the country, one realises the hardships involved for the Roman soldiers. 'There was everything', as Livy expresses it, 'to put them on their mettle.' Tough to beat, these hill tribes proved almost tougher to find. 'There were marches through long defiles and constant surprise attacks from a light-footed enemy that just melted away into the shadows of the forest-clad mountains.' The vegetation, it must be remembered, was much denser in Roman times; evergreen bushes clothed the lower slopes, while pine woods covered the heights. Worst of all, it was a country almost barren of any resources and there was 'no hope', as Livy writes, 'but in cold steel and individual pluck'. It took Augustus the best part of ten years to force the tribes to capitulate and to commemorate his victory the Senate gave orders for the building of the famous monument known as *Le Trophée d'Auguste* at La Turbie; La Turbie, of course, being a corruption of *trophia*, or trophy. The monument was a prototype of its kind, and the most magnificent of any built in the antique time.

The foundations were laid in 7 BC and it took just under a year to finish. The great, whitish-yellow blocks of limestone of which it is built came from a quarry about a mile to the west of the present village, and not so long ago, within my memory, one could still see roughed-out blocks clinging to the sides of one of the pits. Of course, the monument has suffered the fate common to most Roman remains. For centuries it was used to supply material for other buildings, some of them as far afield as Genoa, and no doubt it would have disappeared altogether had the local feudal lords not thought of turning it into a stronghold for themselves. Thus encased in a shell of bastions, with small houses sheltering beneath the stout walls, it weathered the years until the wars of the Spanish Succession, when it was blown up by one of Louis XIV's generals. Soon after this, strange stories started to circulate about its ruins which, as local superstition would have it, had become the haunt of no less a person than Apollo himself – an improbable tenant. But it would appear that the Phoenicians had originally chosen the heights of La Turbie as a spot on which to erect a temple to their sun god, and Apollo, angered by the people's neglect of him, and jealous of Augustus's exclusive association with the place, started his hauntings, taking malicious pleasure in keeping husbands informed about their wives' infidelities. Had one doubts about one's wife, one chose an auspicious hour to question what was left of the tower, and Apollo would answer – a strange pastime for the son of Jupiter, himself the greatest philanderer when disguised as a mortal.

Towards the end of the eighteenth century a new church was built at La Turbie. Again the trophy was used as a quarry and from then on the bare skeletal remains, half hidden in cloud, were almost totally ignored by future travellers. Few bothered to make the steep climb, but amongst the few came Napoleon III who gave orders for the removal of any fragments bearing inscriptions. He had them displayed in the Museum of St Germain-en-Laye, and in return sent the church a copy of Raphael's *St Michael*.

It was not until the first two decades of this century that archaeologists started serious digging on the site. Clearing the immediate vicinity of the encumbering houses, they laid bare the site on which the trophy had rested: a large platform of paving reached by inclined stone paths. The actual base was intact, even down to the iron staples joining its great blocks. In demolishing the trophy, the foundations had been covered over with rubble and fallen masonry, and it is in this rubble that the majority of decorative fragments were found. The reconstruction is a remarkable achievement and is the work of Philippe Casimir and an architect called Camille Formigé. After prolonged study they were able to establish the trophy's exact proportions. It had stood a hundred and sixty-five feet high and mounted in three distinct floors, receding as it progressed, the base a giant square, each side measuring two hundred and thirty feet. The first two tiers were square, the third a circular drum faced with twenty-four Doric columns behind which were niches for life-sized statues. Surmounting this huge pile rose a colossal effigy of the victorious Emperor. Carefully sorting out the

material, Casimir and Formigé were able to surmise the different
materials used. The architrave was cut from La Turbie stone, the great
blocks forming the walls being of the same soapy texture, while the
capitals of the columns were of Carrara marble, probably the only
marble used on the building except for the statues which it is thought
represented generals connected with the conquest of Gaul, or possibly
members of Augustus's family. A supposed head of Drusus, Augustus's
step-son, now in a Copenhagen museum, is said to come from La Turbie,
and if true is the only trace ever found of these statues. It is not known
whether Augustus himself was in marble or bronze; a small piece of
bronze has been found in the ruins, but nothing explicit enough to cast
any light on the matter.

Work was interrupted by the 1914 war, but was resumed after the
armistice. Formigé had died, and Casimir was fortunate enough to find
an American backer – a postcard magnate called Edward Tuck – who
financed what remained to be done, namely the intricate piecing together of the official dedication inscribed to the Emperor. Fourteen
letters on four different fragments were all that were known to exist of
the inscription. However, Pliny the Elder had copied down the text,
and it was known exactly how it should read. Cut in letters fourteen
inches high came the dedication to be followed by the names of the
conquered tribes in letters half the size. Knowing the text made it easier
to hunt for further missing pieces, some of which were found built into
the walls of the houses. What had been lost was recut, and like a giant
jig-saw puzzle it now greets one, occupying one whole side of the base,
the side of the trophy that is first apparent as one arrives.

Only a small section of the trophy has been restored, but enough to
give one an impression. One approaches through the narrow streets of
the village and then, suddenly, there it looms, white, and very splendid,
the hugeness of its scale accentuated by the nearness of the houses. At
the time of the building, it was visible for miles around and, indeed,
even in its crippled state still dominates and is plainly discernible from
the terrace in front of my house, some twenty miles away across the sea.
The view one has from between the remaining columns is very splendid;
behind are the Alps receding tier after tier, the furthest peak capped in
snow. To the east stretches the Italian Riviera, while towards France
one looks across the red bluffs of the Esterel, and beyond, to the dusky,
wooded mountains of the Moors. On a fine day even Corsica is visible as
a dark haze on the taut line of the sea. It is hard to imagine a more

splendid sight, and it must certainly have been amongst the most spectacular views the empire had to offer.

It has already been indicated how poorly the provinces had been administered under the Republic. Little had been done to develop their internal resources, and it was left to Augustus, with Cleopatra's carefully hoarded treasures at his disposal, to set the example of liberal expenditure. Many of the grander public buildings in the hinterland owe their beginnings to him; few on the coast, however, can claim direct connection with Augustus. Both Cimiez and Fréjus were important centres, but the reason for their existing was purely strategic; one was a garrison to protect the road into Italy, the other was the last harbour on the Mediterranean for troops that were to disembark on their march into the heart of Gaul, to Britain, and to the Rhine. After Ostia Fréjus was the most important port in the empire. Augustus, however, is more readily associated with places like Orange, Arles and Nîmes. The Romans had never been particularly attracted to the coast; for them it was a convenience – a means for reaching further outposts. Nor were they given to admiring scenery and the scantily clad mountains, pushing almost directly into the sea, had little attraction for them. It was only when they came to the widening plains of Provence that they became really interested, many wealthy Romans settling there in preference to their native Italy.

Perhaps no cultural centre, Cimiez nevertheless was a place of some consequence and could count a population of over twenty thousand people. Primarily a garrison, it also served as a rest station for weary legionnaires, and was supplied with luxuriant baths and an amphitheatre capable of seating a good part, at least, of the inhabitants. There were temples and coloured mosaics and white shafted columns, some of them twenty-six feet high. Of the theatre nothing remains except for a touching inscription to one of the performers. *Saltavit et placuit*, it reads – 'he danced and pleased'. One imagines a poor lad, perhaps a captive from the north, hired by some theatrical manager to appear on the stage at Cimiez where he died at the height of his success. It is known also that the governor of the province had his palace at Cimiez, situated, in all probability, where the eighteenth-century Villa des Arènes now stands.

Weathering various changes, the city remained intact till comparatively late; it was sacked, eventually, by the Lombards in the sixth century. Slowly, then, it crumbled away, all except for the wreckage of the amphitheatre which was traversed by a road. In 1787 a German obtained permission to dig in its ruins and found two small bronze statues. A Polish princess, following in his footsteps, proved even more successful, unearthing a figure of Jupiter. Since then a quantity of material has come to light: sepulchres, urns, ivories, fragments of marble columns and a considerable number of statuettes, and work still goes on, every year bringing some new detail to the fore.

Of the two towns Fréjus, or Forum Julii as it was called after Julius Caesar, its founder, is the more interesting. Standing at the entrance of a rich valley watered by two rivers, it also had the advantage of being within easy reach of the Aurelian Way and another strategic route that branched off to Riez and Forcalquier, right to the very heart of Provence. It was the first natural harbour after the Alps by which it was possible to communicate directly with the hinterland. Marseilles was too far from Rome, besides which Caesar had not forgotten the role that city had played in the wars of 119 BC and felt that it might be unwise to trust the Greeks should any emergency arise. Much better to have a port of their own and one that could be self-supporting. To this day the plains of Fréjus are well known for the fertility of their soil, and besides the crops that could be produced there were the newly discovered quarries of green and greyish-blue porphyry in the nearby Esterels. Drive inland from Agay, to Les Caous, and one can still see the quarry sites, and in them the remains of twenty-five-feet-long columns roughed out but never completed.

As it turned out, Caesar, for all his far-sightedness, had made one serious mistake in the choice of his harbour – had built it at the mouth of a river, and further to complicate matters, in an all but tideless sea. It was inevitable that silting should occur. Vitruvius, Caesar's military engineer, had written a treatise on the subject, and it is difficult to believe that Caesar was not familiar with the work. He must have chosen to ignore the warning, arguing, no doubt, that Rome had an unlimited number of captive hands at its disposal to dredge if and when the need arose. Of course, as predicted, the Reyran and Argens gradually filled up the original coastline with alluvial deposits, driving the sea back to a distance of several miles. However, these were not problems to bother the Romans, and Forum Julii, in Augustus's time, provided an adequate anchorage not only for the fleet protecting Mediterranean Gaul, but also the additional two hundred large vessels captured from Antony at the battle of Actium. At the peak of its power, the empire built state transports of well over a thousand tons, but by and large

Antony's Egyptian fleet boasted larger ships than were usually found, and those anchored at Fréjus represented Augustus's most glorious trophies.

The Romans were not good sailors and were at their happiest in light transports that would make short runs hugging the shore, and could be hauled up onto the beaches at night. As to their battleships, they were little better than lumbering cargo boats into whose holds were crammed soldiers, horses and military stores. Propelled by oars, they were difficult to handle in rough seas and impossible when contrary winds were blowing. Fortunately the Ligurian coast is well supplied with protected anchorages, but Forum Julii at this particular moment in history, was the only real harbour, and its past importance is reflected in its ruins.

First on the list comes the aqueduct that caterpillared some thirty-five miles along the Reyran Valley. Winding past hills it leaped several gorges and entered the town through the Porta Romana, the most important of the four gates. Bullock Hall,[1] spending his winters in Fréjus in the late nineteenth century, remarks on the similarity of the countryside to the *campagna* near Rome, and at times finds it hard to believe that the mellow arches striking across the plains were not those built in Claudian times – a similitude lent by the clumps of umbrella pines.

Much has been written about the glories of Fréjus's supposed lighthouse. It is said to have stood on what is now known as the Butte St Antoine, and was modelled, one is told, on the famous *pharos* at Alexandria. Bright fires were kindled in its belfry at night while damp straw sent up clouds of smoke during the daytime. But Paul Février, in charge of the present diggings, is very sceptical on this point and thinks that the foundations (thought to have been those of the tower) are connected in some way with the remains of a large villa on which he is now working. The so-called *lanterne d'Auguste* is also a misnomer and was probably only a guiding mark for captains to steer by when coming into harbour. M. Février is a very knowledgeable guide, and walking round the ruins with him made things come to life, but even accompanied by so forceful an interpreter, it is almost impossible to visualise the port as it must have been. The railway now runs close by, across what had been the basin, and cows graze where once joggled a forest of masts.

One reads that Fréjus was still a naval headquarters up until the sixteenth century, but constant dredging was necessary to keep it free of sludge, and by 1663 it was already dangerous, even for light barques. By 1704 it had become little more than a pestilential swamp drained by canals to keep it free of mosquitoes. Judging by early-eighteenth-century prints, the Roman fortifications were in a far better state of preservation than we find them today. Even so, they are quite extensive and have been worked on considerably, particularly during the last few years.

Interesting though Fréjus might be, it draws our attention more by association than by its actual sites, and these cannot be compared to the Roman remains further north which are of an astounding quality, quite as good, if not better, than many of those to be found in Italy.

To reach Arles, the capital of Roman Gaul, and the most lavishly endowed of its cities, one can still travel, if one takes the old 'Nationale 7', over the exact route followed by the famous Via Aurelia. Originally it left Rome by the Janicular Gate, made for Lucca, then Pisa and, hugging the coast, passed above the present Monaco. Crossing the shoulder of the Alps at La Turbie, it cut down the valley of Laghet to Cimiez, thus avoiding the difficult terrain behind Eze and by-passing the Greek town of Nice. Rejoining the sea again at the Var it skirted Antibes and Cannes, and on reaching Frejus turned abruptly away from the coast and, caterpillaring its way over the hills, made for Aix and Arles. From Arles subsidiary routes radiated outward through Gaul, to the Rhine, and southward stretched the Via Domitia to Spain.

It is difficult to give the exact distance from Rome to Arles as traced by the Via Aurelia, or the Via Julia Augusta as it was later called, but it must have been in the region of eight hundred miles and like all roads leading from Rome was measured from a golden spike in the forum – what was known as the *umbilicus Romae*. On an average the roads were about eight feet wide and set with pebbles, packed edgeways on. The large polygonal blocks with which they were paved when passing through towns were seldom, if ever, used once the open country was reached. Sections of the Via Aurelia are still intact, but most of it, as can be imagined, has been either absorbed by the railroad or then simply incorporated into the 'Nationale 7'. The parts of it not scattered have simply disintegrated into mule tracks that are hardly discernible as they wind their way under the olives shading some hillside. There is a section to be seen outside Rapallo, and again another strip that passes along the bottom of La Mortola gardens, protected on both sides by high walls and shaded by the lovely, pale-yellow rambling rose named after the gardens. Most of the local museums can boast of one or two milestones. Nine have been found between La Turbie and Cimiez and until recently others could be seen either flanking the stairs of some town hall or gracing some esplanade as in St Raphaël.

On reaching Arles one is immediately aware of its strong ties with Rome. It is a past that, at times, entirely dominates the atmosphere. When going there, I always stay at the Hotêl Nord Pinus in the Place du Forum, a choice partly explained by the name of the square, besides the charm of the hotel itself which is old-fashioned and attractively furnished. Henry James* disapproved of the place. Not I. The rooms are all named, and mine invariably turns out to be *'L'âme des poètes'* and looks out, appropriately, over Mistral's bronze and hatted head as he stands calmly surveying the shade mottled scene. But the real attraction is something quite different, for sunk into the wall, directly outside the window of what is usually my room can be found a section of cornice and part of a column: remains once forming part of the forum! The past, as I say, is never far distant, even the people one meets in the street seem over-conscious of their heritage. They look you proudly, straight in the eye. They are kind, even courteous, but infinitely superior. *Civis Romanus sum* the look seems to say, and like Madame Darmesteter, when visiting nearby St Rémy, I sometimes feel that I am being regarded as one of the defeated hordes – a barbarian from the north![2]

The city, more than likely, inherits its name from the Celts, *ar-lath* in their language indicating a place of waters, no doubt an accurate description two thousand years ago. As with Fréjus, it was a question of silting, only in this case on a much larger scale, the whole countryside having risen over thirty feet. Take a map and one sees how Arles must once have been a maritime city. The Rhône divided twenty-five miles from the sea and here, at the head of the delta of one of the greatest waterways of Europe, Ar-lath came into being. Under the Romans a great bridge of boats allowed the city to spread to both banks of the river and huge rafts floated on distended skins acted as ferries. The city proper occupied the left bank, while wharves and brick warehouses lined the far side, now the suburb of Trinquetaille. It is here, behind the waterfront of the business section that the rich merchants built their villas, their estates extending several miles down the delta. Old

---

* James does not actually name the hotel in his *Little Tour of France*. There are two hotels in the square but it is quite obvious which one it is that he slanders.

accounts exist detailing the merchandise: an abundance of wheat, corn, oil and sealed amphora of wine: cotton and papyrus from Egypt; from Africa and Syria, spices and silks; whole cargoes of luxuries waiting for transport to the interior. The empire was founded on trade and Jean-Maurice Rouquette, director of Arles's museum, himself an archaeologist, goes so far as to say that Gaul was colonised for the express purpose of creating a market for Roman wines. He does not pretend that it was the only reason, but gives it as one of the deciding factors and to give weight to his argument points to the laws protecting the vintners. Natives of Gaul were forbidden to cultivate vines, and if found growing them were punished by death. The wine itself arrived from Italy in amphori stopped with clay or wax seals, and it was the duty of the port authorities to verify each shipment. But strict as the rules might have been, they were by-passed by the wily inhabitants who, braving the consequences, went ahead producing as much wine as they pleased. In the basement of his museum, Rouquette has a whole pile of amphora with false stamps, squiggles impressed in the clay in the semblance of Roman script. It was all right so long as there was a mark of some kind, for, as Rouquette explains, few of the officials could read. 'You wouldn't believe it', he laughs, 'but at the height of the Gaelic War ship after ship arrived loaded, not as you might imagine with military stores, but with cargoes of wine.' The Royal Naval Museum at Albenga has an impressive exhibit of what a shipment of amphora could be. In 1950 divers working in the harbour located a wreck that must have been carrying anything up to eight to ten thousand amphora, and choosing the best of the specimens, those in charge have put them on exhibit, stacking them as they would have been on the ship, arranged on ledges in the hold, one tier above another like the overlapping of tiles on a roof.

With Rouquette we explore the city, starting with the recent excavations carried out in the basement of the forum. He refers to them as the *cryptoportiques* and we reach them by stairs cut into the foundations of a seventeenth-century Jesuit church. Rouquette thinks the place was used for storing grain, or possibly as a depot for traders with stalls in the forum above. Spacious barrel-vaulted galleries run the length of a vast rectangle, measuring some ninety metres or more from wall to wall. A feeble subaqueous glimmering filters down through the original ventilators and somewhere in the distance an underground spring drips through the natural rock. The air is chilly. It is an awesome sight and one admires the patience of the men who worked down here tunnelling away under shops and hotels. The excavation took twenty years to complete, and one can readily understand the difficulties they must have encountered.

In another part of the town we see the public latrines, built of white marble with ducts for running water. The town's drinking water came from a spring seventy-five kilometres away and on reaching the city was channelled off to the different fountains, baths and villas. It is amazing the speed with which the Romans worked. In something less than six years Arles was given a forum, a group of temples, an immense theatre, an even larger arena, as well as monumental baths. Rouquette explains the building techniques that made it possible: it was a question really of developing a system by which untrained labour could be used. The core of the buildings were formed of bricks and rubble embedded in mortar. The bulk finished, it was then encased in stone. Skilled hands were needed for cutting the stone, but no great talent was called for in the initial part of the operation which was left to the slaves or sometimes even the soldiers who were made to work to keep them out of trouble. Not all the buildings though were given this time-saving treatment, the theatre being an example; an elaborate construction decorated with marbles coming from quarries as far afield as Greece and Egypt.

Arles's amphitheatre is better preserved than the Colosseum in Rome and nearly a century earlier. It was capable of holding thirty thousand, ten thousand more than Pompeii and less than half the number of its equal in Rome. It must have been a fine sight with its thirty-seven tiers shaded by a great awning, the sand in its arena mixed with red dye to stop the blood showing. There is no record of Christians having been tortured at Arles, but the bones of every conceivable animal have been found among the débris, including Africa's great predatory cats.

Few opinions seem to coincide on the number of spectators the theatre could hold; the figures jump from seven thousand to more than double that number. One thing, however, all are agreed on, and that is the quality of what little is left. In its pristine state it must have been amongst the most splendid of the Imperial age. One is told that the scenic wall behind the stage rose to a hundred and thirty feet, higher than a ten-storey building, and made a marvellously resonant background. All that remains of it now are two lonely columns, one of a conglomerate marble from Africa, the other, experts say, from Sienna.

Charles x had made off with their eight porphyry companions which came to grief as they were being floated up the Rhône. They were probably shipwrecked on hitting a sand bank or sunk in shooting the arches of the Pont Saint Esprit.

Another relic shown us by Rouquette was the granite obelisk which now caps the fountain in the Place de la République. It had once been the *spina* of the Roman circus situated on the banks of the Rhône and first came to light during the fourteenth century. Left buried with its point showing, it was used as a decorative element in a private garden. Catherine de Medici, on a royal visit with her son, remarked on it but gave no orders as to any other possible use, and it was not until the seventeenth century that the city council eventually decided to set it up in its present site. It was solemnly dedicated to Louis xiv, his emblem, a shining disc, being fixed to an azure globe at the very apex. Bronze lettering graced the pedestal announcing its state, but with the fall of the Bastille this disappeared to be replaced by lions' masks – emblems of more democratic associations – from which the water now gushes.

Cook, in his book on the Romans, states that the granite for this obelisk comes from the gorges of the Esterel, and assures us that it is the only monolith of its kind which can compare in size with those from the banks of the Nile.

Wherever one goes in Provence the shadow of Rome's first emperor looms to the fore. Four of the major theatres date from his time: those of Vaison, Arles, Fréjus and Orange. He is also responsible for the great arch at Orange, the most successful of the triumphal arches – the prototype of the great arches with three bays that were to spring up in Rome. He is equally present at Nîmes which he founded by parcelling off lots which were divided amongst the veterans returning from Actium and the chained crocodile, symbolising the conquest of Egypt, is to this day incorporated in the arms of the city.

Nîmes is well known for its public gardens, and although pure eighteenth-century they rest on Roman foundations which form a frame for the springs dedicated to Nemausus, the god of fountains, from whom the city takes its name. Originally the place had been settled by one of the many Ligurian tribes attracted by the crystal clear eddies welling up from a fissure in the ground. Not unnaturally the presence of so much water had been regarded as an unusual dispensation, and forthwith the source had been dedicated to Nemausus and the Romans, always showing great tolerance of ancient faiths, adopted the deity as part of their pantheon. The fountain lies in the centre of the gardens and, using the original Roman columns framing what had been the baths of a *nymphaeum* the architect, a military engineer, built on a whole fanciful superstructure of balustrades decorated with cherubs and urns. The effect is pretty enough but I, personally, find there is something lacking. Is it the proportions, or the fact that there are not enough trees to shade one from the glaring Provençal sun? Far more diverting were the antics of two swans gliding in and out amongst Augustus's columns half submerged in the dappled, green-blue, upswelling waters.

Am I wrong, perhaps, about the gardens? But no one could possibly be disappointed with the remains of the adjoining temple dedicated to this watery deity. Here is Roman architecture at its most robust; severe, yet with a simple majesty to be found in most buildings associated with the first century. Another superb example of this early period is the Pont du Gard, also to be counted in the district embracing Nîmes, the aqueduct passing over it terminating in a reservoir near to the fountain. It is a gargantuan job of engineering, composed of three stages, built with enormous blocks of light, golden-yellow stone. The stones are rough cut, some of them weighing several tons, and give the appearance of having been wrenched from the quarries. In fact the architect of the Pont du Gard has achieved his effect by the masterful handling of his material. His arches are of unequal span, and the structure itself is bent in its length which gives it immense vitality. A purely utilitarian structure has thus been converted into an architectural screen of unrivalled beauty – 'the giant work', as Sir Theodore writes 'of a conquering race'.

One should creep through the uppermost storey, a tunnel through which the water actually flowed. Five feet high by two feet wide, it proved a claustrophobic but interesting experience and one welcomed the occasional glimmers of blue sky where the roof had caved in. The channel, already restricted, has been further reduced in width by thick calcinerious deposits left by the water, so thick in places that the sediment has been cut up and used for building purposes, the village church of Bezouce being entirely composed of it. I found the magic of the Pont du Gard very difficult to capture with a camera. One could, perhaps, manage from a helicopter, but failing this Hubert Robert's painting, hanging in the Louvre, gives the most faithful rendering I know. The painting is one of a series depicting monuments in Provence, a commission Hubert Robert received from the king, the first being executed in 1783. The surroundings have changed very little since Hubert Robert's day and, of course, add immensely to the pleasure of one's visit. It was autumn the last time I was there and the Gard, or Gardons as it is now called, glinted through the autumn foliage. We were alone and I walked down to the river's edge, running limpid over the pebbles in front of me. Poplars trembled in the sharp air and further out the deep blue of the water flecked with light as it passed under the great upsweeping arches.

I have purposely left the famous Maison Carrée to the last. It is a subject I approach with trepidation for, although I hardly dare admit it, appraising it with a cold and critical eye my first reaction was definitely one of disappointment, of sadness that I couldn't share in the general enthusiasm. Previous to this I can only suppose that I had been influenced by the mass of adulation that exists for the building. Sir Theodore finds it the finest surviving temple outside Hellenic territory, and that man of taste and discernment, Thomas Jefferson, was equally enthusiastic. He writes to a friend in Paris describing it as 'the most perfect model of ancient architecture remaining on earth', an 'edifice which has been the object of as many pilgrimages as the tomb of Mahomed'. But why this lack of response on my part? Many have criticised the attached columns at the sides, welded as it were to the *cella*. Not a very satisfactory solution, but not a factor in itself that would mar the building as a whole. The fault was more than this, but what exactly? I find it hard to explain. It seemed to lack soul and certainly has none of the fire to be found in many of its contemporaries. It is small and compact and in a near perfect condition, which certainly adds to its interest. One wonders whether this is not one of the factors that so impresses people, this and the richness of its detail, which is admirable and almost gem-like in its precision: the elaborate carvings on the cornice, its friezes and the swirl of rich foliage massed around the capitals of its Corinthian columns. But . . .

It has been said that the temple was dedicated to Gaius and Lucius Caesar, Augustus's adopted heirs who were both killed in the field. The bronze lettering which was originally fixed to the frieze of the portico, proclaiming the temple has now disappeared, and it is from the holes left in the stone that a certain Professor Seguier deduced the names of these young princes. Sir Theodore accepts this theory but not Lenthéric who points out that a letter can be placed in a variety of ways when it comes to fixing a name and argues that its exaggerated refinements are in themselves proof enough of decadence.[3]

Prosper Mérimée, who had the temple under his care as Inspector-General of Historic Monuments, also had doubts about its early date and wrote that it lacked the simple majesty generally associated with products of the first century.

However, whether late or early,* whether worshipper or not, there are various things to admire about this little temple; the most obvious being the subtle divergencies from mathematical exactness which the architects, when copying it on a vast scale for the Madeleine in Paris, entirely ignored, with the result that the overblown replica is dull and cold. Apart from its own decorative elements, which stand up admirably to closer inspection through a pair of field glasses, the Maison Carrée houses a very fine collection of fragments, among them a floral frieze from the forum and some beautiful eagles cut for some architrave. But good though they are, the collection does not compare with the quality of the sculpture in the Musée d'Art Païen at Arles. What is remarkable, given the abuses it has sustained, is the fact that the temple itself is in such perfect condition. By some miracle it was ignored by the invading hordes at the fall of the empire, and for years lay half buried amongst the mass of masonry that had accumulated around it. When first disinterred, it was used as a church, later on becoming a form of council chamber and eventually a private house, various architectural alterations having been carried out to suit the owner. At the latter's death, the Duchess d'Uzes, a local grandee, had plans for turning it into a mausoleum for her family. She was refused permission, but this can hardly have been based on artistic considerations for it was eventually bought by Felix Bruyès, a gentleman farmer, who made a stable of it after having filed away the flutings of the columns to make room for his carts. By 1672 we see it being used as a consecrated burial place by the monks of a nearby Augustinian monastery. It then narrowly escaped being shipped to the north. Ignoring the monks, Colbert had persuaded the King to transfer it to the park at Versailles. Fortunately war intervened, and the temple remained with the Augustinians until the revolution, after which it was put up for auction as national property and was bought by the municipality who were in need of a granary. Not until 1823 did it become a museum.

One more thing about the temple that always strikes me is its

* The *Michelin Guide* dates it the first century of our era.

singularly inappropriate name. Why, one wonders, should this little rectangular building be known to the world as the Maison Carrée? No one, as yet, has come forward with an adequate explanation, and even the *Guide Michelin* is at a loss to explain.

Back at Arles one is hard put to stop writing about it. In any event another visit at a later date in its history is necessary, for its charms are not exclusively its Roman antiquities. For the moment a walk up its avenue of death, the Elysii Campi, or Elysian Fields, which twisted into provincial French has become Les Alyscamps, would seem an appropriate way of taking leave.

Les Alyscamps used to be one of the largest and most venerated cemeteries in Europe. Dante makes mention of it in his *Inferno*, and one finds references to it in a number of equally distinguished works. It lies in a slight impression of rock on a plateau that was out of reach of Rhône waters and would appear to have been used as an acropolis long before the time of the Romans, and continued as consecrated ground even under the Christians – to be buried there was considered a great honour. So venerated was it that all the towns situated on the banks of the Rhône floated their dead down to a special landing stage. Those who could afford it accompanied their defunct, while the poor were just put adrift, attached to a raft with a coin wedged in their mouths. Floating with the current, they were met by those who made a profession of caring for them, their payment being extracted from between the rigid jaws of their charges.

Originally the Alyscamps covered as much ground as the town it served and continuing to grow, spread out in a wilderness of stone, of carved catafalques and urns clustering around the Via Aurelia as it made its way out of Arles. By early Christian times it could boast eighteen small chapels and then, with the Renaissance and the revival of classical learning, the reverse happened; the cemetery started to shrink. The nobles, wanting to make a good impression on the *cognoscente* visiting them, started offering their friends finely carved sarcophagi, and there came a time when no self-respecting museum in Europe was without its 'souvenir' from the Alyscamps. The railway and local industries completed the carnage, and now all that is left of this once proud cemetery is a dusty assembly of the ancients' funerary art. Empty, many with their lids cracked, the sarcophagi line the way of a grassless track leading to the remains of a blackened, Romanesque church. In the end one feels that even death has departed the Alyscamps.

❧9

St Honorat

We return now to the coast, to St Honorat, a little pine-clad island situated in the Golfe de la Napoule opposite Cannes. But first, before embarking for its rocky shore, let us take a quick look at the situation on the mainland. We have seen Provence grow from a loose confederacy of Ligurian tribes to the preferred province of a great empire. So popular had it become with the Romans that by the fourth century AD Constantine had made Arles his chosen seat of power, the Emperor's eldest son being born there. But the days of the *pax Romana* were numbered: Rome's domination had lasted close on to six centuries, it was a long time and the threads were beginning to wear thin. The question of guarding the frontiers, particularly those bordering the Rhine and the Danube, was becoming a major problem. Along with other symptoms of decay there had been a decrease of population, and it was not easy to find the soldiers to police the forts strung out along the dangerously extended frontiers. To counteract this shortage, more and more men were being drafted from amongst the ranks of the conquered people. There are many examples of this form of infiltration, and even the Emperor himself was affected. One reads, for instance, that Constantine's palace was crowded with Franks and that Huns helped swell the ranks of Theodosius's army. The empire had become an odd mixture of barbaric rudeness and Imperial splendour. The question of finance was yet another problem. Vast sums were needed to keep Rome's legions at their posts, and still further funds were absorbed to maintain the court in the oriental pomp which had become almost ritual. To meet these exigencies crushing new taxes were imposed and inquisitorial methods were adopted in obtaining them. The provinces were the first to suffer and whole areas were laid waste, the cultivators having fled to escape the rapacity of the local administrators.

Before his death in 337 Constantine had decided on two momentous moves – the recognition of Christianity, and the building of a new capital at Byzantium: the city of Constantine, or Constantinople. The founding of a second capital was probably a question of tact. Rome and its senators were die-hard pagans and Constantine, not wanting to antagonise them more than was necessary, decided that his recently adopted creed should be administered from a new centre, the site of which, he pretended, had been revealed to him in a dream. As to the actual spiritual side of his conversion, he must have recognised the power inherent in a religion that preached hope and compassion for the oppressed. More than half of his subjects were either freedmen or slaves and a religion that appealed directly to them, rather than to their masters, was bound to have their support. By making it a state religion he was enlisting their services on his side rather than against him, and in a way his policy worked, but perhaps not entirely in the manner Constantine had envisaged. However, the fall of the empire and the growth of the Church as a power is far too complex a subject to broach here; suffice it to say that when the great collapse came, civilisation took refuge under its wing. For hundreds of years the emperor had been at the head of state religion and tradition was too strong to break altogether with the past. Rome remained the principal seat of Christendom, the pope becoming its chief arbitrator, wielding the powers that had been vested in the emperor.

As to the empire, the first rift in the mighty structure came with Constantine's withdrawal of troops from Britain in 307. Twelve years later the Vandals descended on Spain and eventually crossed over to Africa, establishing themselves in the Roman colonies. Then follows the invasion of Italy and the sack of its capital by the Huns. It is difficult to follow the confusion and one must see the fast disintegrating map of the empire as a series of gaping holes divided up amongst various small barbarian kingdoms. Provence, our particular area, had been ravaged in turn by the Vandals, Huns, Lombards and Franks, and it is to this chaotic period of its history that the story of St Honoratus belongs. It is a fascinating story and the importance of the monastery he founded on the island now carrying his name has not always been given the attention it deserves. For generations it was to remain a centre of learning: it was one of the few inviolable asylums of faith and thought that, with the centuries, was to grow into a refuge for the whole of southern Europe. All the more illustrious sees of lower Gaul were filled with prelates who had been reared on St Honorat. It also nurtured some scholars, a few doctors, and a number of saints.

But first, before going any further, let us try and draw a rough outline of the man responsible for it all. It can only be a mere brushing, a formalised composition produced for us by St Hilary, a kinsman of Honoratus's who had worked as his secretary. Towards the end of his life and much against his will, Honoratus had been forced to leave his beloved island and accept the Bishopric of Arles, and Hilary, following him there, had eventually become Bishop on Honoratus's death in 429. It was Hilary who officiated at the burial, and Hilary who wrote the obituary, written in the form of an eulogy. Reading it now, it appears very stilted, but despite its archaic manner it succeeds in capturing the atmosphere of the time; a form of idealism; a feeling of purity that one sees reflected in early Romanesque architecture. Hilary, barely in his thirties when he succeeded Honoratus as Bishop, shows a touching devotion to his departed kinsman.

Hilary intimates that Honoratus came from a distinguished family of consular rank, since believed to have originated in northern Gaul, and says of him that he was serious, handsome and good at sport – the ideal son. His only fault, from his parents' point of view, was an almost morbid interest in the new religion. His father, seeing that he might lose his son to the Church, 'tried to appeal to him with all manners of delights . . . to entangle him in various worldly vanities, and to revive his own youth in a kind of comradeship with his young son'.[1] Honoratus, true to form, became all the more detached, and to achieve complete independence took the orders. One feels for the father in his son's renunciation of the world. 'His luxuriant tresses were cut . . . stiff cloaks covered the beauty of his milk-white neck . . . the handsome face grew pale with fasting . . . Vigour of mind took the place of vigour of limb. Need I say more? So suddenly did he become a wholly different person that his parents mourned for him as a father who had lost his son.'

They were a large family and Honoratus had an older brother who also took the orders. But they were too well known and too much respected by the locals for them to be allowed to lead the retired life they both felt was their calling. The only hope was escape and 'losing no more time in crossing the seas they made for shores where the eloquence of Rome was reckoned barbarous'. The country, of course, was Greece in some of its wilder aspects. From his pulpit the young Hilary continues the story and tells us that the brothers' 'tender and delicate upbringing was poor training for the rigours which they imposed on themselves'. Venautius, Honoratus's brother, died of the effects and alone now, Honoratus travelled to Italy and always in search of the ideal place to settle wandered northwards, and while exploring the rugged, pinnacled coastline of the Esterel came across a sheltered cave situated on what is now known as Cap Roux. Wild though the country appeared, it was still not to be the holy man's ultimate choice. On fine days he would have been able to gaze out across to the Iles de Lérins which, although they had been used as guard-posts by the Romans, were completely deserted, and it was here that he decided to move, choosing the smallest and furthest away of the two: scarcely more than a rocky shelf about two miles in diameter known then as Lérina. It is probable that Honoratus had intended Lérina to serve as a hermitage for himself and perhaps a few kindred spirits. He could have had little idea of founding a monastery, and one that was destined to play so important a role in the country's ecclesiastical history.

The actual settlement of the island is wrapped in the usual vague imagery one comes to associate with the stories of saintly men. We are told that the place was infested with hissing serpents and that at Honoratus's approach they all wriggled to their death in the sea. The lack of water proved equally easy to deal with and, as with Moses, a gushing supply was brought forth from arid rock by a smart tap with a stick. But these were embellishments that detract rather than add to the picture of someone who quite clearly had remarkable qualities. One turns again to Hilary without really transcribing. The phrases are flowery but genuine as he describes the small brotherhood gathered round the saintly man. 'He discerned what was troubling anyone as easily as if he carried everyone's mind in his own', and being a good judge of character planned these men's lives for them, 'no one was burdened by excessive labour and no one grew slothful with too much inaction.' His admonition had immediate effect. 'Those who were worried threw off their distress. Savage characters came to detest their rages. The arrogant loathed their own pride and the lewd adhorred their wantonness.'

Properly speaking, the settlement was not a monastery but a seminary of sacred learning, and as such gained a considerable reputation. It was on the island that St Vincent wrote the commonitorium against heresy, a work still often cited in controversy about the dogma of infallibility. It was also due to the influence of those trained on the island that St

Augustine's writings were finally discredited. Born in Numidia St Augustine was converted and became Bishop of Hippo at about the time Honoratus settled at Lérins. Augustine maintained that man was predestined to good or evil, a doctrine that did away with the necessity of self-control. Rome was inclined to accept his views, and, but for the stubborn bishops of Gaul, it is possible enough that western Christendom would have accepted a kismet as fatal as that of Mohammedism.

The island was also a centre of missionary enterprise, and amongst the better known of its qualified men comes St Patrick, the patron saint of Ireland. The son of Welsh landholders, he was captured by a raiding party from Ireland when about sixteen and carried off to County Antrim, or possibly somewhere in Connaught (Irish tradition is not clear on this point). After six years of bondage he made his escape and boarding a boat which was engaged in the export of Irish wolfhounds landed on the west coast of Gaul. From here he made his way to Lérins. We know none of the details, or how he happened to pick on this particular retreat, but once there he must have stayed long enough to have become inspired with the idea of a missionary undertaking to the country of his captivity. He would have been about twenty-two at the time, and the years he spent on the island must have coincided with the first decade of the fifth century.

It is frightening to think of conditions across the narrow channel of water, on the mainland. Beyond the Alps, the Roman world was falling to pieces; brutal forces were scattering all semblance of learning. Only on this quiet island was it possible for man to escape the convulsions. 'Mental culture, science and literature, can prosper only in peaceful times . . . they are delicate plants and need a clear sky, a bright sun and a mild atmosphere; they droop and wither in a storm.'[2] The Church, in a sense, was their greenhouse, and the Church, fortunately, was held in certain respect or perhaps superstitious dread by many of the marauding tribes, some of whom were already Christians and stood in awe of its institutions. Perhaps Lérins was too out of the way to bother about and, in any event, offered nothing tangible to tempt the would-be spoilers. Whatever the reason, the men who sought refuge there were left to live out their lives amongst their vines and the wind-tossed trees fringing the rocky water's edge.

Even in old age, as Bishop of Arles, Honoratus found time to revisit his island. Regularly every year he would make the pilgrimage and when, in the words of Hilary, 'he fell into his last sleep and passed,

sleeping into the quiet of death' others followed to direct the brotherhood. For five hundred years the monastery remained unmolested, and
as its numbers grew it gradually acquired more holdings on the mainland. Cannes formed part of its fief and paid a form of tax by supplying
the island with its agricultural produce. A flour mill was established at
Mougins, and a sawmill at Pegomas. Biot also came under its sway and
acres of vines were planted at Vallauris. To escape the worst of the
heat, the abbots started spending their summers there and built themselves a small palace. It has weathered the years and its chapel, at one
point used as an oil mill, has now been sheathed by Picasso with
polythene sheets daubed with a fresco entitled *War and Peace*. So
extended became their lands that at one point the island owned tracts
of country behind Bordighera and the authorities went so far as
establishing a mint at Seborga where the monastery coined its own
money. Unfortunately its reputation increased with its wealth, and
it was not long before it became prey to the Saracens whose *feluccas*
were constantly raiding the coast. In 732 five hundred monks were
massacred while attending Mass. Other raids followed, many of the
monks being carried away and sold into slavery. To counteract these
attacks, it was decided to fortify the island, and in 1073 a strong
quadrangular tower was built on the shore facing Africa. This watchout-
cum-monastery has come down to us almost intact and is built round a
two-storied cloister with an entrance door cut high in the wall and
reached, originally, only by ladder. Even the great Vauban, Louis
XIV's avant-garde military architect, had no suggestions to make when
consulted as to any possible improvements in its defences.

During the Middle Ages the island became a famous centre of
pilgrimage, the pilgrims offering up prayers in the chapels strung around
its shore. Of these St Trinité, situated at the eastern point of the island,
is the most interesting and can claim to be amongst the earliest
ecclesiastic buildings in Provence. It is almost impossible to place an
exact date on it. Viollet-le-Duc, when visiting the island with Prosper
Mérimée, attributed it to the seventh or eighth century. It is typically
Copt in style, but the general consensus of opinion these days would put
it much later, some time between the tenth and eleventh centuries.

Once fortified, the monks of St Honorat were able to re-establish
themselves. But the golden age of the island dates from its founding up
until the end of the Middle Ages; from then on its story is one of gradual
moral disintegration. Secular abbots were appointed who cared only for

the revenue to be drawn from their holdings, while the monks under their care were treated simply as serfs attached to the soil. St Honorat, as Lenthéric puts it, was really no longer a monastery, but a 'sort of religious penitentiary for monks who had been turned out of other communities'. He goes even further, dubbing it 'a new kind of Bastille' for minors 'deprived of their inheritance by family intrigue'. It sank so low that finally in 1787 Pope Pius XI issued a bull uniting the abbey to the Bishopric of Grasse. The following year it was suppressed altogether, and when the commissioners arrived to take possession they found their inventories hopelessly overstated compared to the tattered remains. What treasures were found were divided between the neighbouring parishes, the silver-covered reliquary containing St Honorat's bones going to Grasse. At least that is what they will tell you, and a portion of his bones they might have, but the casket in which they repose is certainly nineteenth century, the original more likely than not having disappeared along with a great many other things during the revolution.

Strange to relate, the monastery's next occupant was to be a woman: a well-known actress of the Comédie Française. In 1791 Jean Honoré Alziary, nephew of the monastery's last accountant, bought the place at auction and it was here that his daughter, Mademoiselle Sainval, chose to retire. Sainval had been much admired as the Countess in Beaumarchais's *Mariage de Figaro* and was still comparatively young when she came to St Honorat. Why she came is another matter and no material seems to exist that would throw any light on her addiction to this lonely island. One must remember, however, that it was the beginning of the romantic period and shutting oneself up in a Gothic tower was very much the kind of thing a heroine of the theatre might be expected to do. Thirty years, nevertheless, would appear slightly excessive, particularly since during this enforced seclusion she suddenly sallied forth to do a lightning tour of Russia, appearing again for a brief spell in Paris at the age of sixty-five. There must surely be more to the story than meets the eye. One need not, however, waste too much sympathy on the recluse for the tower in Sainval's lifetime was far from presenting the stark interior that the visitor meets with today. It was not unusual for monasteries to be lavishly furnished, and from the inventory we know that this abbey-fortress was no exception. The ceilings were gilded and painted, and there were galleries, a library, even a ballroom. Mérimée tells us that the guest rooms had overdoors painted with pastoral scenes in the style of Van Loo. Some even pretend that Sainval had engaged Fragonard to paint some frescoes for one of the rooms. Not impossible since he had been an intimate friend of hers, even her lover for a brief period, and Fragonard, in Grasse to avoid the furies of the revolution, we know visited the island with his young wife.

Though change there has been, at least Honorat is inhabited once more by a religious order: *les pères tranquilles* as they are locally known. In 1871 a number of Cistercians from the twelfth-century abbey of Senanque installed themselves on the island, rebuilding, not the tower, but the original monastery and church. Proudly they boast that it is an exact replica of the original, but, alas, what a travesty. However, given the date of their move, it is perhaps asking too much of the good fathers that, along with their other qualities, they should also have been men of exceptional taste.

The best way of visiting St Honorat today is by yacht. Anchor should be dropped in the glass-smooth channel between the two islands, and if early enough in the morning, a glimpse should be obtained of the monks in their black and white habits. Their occupations vary with the seasons and they can be seen as stooping figures, weeding in between their vines or, if it is June, scything their acres of lavender. A distillery in another part of the monastery grounds produces two very potent kinds of liqueur which is bottled and sold under the old name of the island: the yellow Lérina being digestive, and the green very tonic. The exact mixture, of course, is a secret and comes from a yellowed parchment hidden away in the library. Forty-four different plants must be thrown into the mortar, and amongst those which they care to tell us about come lavender, sage, anise, rose-geranium and coriander. The bouquet depends entirely on a correct dosage when mixing, and Father Albert, the alchemist for the past thirty years, has developed such an acute sense of smell that he can tell immediately if there is too much, or too little, of any one particular herb.

Saracens, Crusades and the Middle Ages

Having established the importance of St Honorat, we must now cross over to the mainland and concentrate on Provence and its littoral. We have reached a period when a few broad brush strokes will, I believe, serve our purpose better and give a sharper picture than any detailed study. While reading up on the Middle Ages, I found myself getting hopelessly embroiled in a mass of unimportant detail relating to family trees, marriages, successions, treaties and involvements governing the numerous independent states into which the country was then divided. Volumes rather than pages are needed to explain the situations clearly and, to avoid being tedious, it is better to hack one's way through the maze of lineages, pausing only when some particular incident draws the attention.

With the decay of the empire one finds the old municipal principle appearing again. The colonies had been founded around cities, so when the imperial system gave way it was only natural that power should again be divided. By the fourth century towns such as Marseilles, Arles, Tarascon, Avignon, Brignoles and Grasse had become self-governing, each jealously watching its neighbour, ready at a moment's notice to spring to the defence if they thought their rights were being impinged upon. This municipal principle is a leading characteristic of the Middle Ages in both Italy and Provence and so, by and large, the history of the Riviera can be counted with that of Italy, or more precisely that of Genoa. What is now French territory had little to do with the rulers of France until quite recently. By 1108 Nice had allied herself with Pisa, and Pisa along with Genoa were the most flourishing of the republics. Both were maritime powers, both were at continual loggerheads, skirmishes in which Genoa was generally the winner and in the end, qualifying herself as *La Superba*, came to monopolise the whole of the Mediterranean trade along the Ligurian coast. Further to complicate

matters were the struggles of the Guelfs and Ghibellines, two dissenting
factions that kept Italy in a constant state of war; the Ghibellines
believed in a strong central government; the Guelfs, or opposing
factions, championed the liberties of the republics. The pope, fearing
a united Italy which might control him, supported the Guelfs. It was
to his advantage that the powers should be divided and constantly
weakened by periodical blood-letting. Feelings ran high and street
brawls were a common occurrence. Various distinctions existed which
made it obvious to which party people belonged: in which side of one's
cap the feathers were bunched, even table manners were different. Very
often whole families were divided, and those of Provence were no
exception. The Grimaldis were strong Guelfs, while the Lascaris and
the Dorias supported the Ghibellines. Certain districts also stood for
different loyalties. The county of Nice, for instance, was Guelf, while
the town belonged to the opposing party. In one thing alone were the
different factions united: their common resistance to the Saracens,
those warlike zealots who had destroyed the Roman civilisation of
North Africa and poured into Spain. By 719 they had crossed the
Pyrénées and invaded southern Gaul. After taking Narbonne they
seized Carcassonne, ravaging the valley of the Garonne. Checked at
Toulouse they turned a few years later on Beziers and St Gilles. Both
Nîmes and Arles opened their gates to them, and with nothing to
check their advance the flood ascended the valley of the Rhône,
burning Autin in 725. There were marches and counter-marches and
in all more than five hundred thousand Saracens crossed the Pyrénées;
a human tide that was at last stemmed at Tours by Charles Martel.
The battle of Poitiers put an end to any idea of conquering Gaul. It
did not, however, clear the Arabs from the Ligurian shores.

Halted in Gaul, they enlarged their navy and took to the sea. Already
occupying the great Mediterranean island of Rhodes, Cyprus and Crete,
they attacked Sardinia and Corsica and before long made a bold descent
on Italy. Landing in the Bay of Naples they ascended the Tiber but
made no permanent foothold, rather concentrated their efforts to
plundering by sea, making frequent raids on the coast of Provence. In
848 they disembarked in the Camargue and devastated the plains of
Aix. Their raids were sporadic and no attempt was made at settlement.
Only in one place, where the corsairs had been shipwrecked, did they
attempt to dig themselves in. Struck by the wildness and the natural
isolation, they decided to make a landing and occupy the mountain

range which now carries their name – Les Maures. Forts were built on the heights converging on a central elevated spot dominated by a large fortress, the present village of Garde Freinet, a derivation of *frasinets*, the Provençal for stronghold.

For nearly a century and a half, the Saracens were entrenched in their thickly wooded enclave, and not until the second half of the tenth century was a concentrated effort mounted against them. The venture was a success, but nothing much is known of the details and there are no remains at Garde Freinet to help the historian. In fact, there are no obvious remains to be seen anywhere along the coast. It seems strange that the Moors should have proved such wonderful colonisers in Spain, leaving behind them a high degree of civilisation, and in Provence nothing; fire-side tales of slaughter and incendiarism, trade in cork, porous water-jars and perhaps the date palm, not that the fruit ever ripens.

Expelled from the land the Moors still continued to infest the Mediterranean, and for centuries the Knights of Malta struggled unsuccessfully to suppress their piracy. In the end it was Napoleon's expedition to Egypt and the conquest of Algeria by France that put a stop to it. But to revert to the chronological order of things, events have brought us to the end of the tenth century, and a hundred years later, in the spring of 1097, we see the first gathering of princes at Constantinople ready to embark for the Holy Land. Having conquered at home, they were now carrying the offensive to the enemy. A series of campaigns ensued occupying the best part of two hundred years. There were eight crusades, and one speaks of them by number, but more exactly they were one continuous armed pilgrimage with Jerusalem and its holy places as its ultimate goal. No spectacular victory can be claimed. The sepulchre of Christ was taken, retaken and ceded several times, and there was no question of occupation, of the east being invaded by the Christian west. Almost the reverse happened in so much that the Ottoman Turks over-ran Bulgaria, and later, under Soleiman the Magnificent, were to be seen laying siege to Vienna. But whether successful or not, it was a period of noble aspirations and the crusades must be seen as the offensive side of chivalry. Man is shown struggling towards an ideal. The ages were not entirely dark, and on the whole the crusaders can lay claim to not a few minor civilising influences: new plants and fruits such as the melon, unknown in Europe until the crusades. There were also the sherbets which the Saladin had served to him, made from the snows of Lebanon and flavoured with different syrups. Sugar was another commodity, and in the baggage of those returning could be found mirrors, face powder, bolts of cotton and muslin and lengths of damask. The colour lilac was another innovation, and we are told that even the use of a rosary for the telling of prayers was a habit picked up from the Muslims.

Reading about this period one's interest becomes centred on certain isolated figures: Eleanor of Aquitaine, wife of Henry II, who embarked with her first husband on one of the crusades, a self-willed woman who, before she became Queen of England, had ruled over France. Her son, Richard Coeur-de-Lion, the troubadour King, is another, but it is King Louis IX of France, or St Louis as he is more often called, who really concerns us. It was St Louis who founded Aigues Mortes, that little fortified town to be found in the quagmires of the Rhône delta, where the great river loses its power and dies lost to the sea; a sad, haunting country known as the Camargue; a land of upside down skies caught reflected in the flatness of endless marshes.

France at that early date had no outlets giving onto the Mediterranean, and St Louis, planning the seventh crusade, felt it unwise to embark from a port that did not form part of the crown. His agents, searching for a suitable place, managed to acquire a small hamlet belonging to a religious order settled in the Camargue, and in 1240 the royal architects started on its defence, namely the rectangle of curtain walls that now greet one as one approaches across the surrounding flatness. At the time of its building a broad canal led from its gates to the sea, but again, as with Fréjus, we have the same problem. Built at the mouth of a river, the slow, sand-filled waters of the Rhône, flowing into a tideless Mediterranean, have gradually pushed the coastline further and further away, with the result that Aigues Mortes now lies incongruously stranded on a dusty expanse that has no need of these complicated fortifications. The place, however, presented quite a different appearance in 1248 when St Louis appeared on the scene. The town was not sufficiently advanced to house all the troops and tents that were pitched under the walls. Flags slapped in the wind, the lion of Venice and the leopard of England floating high besides the fleur-de-lys. A little beyond the walls a fleet of thirty-eight ships rode at anchor, sails furled, waiting. They had been assembled in Genoa and were roomy enough to hold from five to eight hundred men. Persons of mark were housed in the poop and St Louis's quarters, and those of his Queen, must have been uncomfortably overcrowded. Not only had accommodation to be found for their suite, but room had to be made for a chapel. The *Michelin Guide* informs us that all passengers were obliged to embark with their own lockers, 'a convenience which served as a trunk, a bed and, in the case of death, as a coffin'. A barrel of fresh water and a chamber-pot were the other requisites. Illuminations exist depicting the scene, and like all representations of the period the proportions are wilfully distorted; the ships appear a collection of walnuts with light wavelets spanking their rounded keels. From the crow's nests, fishtail fannions float sinuously in the salt breeze, and below pinheaded men can be discerned with a bristle of lances. The admiral waits on the weather, for there is no tide to dictate their departure. It is a matter of hours before the winds will be thundering in the canvas, and once at sea the great snub-nosed ships will advance at the speed of a tortoise, a passage to Cyprus in those days taking just over three weeks.

For two years enormous stores of provisions had been collected in Cyprus, and once arrived St Louis would be joined by the rest of his fleet, some eighteen hundred vessels in all.

St Louis's first crusade had been aimed at taking Egypt. Failing in this, he set sail again many years later; this expedition was also doomed to failure. Hardly had he landed in Tunis when he sickened and died, his last words barely whispered: 'Jerusalem, Jerusalem'.

There is little doubt that many of those taking part in the crusades were men cast in a romantic mould. They had ideals, and from a social point of view they must have been shocked by the Mussulmen's attitude towards their women. Never in any society in the ancient world were they so little regarded, and this at a moment when western women were beginning to come into their own; a new reverence that had been engendered by a recent revival in the worship of the Virgin Mary. In Europe, and especially in Provence, this idealisation of womanhood was reflected by the growth of a particular school of poetry which found its expression in the troubadours. And who, one might well ask, were these troubadours? The word is probably a derivation of *trouver*, to find. Others would have it stemming from the low Latin *tropus* meaning an air, or melody. Both interpretations, as will be seen, are equally applicable. As to the troubadours themselves, they were a mixture of poet, musician and entertainer. Highly professional, they attended music schools, were carefully trained in articulation and the placing of vowels, and above all how to breathe properly. The songs, concentrating for the most part on the lyrical side of things, were sometimes in French but more often the verses were written in the Midi's cherished *Langue d'Oc*, the vernacular of France south of the Loire. As to the music, it had a decided oriental flavour, influenced certainly by the tantalising arabesques practised by the Moors when in Spain; and lastly, matching these lark-like trillings, came their clothes which would seem to have been almost a uniform: 'red shoes, saffron lined breeches and a flowing mantle of green and crimson Flemish brocade'.[1]

One is well aware of the primitive conditions obtaining during the Middle Ages, but here was a performer who could slip airily above the crude limitations, and he did so by a clever blending of poetic imagery. The troubadours drew on legendary lore and could spice their tales with the perils attending the crusades. The supremacy of love, however, was the key-note of the troubadour's lyrics, and listening to their songs one could escape into a wonderful world of make-believe, an arcadia where passionate men were seeking an ideal love; it did not really matter if the loved one was purely a figment of the imagination.

There are slight nuances in the interpretation of the role actually played by the troubadours. They were court poets under a patron lord, but dependants, nevertheless, though of a superior order. One imagines that they can be compared in rank to a private tutor in a present-day household. Their duties, though, were entirely different. It was the troubadour's job to keep the family amused, especially during the long winter evenings, and his presence must have been a godsend, particularly to the women. High-born ladies of the Middle Ages seldom married for love. The daughters of territorial lords, their unions were generally based on sound common sense and were concerned with the union of fiefs, or the pooling of family estates. They were much appreciated and paid courteous respect, but more often than not it was the troubadour, with his gifted turn of phrase, who administered to their vanity. He complimented them, making them play the role of idolised lady-mistress. Usually beneath the ladies in social status, they wrote in a most guarded and respectful style as though they had very little hope of having their love requited, and the lady in return gave her suppliant a gift of ribbons, gloves – even a kiss, but rarely more than a chaste brushing of the lips. There must have been moments, however, when this professional lovemaking went beyond bounds, though transgression, one feels, must have been a fairly rare event. Most women must have understood the value of the relationship as an ideal.

The troubadours originated in Provence during the eleventh century, their art dying out some two hundred years later when their country was absorbed by France. A few amongst them have left us their names: William de Balaun, Peire Vidal and Bernard de Ventadour who sang Queen Eleanor's praises. Ventadour was the troubadour so much admired by Petrarch, the great Petrarch whose poems owned not a little to the troubadours in so much that all the odes and sonnets deal with a chivalrous, unrequited love; a story that in any event concerns us here, for it is in Avignon, one spring morning, that he was to meet the beautiful Laura de Sade, a meeting that was to kindle a hopeless passion that lasted twenty-one years and continued even after the lady's death. He describes the tortures he was to go through in the *Canzoniere*, and along with Dante, he must be counted the first distinguished writer of modern times to concentrate on amatory verse and the love he describes is touchingly beautiful. No mood of his lasts very long, and his poems are filled with inconsistencies. At times one feels that his sufferings are a product of the imagination. At others one is convinced of the hopelessness of his passion. In short, he is subject to all the grief and ecstasy that all who have really loved must experience.

On reading Petrarch's life, it seems unfair that his *Canzoniere*, which he deprecated, should remain the one work by which he is best remembered. He was, after all, a man of almost inestimable learning. Symonds in his study of the Renaissance goes so far as to name him 'the Columbus of a new spiritual hemisphere, the discoverer of modern culture' and hails him as the founder of humanism.[2] He was the first scholar to understand the importance of libraries, coins, inscriptions – anything that could be regarded as a source of accurate historical information. The majority of his own works were written in Latin and initially it was for his fame as a rhetorician and his compositions in that tongue that gained him recognition in Rome, when in 1341 at the age of thirty-six, he received the laurel crown; the equivalent, one supposes, to being voted England's poet laureate. No, as already mentioned, it would seem almost ironical that it should be his *Canzoniere*, written in Italian, for which he is known and admired. Ironical, perhaps, but hardly surprising. Read his poems and they are like enamels. It would seem that he revised them constantly and boasted as an old man that he could correct his works and improve them 'all except my Italian poems, where I think I have reached the highest perfection I can attain'.

G.R.—5

Printing was first started in Germany, at Mainz, in about 1450; therefore the *Canzoniere*, when they appeared, were circulated in manuscript form. They had an immediate success, but from the nature of things enjoyed a limited distribution. The first printed edition appeared in Venice in 1470 to be followed in quick succession by others. Thirty-four editions can be counted before the close of the century, and three times that many during the century to come. Reprints have been constantly called for, and the demand still keeps up. There have been several English translations, the first by the Countess of Pembroke in 1565; others have appeared subsequently, and amongst the more recent is that of William Foulke. Since Petrarch's memory has become an integral part of this country, and since I have no Italian, it is Mr Foulke's translation that I intend to use here. It would be impossible not to quote from some of the poems, particularly as the touching idyll they describe is set for the most part by the banks of the Vaucluse, near its limpid source, which in itself is one of the most remarkable natural phenomena the country has to offer.

In his introduction Foulke tells us that Petrarch is still largely unknown in other lands than his own, and as a reason he gives the difficulty of capturing the beauty of his language in another tongue. 'No kind of literature is more difficult to translate', he writes, 'than lyric poetry, and this because its beauty depends so largely upon its form, including the metre and rhyme employed. In epic and dramatic poetry, as well as prose, other things predominate – the story to be told, the thing to be described, the character to be delineated.' 'And', Foulke continues, 'no lyric poems ever depended more for their beauty upon their form and their metre and rhymes employed than those of Petrarch.' He was not so much distinguished for his originality in thought or portraiture 'as for his delicate taste and the exquisite form in which his thoughts are embodied'.[3] Foulke complains of the words with different meanings employed for rhyming purposes and the difficulty of reproducing them exactly in English. However modest though Foulke might be, he has accomplished his task with tact and great feeling, and the *Canzoniere*, even in another language than their own, are wonderfully moving.

Petrarch comes from a respectable background, his father having been a successful notary in Florence. Banished for supporting the Ghibelline cause, the family moved to Arezzo, a township which espoused the same cause, and it is here in 1304 that Francesco was born.

The family name, according to Tuscan usage, should be spelt di Petracco, and it was the great poet in later life who altered it to Petrarch for the sake of euphony. From Arezzo the family moved to Pisa, and in 1313 moved again to Avignon, then the pope's place of self-imposed exile. For a period of nearly a hundred years it must be seen as the hub of the Christian world, which meant that Petrarch grew up in a bustling, cosmopolitan town of culture and learning. While there he attended three years of law school at Montpellier, and on the death of his father in 1326 returned to Avignon. Banishment and the fraudulent administration of his father's estates had left the young man almost penniless, a Cicero manuscript saving him from total penury. With little or nothing to fall back on, Petrarch took to the Church. His exact functions in that institution have never been clearly elucidated, but in any event he seems to have been on good terms with the hierarchy, in particular with the powerful Giacomo Colonna, the future Bishop of Lombay, who was to remain one of his life-long friends. By all accounts Petrarch was handsome as a youth before he grew paunchy; tall, with the kind of looks that, despite his impecuniosity, made it possible for him to cut an elegant figure at the pontifical court. It is as something of a dandy then, that we must see him on that fateful Good Friday morning in the church of Santa Clara, when first he laid eyes on Laura de Sade, the beautiful Laura of the *Canzoniere*.

Born a de Noves, Laura was of noble Provençal stock, and it was probably the family who had persuaded her to marry de Sade, a rich bourgeois merchant. She was sixteen when she married, and only eighteen when Petrarch first saw her. 'I beheld a lady', he writes, 'habited in a green mantle interspersed with violets.' A profusion of golden hair fell round her shoulders. One gets an impression of pale, delicate hands and small tapering feet, and a lofty, graceful carriage. From reliable sources one learns that contemporary painters were so taken by her beauty that they used her on several occasions as their model in both paintings and frescoes, notably in the fresco Simone Martini executed for the porch of Nôtre Dame des Dômes at Avignon. Having been exposed to the elements, the fresco is all but obliterated and what remains has been removed to the palace for safe keeping. In its original state it represented the Virgin, enthroned, surrounded by angels. Below St George charges a dragon, and besides him kneels a beautiful young woman who, according to Lenthéric, is Laura posing as St Marguerite; St George being none other than Petrarch himself.

Simone Martini was a pupil of Duccio's and is mentioned by Petrarch in his sonnets, which leads one to suppose that there is some truth in Lenthéric's story, also the fact that Martini is supposed to have limned a miniature of Laura which the poet carried around with him on his journeys.

The Abbé de Sade's life of Petrarch[4] is accepted as the definitive work on the poet, but there are those who hold different opinions when it comes to some of the details, particularly regarding Laura's identity. Baring-Gould in his *Troubadour Land* pretends that the beautiful woman of the sonnets is not de Sade's wife but his daughter, and claims that there is abundant evidence to prove his point. Sir Theodore Cook has yet another theory, and maintains that she was a country lass living in modest circumstances, and quotes from Petrarch, building up quite a different image from the stately woman of the sonnets. He would have her 'the rose born in the harsh briar' living in a squalid farm, and points to some given line, reading into it the meaning that fits his argument: 'The dark and vile prison', the 'mean drudgery' of her life, 'the unworthy environment'. These phrases could very well refer to the corrupt life of Avignon which Petrarch was always decrying. As to the Abbé's carefully researched work, Sir Theodore just writes it off, claiming it only natural that a distinguished family of the region should want to appropriate the enchanting heroine of the sonnets, pretending that she was the daughter of their house. In any event, this theory that she was a country girl is constantly disproved, for all through the sonnets Petrarch goes to some lengths to describe her clothes: the richness and colour of her dresses, her jewels, her constantly changing coiffure and 'her tresses now wound in pearls and gems . . .' There was also another theory, and this one current during Petrarch's lifetime, that Laura was not flesh and blood at all, but a woman in the abstract. A letter exists, however, written to Giacomo Colonna which makes it quite clear that she existed. 'Would to God', Petrarch writes, 'that my Laura was an imaginary person and that my passion for her were only feigned! Alas, it is a madness! How difficult and grievous it would be to feign it for a long time, and what extravagance to act and play like this!'

But what further details do we know about Laura? Very little except what one gathers from the sonnets. Hugues de Sade, her husband, appears to have been a rather mediocre person. She gave him eleven children, nine of whom lived, and when she died of the plague in 1348 he remarried almost immediately, which suggests a certain lack of sensibility. Although deeply moved by her ardent admirer, she was never unfaithful to de Sade. Indeed the sonnets show that the intensity of Petrarch's feelings upset her considerably and it is supposed that seeing how his advances troubled her he started to put his thoughts into words, and thus began the deluge of sonnets and ballads which one reads with growing fascination, Petrarch all the time adding touches to his evocation of Laura:

> Lady, I have not seen you draw aside
> In shadow dark or under skies serene
> The Veil wherein your gracious face doth hide

and a few lines further on in the same ballad he writes:

> I saw compassion in your face revealed,
> But often Love his yearning doth betray,
> A veil around your golden locks you threw,
> And your kind glance within itself withdrew.
> What most I cherish now no more I see –
> So close that heavy veil restraineth me,
> Which both in summer airs and wintery skies
> Doth darken the sweet light of your fair eyes.

He chides her for allowing her mirror – which he refers to as my 'glittering rival' – to see her beautiful face.

Petrarch travelled widely all during the time he was pouring out his sonnets. In 1330 he was in Flanders and Germany; he may even have paid a visit to England. Back in Avignon he climbs Mont Ventoux with his brother. The ascent was rough but wonderful views were to be had of the Alps, the Rhône and the surrounding mountains. Later he pays his first visit to Rome, and in 1337 he establishes himself at the Fontaine de Vaucluse. 'Here is a place', he writes, 'most suited to my nature . . .' For this first visit Philippe de Cabassole had lent him his château which still stands in ruins above the famous spring, one of the most forceful upsurges of water in the world. The outlet is the beginning of the Sorgue, a subterranean river fed by the rains which seep through the porous plateau of the Vaucluse. The gorge through which the waters run for the first part of their way was wooded in Petrarch's time, and now its approaches are disfigured by two hideous, but fortunately defunct, paper mills. One simply has to shut one's eyes to this inexplicable vandalism and make for the spring itself, which is spectacular. The blue-green water wells up silently from the depths beneath a vast towering wall of rock, mounting some thousand feet into the sky. From a troubled current it spills to become a furious foam, and the contrast between the stillness of its basin and the agitation of the waters directly after it has overflown are fascinating to watch. Charmed by the sylvan scene, Petrarch settled down to live in the valley, and for the next sixteen years it is his home. It would seem that Petrarch and Laura had met here on several occasions, and the memory of her presence there gave rise to some of the most charming lines in the whole *Canzoniere*. He writes of his love surrounded with the natural beauties.

> I hear her as the summer breezes pass,
>   In rustling leaves, in songs that fill the glades
> And in the brooks that murmur through the grass.

In another sonnet he gathers the flowers she brushed aside in 'wandering between the mountain and the stream':

> What miracle to see her on the grass,
>   Where like a flower she sits! Or watch her press
> Her breast on that green bush; or mark her pass
>   In the fresh springtime, in her loveliness,
> By her own thoughts attended, chaste and fair,
>   Twining a garland for her golden hair!

One gets these euphoric moods and then in another of the poems Petrarch is restless, unable to sleep and plunged in gloom.

> No truce in sighing have I with the sun,
> And when at night I watch the flaming stars
> I go lamenting, longing for the day.

And again he cries:

> What was my foolish will
> That I so held them fixed on one fair face
> To sculpture it in fancy in a place
> Where it can ne'er be moved by force or skill
>   Till I shall be the prey
> Of death that endeth all? Nor do I know
> If even on him my trust I may bestow.

Petrarch even prays for deliverance from his hopeless passion.

> 'Tis now O Lord, the eleventh circling year
> Since I am fettered by this pitiless chain

Then Laura, never very strong, starts failing in health. It is twenty years since they have known each other, and leaving for Rome Petrarch has forebodings; forebodings that he expresses when he tells of Laura visiting him in a dream to bid him adieu.

> 'Dost thou remember not,' I hear her say,
> 'That final evening when we needs must part?
> Late was the hour; I could no longer stay,
> And left thee tearful, but I had no heart
> To tell thee then what now is proved and plain:
> Hope not on earth to see my face again.'

The dreaded event is all the more poignant for shortly before Laura's death their relationship had undergone a change, gone was Petrarch's desperation and they had become friends.

> At last my blossoming and vernal age
> Was passing, and I felt my youthful fire
> Grow calmer. Life had reached its crowning stage
> And soon would seek the valley and expire.
> Little by little my dear enemy
> Began to win assurance from her fears
> And her pure heart and stainless honesty
> Would take in fancied jest my sighs and tears.
> For it was near the time when love doth walk
> With chastity, and lovers may have leave
> To sit together and in friendly talk
> To tell how they did dream and yearn and grieve.

Laura died while Petrarch was in Italy, and after her death she keeps appearing to him in dreams, and it is these ephemeral visits that the poet claims keep him alive.

> And how intently doth she lend her ear
> To the long story of my suffering.
> Until the garish daylight doth appear!
> Then – for she knows the way – she seeks the skies,
> The tears still glistening in her tender eyes.

In another verse he imagines her entrance into heaven, the angels are marvelling among themselves!

> 'What light is this? What beauty rare and sweet?
> So fair a soul, such queenly majesty
> Ascending from the world to this high seat,
> Never before in heaven did we see.'

The *Canzoniere* close with his celebrated 'Hymn to the Virgin' in which he begs forgiveness for his simplicity. He realises the things that charm this world are idle dreams and the tenth verse expresses his sentiments quite clearly.

> Virgin, how many were the tears I shed,
> How many years I prayed and longed and sighed!
> What was my guerdon! Grief and sorrow vain.
> Since I was born where Arno's stream doth glide,
> From land to land my restless feet have sped,
> And life was naught but bitterness and pain.
> For mortal charms and gracious ways and dear
>   Have clogged my heart and mind
>   O Virgin holy, kind,
> Delay not. Haply 'tis my final year.
> My days like flying arrows speed away!
>   In sin and misery
>   They swiftly flee
>   And death alone doth stay.

It was to stay a few more years, during which time Petrarch moved from Vaucluse to another hermitage in the Euganean Hills, near Padua: the village of Arquà. In 1374 his people found the old poet and scholar dead among his books in an upstairs room with a view out over some fields facing towards the Adriatic. The house still exists and they have managed to preserve some of his furniture; even his cat, which is now a desiccated mummy.

I have purposely concentrated on the part of Petrarch's life that links him most intimately with Provence. Nothing has been said of him as a public figure, and I feel it would be a mistake to let him slip from these pages without trying to fill in at least some of the gaps. First how does one classify him? As priest who penned poem after poem to a woman he adored; as a man of letters, diplomatist or monastic saint?

Selfless citizen, one supposes, is the label which suits him best. Like his father before him, he was a staunch supporter of the Ghibelline party and the major part of his energies were dedicated to the Italian liberties. Forty years of letters and dissertation poured from his pen demanding a united Italy to be ruled jointly by an emperor and a pope; their centre of power to be the city of the Caesars. Paradoxically, considering his leanings, he was repeatedly offered a papal secretaryship, and there was no great house in Italy that would not have counted themselves lucky to harbour him under their roof, even the very despots who were destroying the freedom of Lombard cities. Petrarch must have enjoyed the pageantry while the Gonzagas, the Estes and their like probably viewed his political theories as of no particular importance and fêted him instead as a poet; the greatest in Europe, the author of the *Canzoniere*; the sad, human figure who made something of a cult of melancholy and could humbly write 'no sparrow on any roof could ever be lonelier than I . . .'

✺11

The Palace of the Popes

An observant traveller passing through Provence at the time of which we are writing would certainly have been struck by the amount of building going on. All round would have risen walls of tawny coloured stone screened by scaffolding; new bridges spanned the rivers, and off, in amongst the trees, would be some isolated settlement where a new monastery had come into being. If a man of discrimination, he would have made detours to include the monuments left us by the Merovingian kings, principally the various baptistries, one at Venasque and others at Aix, Riez and Fréjus. Plain square structures from the outside, their interiors were octagonal in plan and solemnly splendid; domed roofs of pale brick reposed on fine columns; black granite with marble capitals, or a grey-green schist capped with the foliaceous remains of a second-century Roman temple. Sunk into the floor and centred under the dome comes a copper or marble basin – the bath into which the baptised were immersed. A curtain fixed to the columns, now worn to a soapy smoothness by age, would have surrounded the font. The fifth-century baptistry at Fréjus can be cited as an excellent example, and when standing in one of these early interiors one is conscious of a certain stillness; a complete feeling of peace seems to dominate the atmosphere: a feeling which stems, one supposes, from age, from associations, but also greatly helped by the controlled simplicity, the colour, and the satisfying texture of the marbles used in conjunction with the soft brick. The same atmosphere predominates in the imposing twelfth-century Cistercian monasteries of Thoronet, Silvacane and Senanque, all situated within a hundred mile radius. The abbey of Thoronet lies north-east of Brignoles and Silvacane just south of Cadenet. Senanque, the last of the three, is hidden away in a rocky ravine north of Gordes, a handsome village perched on the edge of a plateau in the Vaucluse. The approach to these abbeys is usually bleak. To reach Thoronet one takes a small road which dips and turns through hard, stony country, sparsely covered by struggling vegetation. Passing a semi-deserted village, one descends to a wooded valley and there, unexpectedly, appears a small pointed belfry rising above the trees. The Cistercians are an austere order and practise the rigid self-abnegation which is reflected in all their actions, extending itself even to the choice of the site on which they built their settlements. St Bernard, abbot of the first monastic colony, was a stern disciplinarian and disapproved of the lavish display evident in the majority of the religious institutions of his day. His dictates were harsh: his followers must be entirely self-supporting and should depend for their livelihood on the land, and the abbeys they founded were planned with a view to accentuating this rigid mood: everything must be functional – no unnecessary turrets or pinnacles, no stained-glass in the windows. The windows, in consequence, remained undivided. The theme throughout was the renunciation of the world and its riches and, of course, this great simplicity and the harmony it creates is what one finds so moving about the abbeys of Provence. Thoronet and Senanque have been carefully restored and it is pure chance that Silvacane has come down to us more or less intact. Immediately following the revolution, it was bought by a contractor who proposed to use its beautifully cut stones to build a bridge over the Durance, at Cadenet. Mercifully, he sold it to a farmer instead, and the man's descendants were still occupying its half Gothic, half Romanesque galleries as a stable until well after the turn of this century.

There are a number of buildings dating from the same period as these Cistercian abbeys; amongst them the remarkable twelfth-century church of le Thor and the beautiful abbey of Montmajor dominating the plains of Arles. Montmajor was much added to during the eighteenth century, but a great deal remains of the original. At Arles itself comes St Trophime, one of the most splendid Romanesque churches in all of France. Within the shadow filled arch of its portal crowd scenes from the Last Judgement. The Redeemer in majesty surrounded by the symbols of the Evangelists is seen receiving the elect to the calm of paradise, while on his left the damned, enchained by demons, are being led, naked and weeping, to immediate combustion in the flickering flames of an all too evident hell. The reliefs are heavily encrusted with grime, but the restorers dare not clean the age-blackened stone for fear of it flaking. Fortunately, the stylised figures of the Evangelists portrayed within the quiet of the cloister are in much better condition. Screened from the soot of the city, they are highlighted by the sun which, in sundial fashion, glides slowly over the multiple pleats of their robes, lending them the gleam of old ivory.

Some twenty miles away, on the far side of the Rhône, comes St Gilles, a splendid echo of St Trophime. Here the portal is three-fold and even richer in its carvings. Majestic, almost life-sized figures of the apostles frame the central door, and above them runs a frieze of swirling, baroque foliage; a jungle in which beasts devour the wicked and camels rub noses with monkeys. The whole is fantastically imagined and at times almost pagan in feeling.

It is not by chance that the Rhône valley produced so many fine examples of the Romanesque. In Provence Rome had never been forgotten, and its building style lingered on far beyond the date of its domination; besides, its people had never taken kindly to the pointed arch. It was left to the north to design richly traced windows inviting the light. In the south, the sun was avoided and thick walls pierced by small windows and dimly lit interiors seemed natural and convenient. They wanted no change, and hours can be spent in exploring the little Romanesque chapels with which the countryside is so liberally endowed.

Mention has been made of the observant traveller and, of course, no place would have intrigued him more than the city of the popes at Avignon. Already in the last chapter within a stone's throw, as it were, of this Rome in exile, all that was necessary to reach its walls was to follow Petrarch's swift, weed-grown waters and with them merge into the slow, upswelling twists of the Rhône. Naturally, there is a more direct way of reaching the city, but at least this imaginary detour allows one a more telling glimpse of the country and helps one to a better understanding of the great river. Conditions have been far from stable as far as concerns the Rhône. For years it snaked as it pleased over the width of its course, forming and reforming islands which in the vicinity of Avignon show as a flatness of pebbles grown over with trembling-leafed poplars. At the time of which we are writing maps indicate the main flow of the river as passing along its western bank: in other words, the water was navigable beneath the tower of Philippe le Bel, whereas the bank beneath the Rocher des Dômes and the popes' palace was shallow and deserted. Exactly the contrary is the case today, and thanks to improved methods of damming, the flow can now be directed at will.

Keeping always to our period, the early Middle Ages, the first land-mark to catch one's eye on arrival would have been the famous Pont d'Avignon, better known locally as the Pont St Bénézet; the bridge on which, so the famous song tells us, *'tout le monde danse . . . y danse tout en rond!'*. These lines always puzzled me as a child, but as Mary Darmesteter so amusingly comments in an article she wrote on Provence, 'Make an effort to cross the Rhône when the mistral is blow-ing, and you will arrive at any rate at one explanation'.[1] One figure, perhaps, could have spun like a top whipped by the wind, but not a whole troupe, for as the *Michelin Guide* sensibly points out, there was no room, the bridge is far too narrow.

As it stands, the Pont St Bénézet is reduced to four gracefully sweep-ing arches,* but at the time of its building it sprang across twenty-three carefully constructed piers and was considered so outstanding an achievement that a legend had to be invented to explain its existence. Not even the Romans had dared to construct a permanent crossing over this turbulent river. Almost a thousand yards long, it was set at an obtuse angle against the stream, a precaution the architect had taken to give it added resistance when the currents were strong. Another security measure were the especially low piers, carried on great boat-like projections which for additional security were pierced by arched open-ings through which high waters could stream without hindrance.

It is not difficult to imagine the effect this bridge must have had on the people of Avignon.† Not unnaturally, they took a great pride in it. It even became a subject for pilgrimage, and was so venerated that the general public insisted on attributing supernatural powers to its build-ing. With a perfectly straight face the pious would tell you that its architect, Bénézet, had been a shepherd of twelve from the Ardèche, and like Joan of Arc, subject to voices. One day, while tending his mother's sheep, the voices informed him that he had been ordained by God to build a bridge. 'Go to Avignon', they ordered, 'and present yourself to the bishop.‡ Fear nothing, we will accompany you.' An obedient boy, Bénézet departed and arriving at the city sought out the august cleric. As it happened, he was in the process of giving a sermon, but nothing daunted, Bénézet interrupted him, piping out his mission.

* It was cut for defensive purposes in 1395, rebuilt again, and then gradually fell away, arch by arch, for lack of attention.

† Started in 1177, it was finished in 1188 and undoubtedly stands as one of the most remarkable pieces of architecture in the entire Rhône Valley.

‡ It was before the days of the popes.

The bishop, quite understandably furious at the child's seeming dis-
respect, had him arrested, and it is the guard who, judging it an unusual
situation, decided to test the boy. Pointing to the broken architrave of
a Roman temple, he told Bénézet that if he managed to move it he
might possibly reconsider his story. Bénézet, remembering the angels,
knelt and said his prayers, and then with perfect unconcern seized hold
of the block and lifted it as easily as if it had been a small stone.

Lenthéric, always so sensible and reassuring in his calm judgement
of things, puts the story down to an excess of imagination, but agrees
with his fellow historians that there is no doubting Bénézet's existence,
or the part he played in building the bridge. It is just his age that this
wise Frenchman calls into question. Instead he offers quite a different
explication: Bénézet was no child, but rather the leader of a group of
churchmen forming a brotherhood known as *les Frères Pontifes*. As to
the sheep, he sees them as an allegoric interpretation of the facts:
Bénézet's herd are the brotherhood over which he had charge, and the
colossal stone a symbol of faith. No one before him had believed it
possible that the river could ever be spanned.

Les Frères Pontifes, or the Brothers of the Bridge as they were called
in England, were an order founded in Rome. The brothers were not
only highly trained masons, but also practising doctors specialised in
nursing whose job it was to care for the travellers and pilgrims. To
single them out they had been given striking habits consisting of white
robes stitched with scarlet arches surmounted by a cross. Perhaps no
saint, Bénézet must, nevertheless, have had remarkable qualities apart
from the fact, of course, that he was a highly competent architect. It
surely needed great powers of persuasion to argue the prelates and
burghers of Avignon into parting with the large sums of money needed
for financing his project, particularly in view of what must have been
considerable prejudice, since the project had no precedent. We know
from different contemporary accounts that Bénézet exercised an almost
mesmeric control over his brothers, and when addressing a crowd had
almost the same powers. He was also an excellent nurse and was
believed to have been a healer. Small wonder that when he died in 1184,
four years before the bridge was finished, the populace acclaimed him
a saint – the building, it must be explained, had advanced sufficiently
for it to be judged a success. Very fittingly his body, encased in a stone
sarcophagus, was laid to rest in a little chapel that had been erected
on the third pier. Canonised, he lay there for close on five centuries,

and only after the disastrous winter floods of 1669 had seriously shaken the structure of the bridge was his body moved to a chapel on the mainland, situated at the bridgehead leading into the town. During the move the coffin had been opened to make sure that Bénézet was safely inside and, as with most saints, it was found that the body was in an almost perfect state of preservation. More moves were to follow and from the chapel Bénézet was carried to the church of the Celestines where he remained until the revolution and the suppression of religious orders which entailed a further shuffling around. The parish church of St Didier gathered in the remains, and there they now rest, but not without having undergone further misadventures in the interim at the hands of the refractory soldiers who had escaped from a nearby detention camp. Breaking into the church, they had desecrated the tombs but, fortunately, had not bothered themselves with their contents.

From the bridge we now wander into the city, of great interest to us, for what remains of the old Avignon dates almost entirely from the Middle Ages. Few cities, in fact, can show so many, and such pure examples of fourteenth century military architecture. Starting with the fortifications of the town one moves to the great palace-fortress of the popes, and from there across the other side of the river to the tower of Philippe le Bel with, behind it, the golden mass of rounded towers that compose the fort of St André. Most painters have shown us Avignon from this side of the Rhône, opposite the town. It is undoubtedly the finest view and dominating it always is the block-like papal palace.

The city has seen far too many changes for us to dwell on its history in detail. Occupied in turn by the kings of Burgundy and Arles, it then became a republic, but only for a short period. By 1251 it was again forced to submit to armed forces, this time those flying the banner of the counts of Toulouse and Provence. Then, in 1309, came the hour of its glory. For nearly seventy years it had the good fortune of being the capital of the civilised world, a brief flowering that coincides with the exile of the popes; an exile that was a question of power politics.

The papacy, feeling itself firmly established in the insecure world of warring factions which divided Italy, had made the grave mistake of taking too active a part in affairs of state. During the second half of the thirteenth century the French monarchy enjoyed undisputed supremacy amongst its neighbours, and Urban IV, a Frenchman by birth, determined to destroy the power of the Hohenstaufen in Italy, offered the

kingdoms of Naples and Sicily to Charles d'Anjou in consideration of a
yearly tribute. Charles d'Anjou, it will be remembered, was the seventh
son of Louis VIII of France, and in accepting and fighting for the crown
of the two Sicilies became one of the most powerful sovereigns of
Europe. It was a rash move on the part of the Church and the following
pope, Boniface VIII, was to reap the consequences. Quarrelling with the
Capetian dynasty, he found himself the prisoner of the recently crowned
Phillip IV, an indignity which drove him insane. Phillip had little
difficulty in finding a nominee of his own to succeed the broken-hearted
Boniface, and Bertrand de Got, Archbishop of Bordeaux, was elected
to the Holy See. Crowned Clement V, he moved to Avignon, the excuse
for the transfer being the disturbed state of affairs in Italy. Understandably, the papacy suffered somewhat in prestige, but the transfer of its
central seat had less effect than might be supposed. Its hold over men's
imagination was too deeply rooted for any temporary change to really
harm it. The real crux of the matter, as already stated, was a question
of politics: which of Europe's numerous ruling dynasties were going to
pull the strings, manipulate it? Quite obviously, France.

Avignon saw the reign of seven popes, all Frenchmen from the
southern provinces. Of these only two can really lay claim to being the
originators of the palace. Clement V, the first pope, always expecting to
return to Rome, undertook no building and spent his pontificate as the
guest of the Dominicans. John XXII, his successor, went one step further
by installing himself in great state in the episcopal palace hard by the
cathedral, but any changes he might have made were purely superficial,
and it was thus left to his two successors, Benedict XII and Clement VI,
to do the real building. Rich and in a position to command unlimited
labour, the popes were able to build at great speed. Benedict XII
concentrated on transforming the existing palace built on the Rocher
des Dômes and onto this Clement VI tacked the new ramifications
dominating the town. What they achieved is quite prodigious. The
buildings were enormous and both palaces were completed in the space
of twenty years.

Of the two builders, Clement VI is the most interesting character.
Born Roger de Beaufort, he came from a noble family and was a man
of taste with an understanding of luxury. There is no question that the
palace must have appeared at its best under his auspices. He had the
great, echoing chapel hung with cloth of gold to deaden the sound,
while the smaller apartments he filled with good furniture, hanging their

walls with tapestries. New plants and strange animals appeared in the garden. But surely the most sympathetic and, incidentally, all that is left to us by which to judge the taste of this *bon viveur*, are the rooms he decorated for himself in what is known as *la Tour de la Garde-robe*. The walls are covered with frescoes representing pastoral scenes which were only discovered recently under coatings of whitewash. Gazing up at them, one wanders off into a delicious world of green-blue woods, noisy with birds, and sprigged with flowers. Between the slender trunked trees zig-zags a hare, hotly pursued by labouring hounds. Some local grandee, possibly the pope himself, his hand heavily gloved, holds aloft a hooded hawk. Other, lesser, beings are to be seen catching fish in a tank half hidden in a glade of leaf-cool shade. Opening off this comes the pope's bedroom, dust-blue in colour and netted over with a trellis of sepia leaves, their convolutions tenanted with warbling birds.

Matteo Giovanetti, an Italian from Viterbo, is commonly acknowledged the painter of these frescoes, but André Villard, in his book, *Art de Provence*, attributes them to quite another source and believes them to be the work of a painter from the north known to have been engaged in the palace and referred to on the lists of artisans as Robin des Romans. Certainly the frescoes are entirely Nordic in feeling, reminiscent of the Flemish tapestries just beginning to be fashionable at the time these walls were being painted – sometime around the mid-fourteenth century.

Clement vi is also responsible for the fortification of the city, restored by Viollet-le-Duc in the nineteenth century. They are not very impressive as battlements go, but were thought to be sufficiently high to act as an outwork in front of the palace which in itself was considered impregnable. They were, as the saying went, 'an ornament rather than armour', but it must be remembered that originally they were accompanied by a moat, the space where the water once flowed now being filled in and serving as a broad accompanying *boulevard extérieur*. To build them Clement vi had put an extra tax on salt and wine, a privation which the citizens seemed only too willing to endure; for at least the walls were some protection from the marauding troops constantly ravaging the countryside; a state of lawlessness for which the Hundred Years' War was responsible. Having suffered repeated defeats at the hands of the English, the French troops found themselves without pay. Destitute, their king in prison, they took to the highways, pillaging and ransoming rich cities. None hoarded a greater treasure than Avignon: in fact, hardly had the walls been started when Arnaul de

Cervoles, Seigneur de Castelnau, Froissart's Sir Arnauld Cervoll, appeared with four thousand horses before its gates demanding the enormous sum of forty thousand *écus d'or*, and it was not only a question of money for remembering his birth and position, the brigand also demanded a private audience with the pope in which it was understood he expected a free pardon. Perhaps amused by the man's audacity, Clement VI accepted the challenge, going so far as to invite the bandit to sup with him.

Of the different popes, Clement VI's reign makes by far the best reading. It was also Clement VI who negotiated the deal by which Avignon became a papal holding, property that subsequently remained a part of the Holy See until the revolution. The manner in which the transaction took place makes fanciful reading, as indeed any incident connected with the celebrated Queen Jeanne is apt to do. Queen Jeanne, or to give her her correct title, Queen Joanna I of Naples, was also Countess of Provence, and Avignon formed part of her holding. Contrary to what might be expected, however, her connections with Avignon have no immediate bearing on this particular case. Her presence at the papal court was not an affair of state, rather was she appearing to plead her innocence, it being maintained that she had murdered her husband.

Queen Jeanne was a remarkable woman and her court at Naples could be counted a small Florence. Petrarch corresponded with her and Giotto's pupils were commissioned to paint her walls. It was for Jeanne that Boccaccio wrote his filthy tales which he afterwards grouped together, entitling them the *Decamerone*. As seems only fitting she was both witty, beautiful and 'spirited; at the age of twenty a humanist unrivalled by the scholars of the Sorbonne; and above all unbridled in love'.[2] She married young to a prince of the north, a taciturn fellow called André de Hongrie, and it is this prince that she is reputed to have poisoned in favour of her cousin and lover, Louis de Tarente. All would have been well had her ex-brother-in-law, the King of Hungary and Poland, not been so determined to avenge his brother. Marching on Naples, he stormed its defences, and on entering its gates demanded Jeanne's death, or at least that she be put to trial. Fortunately for the queen, the affair was referred to the pope, and Jeanne, in perfect command of the situation, made a triumphal entry into Avignon, accompanied by her new husband. Being the legitimate ruler of the place, the people crowded the streets to acclaim her, and with the crowd stood a delegation of eight cardinals to bid her welcome, at the same time offering her an escort and a canopy of cloth of gold under which she rode up to the palace.

The trial took place in the great *salle de conclave* and Queen Jeanne, sweeping regally into the hall, was placed directly opposite the pontifical throne. She pleaded in Latin and for four hours kept the assembly spellbound by her eloquence. She was fortunate, of course, in her audience for the pope was a man of the world with an eye for the ladies: the sort of man that would have appreciated her performance. It should also be remembered that he had everything to gain by lending a sympathetic ear to her cause – namely Avignon, which he acquired from his royal prisoner for a formal absolution and a derisory sum of money, a sop, no doubt, to public opinion.

Succeeding Clement vi came Innocent vi, and he it was who completed the southern front of the palace, at the same time finishing the great chapel. The next pope on the list, Urban v, levelled the square which forms the *Cour d'Honneur* – but these are minor additions compared to what was accomplished by their forerunners; a gargantuan task, the magnitude of which can only be fully appreciated by those who have been taken on a tour of this rambling piece of masonry. It is an exhausting experience and one for which a guide is necessary if any sense is to be made of the building. The palace grew with no settled plan, various blocks being placed where needed; a haphazard way of doing things, but one that gives the place a certain vigorous appeal. Of course, what really strikes one more forcibly than anything is the incalculable amount of damage done during the revolution, particularly violent in the south, and at Avignon the crowd seems to have vented their 'intelligent fury' on this one particular building. The Musée Calvet is full of shattered fragments, and perhaps the most flagrant example of this wilful destruction is the pinnacled tomb of Pope John xxii in the cathedral church of Nôtre-Dame des Dômes adjoining the palace. It was completely decimated, but fortunately enough remained for the restorer to work on, and it was reassembled during the reign of Louis Philippe. Only the pope's recumbent figure was missing, and this has been substituted by some unknown bishop who masquerades as the wearer of the triple crown. Serious as this damage might appear, by far the most devastating loss are the frescoes which once covered the walls and ceilings of the grander apartments, and these, it must be admitted, disappeared through no fault of the revolution but

during the first quarter of the nineteenth century when the palace
became a military barracks. To make room for the billets, the great
halls and chapels were sectioned off into floors, and amongst the
regiments occupying them were a contingent of men from Corsica, later
accused by Prosper Mérimée[3] of being the real instigators of the crime.
He argues that intrinsically Italian by birth, they would have been the
ones with an instinctive understanding of art, or anyway, of its value.
The French, he feels, would probably have just whitewashed the
prophets and saints while the Corsicans, having a more venal turn of
mind, preferred to sell them. This, at least, is Mérimée's contention
and he is probably right for it is known that one of the regiments,
including the officers, made a regular business of disposing of fragments
to unscrupulous travellers. Heads, hands, or some likely section of
drapery were expertly detached from the walls by specially made
knives; a profitable trade that took care of all the best frescoes which,
if one can judge their quality by what remains, must have been of
remarkable beauty.

Another connection with the papal court is the grandiose Chartreuse
du Val de Bénédiction, situated on the far side of the river, at Villeneuve. Innocent VI, Clement VI's successor, bought a small property
there and it is his original holding that through the years grew into a
splendid monastery. Little remains that can claim direct descent from
the popes other than Innocent's lace-like tomb. It is, nevertheless, a
place that should be visited, and in particular note should be taken of
its handsome mid-seventeenth-century gateway leading in off the road,
a splendid piece of bombast. The last time I saw it, it was wreathed in
smudges of smoke spiralling upwards from a bonfire of autumn leaves.

Also not to be missed while on this side of the river is the beautiful
polychromed ivory Virgin and Child to be found hidden away in the
sacristy safe of Villeneuve's church of Our Lady. The church was
founded by John XXII's nephew and the ivory is contemporary with
the exile of the popes and must certainly be the work of a master. If
around, the sacristan will unlock the door and pressing a button will
make the Virgin revolve slowly on a small turn-table. The sculptor
has taken full advantage of the curve in the tusk and the figure is
forced backwards in a charmingly stylised position, which leans the
Christ-child with his weight up against his mother's chest. Crowned as
a queen, she is richly dressed and her slit eyes give her an almost
oriental expression.

While in Villeneuve one must also visit the museum, housed in the Hospice. In it hangs the splendid *Coronation of the Virgin* by Enguerrand Charonton, a master of the early French school. The painting, commissioned in 1453, antedates the popes, but as Sir Theodore points out it no doubt exists due to the impulse first given by Innocent VI. In the same museum used to hang the *Pietà*, now also attributed to Charonton. Some years ago it was sent to the Louvre for an exhibition of primitives, and while there was judged to be of such remarkable quality that the curators refused to return it. Another painting belonging to this period is the mysterious *Annunciation* hanging in the church of St Mary Magdalene at Aix. The painter is unknown, but here one is immediately in a different climate. Grey, attenuated arches suggest the Flemish north, while the view hinted at through the divided window behind the figure of the Virgin gives a promise of soft skies and a heavy, green vegetation. I much prefer the bright landscape that crowds in at the bottom of Charonton's *Coronation*. It reveals a bird's-eye view of Avignon and the Rhône delta and there is no mistaking its Mediterranean setting. Charonton was born at Loan near the Flemish border, but having worked for a good part of his life in and around Avignon, he can by rights be claimed a painter of the Southern school.

Visiting Avignon today, touring the palace, it is difficult to visualise it as it must have appeared at the time when the papal court was considered a byword of luxurious living. At least the works we have glimpsed – the frescoes, the paintings and the fragments of sculpture – should give some indication; help soften the effect the now austere, echoing rooms of the palace must have on one. If in a mood to evoke the past, it would be a question of timing, and travelling back through the years care must be taken to arrive before Innocent VI's death. When he died in 1362, the culminating point had been reached. Following him came Urban V and Gregory XI, the last two pontiffs in the undisputed Avignon line: both were intellectuals, both retiring, Urban V being generally accounted a saint. The panache had gone; besides, the political situation in France had entirely changed and each pope now entertained the thought of returning to Rome. Turning a deaf ear to the French cardinals and a weak king, Urban V actually made the move, leaving Avignon in 1367. Unfortunately he failed to deal satisfactorily with the highly complicated situation in Italy, with the result that within less then three years he was back in Avignon, dying of exhaustion a few months later. Gregory XI, his successor, nephew of the sympathetic

Clement VI, was a sickly young man of thirty-nine. Bad health delayed his return to Italy, but it was a step that had to be taken if the Church was not to lose hold on its Italian estates. Accompanied by thirteen cardinals, the departure was set for 13 September 1376.

On state occasions it was the custom for the pope to ride out on a white mule, but when travelling, a horse was considered more suitable, and in this case his Holiness's mount could not have been carefully enough chosen – the horse refused to budge from the palace courtyard. Consternation all around, and the pope was forced to change mounts which was considered a very bad omen.

Exhausted by the journey, Gregory XI made his entry into Rome on 17 January 1377 and died in the Vatican in March of the following year, his last hours made uneasy by the doubts he had about the future of the papacy. Indeed, by the turn of the century Christendom was to behold the astonishing spectacle of two popes wearing the triple crown at the same time. Rival popes hurled ecclesiastical thunder at one another, each denouncing his rival as anti-Christ, and each excommunicating his rival's adherents. France, Spain, Scotland and the two Sicilies acknowledged Clement VII, while Germany, Hungary and England and a major part of Italy recognised Urban VI. Two of the rival popes were actually to issue their bulls of Excommunication from the palace at Avignon, the tenacious Benedict XIII barricading himself behind the formidable walls of the Rocher des Dômes and eventually making his escape by means of a secret passage leading to the banks of the Rhône. With his flight to the Iles de Lérins, the palace had seen its last pontiff.

Mention has been made in these pages of the painters belonging to what is termed the Avignon school, and it would be unfair, when writing about the coast, not to include the Nice primitives. They are a little later in date, but strictly speaking belong to the same school, though the influence is Italian rather than Flemish. Robert Doré, in his book *L'Art en Provence*, tabulates them as being of minor importance and writes perfectly accurately that '*ces tableaux sont des reflêts et non pas des oeuvres mères*' [These pictures are merely reflections and not the great works that inspired others].[4] There is no question, in fact, of comparing them with the splendid Avignon paintings and at best they can be considered superior folk art, or rather crude interpretations of a superior school. They do, however, have a certain originality and deserve some attention, especially since to see them generally involves expeditions up the picturesque valleys spreading out behind Nice.

The school is composed of several painters, and the first to be known about seems to be Jean Mirailet or Miralhet from Montpellier. He was working in Nice round about the 1420s and a triptych of his exists in the Bureau d'Aide Sociale of that city. Particularly pleasing is a panel in the *predella* representing Christ appearing to Mary Magdalen. They are shown in a flower-sprigged enclosure railed off by a picket fence. The landscape of gently rolling hills and the trees are burnt umber, and the sky burnished gold leaf.

Jacques Durandi is another of the same school, Durandi being actually born in Nice. A signed triptych of his is to be seen in the cathedral at Fréjus, and another, thought to be by him, hangs in the Musée Masséna at Nice. The Masséna triptych comes from the mountain church of Lucéram and is dedicated to John the Baptist in company with eight other martyrs. The saints have almond-shaped eyes, and amongst them are two elegant ladies in high-waisted dresses covered with voluminous capes. They wear beatific smiles and at the same time present their mutilations: Saint Agatha with her pink breasts sliced like a melon, and Saint Lucia with her eyes gouged out with a dagger. Durandi, however, has had the taste to represent Saint Lucia as she appeared before the mutilation. The gouging is only suggested by a spare pair of eyes, as it were, which she holds before her on a plate.

Of the various painters, the Bréa family seem to be the most popular. The family were coopers by profession, and they were all born in Nice: Louis, his brother Anton, and Anton's son François. Louis is the best known of the family, although his nephew François painted the most successful of the many triptychs attributed to them, known as *The Virgin of the Misericorde*. It dates from the last quarter of the fifteenth century and is to be found in the village church of St Martin d'Entraunes, high up in the Var valley. The drive alone is worth it. Twisting and turning through a series of red gorges, the road emerges amongst razor-edged peaks and lush meadows backed by dark pines – a typical alpine landscape. Even the farms wear steep roofs weighted down against expected falls of snow.

Of the Bréa family's many paintings my own particular choice is Louis' *Pietà* in the monastery at Cimiez, the first signed work by the artist, and dated 1475. My fondness for it depends largely on one figure, that of St Martin, mounted on a white charger and forming the narrow

left-hand panel flanking the dead Christ. The young saint looks down
in compassion at a trembling child beggar on crutches who tugs at the
red lining of a brocaded coat. It appears as if St Martin is about to slice
the garment in two with his sword as an offering to cover the child's
nudity.

At Biot there is another triptych of Louis Bréa's: *The Virgin of the
Rosary*, but as already mentioned the majority of his and his nephew's
works, or attributed works, are to be found in the steep mountain
valleys converging on the plains of the Var behind Nice. Moving fanwise
across the map, one can name a seemingly endless list of mountain
villages, all of them with parish churches and most of them boasting
of gilded and monochromed altars: St Martin des Trônes, Lieuche and
Pûget-Théniers; St Martin Vésubie, Lucéram, Sospel and La Brigue.
Seeing them now, one wonders how these villages were ever rich enough
to afford the painters who worked for them. The soil is stony and
difficult to cultivate, and communication, even today, is precarious.
Nice itself was dependent on small coasting vessels for the transport of
its immediate necessities. Other commodities arrived by mule carried
over *le chemin du sel*, the only trading route of any importance connecting the coast with the hinterland and the prosperous cities of Lombardy.
Leaving Italy it branched off at Sospel and following the Col de Braus
met up with the Paillon, and so on down to the Baie des Anges. At a
later date it was widened by the Prince of Savoy, thus turning it into
a road fit for carriages – the first to cross the Alps. But to revert to the
question of the villages, on closer inspection one sees that the country
was once much more densely populated, a fact borne out by the number
of abandoned terraces. A place like Utelle, or Lucéram, must, in their
day, have numbered at least three thousand inhabitants. They were
numerous enough to afford their elaborate churches. Now five hundred
is the most that can be counted; hardly surprising, for there is little to
attract the young. The brick-paved streets are too narrow for any form
of transport other than a clatter of hooves, while the houses, closely
packed, receive the minimum amount of sun. Certainly the villages are
picturesque with their tiled roofs clustering round a hill-top manor or
castle. But the old splendours are gone. The seignioral domain is now
a crumbling ruin and its occupant long since flown to the towns by the
sea. One should be grateful, I suppose, that so little has changed: but
the depression, I find, is all engulfing. I so understand the young. The
smell, a mixture of dampness and manure, would alone be enough to

send me headlong down to the open plains – even to the ugliness of reinforced concrete. However, I do not intend to damn all mountain villages. They are not all doomed to depression. I can remember one expedition we made to Lieuche. It was after lunch, and the younger members of the village were playing a local form of *pelote*, hitting a ball with bound hands rather than the ordinary curved basket. Incidentally, it is not a game usually associated with this part of the world, unless it can claim Italian parentage. They were hitting the ball far up into the distant reaches of a narrow street, curving away from the central square, and it was returned them by unseen hands posted somewhere beyond the curve. It was a difficult game to understand. The whole village, some three dozen in all, had gathered to watch, all except for one woman who swayed into view down one of the converging passageways. She was clothed in dull blues and earthy reds, and with arms akimbo advanced balancing a basket of washing on her head.

❧12

King René and the Saint Marys

As the Middle Ages draw to a close we meet with one of the most sympathetic characters of Provençal history – le Bon Roi René, Duke of Bar and of Lorraine, Duke of Anjou and Count of Provence, also titular King of Sicily. For nearly two centuries the counts of Provence had reigned both sides of the Alps. It had cost them dear, and by 1442 René had lost all hold on Naples, a city he had never properly ruled. In reality the majority of his titles were but empty boasts, for in the end he was despoiled of most of them, all except for Provence, which fortunately for René was the country of his real affection.

Mention of René has already been made in the opening chapters of this book, the manner in which he travelled by royal barge to his castle at Tarascon. He had a palace at Aix but it was wantonly destroyed during the revolution, which makes Tarascon, on the banks of the Rhône, the logical place to evoke him. The castle had been started by Louis II of Anjou, René's father, and René had finished it in the manner in which it had originally been designed rather than in a more contemporary style. It thus comes down to us as one of the best preserved fifteenth-century castles in France. It sits four square, its corners faced with towers: two square ones which plunge directly into the river, and two round ones at its weakest point, facing the town. Henry James, in his *Little Tour of France*, describes how he strolled around 'the dusky habitation', remarking that it must have taken all René's good humour to light it up. The building, however, is not a castle of the ordinary kind: the chapel is surprisingly elegant, so also are the free-standing circular stairs. The great windows are another unusual feature and unexpected in a fortified dwelling of the period. It is not difficult to imagine the polished gatherings René would have attracted to his Anjou-Provence court. He was a remarkably gifted man, a good linguist, interested in the theatre and the performance of mystery plays, wrote poetry and also dabbled in music, and was proficient enough a painter to have had most of the well-known works of Provence attributed to him, a touching mark of his subjects' affection. There does, however, exist one authentic work from his hand: an illuminated prayer book which is on exhibition at the Bibliothèque Méganes situated in the town hall at Aix. Characteristic also of the man is the fact that one can claim him to be amongst the first in his country to patronise artists working in the new classical revival style just beginning to be popular in Italy. He was responsible for importing Francesco da Laurana, a sculptor well known for his bronze medals and who left behind him the earliest truly Italian Renaissance work in Provence: namely, the tomb of Jean de Cossa in the church of St Martha at Tarascon. Another work of his is an altar in the Lazareth chapel of the twelfth-century cathedral of La Major at Marseilles, a fine piece of carving traced over with a typical Florentine netting of arabesques framing a collection of playful *putti*.

Approaching René from a more personal angle, one learns that he had the reputation of being a good lover. Sir Theodore hints ominously at this side of his nature, but goes no further than to tell us that his temperament 'sometimes led him into paths where kings are best unseen'. At least we know something of his appearance, the best likeness we have of him being in Nicholas Froment's triptych, *Le Buisson Ardent*, hanging in the cathedral of Aix-en-Provence. René and his second wife, Jeanne de Laval, were the donors, and they are to be seen kneeling each side of the Virgin who sits enthroned on a cushion of oak trees twined around with pink eglantine and outlined in a halo of flames; gentle tongues that dare only to lick at the perimeter of the holy thicket. The triptych was painted in about 1468, which would make René a man of fifty-nine at the time. Froment has not flattered his sitter, and we see the King with a square, jowly face, looking not unlike an English bulldog. He obviously inherited none of his mother's famous looks, the beautiful Yolande of Aragon, one of the first great ladies of France to encourage and support Joan of Arc. René appears quite differently in a statue standing at the head of the famous Cour Mirabeau at the entrance to the city. Cast in bronze by a nineteenth-century sculptor, His Majesty has been thinned down and in this guise bears not the slightest resemblance, one feels, to the original. It is just an excuse to advertise his agricultural activities, for he is shown gazing into space holding out a bunch of muscat-grapes – fruit he is said to have imported from Sicily. The introduction of roses, carnations and peacocks are also attributed to him, along with the mulberry tree and the breeding of silk-worms, later destined to become one of the main products of the country. Admirable all this might be: but it is the spiritual side of his nature which is the most interesting. A pious man and a great believer, it was King René who organised a search for the relics of the Three Marys said to exist in the Camargue and found hidden away beneath the foundations of the little fortress church to be known in the future as Our Lady of the Sea. His interest gave new life to a twelfth-century tale which relates that in the year AD 40 a boatload of distinguished refugees fleeing persecution in Judaea had landed in the vicinity of present-day Saintes Maries-de-la-Mer. It was no ordinary passenger list, for seven of the occupants were persons who had actually witnessed the crucifixion: Lazarus and the Virgin's sister; Mary, the mother of James, and Mary Salomé, mother of John the Evangelist. With the two Marys came their colourèd servant Sarah, Lazarus's sisters Martha and Mary Magdalen, also Maximia Sidoine, the man whom Jesus had healed of his blindness. The two Marys, with their servant, are alleged to have remained where they had landed, building an oratory on the site of a pagan temple. Lazarus, it was said, moved westwards to Marseilles and became its first bishop, while Maximia evangelised Aix. Mary Magdalen, living the life of an anchorite, retired to La Sainte Baume, a cave in the mountains, while Martha, sailing up the Rhône, tamed a dreadful dragon known as the Tarasque, his cavern the site of René's Tarascon, the city to which the dragon gave his name. Should one be sceptical about the dragon, Henry James has a perfectly acceptable alternative and suggests that we regard him as a symbol of ravening paganism 'dispelled by the elegance of a sweet evangelist'. Whatever the explanation, the saint's bones lie in a fifth-century sarcophagus in the crypt of the church dedicated to her at Tarascon, and the fact that her remains had tangible form must have urged René on to search in the Camargue. His men started digging in 1448, and in due course they, too, came across some bones. To his mind, there was no question to whom they belonged, and his enthusiasm alone must have been sufficient reason for the pope to grant him a bull proclaiming their identity.

Now whether or not Lazarus and his entourage ever landed on these shores is something we shall never know for certain. There are those, of course, who scoff at the story. Just a legend, they say. But legend, surely, preceding the written word, is a legitimate part of history, and reviewing the facts there would seem to be no valid reason for not believing the story. Marseilles and the Greek towns along the Ligurian coast would have been in constant touch with Asia Minor at the time of the supposed landings, and Marseilles would have been a logical choice for refugees escaping persecution. That they landed on the desolate shores of the Camargue instead of the chosen port is easily explained by a fault in navigation or possibly a sudden storm, in which case the marshy delta of the Rhône, advancing into the sea, would have made a more convenient landfall than Marseilles which lies, well hidden, tucked in behind a foreland. It is possible also, as Lenthéric points out, that the particular people in question, all fervent disciples, were simply carrying out their master's orders. 'Go', He had told them, 'and bring my word to all countries' – and the Greek colonies in Gaul would most certainly have been considered worth saving.

It is a touching story for those who like to believe, and it has been believed by so many for so long that one can easily accept it as truth. In any event this flat, melancholy land of empty horizons makes an ideal setting in which to picture the landing.

One can sense the desperation of those first days. Lazarus, the youngest amongst them, afire with apostolic zeal, struck out full of courage while Mary Madgalen, escaping realities, isolated herself in a dripping, sunless cave. The other two Marys, already middle-aged, must have been worn out by what they had gone through: not so much the journey as the events they had witnessed before leaving their home. It was not easy to forget, and absorbed in their thoughts it seems a perfectly acceptable explanation that they were content to live out their lives watching the silvery light touch on the marshes. But one must know the country to understand the strange pull it exerts. One must have walked along the narrow strips of mud-coloured sand that separate the swamps from the sea. What soil exists is soaked through with salt and only certain saline-loving plants will grow, amongst them the coarse grasses that tuft the hillocks and clump the brackish waters. The only moments of real colour are the Altdorpfer sunsets which slash great rifts in the sky. It is a sad, beautiful country, so poor before man was able to enlist the aid of machinery that one wonders how the refugee women from Judaea were able to exist. Indeed, until recently travellers fought shy of the place, frightened away by the agues that turned one bright yellow and set one trembling like a leaf. But one forgets that the holy Marys had Sarah and her capable black hands to fend for them. But even with their 'darkies' help, it seems improbable

that the oratory they are said to have built was anything more substantial than a shelter made from driftwood gathered on the beach. In
any event, the twelfth-century battlemented church that replaced it is
very much in keeping with the desolate atmosphere of the country as it
used to be. Half castle, half chapel, its austerity awes one. Luck was
with me the afternoon I was there. I had the place to myself and it was
lit by a shaft of sunlight striking through a circular window above the
entrance. Severe, barrel-vaulted, it is built of warm-coloured stone so
grained as to give the impression of wood – wood that with the years
has taken on the appearance of petrification. What relics remain of
the sainted women lie in an iron-bound casket placed high up above
the architrave crowning the apse, in a little chapel added by René and
reached by an exterior staircase. One can climb up onto the roof
amongst the crenellations, but the chapel remains firmly locked. Only
twice a year, as the saints' days draw near, in May and October, is a
great key produced and ceremoniously, using flower-wreathed pulleys,
the remains are carefully lowered into the main body of the church.
Effigies are produced, and on the second day Mary Jacobe and Mary
Salomé are given an outing, paraded through the town accompanied
by a model of the boat in which they arrived. Escorting them is the
Bishop of Aix and a posse of men mounted on white horses – *les
Guardiens*, the cow-boys of the Camargue whose job it is to herd the
black bulls for which the country is famous. Winding through the
streets, the procession arrives lurchingly down to the beach and the
Marys are carried into the waves. Joining her mistresses and following
in the rear is the black Sarah: a strange figure muffled in a wind-blown
satin cape with a diamanté bandeau glinting on her dark gessoed head.
Sarah's effigy is not kept with those of the Marys but lives in a dark
crypt smelling faintly of garlic. Time has emancipated her, and thus
freed of her slavery she has become the patron saint of the gypsies, and
it is these slant-eyed followers who carry her swaying on their shoulders.
The men with their raven hair and the women striking out in heavy
skirts that swing out in pleats from their ankles look quite as dark as
their saint, and at times could be taken for Indians, especially the
women with their silver jewellery lying greasy and warm against their
coarse skins.

  It is not a task I relish, but I feel that I should perhaps warn some
future traveller not to expect too much from Les Saintes-Maries-de-la-
Mer. The church is magnificent, and of its kind possibly the most

beautiful in France, if not the whole of Europe. It is the surroundings, which not so long ago were simple fishermen's dwellings, that I find inexcusable. On my first visit a number of years ago, they had already started building, but the houses, topped by sunbaked roofs and washed in pale colours, were comparatively inoffensive. The stone pavements shone like polished bone, and canvas awnings stretching across the streets gave a pleasant luminosity. Now the place is better not described, and spreads like some hideous parasitic growth between the church and the sea. One has simply to shut one's eyes to the criminal desecration, and by an effort of will isolate the church – remember the country only as it appears in its wilder stretches. Drive down the straight roads bordered with feathery, golden-brown reeds and, if it's winter, look out over the muddy waters of the empty rice fields – square patches of dulled taffeta shot with the sky. And always this flatness of landscape, everything beaten down by the wind; only the umbrella pines seem to resist and grow in great clumps like freak toadstools. It is a bleak, beautiful country, an emptiness of strange mirages: migrating drifts of flamingoes, black bulls and white horses – and the immortal saints!

The castle church of Les-Saintes-Maries has focused our attention on three of the companions landing from Judaea, and another building, the basilica of St Maximin twenty miles to the east of Aix, brings us back to the beautiful, repentant Mary Magdalen. St Luke in the Bible tells us of her beginnings, and Lacordaire, the nineteenth-century Dominican preacher whose eloquent sermons so delighted Paris, finishes the tale in his *Vie de Sainte Marie Madeleine*, and it makes very sad reading.

For the first few months Mary Magdalen was content staying with her brother, Lazarus, but after a while, wanting complete solitude, she wandered off into the fastnesses of the Saint-Baume, a mountainous region rising behind Marseille. Exploring the different valleys, she found a grotto in the face of a vertical cliff. It faces north-west, gets little sun, and must be excruciatingly damp. It can be visited, and seeing the gloom one wishes that sometimes these inspired anchorites had taken more trouble about their habitations; but then deprivation is undoubtedly an essential part of the mystic and St Magdalen must certainly be counted amongst the most exalted in this respect. Lacordaire goes into Proustian details about the dripping water and the year-round leakage pouring down from the fissures in the ceiling, the only dry place being a little ledge forming a lip at the entrance of the cave.

At night icy winds rage through the valley, and down below, in the shade cast by the mountain, grows a matted forest of powerful-limbed trees – an eerie spot where the Ligurian priest once offered up human sacrifices. It is here, in indescribable misery, that the unfortunate Mary Magdalen is supposed to have wasted her life, kept alive by what she could find in the woods. Small wonder that she became subject to visions, imagined herself to be in the company of angels, and even in direct communication with God himself.

At her death, her remains were carried down and buried at St Maximin, in the Christian funeral vault of a Gallo-Roman villa. Its handsome marble sarcophagi can still be seen as they originally stood, two to each side of the wall, and in one of these, as I understand it, rested the body, remaining there until sometime during the eighth century when it was hidden away lest it be desecrated by the Saracens who were plundering the countryside. One hears no more of the sacred relics, and for three centuries they appear to have been forgotten about, until Charles de Provence exhumed them in 1279. At this point things became somewhat complicated, for counter claims are put forward by the Burgundian monks of Vézelay. Charles's body cannot be that of the saint, for Mary Magdalen, they declare, lies under the high altar of their abbey, where they pretend it had been lodged at the time of the Saracen raids. On the strength of their claim, Vézelay became a popular place of pilgrimages, hardly a state of affairs that could be accepted by St Maximin, which town firmly believed they still harboured the saint. To prove this point Charles de Provence had the tomb he had exhumed reopened, and on close inspection came across a painted missal that left no doubt as to the occupant's identity. Not wishing to risk a repetition of this kind, Charles gave orders for the dismembering of the saint's remains, the several pieces to be enclosed in different reliquaries. The head was placed in a golden bust, the actual face being made as a detachable mask that lifted off, exposing the skull behind the protective layer of rock crystal. Charles's father, the King of Naples and Sicily, sent his own regalia to adorn the reliquary, and thus glittering in jewels it was taken to Rome, where Boniface VIII gave it his official recognition, at the same time authorising the construction of a basilica over the tomb, to be cared for by the Dominicans: the tomb, naturally, being the original Gallo-Roman funeral vault in which Mary Magdalen had been first laid to rest.

The church was started in 1295 and took two centuries to build.

Never entirely completed, it still lacks its façade, but this, in a way, heightens the shock when first entering its pale honey-coloured interior, constructed in one soaring, attenuated aisle. There in front of one, glowing in light, is the most beautiful example of the pure Gothic style to be found in Provence.

Mary Magdalen has always been very popular in the south and much courted by ruling monarchs. Louis XI proclaimed her *'une fille de France'*, and a succession of crowned heads continued to encourage the cult. Louis XIV was the last to actually pay a visit in person to *les Saints Lieux*. As can be imagined, the church of St Maximin amassed a considerable fortune in its sacristy cupboards. But as is usual, everything disappeared during the revolution, including the reliquary. Mary Magdalen's head, however, still lies enshrined behind its crystal mask, but the gold head and shoulders look blatantly brassy and certainly date no earlier than the late nineteenth century. As in so many cases, one should be grateful, I suppose, that anything remains at all since the church itself was scheduled for destruction and was only saved by the timely intervention of Lucien Bonaparte, Napoleon's younger brother, who held a modest post in charge of military stores at Marathon, the revolutionary name for St Maximin. He turned the basilica into a warehouse and saved the great organ by having the villagers perform on it, on one occasion encouraging a young patriot to thump out the *Marseillaise* on its keyboard. The whole complex, monastery and church, was subsequently auctioned as national property and bought for a paltry sum by a Madame Tan, who returned it to the authorities at the Restoration.

❧13

The Renaissance

Strangely enough, Provence is very poor in good examples of Renaissance architecture and no important ecclesiastical buildings exist of this period. However, two notable private houses can be singled out, one the Château d'Armillière in the Camargue, built in 1604, and the other, the Château Tour d'Aigues begun in about 1571 and standing in the middle of the village of that name about five miles north-east of Pertuis in the Vaucluse. They are not often visited and should be better known, particularly the magnificent remains of the Tour d'Aigues which was burnt down, alas, some time during the eighteenth century, a disaster that for once cannot be blamed on the revolution. Little is left, but what remains is enough to prove it the most splendid of all the Provençal châteaux, an equal to any of the great châteaux of that period in the north of France. Its architect was a Piedmontese called Ercole Nigra, a very apt interpreter of his Roman ancestors and obviously a great admirer of Palladio. The detailing is splendidly vigorous, especially in the frieze running across the entrance portico, carved in deep relief with a series of trophies. The four corinthian columns framing the entrance are without flutings, unusual in France at this period and typical of Palladio.

Driving from Ménerbes, I happened to arrive at Tour d'Aigues just as the sun was setting and the building was flooded with metallic light, sharpening the details. It is an impression I shall never forget, and if one could collect architecture as one does paintings, this isolated portico would certainly be amongst those I most covet.

Armillière, the other château, is interesting but somewhat on the quaint side when compared to Tour d'Aigues. It stands in its own fields adjacent to the Rhône, and is an unusual mixture of Henri iv and Louis xiii. It gives the effect of being the work of a gentleman architect rather than that of a professional. The long windows set in its flanking towers are framed with great garlands of fruit tied into extravagant bouquets and hanging from the wall on knotted ribbons. Other entertaining details are the cannons forming waterspouts jutting out from its arched cornice. Something must have happened to the roof which is now flat and invisible behind the cannons. Crowning the edifice is a watch-tower from which its original owner must have watched the shipping as it battled its way against the Rhône's eddying brown waters on its way up to Arles and its markets. For a moment I was reminded of the great plantations lining the banks of the Ashley and Cooper rivers in South Carolina. It was the nearness of the river, I think, and the flatness of the country.

Tour d'Aigues should most certainly be paid a visit, but Armillière is privately owned and is not generally open to the public.

There are, of course, different representations of this classical period, but as with the Gothic, one is obliged to hunt for them: a crowded triptych carved in high relief at Seillans and the handsome wooden doors of the cathedral at Aix, another door at Fréjus and a charming little pavilion attributed to Queen Jeanne at Les Baux, which was so admired by Mistral, the nineteenth-century Provençal poet, that he had a copy of it made for his tomb at nearby Maillane. Les Baux itself, a haunted place of empty façades, has the remains of several handsome Renaissance buildings, and it was here that the Seigneurs des Baux had their great castle. An important family, they proudly claimed descent from Balthasar, one of the Magi – a singular honour which is commemorated, blazoned on their arms, by a silver sixteen-rayed star, the Star of the East! Legend also has it that when Adelicia des Baux, the last of the line, lay dying, the star shone in her chamber and vanished into the night for ever as she drew her last breath.

Sir Theodore Cook, who has written at length on Les Baux, tells a fascinating story about the body of a Florentine princess found buried in the vault of the church. Repairs were being carried out, and while working on the floor they came across a stone dated 1471. It carried no name, and puzzled at what it might be, they carefully levered it up to expose a coffin containing the body of a beautiful girl with long shining hair. Her dead hands were holding a Book of Hours, and within seconds the vision crumbled to dust leaving only the golden hair, which Cook assures us is to be seen in the Museon Arlaten at Arles. I have to admit that I was never able to trace this hank of gold, but **this does not** necessarily damn the story, for the same thing has **happened in England** with the remains of a Saxon girl, although, if I remember correctly, the hair in this case vanished with her body.

Les Baux's pale rocks are drilled and fretted by the all-prevailing mistral, and clambering amongst its ruins is to explore a monstrous gruyère. How often have I wandered up there at night when the crowds are asleep. Snatches of history keep recurring, as fragmentary as the rocks over which one scales. A broken wall suddenly recalls the Grimaldis, for they also have a hand in its past. By the mid-seventeenth century Monaco was occupied by the Spanish, and Louis XIII, not wishing to see them planted so close to his borders, made a treaty with the young Honoré II of Monaco. The Grimaldis, usually allied with France, had sided with Charles V in the war of the Reformation, and were now once more seeking French protection. It was agreed that if Honoré managed to oust the Peninsula troops, France would guarantee him his principality's independence and confirm her *droit de mer*; a law by which Monaco had the right to claim two percent of the value of the merchandise in ships passing within sight of her fortress. Lands in France were also promised to compensate for any lost the far side of the Alps. Honoré fulfilled his side of the bargain, and forthwith was given the Duchy of Valentinois, followed in 1643 by the marquisate of Les Baux. The Grimaldi pleasure house – for it was never more than this – lay adjacent to Adelicia des Baux's feudal castle. The castle was destroyed at Richelieu's order in 1641, while the Grimaldis' pavilion disappeared during the revolution.

The trouble with this kind of book is the mass of material unearthed during the writing. How does one correlate it and still keep the reader interested? Again it is a question of concentrating on isolated incidents, and the one that immediately springs to mind at this particular moment of history is the so-called conference of 1538 between Pope Paul III, the Emperor Charles V and France's Francois I: a meeting that in the strict sense of the word never took place and is commemorated by the Croix de Marbre in Nice which stands in what is now the rue de France. The cross marks not so much the meeting as the spot where its instigator, Paul III, lodged in a monastery once situated on the right bank of the Paillon. It represents quite a landmark in Nice's history, and during the revolution the cross was hidden away for safe keeping, to be replaced by the Comtesse de Villeneuve in 1806.

The occasion, then, is of some importance and was manoeuvred by the Vatican. The Pope, feeling menaced by the wars of the Reformation, had brought all his power to bear to put an end to the constant bickering between Emperor and King, and it took all his skill in diplomacy to persuade the two antagonists to agree to a meeting. Paul III, who as Alexander Farnese had been Bishop of Venice, chose Nice as a convenient place. The Emperor was the first to arrive in the *Saint-Jage*, a luxuriously appointed galley which dropped anchor at Villefranche. Paul III had hoped that they would meet in the Duke of Savoy's castle standing on its rock above Nice. The Duke, however, seemed to have mistrusted the whole procedure, and in any event refused any form of hospitality. The Emperor, no doubt feeling it to be *lèse-majesté*, decided not to leave his floating palace and announced that if a meeting were to take place it should be staged between decks, on his galley. Accordingly, a wide gangplank, the width of a bridge, was hastily improvised connecting the imperial quarters with the shore. François I, equally proud, and hearing of the complications, delayed his arrival and on approaching refused to advance any further than the castle of Villeneuve-Loubet, some ten miles west of Nice, where he took up residence with his suite. Though Charles and François never met, the French King could not very well forbid the Queen from paying the Emperor a visit, since Eleanor of Austria, François's second wife, was the Emperor's sister. Arriving in Villefranche suitably escorted by numerous courtiers, the Queen prepared to embark, and in solemn pomp the cortège began winding its way onto the galley. Too numerous for the improvised gangplank, there was suddenly a loud rendering of breaking wood and pages and ladies-in-waiting were unceremoniously dumped into the sea. Fortunately, the Queen had already reached the safety of the deck when the incident happened.

One can imagine the stir caused by the proceedings, not only amongst the onlookers in Villefranche harbour, but the whole of the Comté de Nice. The natives could hardly have been accustomed to playing host to persons of such august standing, personalities who were proving themselves so ridiculously childish. The admirable character in all this, of course, was the Pope who all along showed great tact and persuasiveness. It could not have been a pleasant task for this sixty-five year old patriarch, bearded and fragile as we see him in Titian's portrait, to have played the role of pontifical messenger-boy, and the fact that he was willing to act as go-between shows his concern at the situation. As it happened, nothing came of the venture, but in July, a month later, the 'powers' did meet at Aigues Mortes and there signed a ten years' truce. King and Emperor embraced, and the meeting seemed completely successful. It was a short-lived success, however, for by 1543 both sides were at each other's throats again, François I allied, this time, with the Turks.

One should, perhaps, mention that prior to the meeting at Aigues Mortes, there had been a series of engagements and twice Charles v's troops had crossed the Var, penetrating as far as Marseilles. It was after one of these campaigns that François I employed an engineer of Arles named Mandon to fortify the little town of St Paul de Vence, chosen on account of its strategic position. It not only controlled the approaches to Provence, but also could act as a 'watch-dog' for Nice. Its foundations go down to living rock, and building onto this Mandon encircled it with massive walls, giving it only one gate, which he then armed with twin bastions: the result being one of the finest specimens of *villes fortes* in existence.

What further incidents catch the eye? One is surprised, perhaps, to hear that Catherine de Medici had contemplated building a royal villa at Hyères, particularly as this part of the coast had been almost forgotten since the departure of the Romans. She was travelling at the time with her sons, Charles IX and his brother the Duc d'Anjou, and reports have it that they came across a giant-sized orange tree growing where the Queen would have liked her garden. It was of such proportions that the royal brothers were scarcely able to encircle the trunk with their arms. Astonished, and impressed with its crop of a thousand oranges, Charles IX gave orders for an inscription to be cut into the bark: '*Regis amplexu glorior*' it read in the shining white of the wood.

Another link with the Valois is the astrologer of Jewish descent born at St Rémy – Michel de Notre-dame, better known as Nostradamus. Patronised by Catherine de Medicis, he is still remembered for his remarkable faculty of foreseeing the future. Casting his moments of lucidity in the form of rhymed prophecies, he published them in book form under the title of *Centuries*, a work dedicated to King Henri II, himself victim of one of the poems, Nostradamus having predicted his miserable death by a wound in the eye at a tournament.

Nostradamus started life as a doctor and one day, while administering to some plague victims, dosed them with a new 'miraculous powder'. By some stroke of good fortune they recovered: the news spread and in gratitude the town of Aix granted him an annuity, an honour which brought him to the attention of the royal family, and eventually procured him the post of physician-in-ordinary to the court. No further miracles are recorded and it is for his predictions that he is best remembered. So famous were they to become that already, only forty years after his death (he died at Salon in 1566) his rhymed prophecies were being used as school primers. Amongst his predictions comes Charles 1's execution, and Pepys mentions him in this connection in his diary.* ——

We talked much of Nostradamus, his prophecy of these times, and Sir George Carteret did tell a story how at his death he did make the town of Salon swear that he should never be dug up or his tomb opened after he was buried; but that they did after sixty years do it, and upon his breast they found a plate of brass saying what a wicked, unfaithful people the people of that place were, who after so many vows should disturb and open him such a day and year and hour.

Stepping forward in time we meet Henri IV at Avignon and Lady Blessington, who is to be our guide in a later chapter, takes us on a visit to the Hôtel de Crillon where the King stayed. How he came to go there is an amusing story. 'Since that epoch', Lady Blessington writes in 1822, 'the house has been sold and is at present divided into two: but though its pristine splendour is greatly impaired, it still retains many marks of its former grandeur.' It is known today as the Hôtel de Berton de Crillon and stands in the rue Roi-René, a narrow little street which makes it almost impossible to see its handsome façade. Its interior is equally inaccessible. However, Lady Blessington, accompanied by the Marquis de L. and Monsieur Revoil, the painter, fared much better. The entrance was paved in marble and she found some of the panelling left in the hall and inner salon which she describes as vast and giving onto a gallery. Off this opens a colonnade 'decorated with old busts placed on curious brackets'. The principal rooms front the garden, 'which bears marks of having been worthy of the mansion', and in the great salon on the ground floor Lady Blessington describes 'a very handsome mantel-piece of enormous dimensions, supported by female caryatides' where, as her Ladyship puts it, 'Crillon had whole forests ablaze to welcome his gallant Sovereign'. And what tact Crillon showed in entertaining his royal friend. Hearing that Henri IV intended to visit Avignon, Crillon immediately put his house at the King's

* 3 February 1666.

disposal. 'Henri declined not wishing to put his favourite to the heavy expense of entertaining him and his suite; and declared his determination of resting at the principal auberge. Crillon guessed the motives of the royal refusal' and immediately placed over the door of his hôtel the sign of the fleur-de-lys, with the following inscription:

BON LOGIS

aux

FLEUR-DE-LYS

'Afterwards, he arranged that the king should be conducted to, and received at the Hôtel Crillon, as if it were an inn; and Henri never discovered the delicate deception until he entered the *grand salon*, the magnificence of which undeceived him.'

Admittedly, one is amused by vignettes such as the foregoing episodes, but by and large I find contemporary accounts dealing with local history during the sixteenth and seventeenth centuries hopelessly involved. Try as I will, I have been incapable of persevering beyond the first few pages. Take Nice as an example. François has allied himself to Soleiman 'the Magnificent', and in 1543 attacks the port with the Turkish fleet under the command of Khizr-ud-Dian, better known as Barbarossa. The fortress held out, but the lower town was taken and over two thousand prisoners carried off. By 1600 we see her again being besieged by the Duke de Guise. A century later she is restored to Savoy and retaken by France nine years later. This time both her citadel and ramparts are demolished. Under the Treaty of Utrecht in 1719 she is returned to Savoy. Thirty-one peaceful years follow, and during this time the new town is built. From 1744 to the peace of Aix-la-Chapelle in 1748, French and Spanish were again in possession. In 1755 she passes to Sardinia, to fall again in 1792 to the armies of the French Republic, and continues to be counted French territory as long as this insecure empire lasted. With Napoleon's fall she reverts to Sardinia, being finally transferred to France by a treaty concluded in 1860 between Napoleon III and the King of Sardinia. The mind boggles at the constant changes, and unless a professional historian, an insular one at that, one is quite frankly bored by it all. It is not until the second half of the eighteenth century that the city and her immediate surroundings really starts to become interesting and, despite the ambiguities of its political structure, starts its reign as a popular health resort – the beginnings of the Côte d'Azur as we know it today.

✋14

The Eighteenth Century

We now come to the eighteenth century. Suddenly the coast comes to
life, in particular Nice. According to Horace Walpole, forty thousand
English travellers were estimated to have passed through Calais alone
in the two years after the Peace of Paris of 1763. A majority of these
were en route for Italy but by way of Provence, since it was one of the
main routes from Paris to Rome. The English, anyway, had a fondness
for Provence. 'It made a ready appeal to their tastes; it was wealthy
in classical monuments, and its climate was suited to invalids. There
were English colonies at Montpellier, Avignon, Toulouse and Aix.'[1] The
Riviera itself was slow in developing, but this, too, thanks initially to
Smollett, was soon to come into its own.

A great many people have left us accounts of the journey south, yet
others of lengthy stays in one particular place en route. Among these
Lady Mary Wortley Montagu ranks high on the list, and reading her
letters it would seem almost impossible not to include her description
of Avignon. They form a part of the general atmosphere and, despite
the delay, help round off our impressions of the hinterland before
actually attacking the coast.

Lady Mary was in her early fifties when, in 1742, she settled in
Avignon for a stay of nearly four years. A woman of character and
decided in her views, her impact on the town must have been considerable. On intimate terms with the court (she was a great friend of the
Princess of Wales, afterwards Queen Caroline), and as the wife of the
one-time ambassador to the Porte, she was a real *grande dame* in every
sense of the word. A portrait of her exists by Jonathan Richardson,
showing her shortly after her return from Constantinople. She is dressed
in Turkish robes and wears a turban with an osprey feather stuck
jauntily to one side. She had obviously been a good-looking woman, and
according to Joseph Spence was still not without charm during her

G.R.—6*

Avignon period. Spence, a friend of Pope's, met her in Rome a year before she moved to Avignon, and describes her as 'one of the most shining characters in the world'. She shines like a comet, but he confesses that she has certain irregularities and can be 'the most wild, most imprudent, loveliest, most disagreeable, bad natured, cruellest woman in the world; all things by turns, and nothing long'. Pope at one time had thought himself madly in love with her and, desperate at the contempt with which his declarations were received, had ended by hating her. Under the circumstances, Spence's summing up is probably fairly accurate and, given his affection and loyalty towards Pope, remarkably unprejudiced. Lady Mary herself admits that she is hardhearted, and in one of her letters doubts whether she can ever really love. Nor, she confirms, is she very fond of women, but despite this thinks that she can be a good friend. Amusing when read in conjunction with Spence's description of Lady Mary is Horace Walpole's waspish letter to Conway dated September 1740 after he had met the lady in Florence. He makes her out as a stingy, badly-dressed comic whose 'impudence must amaze anyone who never heard her name'. He tells us about the scruffiness of her clothes, and even accuses her of never combing or curling her hair which hangs, according to Walpole, in greasy black locks. Her face, swollen on one side, is daubed with white paint 'which for cheapness she has bought so coarse, that you would not use it to wash a chimney'. It is quite obvious that Walpole is exaggerating. Lady Mary had probably slighted him at some time or other and, not being the best intentioned of men, this was his way of getting back at her. One can well believe that she was untidy, a usual trait in intelligent women, but that she was the laughing-stock of Florence's *beau monde* is hardly likely. It is difficult to cast the woman who had had the courage and foresight to introduce London to the entirely alien practice of inoculation against smallpox, as a comic. Certainly her behaviour in Avignon would make Walpole's description of her appear somewhat futile.

The reasons for Lady Mary leaving England have never been explained, and her letters to her husband give us no hints for they imply that she still remained on friendly terms. However, this is not our concern here. She had waited twenty-one years to cross the Channel, and once having made the move did not return till after her husband's death, and when she herself was a sick woman of seventy-three. From Venice, she moved to Florence, then Rome and Naples, and crossing the Alps to Geneva, appeared in Avignon. She found the people 'very polite and obliging to strangers. We have assemblies every night, which conclude with a great supper; and comedies which are tolerably well acted. In short I think one may while away an idle life with great tranquillity; which has long since been the utmost of my ambition'. Later in the same letter we hear of several English ladies, 'none I ever saw before, but they behave with decency, and give a good impression of our conduct, though their pale complexions and stiff stays do not give the French any inclination to imitate our dress'.

Society, Lady Mary tells us, evolves round some two hundred houses, two of which were ducal: Crillon and Guadagna, the last being an Italian family. 'The Count of Suze, who values himself very much upon his pedigree, keeps a constant open table, as likewise so do others.' Avignon, it must be remembered, was still a papal holding and Lady Mary is somewhat scathing when writing about the vice-legat's court. He is surrounded by priests 'and sees little other company; which I believe is partly owing to the little respect the nobility show him, who despise his want of birth. There is a new one expected this spring, nephew to Cardinal Acquaviva: he is young; and, they say, intends to live with great magnificence'. Alas, Lady Mary had left by the time he arrived. Lady Mary finds the price of living 'exceedingly cheap' but only for those of the country 'for strangers the price of everything is high' – a familiar echo! The climate is as fine as that of Naples, if it were not for the north wind: the famous mistral 'which is almost a constant plague. Yet by the great age of the inhabitants, and the surprising health which I see many of them enjoy, I am persuaded the air is very wholesome. I see some of both sexes passed eighty, who appear in all the assemblies, eat great suppers, and keep late hours, without any visible infirmity'. Lady Mary makes little mention of the heat and appears always lively and energetic. 'My cure for lowness of spirit', she tells us, 'is not drinking nasty water, but galloping all day, and a moderate glass of champagne at night in good company.' She finds it hard, however, to make intimate friends: 'they are as impossible to obtain in France as orange-trees on the mountains of Scotland'. Thrown back on herself she passes the time 'with reading, working, walking, and what you'll wonder to hear me mention, building'. Talking one night to a member of the town council, she happened to mention an old tower that she had seen on the Rocher des Dômes. She describes it as situated above the vice-legat's palace, with a wonderful view out over the provinces; in the distance the mountains of Auvergne, and below the near meeting of the Durance and Rhône which flows at its feet. The tower stood on the site of a temple dedicated to Diana 'whose ruins were turned into a fort'. Reading this I remember a theory held by a much later writer who claimed that Avignon owed its name to this temple, Avignon being simply a corruption of the *Ava Dionaea* which the sailors intoned as they passed under the spot sacred to the divinity.[2] While discussing this tower she vaguely mentioned what an agreeable belvedere she could make of it. 'I expected no consequence from this accidental speech of mine' and much to her surprise, the following day, the Hôtel de Ville made her a present of it. Immediately she starts settling in, adds a dome and obviously faces the entrance with columns, for when finished she refers to it as 'a little rotunda which Lord Burlington would call a temple'. She used it as a library-drawing-room and writes that it was where she passed her evenings, 'walking there, for the height made it inconvenient for the carriage of mules'.

In another letter Lady Mary tells us of a ball she attended at Nîmes given for the Duke of Richelieu, Governor of Languedoc. 'It is but one day's post from hence, and the Duchess of Crillon, with some other ladies of the town', forced her to join them. Not gregarious by nature, she believes that providence had a hand in her going. 'The greater part of the town of Nîmes', Lady Mary explains, 'are serious Protestants and are still severely punished according to the edicts of Louis XIV whenever they are detected in any public worship. A few days before we came, they had assembled', with the result that their minister and about a dozen of his congregation had been arrested. 'I knew nothing of this; but had not been in the town two hours, when I was visited by two of the most considerable of the Huguenots, who came to see me with tears, to speak in their favour to the Duke of Richelieu, saying none of the Catholics would do it, and the Protestants dared not.' The Duke of Richelieu, they assured her, was too well bred to refuse to listen to a lady, 'and I was of rank and nation to have liberty to say what I pleased'. Moved by the situation, Lady Mary promised to help, 'though I had little hopes of succeeding'. Carefully planning her coup she refused the supper but 'went in a domino to the ball, a mask giving the opportunity of talking in a freer manner than I would have done without it'. Once there she had no trouble in engaging the Duke in conversation: 'the ladies having told him about me'. Immediately he advanced towards her and compliments flowed. After a time and surely not without trepidation, 'I made my request for the liberty of the poor Protestants'. With great courtesy the Duke told Lady Mary that 'he was so little a bigot, that he pitied them as much as I did, but his orders from the court were to send them to the galleys. However, to show how much he desired my good opinion . . . he would solicit their freedom', which, Lady Mary writes, 'he has since obtained'.

From Avignon Lady Mary moved to Brescia where she bought a shell of an old palace and 'fitted it up'. She explains her move in a letter to Lady Oxford. 'Avignon has been long disagreeable to me on many accounts, and now more than ever, from the increase of Scottish and Irish rebels that chose it for their refuge.' She complains that they were under the vice-legat's protection and 'it is impossible to go into any company without having a conversation that is improper to be listened to, and dangerous to contradict'.

So much then for Lady Mary's impressions of Avignon, and having included them, it would seem a pity not to round them off with those of Lady Blessington's. They are slightly later in date but the scene, apart from the change in fashions, appears very similar. Gone are the stays, and ladies apparelled for a ball now wore high-waisted, clinging robes of organdie and tulle, delicate shoes and elbow-length gloves. Lady Blessington compared the two countries, and finds 'a much greater degree of prudery in France with regard to dress';[3] busts are more tightly contained and less is seen of the shoulders, perhaps not a bad thing since her ladyship finds this particular part of their anatomy 'vastly inferior to the English'. Modest about their clothes, they seem to have had no reticence about their dancing 'and ladies and gentlemen trip it on the light fantastic toe at an age when the gout precludes such amusements for men in England'. She admires their social graces, finds them witty, playful and brilliant 'but rarely, if ever, thoughtful, and never thoroughly erudite. Of humour, they appear to be not only deficient, but ignorant. A *bon mot*, an epigram, or a lively sally, they comprehend at a glance; but broad or sly humour, which is so well understood, and duly appreciated in England, has no attraction for them. I refer, of course, to the many'. And then a more serious note creeps into Lady Blessington's diary; at one of the soirées she meets Madame de Villume, 'the celebrated Mademoiselle Sombreuil, whose celebrity is among the most honourable that ever was acquired by woman'. She describes the lady in question as still strikingly handsome 'though her countenance is tinged with a soft melancholy that denotes the recollection of the bitter trials of her youth'. Lady Blessington tells the story: her father was Gouverneur des Invalides at the beginning of the revolution, and when the crowd broke in intending to do away with him, his daughter threw herself into his arms offering herself in his stead. 'Her youth, her beauty, and her self-abnegation touched even the callous hearts of the murderous band' and they consented to spare the Governor's life 'provided she would, on the spot, drink a goblet of human gore fast pouring from the slaughtered victims around! She swallowed the fearful draught, and saw her father led back to prison; whence, in June 1794, he was consigned to the scaffold by the revolutionary tribunal, more cruel than the sanguinary band from whose vengeance his daughter had rescued him.' Lady Blessington concludes the episode with a slightly macabre twist, telling us 'that Madame de Villume cannot bear to look at red wine, which is never brought into her presence'.

Another awesome note is struck by her visit to the great theatre at Orange. To examine the interior of one of the *vomitoriums*, they were led through a wretchedness of hovels that had collected under the arches.

> Nothing could exceed the dirt, except the misery of the habitations: it was of cimmerian darkness, and the lamp carried before us threw a lurid gloom over the black walls and visage of the beldame who led us through the tenebrous passages, and up the various flights of steps: giving to her weird and haggard face something so unearthly, that it required but little stretch of the imagination to fancy her some ancient sibyl, muttering incantations as she strode on, pointing out with violent gestures and in tones whose intonations were painfully harsh, the objects worthy of notice in her wretched abode.

Reading Lady Blessington reminds one of similar descriptions referring to the amphitheatre at Arles. During the Middle Ages it became a fortified village, a kind of stronghold within the town, and as with Lady Blessington's theatre one walked down narrow streets crowded in between the galleries of the original building. There were two chapels and four towers at the cardinal points. Most of Rome's great ruins suffered the same fate. Take the sister arena at Nîmes. In turn it became citadel – dungeon – thieves' kitchen. Every archway held its nest of human outcasts and, as Sir Theodore writes, 'such was the place in which the plague broke out in 1640'. Already cut off socially from the rest of Arles, the inhabitants of *les arènes*, as they were called, were now shut off from all communication. A cordon of militia was drawn up at a safe distance outside, and orders were given to shoot without pity any who attempted to escape. There was no means, within that fatal circle, of burying the dead, of getting fresh water, or of procuring medical assistance. Day by day, the corpses were seen, beneath the walls, of women who had cast themselves down at night to easier death than they could find inside. Morning by morning the soldiers shot down one child after another who tottered out towards the fresh air and the water of the town, that had never before refused him either.[4] His evocation does not end here but goes on, becoming even more harrowing, and I have to admit that these descriptions have always remained with me ever since that first evening, long ago, when I read myself to sleep with them.

One might add that the arena was first cleared between 1826 and 1830, and at that date there were still some two hundred houses. Restored to its near original state, the first fête held within its walls commemorated the fall of Algiers in July 1830. Slightly larger than the arena at Nîmes, it can hold twenty thousand and ranks about twentieth among the amphitheatres of the Roman world.

But enough of guide book information: we must return to Lady Blessington in one of her more sunny moods. She is essentially an optimist and clever in the way she suggests atmospheres. How aptly she describes the Rhône: 'its turbid waters, of a dull yellow colour, resembling gold that has lost its brightness'. On another day she tells us that nowhere is the great river to be seen at greater advantage than at Avignon, 'where it sweeps along with a rapidity and grandeur that gives the boats that glide over it the appearance of being hurried on by some irresistible influence: like those vessels we read of in fairy tales, that skim the waters with magical swiftness, but cannot retard their course'. When describing the mistral, one can almost feel its buffeting, and she refers to it, as many do, as the *vent de bise*. 'Nothing can be more detestable or perfidious; for while a bright sun lures one from the fireside, this treacherous wind rushes from behind the corner of the first street you enter and penetrating through every muscle of the frame, making the cheeks blue, the nose red and the eyes tearful.' Women, she complains, become gorgons, their hair like so much seaweed and their draperies 'driven from the limbs they were meant to cover'. And how pretty her dance of the pink umbrellas when it rains. 'They

use umbrellas of a deep rose colour on a wet day and the streets
resemble vast beds of damask roses put into motion.' Incidentally, in
my notes on the mistral I came across the following entry. It is not
known from where it comes, but it pre-dates electricity and has to do
with guests at an inn. They complain that on a night of the *bise*, they
are charged extra in the bill for candles. Blown every which way, I
suppose they gutter themselves away in half the time it would take to
burn out when the air is still.

Of all the different situations in which one can visualise Lady
Blessington, I think I admire her most when mounted side-saddle on
her Arab charger, Mameluke. She doesn't tell us how she is dressed,
but I imagine her in a velvet habit with a plumed beret set on the
side of her dark Irish locks. Mameluke was a recent acquisition and
replaced an English thoroughbred which she found not being quite
steady enough for her daily rides; sorties which she describes as galloping 'over the hills and far away'. Mameluke had belonged to a Comte
d'Hautpoul, a colonel of the Ninth Chasseurs who had accompanied
the Blessingtons on part of the journey. Lady Blessington hardly
mentions him except to say that he was 'learned and a brave soldier',
and one presumes that he had joined the party for their protection;
an unfortunate day for the colonel, for the moment her ladyship set
eyes on his charger she was determined to have him. Bullied and charmed
by turn, one feels that the poor man eventually felt obliged to part
with the proud animal. Delighted, Lady Blessington clatters off across
the Rhône up to the fortress of St André. The road, cutting into the
rock, is extremely steep and very slippery and scoured with deep ruts
made by the carts rumbling up to the castle. 'Mameluke carried me up
and down without making a false step, to the wonder of many spectators,
who seemed embarrassed which most to admire, his steadiness and sure
feet, or the courage of his mistress.'

Following Lady Mary and our Irish Amazon comes a whole list of
literary gentlemen who add to our impressions of Provence and the
coast: Laurence Sterne, Tobias Smollett and Boswell on his Grand
Tour; Philip Thicknesse, and amongst them a Frenchwoman – Madame
de Genlis, who accompanied the Duchesse de Chartres, wife of Philippe-
Egalité, as lady-in-waiting. Also to be included are Lady Polwarth and
her sick husband; Dr Rigby and Arthur Young, famous for his agricultural *Tours* of the English countryside. There is even an American,

a lieutenant-colonel called Pinkney – and during the early years of the nineteenth century we again use the beautiful Lady Blessington and the sympathetic Way family, Way being a minister of the church and one of Nice's great benefactors.

Intelligent, accurately observant, they give us graphic descriptions of the journey. Arriving from England there were regular cross-Channel services by a number of routes; Rye-Boulogne and Brighton-Dieppe, but Dover-Calais seemed to be the most popular on account of the Hôtel d'Angleterre, an excellent inn run by a man called Dessein who is said to have made a fortune out of the English. No one has a kind word to say for the Channel. In normal weather, the packet crossed two or three times a week. There were also the private charters. The packets were far from comfortable and usually crowded, sleeping up to thirty in a small cabin. As to the crossing, it took anything from two and a half hours to a couple of days if there happened to be a storm. If the tides were low, the traveller had to transfer from the packet into a small boat, following which came a long walk of some half-a-mile across ribbed sand. Sometimes the captain timed his arrival wrong and the packet got stuck on a sandbank and had to wait for the turn of the tide.

Once safely landed, 'the traveller, unless he had brought his own carriage, had to consider his means of transport. He could go to Paris by diligence, or he could hire a post-chaise',[5] or two post-chaises if the party was numerous. Cobbett strongly advocates the post-chaise and likens travelling by diligence to being 'hurried along by force, in a box, with an air-hole in it'. He points out the dangers of broken limbs and, in fact, strongly advocates travelling by ship: 'it is infinitely safer and certainly less noisy'.[6]

All seem to be agreed that French transport compared very badly with the English. The coaches were poorly sprung and nearly always overcrowded and, as Sterne points out in *Tristram Shandy*, something invariably went wrong with the post-chaise. On the other hand, the roads were judged excellent, far better than those in England. That old chauvinist Voltaire goes so far as to boast that they are the only ones in Europe 'worthy of antiquity', while Pinkney, our American colonel, longs for an honest to goodness mail coach. 'How they would roll', he sighs. However, despite the roads, it was a long haul from Calais to Nice: a good two weeks; seven days from Calais to Lyon, three from Lyon to Avignon, and four from Avignon to Nice. The timing improved somewhat after the revolution, the empire having spent a great deal on communications. The Paris-Nice run which, in 1770, could count eighty relays, boasted one hundred and twenty-four by 1815.

The route taken was nearly always the same. Reaching Chalon-sur-Saône, most of the travellers preferred to embark on the *coches d'eau*, great barges which were towed along by horses. At Lyon they transferred to the Rhône. Thicknesse describes their cabins, complains their stuffiness and eschewing the motley crew of priest, monks, friars and milliners, prefers to stay on deck, seated in his own cabriolet where he could enjoy the view. The *coches d'eau* were understandably popular, at least one had a smooth ride, and when night came there were the inns in different towns along the banks to stay in. From Lyon to Avignon took four days, and during the trajectory came the excitement of being sucked under the famous Pont St Esprit. The bridge spans forty arches but only the central arch was navigable and great skill was necessary when the current caught one, hurtling the barge at a prodigious speed under the vault.

As far as concerns highwaymen, the roads appeared to be safer than in England, the countryside being patrolled by a form of mounted police. When caught, the miscreant was given a public execution: the cruel 'breaking at the wheel' which wrenched every bone in the unfortunate's body. Only one run was always considered dangerous: the wild reaches of the Esterel, a distance of about fifty miles through the mountains just before reaching Cannes. ⁓

Reading the different accounts, one remembers certain details; one the question of customs officials. At Calais Lady Mary's things were examined and sealed and 'they took from me a pound of snuff but did not open my jewel boxes, which they let pass on my word'. At Boulogne Smollett was obliged to pay duty on some silver spoons. Worse still, his books were temporarily confiscated and had to be gone through to see 'whether they contained anything prejudicial to Church, or State'. Complaining most of the time, he also passes comment on the question of clothing and warns the newly arrived Englishman that unless he wants to feel a perfect ass, he must adopt French fashion and forthwith 'send for the tailor, perruquier, hatter, shoemaker, and every other tradesman concerned with the equipment of the human body – must even change his buckles, and the form of his ruffles'. A practical man, Smollett also advises on travelling expenses. The journey from Calais to Nice, 'four persons in a coach, or two post-chaises, with a servant on horseback, travelling post, may be performed with ease for about 120 pounds, including every expense'. He adds that a coach or berlin can be purchased for thirty or forty guineas. This, however, is not quite as reasonable as it may appear to the presentday reader, for the different values must be taken into consideration.

Agreed on the roads, the travellers are also in accord on the question of accommodation. The French will have it that the Hôtel de la Couronne at Chalon was excellent, very luxurious with its silver plate and silk covered beds. The Hôtel de Malte at Marseille was also warmly recommended, but apart from these the inns seem to have been pretty bad, all except for the food which was generally considered excellent. Even the smart Lady Blessington agrees with this and writes that a bad inn 'where the sleeping and sitting room are destitute of all comforts' can generally be relied on to produce a passable meal. 'In England,' she continues, 'it is precisely the opposite.' The soup, she complains, tastes of nothing but pepper, the fish is too old and always to follow comes the inevitable beef-steak, or, then, an unsuccessful attempt at *côtelettes pannées*, half-boiled vegetables and a stale tart. 'And all this melancholy resemblance of a dinner,' she writes, 'is introduced with a flourish of gaudy plate covers borne by two or three well-dressed waiters headed by the patron or mistress.' In France it is precisely the opposite: the table linen is coarse, the knives bad, there are no 'richly chased plated covers', but, at least, the soup is good and is followed more often than not by a *fricandeau à l'oseille* or chicory with *côtelettes à la minute*, *poulet à la tartare*, *pommes-de-terre à la maître d'hôtel*, and a smoking hot *soufflé à la vanille*. Upstairs the lofty beds of silk and satin were impossible to sleep in on account of the bugs. Arthur Young, travelling with the Duke of Liancourt and his family, adds a few details about the general decoration: papers of different sorts in the same room and the furniture such that an English innkeeper would light his fire with it. Doors give music as well as entrance, and windows that are always difficult to open and when open, impossible to shut. 'Bells there are none, the *fille* must always be bawled for, and when she appears, is neither neat, well-dressed nor handsome.' Colonel Pinkney also has some complaints to make about the plumbing, it was usually poor and 'there is neither soap, water nor towels. A Frenchman,' he assures us, 'has no idea of washing himself before breakfast'.[7] Pinkney, it must be remembered, is writing during the early part of the nineteenth century, but even so is able to claim better inns across the Atlantic. 'In no country but in America and England have they any idea of that first of comfort to the wearied traveller, a clean, well-made bed. I speak from woeful experience when I advise every traveller to consider a pair of sheets and a counterpane as necessary a part of his luggage as a change of shirt.' I presume the colonel to be a member of that well-known family who settled in South Carolina, and being a Southerner it is only natural that he should feel in a more lenient mood when reaching the Rhône valley. 'I know nothing,' he writes, 'more pleasing than to pass a night at one of these provincial inns.' Obviously he has his own bedding. 'The moon shines through the casement with a soft and clear splendour unparalleled in humid climates.' In the morning he throws open his casement 'to the singing of birds', and leaning out, sniffs 'the perfume of flowers'. ⁓

An amusing detail while on the subject of inns is the manner in which the clients were categorised. During the twenties, when I first started to travel, I was given to understand that the hall porter sized up new arrivals by their luggage; the owners of the ugly but somehow appealing brown Louis Vuitton suitcases with their brass corners were automatically singled out for special attention. Nowadays, alas, they have become a matter of standing and are mostly in the possession of the wrong people. They nevertheless still indicate a certain affluence. During the eighteenth century no such snobbishness existed, and the inn-keeper was obliged to rely on the postillion to give him adequate warning when a private carriage arrived. A subtle language of whip cracks was used, their number indicating the generosity of the occupant.

It goes without saying that only the wealthy or moderately well-to-do could afford to travel abroad during the eighteenth century, and this question of whip cracking brings us to what might be called the real ton: those in a higher bracket of affluence, and with them, perhaps, a few eccentrics. Madame de Genlis, travelling with the Chartres, must certainly be considered amongst the ultra chic. The Duchess, of course, was made much of and at Antibes they came across the nicest kind of people, amongst them M. de Rouffignac who had already entertained them at Angers. This gentleman seems to have gone to great pains, for Madame de Genlis writes that knowing they were passing his way she had advised him that they would stop at his door, and although late at night, she hoped he would receive them with a hot cup of soup. The bouillon was not only waiting for them but when served turned out to be a concentrate of bear meat. M. de Rouffignac, the owner of a tame bear, had heard that their flesh made especially good eating and being overcome, no doubt, at the thought of entertaining so august a party, he had had the unfortunate animal boiled down for the ladies. At least they appreciated his extravagant gesture for, although the bouillon appeared very red, Madame de Genlis admits that she had never tasted better.

Madame de Genlis's memoirs provide a typical example of travelling in the grand manner. The Duke had left his ladies to embark on some naval manoeuvres and, thus abandoned, the Duchess and Madame de Genlis had decided to prolong their journey and carry on into Italy. Being intrepid by nature (though one feels that Madame de Genlis was the most adventurous of the two) they set out from Nice to Genoa, not by boat, which would have been the normal procedure, but overland by carrying chair: a perilous voyage winding over the mountains. At the time Madame de Genlis was writing no proper road existed, and being slung in between two mules or riding pillion was the only way of crossing the Alps. Spoilt as they were, it was brave of them to undertake such a venture, and Madame de Genlis's descriptions evoke it all with great spirit. At Antibes they had made friends with a certain Marquis de Clermont d'Amboise. The Marquis had been appointed ambassador to the court at Naples, and with him he had two young men who were to act as his secretaries. With an eye to the usefulness of the young men and finding the Marquis agreeable company, the two ladies persuaded their new acquaintance to join forces with them for Italy. Despite these male reinforcements, Madame de Genlis went on being responsible for the travelling arrangements and writes of an interview she had in Nice with the man who was to supply the mules. She questioned him, wanting to find out exactly how dangerous he considered the crossing to be and rather ungallantly he told her that it wasn't themselves he was worried about but his mules. Last year he had lost two of them, crushed by falling stones. Hardly a recommendation!

When all was in readiness, the maids, their baggage and various household effects, including Madame de Genlis's harp – for a musical education must be added to her other accomplishments – were shipped off by boat. The men of the party rode mule-back and the two ladies took to their litters. It all started off gaily enough, the commandant of Nice having arranged a charming alfresco picnic served under a flowered arbour up at La Turbie. They must, along with many others, have exclaimed at the view, reaching way out, the blue sky fading to a golden haze as it met a waveless sea. Then begins the climb: they slept the first night in a farm, the Duchess bedded down on a pile of cornstalks covered over with mule blankets, while Madame de Genlis passed a few restless hours semi-reclining on a pile of shifting grain. As to the porters, they appear to have been real ruffians, drinking and arguing and speaking only an unintelligible patois. Uncomprehensible though it might be, 'it was difficult,' Madame de Genlis writes, 'to be indifferent to their quarrels, especially when balanced precariously on the edge of a precipice'. At times the road was so dangerous that they decided to make the descent by foot. 'Quite literally by foot, for the rocks had torn our shoes to threads!' On the Italian side, one particular shoulder of mountain sent the party scurrying down to embark on their boat which slowly followed their progress. However, undaunted, the obstacle passed, the ladies regained their litters and, as Madame de Genlis writes, despite the hardships their week's trek over the Alps proved a fascinating venture. —

Perhaps belonging to a ducal party could be considered as moving in the right circles, but undoubtedly of all the travellers the Blessingtons were those with the most panache. Blessington was an Irish title, and with it came a large slice of land – Mountjoy Forest in County Tyrone. Created an earl in 1818, Blessington had married Margaret Powers, a beautiful young girl from Tipperary, and together they made a handsome couple; he very rich, with a passion for magnificence, and she lovely and one of the most widely read and best informed women in London society. She was thirty-three when they embarked for France and Blessington but a few years older. With them they had Lady Blessington's younger sister and later, at Avignon, they were joined by the amazingly handsome young Count d'Orsay, that *arbiter elegantiarum* whom Byron describes as looking like a *cupidon déchaîné*.* Arriving in Paris, Blessington busied himself with the preparations for the journey. He engaged a chef, once in the employ of Napoleon, and bustling around turned up with a battery of kitchen utensils sufficient to feed a club. The retinue of servants was enormous, and added to the coaches there was a *fourgon*, or wagon, for the heavy luggage. On the morning of their departure, Lady Blessington, looking out of her bedroom window, is embarrassed at the ostentation of their cavalcade. She describes the courier in his *habit de voyage*, bustling from carriage to

* 'a dissolute cupid'.

carriage testing the springs, the ladies' maids packing and the valets and footmen grumbling. The commotion must have been rather more than was usual, for Lady Blessington heard a passer-by remark on the extraordinary habits of the English. 'One would suppose,' he grumbles, 'that instead of a single family, a regiment at least, were about to move.' She sees his point but wistfully decides that she would find it difficult to relinquish her 'specially equipped coach with its library, soft cushions and eiderdown pillows, its china safely stowed in the well'. But this is only one small item in the general list which included not only a writing desk but also a comfortable sofa, then quite a modern invention. At Vienne, on the third or fourth night out, they engaged nearly the whole inn to themselves at an exorbitant price, and further to illustrate the grandeur in which they travelled, one learns that they were in the habit of sending the courier ahead of them to prepare things so that when they arrived at a new hotel they found a wood fire blazing and dinner all ready. Later on, when Italy had been reached, Mathews, a young architect pupil of Pugin's, is added to Blessington's staff, and reading his letters gives us yet further proof of the *luxe et indigence*. On account of some floods, they had been obliged to spend the night at Borghetto, a miserable little town, and Mathews describes the following morning with Blessington sitting up in his bed coiffed in a flannel nightcap, with a travelling shawl over his shoulders. All round are strewn his books and drawings, and by his side his breakfast, served on the silver accessories of his travelling kit. On another rickety table are some cut-glass bottles belonging to his crested dressing case. In each stopping place the scene is repeated, and added to the clutter comes the luggage: imperial piled on imperial, completely obstructing any free passage along the corridors leading to their rooms. One gathers that her Ladyship spoke up when things were sloppily managed, and on arrival at Nice she is critical of their hotel which is 'deficient in not only the elegancies, but all the comforts of life. It seems strange for us English,' she writes, 'to be compelled to sit and take our repast in a bedroom'. She remarks that all the rooms have two or more beds, and that they were obliged to pay extra to have those encumbering their would-be salon removed. Even then 'the landlord felt he had the right to turn the room to his profit during the day and only by threatening to leave did we obtain the room for our exclusive use'. They stayed two weeks in Nice and owing to the mistral Lady Blessington was somewhat scathing about it. From Nice the party wound its slow way to Genoa, where Lady Blessington meets Byron, the outcome being the famous *Conversations*.

The Thicknesses, though not to be compared with the Blessingtons, must, in their own way, have caused an equal commotion when travelling. A self-confessed 'eater of opium', Thicknesse is a real English eccentric, his wife no less so. She was the beautiful Ann Ford, niece to the Queen's physician and another of those accomplished women musicians quite common during the eighteenth century. Playing the viol de gamba and the guitar, she would accompany herself, and gave several concerts in London, one in which she played on musical glasses. Her father, disapproving of these public appearances, tried on several occasions to have her arrested. It goes without saying that nice society found her 'unmeasurably affected'; a fine match, in fact, for her husband. Thicknesse, having served in America, transferred to Jamaica and in 1752 bought himself the lieutenant-governorship of a post in Suffolk. He seems, also, to have dabbled in the arts, styling himself Gainsborough's original patron. His main talent, however, seems to have been rubbing people up the wrong way, 'increasing the number of his enemies'. But whatever his faults he was an original writer and published several books on his travels. On one of his visits to France, he sets out with the beautiful Ann and his two children.[8] Travelling on 'the frugal plan' he buys a heavy French cabriolet and fills it with every conceivable contrivance, including a large wooden drinking bowl for the horse and all kinds of musical instruments. Besides this interest in music they were both great animal lovers, and Mrs Thicknesse must be seen with a parakeet perched on her shoulder. Their monkey, Jacko, Thicknesse tells us, was dressed as a man 'with a pair of French jackboots and his hair in a pigtail,' and adds that the revolting animal 'rode postilion upon my sturdy horse some hours every day'. Thicknesse might have found this all perfectly natural, but the towns through which they passed were not quite so blasé and their appearance quite upset the locals, especially as the family were in the habit of picnicking by the roadside and, while waiting for the kettle to boil for tea, would play and dance to the guitar – all very tiresome.

Others of the same ilk, only less rumbustious, and to me far more sympathetic, are the Way family. They have none of the exhibitionism so evident in the Thicknesses, though I doubt whether they would have been any less conspicuous bowling along the dusty Provencal roads on their way to Nice. It was autumn, 1822, and the Ways consisted of a family of twelve all stowed away in a phaeton and a carriage nicknamed 'the heavy'. The Reverend Way, with his eighteen-year-old daughter Drusilla, led in the two-wheeled carriage, and behind came Mrs Way (affectionately known as Bombie) with her other four daughters, her son Albert, his tutor, and a governess called Phebsey. On a seat at the back, in the open, sat John the butler, and next to him Betty the cook. A great deal of luggage followed after them, shipped on the *Dash* and accompanied by Bill Drewe, Mrs Way's nephew. Included in the luggage were a quantity of Devonshire hams, a harp and Mrs Way's piano, as well as four of the children's ponies. The *Dash* sailed on the 15th of December and docked at Nice a few days past the month. The voyage shouldn't have taken so long, but they had been held up by a series of unfortunate storms, in one of which the ponies had been jettisoned. Terrified, the poor animals had jammed themselves up against the side of the ship, causing a dangerous list, and the captain had been obliged to dispose of them.

But to revert to our collective travels: one aspect of the voyage all pay especial attention to is the final haul through the Esterel, a strange, beautiful country, different in form and colour from all other parts of Provence. Of volcanic origin, these mountains erupt in a great upheaval of red porphyry, pointed and crested as in some Chinese wash drawing. Bare peaks tower above wooded valleys, and advancing towards the sea its shoreline is as tormented as the rest of the range. Waves rush noisily into tortuous indentations, lashing the hard rocks, boiling across their knife edges in a froth of white foam – a restless lashing that for countless ages has made not the slightest impression on the obsidian-like hardness of the porphyry. At certain hours the Esterel look as if they are ablaze against the hard blue of the sky, and then towards sunset the colours slowly begin to fade, darkening to purple, the mountains becoming a dusty silhouette outlined against a dying horizon of amber. According to Lenthéric, the ancients were frightened of the district and had as little to do with it as possible. Odd, for the origin of its name seems to belie these sinister suppositions, stemming as it does from a certain beneficent spirit known as Esterelle, a familiar who was believed to haunt these hills and to whom barren women made offerings in the hopes of producing offspring. Whatever its beginnings, good or bad, it was to become a place of very evil repute, and the road to the coast cut through its bare rocky masses only out of necessity. There was nowhere else it could go. The evil was, of course, the bandits, and it was in-

variably while on the Esterel road that hold-ups occurred. That the
bandits congregated here is easily explained: first the country furnished
ideal hideouts, and secondly it was in the proximity of Toulon, at that
time, during the seventeenth and eighteenth centuries, the most
important convict establishment in France. This was brought about by
Louis XIV's concern for his fleet. To strengthen it, large warships were
needed, and to assemble them new workshops and dockyards were
necessary, the building of which was entrusted to Vauban, the King's
military architect. To provide the manpower, prisoners were transferred
from the different gaols, in particular from that of Marseille. In addition
to the ordinary run of criminals, there were also the galley slaves for
which Toulon was noted, poor wretches who spent their lives chained
to an oar, sometimes six in a row in large galleys. For hour after hour
they were kept sweating together, not sitting, but leaping on their
benches to give them more purchase. Small wonder that these men
made every possible effort to escape, and when they managed to
do so would hide in the most inaccessible of places. The wilds of the
Esterel proved ideal for their purpose, and once there they would form
bands that could live off plunder ransomed from travellers. In 1787
Saussure, the celebrated Swiss naturalist, visited the Esterel to collect
plants, and one gathers from his writings that his enthusiasm was
somewhat tempered by uneasiness about his safety. He describes the
main road as being entirely exposed and dominated by salient rocks 'on
which the brigands plant their sentinels'. They would wait until the
traveller had advanced into the trap and then pounce. It was no use
trying to catch them, the undergrowth was far too dense, there were no
paths, and unless one knew the woods as well as the brigands themselves,
it was advisable to remain on the road.

The best known of these desperadoes was a man called Gaspard de
Besse. Somewhat of a show-off, he would perform his hold-ups wrapped
in a magnificent red cape. He became quite a notability, even featuring
as a hero in a nineteenth-century drama laid in the Esterel. The play
was named after the local inn, *L'Auberge des Adrets*, and the place still
exists and sits at the highest point of the road in the very heart of the
mountains. George Sand mentions it in her *Letters d'une Voyageuse*,
written for the *Revue des Deux Mondes* and dated 1868. Suffering from
anaemia, she had gone to stay with friends at Golf Juan, and was
taken on an expedition through the Esterel in a great lumbering
carriage drawn by three stout horses. She found *'les corniches verti-*

gineuses' and, of course, stopped to have a look at the *Auberge*. Knock-ing for a long time at an iron-bound door, she was finally taken in. The proprietor seemed ill-disposed to receive her and grudgingly led the party to what she called the dance hall: a dark room, dirty and smeared with indifferent frescoes representing rather primitive hunting scenes. Today the 'Nationale 7' goes right past its door but now, with the new autoroute, few bother with it – only those who, like George Sand, have a morbid curiosity. It was early in the year when I was there, and the place hadn't yet opened for the season: however, as luck would have it, an Algerian woman with blue tattoo marks on her forehead was busy spring cleaning. She showed me the downstairs rooms: no sign of the frescoes, but in the old part of the building I found what must have been the original oaken door with a peep-hole through which the traveller could be scrutinised before being admitted. Oblique loopholes cut in the walls commanded the entrance, and I noticed that the walls were unusually thick. It was obvious the place had been built with an eye to defence.

The village after which the *Auberge* is named lies a mile or two off the main road, and dates from the end of the eighteenth century. It was built as a military camp to keep guard over the neighbourhood, but as brigandage is now a thing of the past the village has lost its im-portance. Despite its isolation and its sinister associations, it is a cheerful little place with houses built of porphyry; roughly hewn blocks of stone ranging from yellow ochre to almost plum-red. Stray evergreen oaks grow in amongst the buildings, and a little way off comes the forest composed largely of arbutus, cork, oak and Spanish chestnuts. When freshly stripped, the cork trees look very red, almost raw, as if they were of flesh and had been flayed. Wedged between the other trees are drifts of an antipodean acacia, an underplanting that has seeded itself within the last eighty years, forming a silvery, feather-like vegetation in contrast to the somewhat dusty, tough-leaved indigenous things.

While on the subject of robberies, I must cite one particular case – that of the Bute diamonds. It occurred during the early years of the last century, near the village of Lucéram, in the mountains behind Nice: and although not, strictly speaking, relevant to the Esterel it belongs, at least in atmosphere, to the general subject matter. The story appears in Augustus Hare's book on the Rivieras, and he tells how Lady Bute 'was waylaid by a notorious band of brigands who had long baffled pursuit'.[9] They made off with all her valuables, including her jewel case and a smaller bag containing all her bottles, among them her vials of laudanum which her ladyship used to help induce sleep. It was mid-day and one imagines probably sunny, and gaining a plantation of olives, a safe distance from the scene of the crime, the robbers took their ease. Luck was on Lady Bute's side, for the men, mistaking her laudanum for some hitherto unsampled liqueur, gulped the lot. Overcome by sleep, they settled down amongst the gnarled roots of the trees, where they were discovered by the police, the famous Bute diamonds stuffiing their pockets. It came out later that the band was composed largely of members of the best families in Nice. For years, if seems, they had been living handsomely upon their illgotten gains, even inviting the unsuspecting authorities of the town to their banquets. ―

15

Smollett's Nice

This brings us now to the coast, and since we are still in the eighteenth century, to Smollett's impressions of Nice, the only settlement of any considerable size along the Riviera existing at that date. It has been described already how it came about that Smollett picked on Nice as a place to which he could escape when circumstances became too much for him. No mention, though, has been made of him as a person, or of the sequence of events which led him to the ground floor apartment in the street which today bears his name. Since he is to be our guide for the next few pages, it would be as well to enlarge on the subject.

In his youth Smollett served as a medical officer in the navy, and while stationed in Jamaica met the daughter of a West Indian planter. She was very beautiful, and later on returning to England he married her and by this marriage had a child – Elizabeth – whom Smollett adored. Seeing no future at sea, the young father set up a practice in London. It was a mistake: he hadn't the necessary charm, and was far too outspoken to please the rich clientèle he had hoped to attract. As it happens, the irascible doctor had another profession open to him – that of a man of letters. His caustic pen pleased the public more than his tongue, and he had an immediate success, in particular with his novel *Roderick Random*, a semi-autobiographical work dealing with his experiences in the navy. Other books followed, including a thirty-eight volume translation of Voltaire. A hard worker, he was also a liberal spender and the strain of living beyond his means was not helped by bouts of chronic rheumatism, a state of affairs that brought on ulcers, which he neglected. Nervous, worried and prone to a dangerous lung condition, he broke down completely when his daughter died, aged fifteen. Acutely unhappy and wanting a complete change, his youthful memories of Nice seemed infinitely attractive, and further encouraged by his wife, they left for the warm shores of the Mediterranean. Nice became their headquarters for nearly a year and a half, and it is Smollett's description of his stay there, appearing in book form under the title *Travels through France and Italy*, that first drew attention to the place.

Smollett must have been an odious travelling companion, but he writes ingenuously of himself and his bad health, pokes fun at his asthmatic cough, his spitting and general restlessness. Hardly a day passed that he did not have an argument of some kind with a landlady or one of the postillions. At one place he mistook a kindly gentleman farmer for an insolent lackey and slammed the coach door in his face. He laughs at himself 'the truth is, I was that day more than unusually peevish', and he excuses himself, blaming the man's clothes, but 'I daresay my appearance seemed as uncouth to him as his travelling dress appeared to me'.

It was mid-November by the time the Smolletts reached the south, and the twisting, tortuous road crossing the Esterel. The ascent took four hours, a little less being needed for the journey down once the top had been reached. The night was spent at the famous *Auberge des Adrets* situated at the highest point of the climb. Smollett mentions the 'desperate *banditti*' but talks of them as a thing of the past. They were far from obsolete, but believing them to be so, it was only the cold in the room in which they dined that set his teeth achatter. Their bedrooms faced south, and opening the window the next morning Smollett 'perceived, within a yard of my hand, a large tree loaded with oranges, many of which were ripe'. But surely Smollett is anticipating things. *Les Adrets* is too high for oranges, and even allowing that a tree grew there, the fruit would still have been green and only just beginning to change colour at the time of year Smollett was writing. As they start their descent, we have the usual reactions of a man bred in the north; the rapt admiration for 'glimpses of blue' seen 'between the cones of the mountains'; and then the exclamations over the plants – 'laurels, cypress, sweet-myrtle, tamarisc, box, and juniper, interspersed with sweet marjoram, lavender, thyme, wild thyme and sage'. The first night by the sea they spent at Cannes, 'a little fishing town agreeably situated on the beach'. In the morning they bound along the coast to St Laurent du Var, not yet a suburb and noted for its muscadine wine. It is all so familiar and Smollett describes it well; the milky blue sea lapping gently on a beach of white pebble, and the 'sunshine as warm as a May day in England'. Then comes the Var and the frontier to Italy;

the Var nowhere near so fine a river as its huge bed of gravel would lead one to suppose. Few rivers, in fact, are more capricious. It either flows in a gentle trickle or then comes rushing down from the heights in a raging torrent. Its floods are sudden and violent, and both the Var and the Paillon, on which Nice is situated, had special guards who watched over them. If a sudden fall of snow was thought to be imminent in the mountains, men mounted on horses would gallop ahead, shouting a warning. There was no question, as with the Nile, of the floods building up alluvial deposits. Engineers were consulted, and even the august Vauban declared the river 'so mad and ill conditioned' as to be beyond improving. Modern engineering, however, has been able to solve the problem and at great cost has encased the lower reaches of the river in a corset of parallel dykes.

When Smollett crossed the Var in the autumn of 1762 it was still untamed, but too early in the year for it to be in flood. There were, however, no bridges 'and a set of guides were always in attendance to conduct you in your passage across the river'. Armed with poles and naked to the waist, six of these fellows waded each side of the carriage. The poles helped them in feeling their way across the different channels, and woe betide the poor wretches if any traveller were drowned, for they were immediately hanged. In Smollett's case there seemed no need of their services. He regarded them as a form of perquisite and advises travellers to tip liberally. The government only allowed them three pence a passenger and 'if you do not gratify them they will rummage your trunks, and turn all your clothes topsyturvy'. Smollett explains that bridges had existed, and tells us that he met people who remembered 'three such wooden constructions thrown over the Var and as often destroyed, in consequence of the jealousy subsisting between the kings of France and Sardinia'. Far-seeing Smollett predicts the corniches and laments the fact that the mule tracks winding over the mountains have not yet been made wide enough to take wheeled carriages. 'I am very confident', he writes, 'that all strangers who now pass the Alps on the way to and from Italy, would choose this road as infinitely more safe, commodious and agreeable. This would also be the case with all those who hire *feluccas* from Marseille to Antibes and expose themselves to the dangers and inconveniences of travelling by sea in an open boat.' The Alpine route he refers to passed via Paris, Dijon, Geneva and Milan, and as to the inconveniences of travelling by *felucca*, one has only to refer to Madame de Genlis. She was held up in Antibes for ten

days not being able to embark for Nice on account of the mistral, and
when finally the party sailed they had to be escorted by a second *felucca*
carrying an entire regiment as safeguard against possible attack by
pirates. Hers, we know, was a special case, but nevertheless it is an
indication of the risks incurred.

While house hunting in Nice the Smolletts lodged at an inn, and
within a week managed to find a ground floor apartment with a garden
for which they paid twenty pounds a year. 'For this I have a floor
paved with brick, a kitchen, two large halls, a couple of good rooms
with chimneys, three large closets, which serve as bedroom and
dressing-room, a butler's room and three apartments for servants.'
Lemons, oranges and figs grew in the garden, and they had their own
well. One gathers it wasn't furnished.

In Smollett's day the town numbered twelve thousand inhabitants,
and was just beginning to attract a small English colony. He mentions
only two houses 'without one of the gates', and these very expensive.
More than likely he is speaking of the Croix de Marbre district, which
lay the far side of the Paillon; open country which by the mid-1780s
was to become the fashionable *faubourg* patronised almost exclusively
by the British.

Smollett is critical of the country houses and writes that they are
generally without chimneys, damp in winter, and infernos during the
summer, and further rendered impossible by vermin.

The Nice Smollett knew ran roughly from the harbour, round the
base of the citadel as far as the Paillon – now entirely covered over – and
was fronted by that part of the Baie des Anges, known today as the
Quai des Etats-Unis. On the land side it ran back to the present
boulevard Piena Sola, the heart of the town lying to the left of the
citadel and between it and the Paillon. La Vieille Ville, as it is now
called, has changed very little; the streets are narrow and the buildings
six storeys high. There were perfectly valid reasons, however, for this
seemingly negligent planning; narrow thoroughfares induce draught and
help exclude the sun, not so avidly sought after in Mediterranean
countries before the second half of this century. The question of height:
the canyon-like character of the buildings is explained by the necessity
of having to crowd within walls. Cramped and sunless, the streets do
certainly stay cool during the hot weather, but, as Prosper Mérimée
points out, at what price! Walk down the slippery stone-paved rue de la
Boucherie, or the rue Pairolière, 'condemned for eternity to the shades',

ABOVE *1* La Fiorentina: 'A
tangle of stone pines
tortured by the wind into
weird Rackham-like
shapes.'

LEFT *2* La Fiorentina: the
shallow grass steps leading
down to the sea.

ABOVE 3 La Fiorentina. The solution to our problem: the entrance façade copied from Palladio's *Rotunda* outside Vicenza. The columns at the gates are those that originally supported a loggia fronting the house.

RIGHT 4 La Fiorentina. The loggia in which we lunched during the summer.

ABOVE 5 A quick impression of the author's mother with the caption as it appeared in the American *Vogue*, 'The Countess of Kenmare at her villa, perhaps the most beautiful on the French Riviera.'

LEFT 6 'The monument was a prototype of its kind, and the most magnificent of any built in the antique time.'

LEFT 7 Caius Marius, a portrait head of him from the Vatican Museum.

ABOVE 8 An altar which is thought to have stood before the stage in
Arles great theatre. A good example of the fine quality of carving
being produced during the first century of the Empire.

9 Octavian as a young man, shown wearing a beard, considered as a sign of mourning by the Romans. A head found in the substructure of the Forum at Arles while work was in progress during the early nineteen fifties.

ABOVE *10* The Temple of Diana at Nimes. 'Here is Roman architecture at its most robust.'

BELOW *11* Aiges Mortes now lies incongruously stranded on a dusty, waterless plain.

OPPOSITE *12* Palace of the Popes; a vast complex completed in the space of twenty years.

13 The splendid
Coronation of the Virgin by
Enguerrand Charonton.

LEFT *14* Saint Martin, detail of Louis Brea's *La Pieta* in the monastery at Cimiez.

BELOW *15* Roi René by Nicholas Froment.

OPPOSITE ABOVE *16* Gateway to the Fortress of St André and the road up which Lady Blessington clattered mounted on *Mameluke*.

OPPOSITE BELOW *17* An early engraving of Nice. To the left of the fort lies the port settled by the Greeks, and on the right one sees what is now referred to as the old town. Crossing the Paillon, recently covered over, one comes to open fields, the future Croix de Marbre district.

RIGHT *18* Stairwell of the Palais Lascaris, old Nice's handsomest palace.

OPPOSITE ABOVE *20* *Fading Away*. A photograph by H. P. Robinson, dated 1858.

BELOW *19* Horace Vernet's portrait of his grandfather, Joseph Vernet, showing him lashed to the mast of the *Santa Maria* studying the effects of a storm.

OPPOSITE BELOW *21* A plate from Antoine Risso's *Histoire Naturelle des Oranges*.

This page

22 Villa Thuret. 'One
relives a period as old as
the trees.'

23 La Mortola.

Opposite page

LEFT *24* Lord Brougham
as an old man.

RIGHT *25* Marie
Bashkirtseff, a self-portrait.

BELOW *26* Paganini on his
death bed.

ABOVE *27* The Grand
Corniche showing the
dilligence rounding a
corner above the village of
Eze. In the middle distance
can be seen the Point St
Hospice where the author
lives, indicated wrongly,
here, as an island. The
Esterel heave up on the
horizon.

RIGHT *28* Sarah
Bernhardt's muse, tucked
away round a corner of the
Casino's southern façade.

and the smells are perseveringly present. As with Mérimée, you breathe in a heavy blanket of fermentation that catches at the throat: a mixture of dried cod, leather, unrefined sugar and olive-oil, all heavily spiced with garlic. Look up, and there is Mérimée's ragged collection of clothes; washing hung up like so many banners riddled with shot. The advent of synthetic thread has improved the tatters, but the 'banners' remain. In Smollett's day the windows were generally fitted with paper, but 'the bourgeois', he writes, 'were just beginning to have their houses sashed with glass'. Few of the houses had chimneys except in the kitchens, and even people of condition warmed their rooms with charcoal burned in portable braziers. The best fuel was oak and came from Sardinia, the commonest – olive. Country people burned vine cuttings which they sold made up into bundles. Dried pulp from the wine presses was yet another kind of kindling.

The food sounds anything but appetising. The ordinary meal consisted of sour bread, a little oil, herbs, vegetables and some fruit. Sometimes salt fish was added to the menu, rarely any fresh, and still more rarely meat. According to Smollett the 'noblesse' supped on salad and anchovy. Fish, when it was available, was rated much as it is today: *loup* at the top of the list, followed by *mostelle*; the general public bought sardines and tunny. No mention of lobster. There was little milk and still less butter and cream. The butter came from a distance and has been described as abominable. Goat's milk could be had in reasonable quantities, but most of the travellers found that it spoilt the flavour of tea or coffee and got used to drinking their tea without it. Lady Blessington, writing from Aix in the early part of the nineteenth century, reports only one cow in the town and that the property of an English family. For fruit they had figs, oranges and grapes. Strawberries during the eighteenth century were wood strawberries, and peaches, when they had them, were small, oblong and yellow but delicious in flavour. There were plums but in limited varieties, bad apples and pears. For hot days there were sorbets – iced froth made with either orange or peach juice. A slice of watermelon was another refresher. On the whole, the wine was good when left alone and not cut with pigeon dung or quick-lime. Smollett tells us that it was a common practice to serve a jug of tar water with the wine, many people preferring to dilute it. He also mentions large flasks sealed, not with corks, but with a floating of oil, and I believe this is still a common practice amongst the farmers living in the small mountain villages.

Once settled, Smollett set out in earnest to write about Nice. The estimable Baedeker was not yet supplying the curious with a mass of useful information on the places they visited, and Smollett, to while away the time while he recovered his health, started on a series of letters to an imaginary correspondent. Little escapes him as he prowls around during the siesta hour, a habit he got into for obvious reasons – it was the only time of day when he could be reasonably sure of not being interfered with. He finds the Nissards a lazy lot and describes them lying around in the sun and playing endless games of *boule*. 'They would prefer to starve than do an honest day's work.' He describes the men as swarthy, flat faced and dark eyed and on the thin side, but concedes that they are well made. Character-wise they 'are, in general, such dirty knaves that no foreigners will trust them in the way of trade'. It was common practice for them 'to fill their oil-casks half full of water, and their anchovy barrels with heads of fish'. He admits that he finds them remarkably polite and respectful. As for the women, 'they are not particularly well favoured except for their teeth'. Dr Davis, writing a few years later, is a trifle more complimentary and is struck by the amount of white worn by the women. No mention of this by Smollett, but Davis recollects attending a service in the cathedral on one of the many saints' days and 'being quite dazzled by the snowy display'.

Discussing transport, Smollett implies that it is practically non-existent. 'I think there are two private coaches in Nice, besides that of the Commandant.' There were, however, sedan chairs, and Smollett used them when he went swimming, being carried to the bathing place and back for eight pence, the distance from his house to the sea being about a mile. As to the swimming 'they thought it very strange that a man seemingly consumptive should indulge in such a pastime, especially when the weather was so cold'. The doctors prophesied immediate death, but Smollett thought little of his fellow practitioners and maintained that no doctor worth his salt would bury himself in Nice. He mentions an Italian physician settled at Villefranche, 'a very good sort of man who practises for a salary of thirty pounds a year and this includes an allowance from the King for visiting the sick of the garrison'. As for transport, the man in the street had his donkey, from time immemorial the Mediterranean's primary beast of burden. They carried the olives, turned the presses, were loaded with every form of merchandise and have even been reported rocking a baby's crib and, when they died, generally from overwork, were turned into sausages. Being an

Englishman, Smollett is upset at the way the animals are treated: 'there is not a dog to be seen in good condition' and 'the cats are so many emblems of famine'. He finds both dogs and cats dangerously rapacious and wonders that 'between them they don't devour the young children'. He laments the small birds which he claims have all been either shot or snared. 'Even the *noblesse* make parties to go *à la chasse* to kill redbreasts, tits and wrens which they eat as *gibier*.'

Wandering out into the country, Smollett passes judgement on the local agricultural practices and comments on the lack of any proper manure. 'The farmers have no cattle and the dung of mules and asses is of very little value for this purpose.' Nitrate is what they need and 'they have recourse therefore, to pigeon's dung and *ordures*'. *Ordures* in the sense Smollett uses it means human excrement, and to procure it, 'every peasant opens, at one corner of his wall, a public-house or office for the reception of passers by'. Even in Nice tenements are provided with one of these receptacles, 'the contents of which are carefully presented for sale', Smollett adding that the 'jakes of a protestant family' fetches a much higher price 'than the privy of a good catholic, who lives *maigre* one half of the year'.

As might be expected, Smollett is not the only visitor to comment on the above practice, and something else that seems to strike them is the country people's sense of time, an intuition common to a great many who have to do without mechanical aids. Having neither sundials nor barometers, the peasants regulate their lives by the sun and the stars and at the same time are practically never wrong in their prognostications regarding the changes of weather. A fog at a certain hour, a cloud of a particular colour on the top of some mountain or the flight of chirping birds enables them to gauge the alterations as well, if not better, than any meteorologist.

When it comes to amusements there are the usual somewhat plebeian pastimes of the period: strolling musicians, rope dancers and transient puppet shows, their arrival heralded by a noisy beating of drums. More spectacular were the saints' days. Dressed in their best, the crowds 'danced to the music of fiddles, pipe and tambour'. Smollett describes the hucksters' stands selling knick-knacks for presents; cakes, bread, liqueurs and wines; 'and thither generally resort all the company of Nice; including the nobles' – then follows an unattractive picture of them dressed in their finery mingling with the crowd, 'covered with dust, and sweating at every pore from the heat'.

Besides the street-shows, the commandant held 'a public *conversazione* every evening in his house, where the nobles play cards for farthings'. During carnival time he gave two or three balls a week, arranged by subscription. 'At this assembly every person without distinction is permitted to dance in masquerade; but after dancing, they were obliged to unmask, and if bourgeois, to retire.' One wonders how the 'distinction' was made, particularly as Smollett is scathing about the noblesse.

> Nice [he writes] abounds in marquises, counts and barons. Of these, three or four families are really reputable; the rest *novi homines*, sprung from bourgeois who have saved a little money by their different occupations, and raised themselves to the rank of noblesse by purchases. One is descended from an avocat; and another from an apothecary; a third from a retailer of wine; a fourth from a dealer in anchovies; and, I am told, there is actually a Count of Villefranca whose father sold macaroni in the streets.

A marquisate, he informs us, costs about four hundred pounds and a *lettre de noblesse* about thirty or forty guineas. In the valleys behind Nice he finds descendants of impoverished families

> reduced to the condition of common peasants; but they still retain the ancient pride in their houses, and boast of the noble blood that runs in their veins. A gentleman told me that while travelling through the mountains, he was obliged to pass the night in a cottage of one of these rusticated nobles, who called to his son in the evening, 'Chevalier, as-tu donné à manger aux cochons?'

Few of the good families appear to have been wealthy and, for the most part, lived off small incomes 'arising from the silk, oil, wine and oranges produced on their estates'. One hears of a rich landowner who every year picked more than three hundred thousand oranges and about half that number of lemons, but he seems to have been an exception. Smollett is interesting about the silk-worm culture and tells us that the eggs, or cocoons, when they first appear are washed in wine, and those that float to the top are thrown away; the remainder needing incubation are carried around in small linen bags, 'which the women wear in their bosoms, until the worm hatches'. Another detail, again supplied by Smollett, is the sensibility displayed by these insects. So fastidious are they that he has seen them 'languish and die by the score, in consequence of an accidental bad smell'.

No sign of the silk-worm or the mulberry on which it feeds exists in the Var Valley today, and one wonders how one of the country's major industries can have dwindled to nothing in such a comparatively short space of time. It is the estimable Brangham who supplies the answer, the reason being a larval disease. It first appeared in the mid-nineteenth century and spread throughout Europe, causing such devastation that by 1865 no healthy egg could be found anywhere outside Japan. Pasteur was called in to investigate and succeeded in isolating the infection, but by the time an antidote had been developed the industry had moved elsewhere.

Critical of the nobles themselves, Smollett is hardly more polite about the way they live but concedes that some of the country places are agreeably situated. As to their town houses, he is surprised 'to see a people established between two enlightened nations so devoid of taste ... no tolerable pictures, bust or statues'; even the ornaments in the churches 'are wretchedly conceived, and worse executed'. There are 'no public or private libraries that afford anything worth pursuing', and, according to Smollett, Nice was completely devoid of booksellers. 'How they live in their families I do not choose to enquire; but in public Madame appears in her robe of gold and silver stuff, with her powder and *frisure*, her perfumes, her paint, and her patches; while Monsieur le Comte struts about in his lace and embroideries'. He is not very gallant about the ladies' complexions: 'rouge and fard', he suggests, 'are probably necessary in this country where their skins are naturally swarthy and yellow'. He complains also about the entertaining. 'The Nissard gentry' are not 'given to hospitality'. The British consul, 'a very honest man', told Smollett that he had lived thirty-four years in the country 'without once having ate or drank in any of their houses'. Smollett is scathing also about the so-called gentry's escapades at night in the park, which, presumably, were the beginning of the Jardin Albert 1er, though, no doubt, more street than park in those days, and not over-endowed with trees. 'Here you may perceive the *noblesse*', he writes, 'stretched in pairs upon logs of wood, like so many seals upon the rocks by moonlight, each dame with her *cicisbeo*'. Smollett infers that they were completely amoral 'with not much passion or jealousy'.

It is possible, of course, that he didn't meet the right people: this, at least, is the conclusion Philip Thicknesse comes to when reading his book. I see his point. Smollett does seem to be a little touchy on the subject and, in one of his letters, mentions the cold reception offered him by the Duc de Villars at Aix. In the same letter he gives one to understand that the French have no idea about English class distinctions. For them a man without a title is just an ordinary plebeian 'who warrants not the slightest attention'. Poor Smollett. Thicknesse is not his only detractor. Horace Walpole calls him a 'gross barbarian', and Laurence Sterne, in his *Sentimental Journey*, ridicules him as Doctor Smellfungus, and writes that he set out 'with spleen and jaundice' and the account that he wrote about his journey ''twas nothing but the account of his miserable feeling'. After reading *Travels through France and Italy*, one is obliged to admit that he is very critical about Nice. Much of what he says was probably justified, and reading him is nearly always diverting: however, one understands Lord Shelburne's subsequent reaction. Shelburne was Secretary of State under Pitt, also an acquaintance of Smollett's, and, on returning to England, Smollett – according to Arthur Young – had applied to Shelburne for the post of British consul at Nice. Rather sensibly the latter had replied that the applicant's recently published account of the city must have so enraged its citizens that they would undoubtedly tear him to pieces if he ever put in another appearance. A kindly man, Lord Shelburne softened the blow by adding that 'he could not but show himself so little a friend to a person of genius by acceding to his request'. It must have been a bitter blow to any hopes Smollett had entertained of ending his life on the sheltered shores of the Mediterranean. His outspokenness had blighted what might have been a successful medical career, and now it had put paid to the beginnings of another venture. It would not be fair, however, to leave him with the reputation of being a complete denigrator of the place he discovered. If Cannes is to be considered the creation of Lord Brougham, Nice is no less that of the doctor's. Critical he might have been, but he was obviously fond of the place. 'Such is the serenity of the air', he writes, 'that you see nothing above your head for several months together but a blue expanse of sky.' Another time, while standing on the ramparts, taking in deep breaths of the air that had temporarily cured him, he looks around admiring the country spread out before him 'cultivated like a garden'. The trees are green and loaded with oranges, citrons and bergamots. On a closer examination of the gardens, 'you will find plantations of green peas ready to gather; all sorts of salading; roses, carnations, ranunculus, anemonies, and daffodils, growing in full glory, with such beauty, vigour, and perfume, that no flower in England ever exhibited'. These are hardly the observations of a 'gross barbarian'.

16

A Growing Colony

Up to now, there has been a tendency to escape from the coast. Events have kept us mainly in the *arrière pays*, in the real Provence. With Smollett the contrary has happened, and more and more one finds oneself concentrating on the shoreline: the sea-washed base of our triangle – the future Riviera. There is no doubt that Smollett's *Travels through France and Italy* had the effect of drawing attention to Nice. Arthur Young, writing a decade or two later, reports fifty-seven English families wintering there, and already the literature of the day is comparing it to an English watering place. The Croix de Marbre district has grown out of all recognition. Fine, detached houses are to be seen fronting the sea and the main road to France, while behind them large gardens give onto a wonderful view of the Alps. Some of them still exist and they are pleasant buildings faced with plaster, with regularly dispersed windows and shutters and, more often than not, sentinelled with palms. Generally known as New-borough, this district was often referred to in jest as *le petit Londres*, and for years to come any foreigner, despite his accent or appearance, was considered to be an English 'milord' – someone who came from a far distant city, one that was wreathed, so reports would have it, in perpetual fog. The names that occur are distinguished: the Dukes of Bedford and Manchester, the Cavendishes, Chesterfield, Ashburton and Sandwich. In 1764 the young Duke of York, brother of George III, passes through Nice and three years later is carried off a warship to die in the palace of Monaco. As Vice-Admiral of the Blue he had contracted a fever while his battleship coasted off the Alpes Maritimes and, fearful of his life, they hoved to in Monaco harbour where Prince Honoré III had him carried up to the palace. Boswell gives us a contemporary view of this place; he admired the court but was not impressed with the interior, though he admits to having seen 'some very good apartments and pictures'. The Prince spent most of his time in Paris, and the palace had an abandoned air 'like the house of a Scots laird who lives in England'. It was fortunate that the Prince happened to be in residence at the time of the Duke's illness, not that it helped the Duke, but at least it must have been some consolation for the royal family in England to know that he had been so well cared for. Honoré had his dying guest installed in the principal state apartment, now known as la Chambre de York. Whether it looked as it does today is doubtful. A *lit d'apparat* hung with Genoese velvet is set back in a gilded and brocade hung alcove. Above it, decorating the ceiling, are allegorical scenes attributed to Annibale Caracci. Not much is known about the Duke's illness. He was attended by the best available doctors and lingered for just over a fortnight, growing steadily weaker, dying on 17 September 1767. 'Great God, Thy will be done', he murmured weakly, then closed his eyes. No sooner was the death announced than cannons rang out in puffs of white smoke. They sounded every quarter of an hour until the arrival of the vessel sent to carry the Duke home. The vessel also let loose a cannonade, sounding off on the minute. Great attention was paid to etiquette, the death chamber being turned into a velvet-hung *chapelle ardente*. The young Duke, aged twenty-eight, lay in state for three days, his coffin spread with a black velvet sheet lined in white satin, heavily embroidered in gold. Silver and vermeil flambeaux flickered away the hours, to be extinguished only when the funeral cortège wound slowly down the hill to the sound of more firing. The coffin safely bestowed, more salvoes rang out as the sails lifted. There was a moment of silence, then, catching the wind, the canvas puffed out carrying the funeral bark across the horizon.

George III was so touched when he heard of the courtesies accorded his brother that, after a decent interval, he insisted on Prince Honoré paying a state visit. Much fêted, the Prince, a keen sportsman and a breeder of horses, also attended several race-meetings at Newmarket, a pastime that must have amused him, particularly as racing had not yet been introduced into France.

An interesting detail concerning the royal Duke is the fact that there exists an entirely different version of his death. It is not the actual death scene that varies, but the circumstances leading up to his presence in Monaco, and one wonders if there is not some truth in it. There could very well be an official version, the other a royal caper that history has thought better to hide and which Horace Walpole exposes in one of his letters. Supposed to be carrying out his naval duties he was, instead, in Paris, and after a brief stay travelled overland through France on his way to Genoa and his ship and, incidentally, an *enamorata* who lived in the same city. Arriving at Aix, he broke the journey in order to attend a great ball given by the Duc de Villars (the duke who had so offended Smollett) in his country château. He danced all night and was in such a violent perspiration that his companions begged him to rest and change his clothes before resuming his journey. But the Duke, in a hurry to regain his duties and his 'love', refused to listen and, instead, stepped forthwith from the ballroom into his post-chaise; the inevitable happened, and in a raging fever he was conveyed to the palace in Monaco.

Given the fact that he was the darling of London society, and well known for his success with the ladies, one finds oneself hoping that what might be a purely apocryphal version is perhaps the true story.

The second half of the eighteenth century was to prove a specially noteworthy period for the English colony in Nice. By 1764 their government at home had imposed peace with France, by which they acquired Canada and a large slice of India. Even the King of Sardinia's troops, stationed in the Comte de Nice, had an Englishman as commander. His countrymen were very *bien vue* and kept appearing in ever-increasing numbers. Two good new hotels, the Croix de Malte and Les Quatre Nations, had been opened, and villas were renting for comparatively high prices. By 1772 the town started spreading eastwards in the direction of the port, what was called le Chemin des Ponchettes, now the Quai des Etats-Unis. A low line of flat-roofed houses ran, facing the sea, their roofs forming a terraced walk reached by terminal flights of stairs. In 1777 a new theatre was opened – the Maccarini – its position being where the present opera now stands. New fashionable suburbs were also spreading out behind Nice, notably in the direction of Cimiez. But despite the changes, the Croix de Marbre district was to remain the popular residential quarters for the British; a colony that had grown to such proportions that it was felt they should have their own cemetery, a plot forthwith being consecrated. It ran between the actual Boulevard Gambetta and the rue Saint Phillipe, and remained in use until 1826 when it was finally disaffected.

Curious how history repeats itself, the prosperity of resort places depending almost entirely on the political situation: thus the war of American Independence, though distant from the actual scene, had its effect. Between 1775 and 1781, during the seven years it lasted, fewer

English than usual were to be seen on the coast. But once the crisis over, things very quickly returned to normal. The winter of 1783 saw the arrival of the Duke and Duchess of Gloucester, another of George III's brothers. They had rented a furnished house belonging to a Madame de Saint-Pierre in the rue Saint-François de Paul. With them they had their children and the children's Savoyard tutor, Albanis Beaumont. Beaumont has left us a charming series of engravings depicting Nice and the surrounding country; a collection that Beaumont had published, dedicating the album to his royal employer. Though beginning to be popular, Nice was not particularly fashionable, and the Gloucesters' presence is perhaps explained by the fact that the Duchess was considered to be in semi-disgrace in London. The King, her brother-in-law, had not approved of the marriage, the Duchess being the illegitimate daughter of the second Lord Walpole, and already a widow when she became engaged to the Duke. Her sister-in-law, the Duchess of Cumberland, was another *hiverneuse*, her marriage being equally frowned on by the King.

The Gloucesters' house seems to have been modest enough and is briefly described by Beaumont, giving an impression of a certain austere charm: curtains and bed covers of Indian cotton, straw matting and whitewashed walls, with a gilded mirror in each room and a great many engravings. Madame de Saint-Pierre was horrified at the state of the linen when re-claiming the house. 'It was in such a disgraceful condition that even the inmates of a home for the poor were unable to use it.'[1] She blamed the royal servants.

From about this same time there exists a considerable amount of unedited material regarding Nice, most of it in the form of letters. Amongst them is to be found the correspondence of Lady Polwarth who was travelling with her consumptive husband. In a letter dated December 1777, she describes their search for a house. She explains that it was a bad year for landlords, but admits that in spite of the war with America, she had left it a bit late to find anything in the country. Together they explored the steep hills behind Nice. 'The roads were passable enough but so rough and jolting they would almost kill a weak patient.' In one of their sorties 'a pair of large gates admitted us into an extensive terraced garden planted with citrus trees. We dragged ourselves up over flights of broken steps and entering through french windows came upon three large rooms, the further room having a chimney'. Cupids 'holding festoons of flowers' floated across their

painted ceilings. Further rooms opened off these 'and only two of the
bed chambers had chimneys. As to the furniture, I had almost forgotten
whether there was any. I only know that it could scarcely look more
dismantled: as if a troop of soldiers had been billetted there, and yet
they said the Count had not left it above a month'. Again, as with the
Cumberlands, one gets this almost spartan emptiness, typical of certain
Mediterranean houses, only in Lady Polwarth's case the walls were
covered with 'a profusion of family portraits'. Though delighted with
'the prospects', the Polwarths did not take the house, and in the end
found a flat next to the Hôtel de la Pension Anglaise in the Croix de
Marbre district.

Lady Polwarth's impressions of Nice are typical of a certain civilised
milieu. She takes tea with Count Gubernatis in his handsome villa at
Cimiez, now housing the Musée Archeologique. She mentions temples
converted into stables and, wandering amongst the Roman ruins,
stoops 'like a hawk on two bits of marble', but in the end throws them
back in amongst the acanthus for 'they were very trifling and only
belong to the commonest kind of cornice'. She did, however, go back
with some coins. In another letter describing the old section of the town,
she criticises the free use of false marbling in the churches and private
houses. 'Marble is the great magnificence of Genoa and these people
not having any, endeavour all they can to imitate it.' On another day,
Lady Polwarth regrets not being able to send home some sketches, 'but
in the neighbourhood of the town you must draw in public and be
pestered with beggars; and the more retired places are not very
accessible'. She writes naturally and things come to life under her pen.
Going to market, she remarks on the peasants' clothes; red striped
aprons and plaited hair wound round their heads 'over that they wear a
piece of white linen which hangs in a triangular shape behind'. She
remarks that the more prosperous amongst them have dangling gold
earrings and crucifixes of the same metal, but unusual in that they are
welded to gold hearts, the whole forming a pendant which they hang
round their necks with black ribbon. In the country the same women
wear large circular straw hats 'which act as a parasol in the summer
and protect them from the rain in the winter'. As to the town 'the ladies
in general dress their head in pretty good taste but wear the strangest,
dirty old fashioned gowns'.

It seems odd that not once in all the letters and diaries that have come
my way have I come across any mention of the Lascaris family, and

yet their house, recently restored, was by far the grandest in Nice and the family one of the proudest in Provence, claiming descent to no less a person than Theodor Lascaris II, Emperor of Byzantium. It is possible, of course, that by the eighteenth century there were no longer any direct heirs. At any rate, one hears nothing of them from Lady Polwarth, and since she spends much of her time visiting one feels that if they had been at all interesting, she would have known them. Amongst the families she names are the Costas and Tonduses, both titled, Baron Tondus playing at the faro table for quite high sums of money. At the Baroness's she met Lady Drogheda 'the best and the most sensible person, and I am sorry to think that she is married to a whimsical Irishman, who has half ruined himself by gaming and could not help losing two hundred pounds, even here'. Already at this early date, Nice had opened a *cercle*, or casino, where foreigners could gamble at faro.

Due to Lord Polwarth's delicate condition, it was impossible for them to move far afield. They took in Villefranche, a 'poor place built on the side of an almost perpendicular hill' and saw 'his Sardinian Majesty's dockyard where one frigate is building by an Englishman'. But most people, those who came to Nice for no other reason than to escape the winter, made expeditions of several days or more. One thing that impressed everyone were the dockyards and fortifications of Toulon. Louis XIV had made it into the foremost port of France, and travellers admired Vauban's star forts with their salient angles, a particular form of defence for which he is famous. There were also the painters' and sculptors' studios, belonging to the men employed in decorating the ships of the line. Foremost amongst the sculptors comes Pierre Puget, with his designs for resplendent poops and opulent figure-heads; a truncated conception of the human figure which started a taste for the caryatids pressed into service on so many of the grander houses in the neighbouring towns. A fine example is Puget's own design for the town hall of Toulon, while others are to be found at Beaucaire, Aix and Fréjus.

Lady Blessington, as might be expected, includes Toulon in her sightseeing and boarded several ships of a hundred and twenty-one guns, including the *Royal Louis*. It was in the *Royal Louis* that the Duchesse de Berri had sailed from Naples when she came to France to marry the Dauphin. 'The ship had been splendidly furnished for the occasion; and the galley that surrounds the state cabin, which she occupied, was filled with the rarest flowering shrubs and exotics.' Lady Blessington also visits the building housing the *galériens*. It is well aired and clean, has a large dormitory and white bedding. She is shocked, however, by the 'staples attached to the foot of each bed for fastening their chains'. Boswell, who inspected the *galériens* at Marseille, gives a slightly different impression and found them working in 'a row of little booths with signs . . . many of them who looked as plump and contented as any decent tradesman'. Among the *galériens* Lady Blessington was shown a man who had been mayor of Dijon. 'He looked like a gentleman and was employed in engraving a coco-nut which he was doing with great skill' presenting it afterwards with a bow and scrape 'that would not have shamed a finished courtier'. A man of some means, he had been married to a woman still richer than himself. Feeling that he should have the handling of their joint fortune, he had tried to persuade his wife to merge her *dot* with his own holdings, and on her refusal, strangled her. Failing to ignite the body, he had been discovered, but the judges, unable to find proof enough to hang him, had sentenced him to the galleys for life.

One picks up further details touching on these unfortunate *galériens*. For instance, on being committed to the galleys each victim was branded. There were different grades of branding: *TF* stood for *travaux forcés* and indicated a sentence of so many years, while *TP* stood for life, the *P* short for *perpétuité*. As uniforms, they wore brick-coloured cotton topped with a red woollen cap, an unfortunate co-incidence that was to cause trouble during the revolution. A member of the Convention, on learning that the red cap of liberty was identical to the woollen cap worn by the *galériens*, rose and demanded that the honourable badge should be removed from their heads; and amidst thunders of applause, the motion was carried, a special commission being dispatched to see that the orders were carried out and the cap confiscated. Unfortunately, the National Commission had made no provision for replacing the men's headgear, and over a year went by before the men were able to cover their heads. When they arrived, the replacements were green. In any case, the fuss over the Phrygian bonnet was a futile issue, for due to sails and improved naval construction, galleys had become a thing of the past, and at the time of the revolution lay rotting at anchor at Toulon and Brest. *Bagnes* these hulks were called, perhaps from the Provençal *bagna* signifying 'moored', and the poor wretches who were left to serve out their term of sentence rotted within their walls, the *Bagnes*, to economise in space, having been turned into prisons.

It is impossible when on the subject of ships and the ports along this coast, not to make mention of the seascapist Joseph Vernet. A native of Avignon, he had, on the advice of Monsieur de Marigny, director of the king's works and brother to Madame de Pompadour, been commissioned by Louis xv to paint the ports of France and amongst them is to be found a charming view of Antibes. Vernet's preoccupation with the sea was a characteristic which completely dominated his painting, and according to the Bénézet dictionary[2] it was while on his way to study in Rome that his real vocation claimed him: that moment when standing on the heights above Marseille he caught his first sight of the sea. A storm at Civitavecchia a few days later really clinched matters – *'ce fut le coup de foudre'*. From then on the sea, one way or another, was to appear in all his paintings, and being a true romanticist, what he gloried in most were its restless moments. He had a special talent for capturing lurid atmospheres and dramatic lighting effects; mounting waves and leaden clouds slashed with forks of lightning. Like Claude, his master in spirit, he always peopled his seascapes, even his storms; and one sees small figures, arms flung skywards, pathetic silhouettes pitted against the forces of nature. A whole room at Avignon's Musée Calvet is dedicated to his work. There are also examples of his son's, Carl Vernet, paintings. Carl chronicled the *incroyables*, but is known, above all, for his horses and his elegant, varnished *caleches*. Horace, the third of the line to follow the family calling, lacked his grandfather's and father's style. His paintings, however, are anecdotal and he is responsible for an entertaining study of his grandfather in which he shows him lashed to the mast of a ship, paper and charcoal in hand, studying the effects of a storm. The painting is large and hangs on the museum stairs, and gazing up at it one can guess at the story. Joseph must have bribed the owners of a *felucca* to take him to sea, and elated by the phenomena, is indifferent to the dangers, but not the poor sailors who, any minute, expect the *Santa Maria* to founder.

We have seen how volatile, how easily affected the English colony in Nice could be, and now comes the fateful year of 1789. The coast would have to wait a further twenty-five years, until after the dissolution of the empire, before the foreigners began to return. Replacing the 'milords' came the French émigrés, and with the fall of the Bastille Nice was suddenly flooded by a distinguished crowd of nobles, bishops, priests, monks, and not least, the vice-legat from Avignon. The town, alas for them, was to prove a very temporary refuge, for by 1792 the revolutionary troops under Napoleon had occupied Italy. Not exactly an émigré, but amongst those who felt not too sure of their position arrived a native of Grasse, the son of a glovemaker – the famous Jean Honoré Fragonard. With reason, one imagines, he judged that his connections at court might brand him as a suspect to the general cause, and feeling insecure in Paris had invited himself to stay with Maubert, his cousin, the owner of a large house in the middle of Grasse.* With him came his son and a number of paintings, including the four large panels Madame du Barry had commissioned from him for her Château de Louveciennes, outside Paris. The theme was love's progress in the heart of a young girl and included the deliciously lyrical *Poursuite, le Rendez-vous, les Lettres d'amour*, and *l'Amant couronne*, now in the Frick collection in New York, perhaps the most important ensemble of French eighteenth-century decorative art in existence. When delivered to Madame du Barry she refused them. No explanation was given, and it is argued that the paintings were a thinly disguised allegory representing the royal love affair, which, if true, would certainly have displeased the king. But it seems highly unlikely that Fragonard would have dared, or have been so tactless ever to embark on such a commission. Indeed, if they are supposed to refer to some given episode, then it is more likely to have been the painter's own adventure with the dancer, Madeleine Guimard. This might well have been the case, for they were painted in 1771–2 and after their refusal had hung in his own studio where they would certainly have been eagerly sought after, if he had wanted to part with them. The fact that he took them with him when he left for the south also suggests some sentimental attachment.

Once arriving in Grasse, Fragonard hung the suite in his cousin's drawing-room and painted a fifth panel, in sepia, entitled *l'Abandon*, to complete the room. For years they formed one of the sights of Grasse until 1898 when, unable to resist the tempting offers† put to them by Mr Duveen, the renowned dealer, the family sold them.

But this is a well known story; less known is the fact that Fragonard also decorated the hallway and staircase of the same house with a monochrome fresco in burnt umbers, depicting strictly Republican

---

* Fragonard stayed in Grasse just over a year, from January 1790 to March 1791.

† At the time the price was considered high, and not only did Duveen pay well for them but also had copies made to replace the originals.

motifs; a work undertaken, one supposes, to curry favour with the local Tribune, reputedly rabidly anti-royalist.

Until recently the house was lived in by an old lady, a descendant of the Mauberts, who, resentful that the state might declare her house national property, barricaded herself in, refusing to allow any visitors. Since her death last year, the situation has improved somewhat and through a friend I managed to see the frescoes. They make a handsome hallway and interesting also is the evidence that Fragonard's son helped him with the painting. If forewarned, one can quickly differentiate between the hand of the master and that of his son. The subject matter should also give some indication: the cannonballs and lictons lining the staircase walls would certainly have bored Fragonard *père* and their execution, though proficient, lacks any obvious flair.

With the revolution appears the thin, nervous figure of the young Bonaparte. Both Gros and David show him as he appeared at the time: burning eyes and a pale, eagle face framed by untidy locks of hair falling in straight meches on a stiff, high-standing collar. He first appeared on the scene in 1793, at the siege of Toulon. Staunch royalists, Toulon's citizens had allowed the English under Admiral Howe to occupy the port. Later Howe was joined by seventeen Spanish ships and subsequently the Neapolitan fleet with a small force of troops. As seen by the French, this build up represented a direct threat to the Republic, and it was decided that their army should counter-attack immediately. The allied British and Spanish fleets, though in possession of the forts, lacked the troops to man them and no large British expeditionary force was available; furthermore, Howe dared not deplete his ships of seamen. To make matters worse, the revolutionaries were constantly receiving reinforcements, and further to complicate matters for the allies there was the question of divided command – the three different nationalities involved. But above all the French had Bonaparte. In the absence of a superior officer he had been put in command of the artillery. His quick intelligence and energetic approach had won him the favour of the Council, and when he appeared before them with a plan of action they listened to him. It was a question of taking the offensive. L'Eguillette, one of Vauban's forts, commanded the roadstead in which the united fleets lay at anchor. Were this occupied by the French, then the squadron would run the risk of being set on fire and would be compelled to quit Toulon. L'Eguillette had a reputation of being impregnable, but the young Bonaparte argued his case so convincingly that his plan for storming it was accepted. In his memoirs, dictated at St Helena, he describes the scene and remarks rather drily that 'success was indeed indispensâble in those days, as the want of it conducted the unfortunate general to the scaffold'. Thus spurred on, Bonaparte was taking no risks. The fort and its works were given a merciless pounding, and at mid-day on 18 December a terrific storm broke. Under cover of lashing rain, a column scaled the scarp and leaping over the embrasures seized the British cannons. By dawn the next day, the *tricolore* was floating over the fort. As predicted by Bonaparte, Admiral Howe and his allies had no choice but to hoist sail, their decks crowded with the Toulonnais who had remained loyal to their king.

Before leaving, the English had blown up Fort Pomé, which they still occupied. Nine gunships and four frigate of the French squadron added to the conflagration. The blaze lasted seven hours, and Bonaparte likens it to the eruption of a volcano, the burning ships crackling like a firework display.

Following Toulon Bonaparte was promoted general and stationed in Nice as commander of coastal artillery. A dutiful son, and with a considerable increase in pay, his first thoughts were for his family, who had been obliged to flee Corsica on account of his sympathies for the 'patriots'. His father dead, he lodged Letizia and her fast-growing brood of daughters in the rented Château Salé at Antibes, and it is here that one gets glimpses of the young general teasingly admonishing his high-spirited sisters, special attention being paid to Pauline, the future Princess Borghese, who was always his favourite.

The coast was to be visited by Bonaparte on various occasions: after his marriage to Josephine in 1796, and again as commander-in-chief of the Army of Italy, and once more after the treaty of Campo Formio when he embarks from St Raphaël on an expedition to Egypt. Following Nelson's victory in 1798 at Aboukir Bay, Bonaparte, leaving his troops, slips through the British cordon and lands at Fréjus. Proclaimed Emperor in 1804, one of his first acts was to improve France's approaches to Italy. Disregarding all difficulties, his engineers ribboned a road along the brow of the Alps and, descending on Menton, skirted the town by building out round the backs of the houses. Previous to this, since old Menton rose almost directly from the water, the narrow Rue Longue had been the main gateway through which all the traffic had to pass. At Garavan, just short of Ventimiglia, another difficulty presented itself in the form of a rift, or chasm, and here the engineers simply slung the beautiful, single arched bridge of the Pont St Louis across into Italy, and until the recent addition of supplementary frontier posts, this bridge constituted the only land approach between the two countries.

The tide had turned when next Bonaparte appears on the coast, again at St Raphaël. The year is 1814 and Bonaparte, now referred to as Napoleon, arrives as a prisoner in a cavalcade of six coaches accompanied by three hundred Austrian dragoons. The allied generals, in full uniform, doff their hats as the Emperor steps onto the boat that rows him out to the frigate bound for Elba. The ship flies the English colours, but the captain orders a salute of twenty guns in deference to His Imperial Majesty.

This first exile is to be of short duration. A few months later, escaping from Elba, Napoleon lands at Golf Juan, a strangely quiet beginning to the dramatic Hundred Days. Under cover of darkness a fleet of five ships appeared as mere shadows off the Cap d'Antibes and rounding the point silently dropped anchor in the shallow bay. By three in the morning a captain and twenty-five horses had landed with orders to reconnoitre. Finding nothing more alarming than the upturned hulks of the fishermen's boats, he took it upon himself to advance on Antibes and entering the town was taken prisoner, an advent which must have passed off with remarkably little fuss, for his absence seems to have made no difference to the Emperor's plans, which went ahead as projected. By five all had disembarked except for Napoleon who was the last to leave the ship. Stepping ashore he rested in a bivouac that had been set up for him amidst some olives, and by eleven they were off. The landing took place on the first day of March 1815, and by the twentieth Napoleon was in the Tuileries, Louis XVIII having fled to Ghent.

The great man's progress as reported in the newspapers of the day makes amusing reading; on first landing he was the Corsican adventurer; the next day the usurper; by the time he reached Grenoble Bonaparte is the distinguished traveller; at Châlons he becomes again Napoleon, and at Auxerre the Emperor reinstated in all his imperial dignity. The south had never been ardently imperialistic, and the villagers en route for Gap had greeted Napoleon with an indifferent shrug of the shoulders. Only in Grasse was there any show of excitement, and that because the landing had been reported as a descent of pirates. A diverting detail is the Emperor's supposed meeting with the Prince of Monaco outside Cannes. Restored to his throne by the Treaty of Paris, Honoré IV was on his way to take possession of his principality. There are various versions of the story, and I find Baring-Gould's the most entertaining. Stopped by the Imperial Guard, the Prince was asked to descend from his carriage, and on being conducted before a little man with clear-cut features, at once recognised the Emperor.

'Where are you going, Monaco?' asked Napoleon bluntly. Honoré told him and the Emperor smiled, 'What a chance encounter. Two majesties in search of a throne', and then reflectively, 'but I shall be in Paris before the week's out and might then be obliged to depose you, my cousin. Come with me instead and I will make you sous-préfet of Monaco if it really means that much to you!' Honoré, hesitating, decided on his throne. 'Even Sire if my reign is to last only two days.'

The Emperor inclined his head and shaking hands the two monarchs wished each other well and went their different ways.

Contemporary with this meeting is Sir Archibald Alison's description of Aix. He happened to be travelling at the time of the landing and notes some of the differences of behaviour since the revolution; for one 'the familiarity of all ranks with their own servants'. He finds it 'most disquieting', but adds that although 'a nobleman will sit down in the kitchen of an inn and converse familiarly with the servants . . . yet he keeps his place most proudly in society, inviting and receiving only his equals and superiors'.[3] He describes a coffee house. All kinds of people are there; 'blackguards and several looking like gentlemen', amongst them one fellow wearing a white cockade in his hat who sits playing draughts with an officer. The cockade suggested royalist leanings and Alison, watching him, admires the precious stones that flash on his fingers and is surprised but impressed at the assortment of seals dangling from his fob. Taking him for a distinguished dandy, he engages him in conversation. 'I was astonished,' he writes, 'at his almost immediately offering me his watch and trinkets for sale.' Alison, apart from being an appalling snob, was obviously slow on the uptake, for again we are treated to the lifted eyebrow 'when a gentleman from the other side of the room called him by name, and bid him bring a cup of coffee and another liqueur. My friend was one of the waiters! Such is the mixture of French society', he sighs. 'Such the effect of citizenship.'

Going back a few years and in contrast to Sir Archibald comes the gangling, six foot two tall Thomas Jefferson who, at the time of his visit to the south in 1787, was serving as Benjamin Franklin's successor as North America's Minister to France. He ignores Nice, but loses his heart to Provence, and being a highly civilised individual it is a pleasure to follow him there. A man of many parts, an expert violinist, an amateur architect, he was also endowed with an excellent eye and considerable taste. It was entirely due to his intervention that Houdon, the eminent French sculptor, was commissioned to execute statues of both Washington and La Fayette; works that were to adorn the State Capitol at Richmond of which he himself was the architect. His designs for this building were based on the Maison Carrée at Nîmes, a building which, as we have seen already, he admired profusely. The Capitol was the first building destined specifically for a modern republican government, and Jefferson took great pains to make it impressive. It was not a straight copy of the Maison Carrée but rather an adaptation, and much larger in scale. He changed the order from Corinthian to Ionic and made the portico, on the advice of Clerisseau, the distinguished author of *Monuments of Nîmes*, only two columns deep instead of three since 'the latter depth would too much darken the apartments'. The other important changes were the omission of half columns and the insertion of windows.

Jefferson was very taken with Nîmes and its Roman past. He writes to Madame de Tassé, La Fayette's aunt, that he is 'immersed in antiquities from morning to night', and 'were I to attempt to give you news, I should tell you stories one thousand years old . . . all the intrigues of the courts of the Caesars'. In another letter he describes how 'wild figs, very flourishing, grow out of the joints of the Pont du Gard'. Arriving at Aix he tries the waters, taking douches for his wrists that were giving him trouble. Unfortunately, he was not drawn to the coast.

❧17

The Invalids

The year is 1822 and Napoleon, lying in a lonely grave on St Helena guarded by British soldiers, is safely out of the way. Breathing a sigh of relief, the people of Europe start travelling again.

The winter of 1821-2 had been a particularly severe one on the coast, and those depending on their citrus crops had been completely ruined. To help alleviate the distress, a member of the British colony had come forward, a man known to us already – the Reverend Louis Way. Having spent several successive winters in Nice, he had noticed that the visitors preferred to walk by the sea rather than along the banks of the Paillon which was the popular parade ground with the townspeople. The shore was rough and pebbly, not very practical for taking the air, and Way, to help the destitute farmers, raised money among his compatriots to employ the men on road-making. They cleared and paved a walk from the corner where the Hotel Ruhl used to stand to the present rue Meyerbeer, a distance of about six city blocks which just about fronted the Croix de Marbre district where all the English lived. This promenade started off life as La Strada del Littorale, but very soon became known as the Camin dei Inglesi, and in 1844 was officially named Promenade des Anglais, the municipality enlarging it and increasing its breadth from six to about twenty-four feet, but despite the improvements it remained without pavements and was incredibly dusty. As late as 1863, Alphonse Karr, the journalist turned horticulturist, was writing to a friend that he could have no idea what dust was like until he had been to Nice where '*au bord d'une Méditerranee d'eau on se promène dans un Océan de Poussière*'. It wasn't until the last decade of the nineteenth century that the promenade was planted and tarmacked and lengthened so that it stretches, as we see it today, echoing the crescent-shaped sweep of the Baie des Anges, as beautiful a bay as its more famous counterpart in the Gulf of Naples. True, there is no Vesuvius, but more often than not smoke from some bonfire punctuates the skyline, hovering in a delicate plume: a perfect substitute for the volcano's subterranean belchings.

Nice was developing quickly. By 1826 the Pont Neuf had joined the two banks of the Paillon. Before long it would become an important city and as a resort was never to lose its popularity with the French, particularly amongst the rich bourgeoisie. There was to be a change, however, amongst the British. Distinguished visitors were beginning to explore the possibilities of other watering places along the coast. In 1834 Lord Brougham and Vaux makes his appearance. In his fifties, and recently resigned as Lord Chancellor of England, he was en route for Italy, and were it not for an intervention on the part of fate, had no intention of tarrying along the way. Reaching the Var, the Sardinian authorities stopped his carriage. Northern Europe was suffering from a cholera epidemic and the Sardinian crown, to isolate herself, had spread a cordon along her frontiers. Brougham, no longer travelling on a diplomatic pass, had the choice of a ten day quarantine, or then the usually lengthy process of waiting for a special pass. Not the best tempered of men, the commotion must have been considerable, but the authorities remained obdurate and 'milord' was obliged to retrace his steps. Cannes, where he had spent the night before presenting himself at the frontier, happened to be free from infection and had he wanted, Brougham could have waited a few days, and reappearing, would almost certainly have been allowed through. Instead, perhaps initially out of pique, but more probably on account of the climate – Brougham had an invalid daughter – he started to look for a house. He was first shown the Château Salé at Antibes, the house Napoleon had taken for his family. Cannes was not much more than a fishing village at the time, and the Château Salé was probably judged the only interesting buy for a rich Englishman. Brougham had a series of interviews with Mr Servelle, the owner, and the deal would, in all probability, have gone through had the local authorities not stopped the sale, claiming historical immunity. Salé, they argued, was not a site that should be allowed to pass into foreign hands. Not easily discouraged, Brougham started hunting round Cannes, the country was very beautiful, besides which his lawyer assured him 'the winters were as mild as Cairo, that frost was almost unknown, and that snow scarcely ever fell nearer than Grasse'.[1] Finally he decided on a narrow strip of land to the west of the village, with a splendid view out over the Golfe de la Napoule. He paid five sous a metre and the house, an Italianate villa, took a little over three years to build. Unfortunately his daughter, Eleanor Louise, died before the house could be furnished, and Brougham, an affectionate father, called the place after her, spending every winter there until his death in 1868. The Villa Eleanor Louise still stands, and on its walls can be found the poems inscribed to the young girl for whom it was built; one by her father, and the others by Lord Wellesley and the Earl of Carlisle respectively.

Brougham's independent turn of mind did not pass unnoticed in Nice, and his countrymen came to look and, impressed with what they saw, followed suit; especially the wealthy. But before exploring this new settlement, there is another element, another strata of society that must be taken into account – the invalids: the invalids, in this case, being the consumptives. Little has been said about them, and it would give a false picture of the coast not to include them, for they are an important part of its history and flocked by the hundreds in the hopes of finding a cure, or at least a prolongation of their frail lives. Pliny's Greek slave, Zosimus, seems to have been the first recorded case. The man had been freed, but was attached to Pliny and remained in his services, and when he started spitting blood Pliny had sent him to a friend's farm at Fréjus.[2] The climate, as we have seen, had agreed with Smollett, but his ills were so numerous that it is difficult to judge to what extent his lungs were seriously affected. Sterne, his contemporary, had left it too late, having already suffered a serious haemorrhage in Paris on his way down. The mild climate only helped those who reacted in time, and even then the discomforts of the journey often proved fatal. Lady Polwarth implies as such in one of her letters: 'Lord P's lungs', she writes, 'were so shook by the repeated jolts of the latter part of the journey that he came here (Nice) with some tinge of blood, though a slight one'. The faintest squall appeared to quicken the invalid's pulse and increase his cough. 'As to the cold we have certainly escaped it, though we continue lighting fires, and burn more wood in a day than the inhabitants of Nice in a week.' This particular letter is dated 20 December, and Lady Polwarth, admitting that there are no frosts, is nevertheless disappointed with the weather. They don't blame the doctors for recommending the climate 'but we do say that they form a romantic idea of it'. Lady Blessington, writing some fifteen years later, echoes the same sentiments. But in all fairness to Nice, it must be admitted that her impressions were gathered during a particularly

blustering attack of the mistral; one of them a pathetic picture of a
fair English girl mounted on a pony, being led by her father or brother
'or one who hoped to stand in a still more tender relation to her'. A
bright, hectic tinge colours her delicate cheeks and she stares with a
lustrous eye which 'betokens the presence of that most fatal of all
diseases'. A gust of wind sweeps the warm cloak 'from her shrinking
shoulders', and then 'that fearful cough which shakes her tortured chest.
A few weeks and such invalids (and alas! there are many) are seen no
more'. Of course, the real trouble was not so much the weather but
rather the want of knowledge regarding the disease. Not until 1882,
when Robert Koch discovered the tubercule bacillus, was it known
what caused the dreadful wasting. Even then the disease had to wait a
further fifty years until antibiotics were to strike it off the danger list.
Up until then it had been one of the major causes of death in most
northern countries, including the United States: something like a ratio
of one in five. However, there is no question that the Riviera climate
was beneficial, providing the disease was caught soon enough and,
although ignorant of the causes of the disease, there were those who
gave very sensible advice.

Following Smollett comes John Bunnell Davis, the next doctor of
any note to have a book published about Nice. The son of a surgeon,
and himself a member of the corporation of surgeons, he had been
engaged as medical attendant by an English family travelling in France
during the Empire. The peace of Amiens had recently been ratified,
and nothing untoward happened to the family, with the exception of
Davis, who for some reason had been arrested on the suspicion of
spying. Put on parole, but not being allowed to leave the country, he
enrolled himself for a course of studies at Montpellier. Concentrating
on pulmonary complaints, he paid several visits to the coast, basing
himself at Nice. By chance he made friends with Doctor Corvisart,
Napoleon's physician-in-chief, and through his offices obtained his
release. Back in England he turned his hand to writing and, amongst
other books, produced his *Ancient and Modern History of Nice*, published in 1807 and written to benefit invalids; an informative guide
supposed to help pass the time while they sniffed 'the air perfumed by
the blossoms of flowering fields'. Davis is full of common sense, and in
his introduction underlines the importance of the care to be taken
when first the 'phtisis' is discovered. 'Consulted by some at Nice, by
others at Montpellier, I usually had to contend with the disease in its

last stages.' Of course, it was hopeless, but caught soon enough, and
provided the patient would listen to his doctor, Davis is quite optimistic
about the chances of recovery. He sensibly advises travellers to patronise the river boats rather than travel down by coach, and once arrived
in Nice begs them to take every possible precaution; laxatives and quiet
and very light food for the first few days; flannel next to the skin;
'a hat lined with fur which would closely encircle the face . . . a fur
tippet . . . and tepid baths produce healthy excitement'. His diet is no
wine, barley water, orange juices, or toast soaked in water. 'Ragouts,
spices and salted aliments must be avoided.' Instead of these he
substitutes 'light soup, vegetables, fish, pandar of bread and biscuits,
new laid eggs, chicken and rabbit'. As to fruit, he considers grapes the
most beneficial. Exercise is important, and Davis lays great stress on
'equitation when the patient is capable of supporting the strain'.
He comments on the Croix de Marbre district, but despite the pleasant
houses to be found there advises against them. He finds them too near
to the sea for consumptives. The best adapted are those on the surrounding hills, where the air is drier, although he admits to the 'difficulty of
access', and reading Davis one is put in mind of Lady Polwarth's
experiences.

The next, and the most remarkable of the physicians on the list is
John Henry Bennet, the first doctor to bring Menton, as a health
resort, to the attention of his countrymen. He opens the preface of the
fifth edition of his *Winter in the South of Europe*[3] by an avowal that he
left England a very sick man: 'I wrapped my robes around me', he
writes, 'and departed southwards in the autumn of the year 1859 to
die in a quiet corner as I and my friends thought'. Instead he made an
almost miraculous recovery, and after only one winter in Menton, was
back again consulting in London. Though a singularly good doctor,
and highly successful in his treatment of pneumonia – reducing the
mortality to nil in uncomplicated cases – he does not seem to have been
very popular with his patients, and still less so with his fellow co-
practitioners. Like Smollett, he was far too outspoken. It did not stop
him, however, from producing a thoroughly engrossing book, and reading it one becomes acquainted with a peculiarly likeable human being,
certainly someone to be counted amongst the authors writing about
this part of the world whom one feels would have been a real pleasure
to meet. He is sensitive, intuitive and observant; unusually intelligent
and obviously a discerning diagnostician; realising, as any good doctor

must, that half the battle is to get the patient's mind off himself. The book is dedicated to the physically afflicted and he opens with a plea to his readers to 'commune with nature', assuring them that by so doing they will find 'the cheerful contented resignation which is all but indispensable to their recovery'. One is in good hands for Bennet himself spent six consecutive winters at Menton, from October 1859 to April 1865, and explored the country thoroughly. He describes it with a knowing eye, loves it, but at the same time is aware of its short-comings as far as concerns the weather. 'The perpetual spring,' he warns, 'the eternal summer, the warm southern balmy atmosphere, described to the reader in such glowing terms, only exist in the imagination of the writers. Although there is so much sunshine, so much fine weather, such immunity from fog and drizzling rain, we are still on the continent of Europe; it is still winter.' Wind, rain, a chilly atmosphere and occasional cold, with snow in the mountains, must be expected. 'It is as well, therefore, that the invalid traveller should be prepared to encounter them. Otherwise, anticipating an Eldorado of balmy zephyrs, he is disappointed.' Only in the temperate zone can one find continuous warm weather in winter – 'those tropical or sub-tropical regions which in themselves present many drawbacks'. Having warned his readers, he then points out all the advantages offered by Menton. 'Its winter climate is warmer than that of Nice or its neigh-bours; indeed it is warmer than that of any part of the northern central regions of Italy. That such is the case is shown by its vegetation. The latitude of Palermo six degrees further south, must be reached to find the same growth – groves of lemon trees growing, without the shelter of walls', and lemons, it should be remembered, are killed by three or four degrees of frost. Bennet is by no means the only one to single out Menton; others also agree that it enjoys a singularly balmy climate for Europe, equalled, perhaps, only in Greece and certain parts of central Spain. Looking at the map, one might question Menton's pre-eminence, for Hyères, Cannes and Nice all lie further south. But in Menton's case it is the folds of the mountains which count and more than counterbalance the few degrees of latitude. Massive arms jut out protecting the town and directly to the back rear up solid walls of sun-baked stone; range after range rising to an altitude of nine thousand feet; a huge curtain that deflects the icy winds. Menton's proximity to the sea is yet another point in its favour, the sea always remaining several degrees warmer than the land.

William Chambers, visiting the place in the 1860s, found it 'a dirty, old-fashioned Italian town with no question of gas lighted streets'.[4] Cannes, by contrast, seems infinitely preferable but was already considered expensive and looked on as highly 'aristocratic'; the very reason, apart from its climate, why Bennet decided against settling there. Nice and Cannes he considered far too stylish, and certainly no place for invalids 'who ought not to be thinking of balls, theatricals and lavish exhibitions of finery'. He cites several examples to act as deterrents, case histories of obstinate patients – pretty young women and gay young blades with only one lung who thoughtlessly waltzed their lives away. –

Though popularised by Bennet, Menton was actually founded in the late 1850s by an English cleric called Morgan, and on Bennet's arrival could already count some three hundred foreigners. Bennet is not as critical as Chambers, but admits that it resembled any other little town along the Riviera with no means 'of supplying the want of foreigners'. The meat was coarse, the bread sour and the butter bad. The only good butter came from Milan and was delivered twice a week by boat from Genoa. Poultry, when they had it, came from farms up in the mountains while the local *gibier*, the entrées of robin-redbreasts and roasted larks, only horrified the English. Fish was scarce and very expensive and was to remain so until the advent of the railway which was slowly inching its way along eastwards. On the French side the Marseille to Nice line had been opened quite some years already, and by 1864 Bennet reports the Italian Government as pushing along from Genoa in the direction of Ventimille. Several thousand labourers were at work and the link-up was only a question of months.

However, despite the conditions, Menton's reputation as a health resort was not long in reaching America, 'where', writes Chambers, 'Doctor Bennet's work is, I believe, fully as well known as in England'. Every season 'fading Americans' made the journey over, crossing and recrossing the Atlantic; one Philadelphian family persevering for eight successive winters.

Gaining status the inevitable happened; first a promenade was added and then a club where members could play billiards and find back copies of *The Times, Standard, Punch* and the *Illustrated London News*. A lending library specialised in paperbacked editions of Tauchnitz, and Willoughby, an English greengrocer, set himself up as house agent. Bennet describes the hotels, many of them existing today. The floors creak a little bit more but the large, grey, shuttered windows opening onto gravelled gardens haven't changed; nor the palm spiked view out over the road onto Garavan's glittering bay. One sees the new arrivals; quickly the old inhabitants sum them up, and with knowing eyes single out the invalids and with accuracy judge even the degree of their illness, which all too often is in its last stages. Bennet describes them as falling 'like autumn leaves before the first blast of winter', and compares his patients to a leaky vessel, 'like Nelson's *Victory* which safe in port may long ride with dignity on smooth waters'. The battle of life, he warns – 'its storms and tempests – must be left to the young and the strong'. He doesn't spare his patients, 'within them lies the seeds of death, they live on sufferance and should act accordingly. The truth should be known, and then bravely recognised and accepted'. Bennet is full of common sense and, judging from his book, basically optimistic. I, for one, would have had confidence in him as a doctor. He writes that it is a mistake for an invalid to accompany strong, healthy, sight-seeing friends or relatives. England should be left during the second week in October and the return journey undertaken towards the middle of May. Bennet does not recommend patients to remain in Menton during the summer and seems always to have encouraged them to return 'to cool, green, England'. He is fully aware that Italy is the country everyone sighs for 'but having made painstaking enquiries' advises against it. The water is bad, 'the plains of Lombardy burning and the snow-covered passes of the Alps pregnant with danger'. In an appendix Bennet gives advice on the journey out. 'It is folly to cross over if the sea is rough.' A night in Paris is advisable or, better still, 'Fontainebleau which is on the direct line to Lyons'. He even lists the times of the trains. The best train leaves Paris at 11 a m. and gets to Marseille at 6 a.m. the next morning, and Nice at 3 p.m the same day. Wagon-lits were still a thing of the future, but there were coupé-lits – three seats in a carriage for which the traveller paid a small supplement. Arriving in Nice, the patient spent the night, catching the diligence to Menton the following morning. These diligences left three times a day and did the journey in under four hours. The coast road had not yet been built and the coach was obliged to wind all the way up to La Turbie before making the steep descent the other side. One can imagine the relief on arrival, the patient being shown into a high-ceilinged room with a southern exposure, especially reserved for him by the careful Bennet. If by chance it was a dull day, a wood fire would be crackling in the grate; otherwise golden sunshine streams in through the open window. Bennet always insisted on his patients being given a southern exposure and was a great advocate of fresh air. Once settled, the doctor goes about his business; Bennet's main concern being his patients' general health, this improved 'the battle is half won'. He warns them against the sudden drop in temperature when the sun goes down. The patient should then immediately wrap up warmly and regain his room and take to his books. Above all, he must fight against the depression that a few dull days could bring. 'In such weather', he writes, 'most of us are indescribably wretched and miserable.' He has a theory about the buoyancy of the spirits – a question of electricity; the moist air is a good conductor, dry air a bad one. Generated by contact with the earth the human body acts as a battery and in dry weather becomes fully charged. This stimulates the nervous system and a certain buoyancy and cheerfulness is the result. In damp weather the contrary happens, the moisture of the atmosphere acts as a conductor, electricity is then at a minimum and mental depression follows. One presumes that Bennet indoctrinated his patients: he also had another theory about nose and throat infections. It sounds convincing; besides, the role he played in the treatment of pneumonia gave great importance to anything he had to say on the subject of breathing and the subsidiary role played by the skin in helping relieve the lungs. One breathes through the skin, and Bennet maintained that the fine weather opened the pores while the cold climate of the north had the opposite effect, clogging the skin's respiratory faculties. In short, the deficiency of oxygen poisoned the blood and indirectly choked the lungs and air passage. 'Hence the colds, the local inflammations and the fevers' so common in the north 'and comparative immunity from the affections in such a climate as that of the Riviera.'

Bennet's theories must have been heartening to his patients and thus buoyed in spirits he advises exercise and sends them out to 'commune with nature' – on walks, or drives and whole day excursions armed with picnics. If one can judge these outings by his own expeditions, they must have been highly enjoyable. Bennet describes them: up at six or seven and after a cup of tea, or coffee, he is off, snugly wrapped up in the back seat of a black leather *vetturino* drawn by four horses. With him he has 'umbrellas, books, maps and provisions; the latter usually consisting of a hamper of biscuits, cheese and fruit'. At nine he stops for breakfast 'which can be obtained anywhere if the traveller is contented with coffee, tea, chocolate, bread, butter and eggs'. At one the horses and driver are fed and Bennet opens his basket, and while the coachman takes his siesta stalks off into the sun-dappled, olive-grown landscape. The carriage is again resumed at three and generally travels until six.

Sometimes his expeditions include Monte-Carlo, then just coming into its own, part of the Principality having been turned over to M. Blanc, the successful operator of a large gambling establishment at Homburg. 'On a fine sunny winter's day it is the most charming excursion.' Bennet admires the newly laid out gardens and listens to the music, played by a competent band, to return leisurely home before sunset chills the air. Perhaps with an eye to the more bigoted of his readers, Bennet lets it be understood that he disapproves of the gambling and finds it a pity that 'this vice should be the means of placing these quiet, health-giving pleasures at our disposal'. Naturally, he forbids his patients the 'gaming saloon', stressing the danger of all such excitements. As it happens, there were quite a number of other expeditions in the neighbourhood: excursions on foot, or on donkey to the mountainous regions, to decayed castles and sun-baked villages such as Castellar and Castillion, and nearer to hand, Roquebrune. For the weak there were endless rocky beaches, which 'with a cushion or two and a rug makes a perfect shelter if out of the wind'. Bordighera, on account of its date groves, was a great favourite amongst the more venturesome. The palms grew specially densely in the gardens of the French consulate (once an old Dominican monastery) and the consul, a friendly man, allowed parties to picnic there. It would appear that the palms have multiplied considerably in the last hundred years, for walking in between the high garden walls in the back streets of the old town one can see to what extent they have taken over. At times one might think oneself in some North African village; they invade the whole mountainside, bunch out over the tops of walls, lean out from the houses, shading one's path with their stiletto-like shadows. The very walls themselves are formed from their notched trunks piled one on top of the other and plastered over with mud. The date, of course, is not indigenous to the coast, and seeing this profusion of growth one is curious as to how they got here, particularly since the fruit can never ripen, needing the heat of the desert to attain its edible stickiness. The explanation is that they are grown for their fronds which are much in demand as commemorative symbols during Holy

Week. The young healthy trees have their tops bound tightly together with hazel twigs, and never seeing the light of day become straw or cream-coloured, anaemic things like plants grown under a stone, and it is these tender vegetable growths that one sees plaited into multiple shapes decorating the churches of the Catholic world on Palm Sunday. How they came to be grown in Bordighera is another story, and dates back to the sixteenth century, to the time of Pope Sextus v. Sextus, an exceedingly devout Christian, was alarmed at the revival of interest being taken in pagan Rome, and determined that as many of the ancient monuments as possible should serve the Church, had ordered the erection of an obelisk on the Piazza San Pietro, its pinnacle to be surmounted by a cross. The obelisk came from Heliopolis and had been brought to Rome by Caligula in the first century AD. Nero placed it in his circus, and there it stood until 1586 when Sextus set it up before St Peter's. However, the raising of a monolith cut to such slender proportions has always been a difficult task as the pictographs incised in the granite facings of Luxor's great temples bear witness. Besides the manpower it necessitated a number of cranes and several hundred metres of rope. Crowds gathered and the pope watched from his balcony as the great monolith was wheeled into place. Slowly it began to rise, then suddenly a halt in the procedure, the obelisk had ceased to move. The workmen had omitted to wet the ropes, and they were visibly sagging. An awful moment of silence and then, from the back of the crowd, came a shout *'Acqua sulle corde!'* 'Water on the ropes!' 'Throw water on the ropes.' Who was this man? Sextus v made it his business to find out and on ascertaining his name rewarded him and his family in perpetuity with the privilege of being the Vatican's special purveyor of palms on Palm Sunday. How this man came to ask for such a favour is another matter. He was a sailor called Bresca, the captain of a fishing smack at San Remo, and as far as one knows had no connection with the land. Another mystery: why should a family from San Remo cultivate palms at Bordighera? This point, at least, is cleared up for us by Edmond Strasburger, one time Professor of Botany at the University of Bonn, who explains that it was all a question of soil. At San Remo it is heavy clay, while at Bordighera it is liberally laced with sand which is just what the palms like.[5]

But what about Menton? Have I painted too cheerful a picture of the invalids' life? Bennet tells us that it was not always easy and that there were those who appeared to derive little benefit from the change, and to be really cured was a slow and laborious process needing considerable force of character. 'Undoubtedly,' writes Bennet, 'the most satisfactory cases of arrested and cured phtisis that I have seen have been among those who have had the power and the will to return again and again; who have adopted my motto, *vivendum est*, "to be or not to be" and have cheerfully made every possible sacrifice in order to give themselves a fair chance of life.' Victorian literature abounds in fading flowers, dainty, pallid sufferers barely able to walk a score of yards unless supported. Each day sees them growing weaker and weaker until the tired limbs can lift themselves no longer from the couch. Quietly then they are borne away to the little graveyard on the hillside facing the setting sun. Cypress and ilex keep guard over their rest. Norman Douglas visiting the Menton cemetery in 1921, 'in a statistical mood', studies the 'sepulchred inscriptions' and comes to the conclusion that sixty per cent were consumptives. I know the cemetery and it's a quiet, nostalgic place reached by steps that wander up through the old part of the town. Formerly a castle of the Grimaldis stood on this hill and there, between the ruins and the encircling wall, a cemetery was built. It had been newly acquired in Lady Blessington's day to make room for the victims dispatched during the revolution, not that they seemed to have paid the victims much respect, their bones having been piled in a heap 'exposed to the elements', while 'rosy cheeked urchins' played with the skulls twining garlands of ivy round 'their bleached brows'. Strasburger, who saw the cemetery at the beginning of this century, describes it exactly as it looks today, and watched a young sculptor 'carving the face of a tender maid on a stone' – and I know precisely to which grave he refers.

Highly professional though Bennet must have been, he was working against serious odds. Only when he had given up his practice in Menton was it definitely proven that consumption was a contagious disease and easily transmitted by sputum, or by way of the respiratory tracts. But even armed with this additional knowledge, the patients were still not being isolated and invalids kept arriving, booking in at the best hotels. Small wonder that the ordinary visitor complained nervously to the management. Despite the seriousness of the disease, it was not until 1900 that a special clinic was built halfway up the Gorbio valley. This allowed the management of the different hotels to refuse a patient without feeling completely inhuman. Many, however, still came to Menton to die, amongst them the young Aubrey Beardsley, who in 1898, at the age of twenty-nine, agonised in a room hung from floor to ceiling with paintings he had collected. In 1920 Katharine Mansfield rented a little house in Menton, though she did not die there since neither her husband, Middleton Murray, nor herself could afford to buy it. She loved the place, and on realising it could never be hers, she wrote to Murray, 'Am I a little mad? You will find Isola Bella in poker work on my heart . . .' Poor D.H. Lawrence had been too ill to have any choice in the matter of where he stayed, and had died in a clinic at Vence. Some time before him Robert Louis Stevenson had rented a chalet at Hyères. But by and large most of the invalids had left, never to return. It was during the twenties that a dry climate and high altitudes were thought to be more beneficial than the damp sea air, and then during the forties both mountains and sea were judged inadequate, surgery having eclipsed the question of climate; a new therapy being used by which the affected lung was collapsed. The discovery of sulphanilamides in 1944 represents the final breakthrough. Except in rare cases, and in underdeveloped countries, tuberculosis has now become a thing of the past.

✺18

The Naturalists

Purposely I have omitted writing about what, to me, is one of Bennet's most sympathetic traits: what, without exaggeration, one might call his passionate involvement with nature. Not only did he preach a general awareness of one's natural surroundings as therapy for his patients, but it was also an occupation he practised more than assiduously himself. There is little doubt that his acute eye and his general interest in everything, as expounded in his book, stimulated others in emulating him. The steady production of excellent botanical works which were to appear on the Riviera over a period of some forty-five years, from about 1865 to the first decade of this century, can certainly be partially credited to Bennet. Reading him one sees that there is little he is not curious about – paths in the sea, currents, and the moon's attraction on tides; rainfall and winds, the rise and fall of temperatures, and the whys and wherefores for everything. It is from Bennet that I learn about *la poudre insecticide* which I had always understood to be a comparatively recent discovery. Not at all, it was introduced into France in about 1850, and Bennet never moved anywhere without it, always sprinkling a teaspoonful or two of the precious powdered pyrethrum on his sheets. He tells us that the daisy is extensively cultivated in Persia but that the best sort comes from the Caucasus and that recently, that is in about 1865, it has been grown in England by a Mr Willemot, hence the *Pyrethrum willemoti* of our botanical dictionaries. He remarks that blackberries grow better on the Riviera than in England, and something I didn't know, that the ordinary *platane*, the plane tree whose mottled branches shade the square of every small town in Provence, was in reality a native of Asia Minor – *Platane orientalis* – and that in its own habitat on the Bosphorus, and in certain parts of Iran, its trunk could attain enormous proportions, anything up to a hundred feet in circumference. Bennet also lists the wild flowers, among them the lovely double *Anemone hortensis* with its slashed scarlet petals. Common once on the coast, it is now seldom met with except when protected by some keen horticulturalist who has had the good sense to naturalise it in his garden. I know a terrace of them under some olives at St César, near Grasse, but they represent a lifetime of collecting and have been gathered from here and there, when making their rare appearance.

Bennet does not pretend to be a professional botanist, and without elaborating further writes that the rarer wild flowers only grow in certain regions 'known to the "initiated" and to some of the donkey women'. He has, however, some pretensions to being a gardener, and during his second year at Menton bought a precariously perched strip of land below the village of Grimaldi. Grimaldi lies just around the corner from the Pont St Louis and Bennet refers to the place as 'warming itself in the sun', and tells us that its presence is made conspicuous by the washing plastered over the mountain-side. With the land came a 'ruined, medieval castellated tower . . . built, no doubt, to protect the coast and town from the attacks of the roving Moors'. No house existed and Bennet only came there to 'bask like a lizard in the sun', to tend his plants and enjoy the splendid view. Others describe the garden, amongst them the one-time Lord Provost of Edinburgh, William Chambers, who refers to it as 'a haunt of artificial beauty'; a kind of open air drawing-room for playing croquet, reading, etc. At one end was to be found a sort of grotto with water and ferns 'and there in a shaded hammock lolled the owner'. On festive occasions 'the Union Jack fluttered on the breeze'. This struck the Lord Provost as 'a rum idea, especially incomprehensible to the ordinary travellers riding in their carriages on the corniche road below'. Intrigued by the descriptions of Bennet's garden, I took the trouble to pinpoint the place and discovered that at the doctor's death the property had passed to an English family who, inspired by the tower, had built a neo-Gothic house on the grounds. Its crenellations are just visible from the old road, but a visit would appear to be out of the question since no one ever answers the bell.

From Bennet we pass to the professional botanists, the best known amongst them being J. Traherne Moggridge with his *Flora of Mentone* illustrated with handsome, hand-coloured plates. Quite a rare book these days, I am lucky enough to own the third edition, published in 1894. Amongst the plants mentioned is the fragile, pinkish-white heath, *Erica multiflora*, which I am interested to see he gathered on our point in November 1866. It apparently grows in profusion bordering the railway near Toulon and Hyères, but once this side of the Esterel is only to be found in three small patches: one in what would become our garden, the others at Bellet and nearer to Nice in the Vallon de Magnau. Moggridge's father had also botanised in the Alpes Maritimes, and Traherne had been one of Bennet's patients. Chambers describes him as the typical English botanist, and met him shortly before his death setting off down the road dressed in a pair of knickerbockers, ribbed woollen stockings and stout ankle boots. A green tin box for specimens was slung from his shoulders, and from his waist dangled two leather sheaths, one containing a large knife and the other a saw. A long pole with a hook at the end completed the outfit. For food he just pocketed a couple of oranges and kept a pipe for when the going got rough, up in the mountains.

During the second half of the nineteenth century several botanists were exploring the steep mountain valleys branching off behind Menton and Nice – H. J. B. Ardoino who produced *Flore des Alpes Maritimes*, the German Oskar Schneider, and a Devonshire man called Robert James Shuttleworth. Many others were to follow, and each in turn located some botanical scarcity: plants such as the extremely rare pomponiam lily found bursting open its brilliantly red, upcurling petals somewhere hidden away on a lost mountain shelf north of the Var valley. Is it a certain professional jealousy that prevents these men from giving precise instructions as to the exact position of the plants they discover? Another reason could be a wish to protect them from possible vandalism and eventual extinction. There is the snowdrop-like *Leucoium nicænese* with its star-shaped flower believed by Moggridge to grow in only one place in the world, and that a narrow strip of land between Beaulieu and Monte-Carlo. He found it in the rocks on the Tête de Chien, and in his description of the plant wonders at the limitations of species, referring to it as 'among the mysteries which surround the origin of all vegetable life'. A gardener friend of mine tells me that he has seen a whole hillside above Grasse covered with the pinkish-mauve flowers of the wild *Paeonia peregrina*. Several times in the spring I have suggested that he drive me up there, but so far he has always found some excuse. I understand him, for it would have been difficult to resist digging up a few of the woody roots. I have done as much with the bulbs of the little candy-striped *Tulipa clusiana* which I once found growing in a field behind Opio. I admit also to having gone to great trouble in collecting plants of the *Lavandula stoechas*. Its violet spikes grow almost four-sided in shape and have a strong aromatic, oily scent, with not much resemblance to the true lavender. It is, nevertheless, a pleasing plant with its softly felted leaves, and amusing for gardeners down here since it is indigenous to the country and particular to the islands off Hyères and the volcanic soil of the Maures where whole tracts are stained with its flowers; in fact, it used to grow in such quantities that the nearby village of Le Lavandou is named after it.

But the most spectacular of all the wild plants of the region is the primeval, almost extinct *Saxifraga florulenta* which has to be hunted for, sometimes for years, and when found, photographed with a telescopic lens. Macmillan confines it, quite rightly, to a comparatively restricted area of the Alpes Maritimes – the Haute Gordolasque, below the rocky ridge of the Col de Fènestre and near a sanctuary which used to serve as a hospice for travellers crossing over the Alps from France into Italy. The country is sparsely populated and not so long ago the inhabitants of the small villages clinging to the sides of these high mountain valleys paid hunters to chase the wolves, sometimes as many as a hundred and fifty being killed at one time. There were also lynxes, particularly hated by the shepherds, but the wolves were more dangerous where humans were concerned and during severe winters could be heard scraping at the doors of the houses. There have been times also, within the memory of living men, when the postman dared not venture up the Vésubie valley beyond the village of Lantosque on account of the eagles – and Lantosque is not much over fifty miles from Nice.

But to return to our plant. Macmillan tells us that this particular saxifrage was discovered in 1824 by an English tourist who sent specimens to Professor Moritti in Padua. Descriptions of it were published, but no accompanying notes as to its whereabouts, and for years botanists searched in vain and were about to give up when, in 1856, it was accidentally rediscovered on the Col de Fènestre by a Monsieur Lisa and soon after him by l'Abbé Montolive, a first-rate botanist and keeper of the Municipal Library at Nice.

It is worth noting that this almost fabulous saxifrage was last seen in July 1972 by Madame Basselaar, an amateur photographer living in Monte-Carlo. Again it was in the haute Gordolasque. Familiar with the plant's history, Madame Basselaar had decided to try her luck and spent several weekends hunting fruitlessly for it and was just about to give up when she saw what looked like a flattened artichoke, a glossy-green rosette about half a foot in diameter, nestling in a wall of rock. It was the fabulous saxifrage! She took her first photograph and returned four times during the next two months, and on the 10 September caught the plant in full flower. The flower stem stood about a foot and a half high; a spike of coral-rose basking in the clear autumn sunshine. What Madame Basselaar did not realise was her luck in discovering the saxifrage in its prime since the plant only blooms every ten to fifteen years.

Once one has begun to take an interest in the life around one, it is almost impossible not to carry the hunt further; besides which, the naturalists and their books are such good company. As an example, follow for a moment the admirable Brangham when writing about the migratory routes of butterflies over the Côte d'Azur. He describes great clouds of the *Vanessa cardui*, or painted lady: an 'exhilarating sight as they pass over the coastal hills from their breeding grounds along the edge of the North African desert' – and an unexpected detail is the fact that these ephemeral wanderings take place 'even in the face of adverse winds'. 'Moths, also', Brangham writes, 'make the great trek in spring and autumn.' He lists the varieties, amongst them the death's head hawk, *Acherontia atropos*, named by the French *le Sphinx tête de mort*. The oleander hawk, or *le Sphinx du Laurier-rose* is another, also *le Sphinx du Liseron*. Comerford-Casey will tell you that 'any beginner who puts a light in his window at nightfall will catch moths which no lepidopterist in Europe can name'.[1] Swallowtails flop around every garden – 'flowers of the air'[2] Strasburger calls them, and Brangham saw a 'dance of blues' just after he had struck the Rhône.* Swallowtails also haunt the giant fennel, and I have seen this with my own eyes. A drift of it grows in a field down by the sea in a new garden I have just made. I brought the seed back with me from Hyères and the swallowtails are attracted to the spot even when the plants are not in flower. Another magnet in the garden is the *Arbutus unedo*, the handsome stringy barked arbutus, or strawberry tree, the haunt of the *Charaxes jasius*, the king of European butterflies. The French call him *le Jason*, or *Pacha à quatre queues*, a name the insect has earned himself from its gorgeous colouring. Sadly the only specimen I have seen was in a museum, but here again it is the question of a migratory butterfly and the *jasius*'s real home is North Africa. Apparently the Esterel is the best

* Francis de Croisset, the author of *Feérie Cingalais*, was nearly smothered to death by a flight of sulphurs while touring Ceylon in an open car.

place to see it, and Brangham describes its characteristics. 'One's interest is first held by the majestic flight of the male, sweeping in wide curves, soaring in splendid circles, then gliding with extended wings towards its feeding place, the excrement of a passing mule, or the juice from an over-ripe fig, but never flowers. The flight of the female is an un-distinguished wavering motion.' From its behaviour, Brangham continues, one would judge it to be 'consumed with curiosity, for the insect will settle again and again on the brim of a hat, and may be captured even. Released, it banks away to return and be caught again moments later . . .' At all events, the male is fiercely combative and has been known to 'chase a small bird from a branch . . .': even will attack a pine cone if thrown in his direction.

Having once been bitten by this bug of naturalising, it is only to be expected that one should be curious about plants growing in one's own garden. One starts with the obvious, and from there branches out. Long ago I satisfied myself about the *Cercis siliquastrum*, and the reason for it being called the Judas tree. Strasburger had the answer: in ancient times it was a favourite in the gardens of Jerusalem and this gave rise to the saying that Judas had hanged himself on one of them. One acquires such a wide variety of unrelated facts. For instance, when out collecting the different euphorbia indigenous to the country, I have learned to be careful of their white, milky sap. Goats fed on them have been known to poison people through their milk, the goats themselves being immune from the toxin. Oleanders are another dangerous poison – flowers, leaf and wood, and to use their branches as a meat-skewer on a picnic may lead to fatal results. The tuberose is another inhabitant of the garden with curious associations. Comerford-Casey informs us that in the Malay states it is referred to as 'mistress of the night' and that its fading flowers emit sparks that scintillate in the darkness following on a sultry day. But no sign of any sparks here. Doubtless one would have to be standing on the lawn of a garden in Kuala-Lumpur or Penang to witness the display, the temperature here not being sufficiently humid.

We all know, I suppose, that the camellia comes to us from Manilla, brought through Spain by a Jesuit father called Kamel, or Camelius, and that the famous Swedish naturalist Linnaeus named the shrub after him, giving it the specific name of *Japonica*, Japan having been its original home before reaching Manilla. What might perhaps have escaped some of us is the somewhat indelicate detail given by Dumas *fils* in his book *La Dame aux Camélias*. It naturally concerns the corsage of his famous heroine Marguerite Gauthier. She was well known for always wearing white camellias, the perfectly formed *Alba plena*, and only during a few days of the month would the corsage change when the pure white flower was replaced by what was probably *Prince Eugène Napoléon*, a deep red variety – a somewhat brash, if not entirely off-putting warning to her rich admirers.

Few gardens down here are without their slender, columnar cypress; tapering spires of the *Cupressus sempervirens* from Italy but which really are not Italian at all, and come instead from the Greek archipelago, northern Persia, Silesia and Lebanon, only making their appearance in Provence some time during the sixteenth century. Their tall, compact shape lends itself admirably to reproduction, and they are to be seen as stylised plumes over half the frescoed wall and marble inlays of Persia and India. Occidental painters have also paid them homage, and amongst them Hubert Robert, Fragonard, and in quite a different mood, Arnold Böcklin. Macabrely concerned with death, Böcklin shows them reflected, rippling across the onyx stretches of water surrounding his much reproduced *Töten Insel*. They were also popular with both Edmond Dulac and Arthur Rackham who use them constantly in their fairytale illustrations; and how many times has one seen them slashed onto Van Gogh's canvases, a dance of black flames whipped by the mistral. As to more immaterial considerations, there seems to be some confusion. For the Greeks and the Romans they were definitely associated with Pluto, god of the underworld, and thus gradually over the years have become a plant related to death: and yet, their symbolic significance is not entirely negative, for there are cheerful overtones – they stand also for fidelity, immortality and the resurrection. In Provence, when planted near a house, it indicates the proximity of water and thus in the olden days stood as a mute welcome to travellers. There are also those who plant them at the birth of a child and believe them to signify prosperity. However, Comerford-Casey found quite the opposite, and writes that the peasants round Nice held them with superstitious dread. The Caseys had wanted to plant them at the end of their garden for shade, 'but the gardener, an honest and good hearted old man, begged me not to meddle with them. "You will suffer", he said, "if you plant a cypress". Thinking that he was afraid on his own account, I asked him to dig them up and bring them: I would plant them myself. I might as well have begged him to bring a tiger, and let it loose in the garden.'

Figs, as already mentioned in an earlier part of this book, are thought to have been introduced to the Riviera by the Phoenicians, and nowadays as many as sixteen different varieties can be counted in the neighbourhood of Nice alone: white figs, green, red, black and brown. The white fig, or *col de dame* as it is called locally, is supposed to have the strongest flavour and, according to Strasburger, was introduced by the Genoese from Syria at the time of the crusades. Figs have always been an important food source amongst the country people and rather naturally certain lores are associated with them. It is believed, for instance, that if you want to swell your fruit and ripen it more quickly, a prick with a straw dipped in olive-oil will accomplish it. Tough meat is made tender, they say, if cooked with their leaves. I haven't tried it, but I have quite often used one or two leaves when boiling potatoes, prior to making a purée. The leaves are removed before mashing, and they give the dish a subtle, unusual flavour.

As to the olives, nowhere do they grow better than down by the sea between Cannes and the Italian frontier. The further east one goes, the more splendid they become, reaching their full growth at about Menton. Inland they start appearing just south of Montélimar but remain puny and squat until one reaches the plains of Aix, where they reach perfection as far as concerns the quality of their oil, though even here they are about half the size of the trees growing down by the sea. Some specimens around us are known to be over a thousand years old, and until quite recently one of these millenarians stood on a corner of the main road passing through Beaulieu. It was a well known landmark and a silver chain bearing a plaque announced its venerability. But, alas, things are never allowed to remain as they are – a block of apartments sprang up behind the tree. The contractors were careful, but given the space they had to work in it was impossible not to cut through its roots. Olives can take a good deal of punishment, but being encased in concrete, on top of being mutilated, proved too much for this particular tree and it started to die. A special meeting was held and at considerable expense the municipality decided to move it. Olive roots are notoriously heavy, and this Beaulieu specimen weighed two and a half tons and called for expert handling. The transfer to the main square duly achieved, a young graft was inserted in its gnarled and hollow trunk, just below one of its twisted limbs – a precaution to ensure new life. As it happens, the tree stands just opposite my barber and I am sorry to report that it looks very sickly, though the graft is perfectly healthy. As a rule, olive roots are almost indestructible; felling them has little effect and burning seems only to encourage the growth, life goes underground sending up new shoots. What is more, there is no limit to the number of times this process can be repeated.

There are dozens of named varieties of olives, and by and large they are mostly centred around the Mediterranean, the Mediterranean countries being responsible for at least three-quarters of the world's oil production which, worked out in round figures, comes to something like a hundred thousand tons a year. First on the list of oil producing countries comes Spain, followed by Italy, Greece and Portugal and, some way down, the North African countries such as Tunisia, Algeria and Morocco. Flowering from April to June, the fruit takes about six months to ripen, becoming black, and falls from the trees between December and January. The fully ripened olive gives more oil, but the oil extracted from the green fruit is of much better quality. The drawback to this, however, is that the green fruit needs harvesting: a laborious process achieved with long poles and much beating, the olives being knocked onto hempen sheets spread under each tree. We used to do our own harvesting, a co-operative arrangement by which we delivered the olives and the mill furnished the oil. One could count on about one litre a tree, but the oil was of poor quality and the labour far too expensive to make it worth while in such small quantities. I speak, incidentally, as the owner of about twenty trees. Fewer and fewer properties down here bother these days with their oil; a pity really, for one has an instinctive respect for the olive: its oil was synonymous with well-being and was a commodity of vital importance to our history. Mr Standish in his book on the olive[3] argues very convincingly that civilisation attended the growing of this tree. Crete, we know, was growing them in about 3500 BC; her whole trade depended on oil, and what, one wonders, would Greece have done without them? Athens was ringed around with immense groves, some of them forty trees deep. Little else would grow on her dry, calcinarious soil. One remembers the olives stretched out below Delphi, lapping the mountains in a silver-green sea. It is rare, however, to see groves like this, for in most cases the trees are grown on terraces – the lie of the land, at least down here on the Riviera, making it impossible for them to be cultivated in any other way.

One last comment I would pass on the olive as regards to the respect it commands in the tree world. It is a rather remarkable fact that even today with the variety of vegetable oils there are on the market, laws still exist to protect them. It is not easy to obtain permission for building on land where they grow, and if it is a question of clearing it can only be undertaken by moving the trees and not cutting them.

We now come to a point that should probably be enlarged on. So far in this chapter, there have been few references to native-born naturalists. A French reader might well take exception, but as it happens it is pure chance that it has worked out this way and is not, I hasten to add, an intended act of chauvinism. Turn to the index of any accredited work, and it will be found that quite a few of the naturalists were natives. Brangham lists them all in his book; first come the Italian botanists from Genoa and Turin: C. Allioni who produced the three volume *Flora Pedemontana* published in 1785, and others like I.G. Molineri, the director of the botanic gardens at Turin whose important collection of specimens contributed to further works in this field. Later comes J.H. Perreymond and G. de Notaris, and Jean-Baptiste Barla with his *Iconographie des Orchidées des Alpes-Maritimes*. Barla was also director of the Natural History Museum at Nice, which is named after him and, together with the Niçois artist Fossat, is responsible for the intriguing collection of moulded and painted plaster models of fungi to be found growing in the environs of Nice. Brangham also cites E. Burnat's monumental seven volume edition of *Flore des Alpes-Maritimes*, published between 1892 and 1931, and a smaller more contemporary work by L. Marret. But of all these books by far the most impressive is Antoine Risso's *Histoire Naturelle des Oranges*. It was published between 1818 and 1822 and is dedicated to the Duchesse de Berry. What makes it so outstanding are its colour plates which were executed by A. Poiteau, *jardinier en chef* to the royal greenhouses at Versailles. The plates are magnificent, and I was fortunate enough to find a complete copy at Maggs while stationed in London during the war. One sometimes comes across single plates selling at exorbitant prices, but seldom the complete volume, which even today must be regarded as amongst the most authoritative works on the subject.

Born in 1777, Risso was a native of Nice and started out life as a pharmacist. When he died aged sixty-eight he had become the most respected of all native naturalists. This particular history – he wrote many others – does not concentrate solely on oranges, but takes in all fruits of the citrus species. However, reading the text, it is quite clear that Risso has a predilection for the golden apple of the Hesperides and refers, almost ecstatically, to the tree in his introduction, calls it 'the most beautiful embellishment of its kind to be found in the world', and points out all its obvious attractions. Touchingly he then pens his dedication to the young Duchess, a woman of extreme refinement with, as Risso points out, a *goût éclairé*. Romantically he hopes that she will enjoy it and that the plates will remind her of the fruit she once picked as a child in her native Italy. Few people I think, particularly amongst northerners, remain unmoved when first confronted with a fully grown orange tree. It has everything going for it, is compact in shape, with wonderfully vigorous, semi-glossy, evergreen vegetation, and shining amongst its leaves a luminous globe-like fruit. To top it all, it flowers and bears at the same time, its blossom producing an intoxicating bitter-sweet smell; 'trees', as Risso puts it, 'which flatter all senses'. I can always remember as a child the excitement at Christmas time of finding an orange wrapped in silver paper, nestling in the toe of my stocking. Too ordinary now to be considered a treat, since growers have so enormously increased the production, they nevertheless remain eminently seductive; as satisfying in shape as an egg, and when on a tree must surely delight everybody? One has only to remember the first lines of Goethe's *Mignon Lied*, lines which have expressed for all time the yearning of the northerner for sunny climes; 'Kennst du das land', it begins:

> Knowest thou the land where the pale citron grows,
> And the golden orange through dark foliage glows.

Risso, very thorough in his researches, delves into the tree's history and reminds us that the earliest mention of oranges appears in Greek mythology, in the labours of Hercules, the eleventh labour set him by Argos's king being the gathering of the golden fruit of the Hesperides. Both Ovid and Virgil agree to placing these gardens in North Africa's Atlas Mountains. More factual is Alexander the Great's account of having seen them growing in Media – in other words, the north-western part of Iran. From other sources we know that the Romans were cultivating them in pots by the first century AD but only the wild variety. Strasburger puts the cultivation of the sweet, edible orange, the *Citrus simensis*, at a much later date, it being supposed that the Portuguese brought them to Europe from southern China towards the middle of the sixteenth century. To bear out this theory he cites the fact that oranges in Italy are still commonly referred to as *portogallo*.

At least it would indicate that Portugal claimed an important part in their distribution, but was not necessarily the first to actually grow them. *Naranja*, from which the name orange derives, is, after all, an Arab word and it is more than likely that they appeared in Spain a good deal earlier than Strasburger would suggest. Columbus on his voyage of discovery in 1492 found them already well established in the Canary Islands, and on his second voyage dug up some young plants and shipped them with him, thus introducing them to the western hemisphere. Bernal Diaz, with Cortez in Mexico, mentions having seen them being planted in Central America.

Lemons, we know, first came to this coast towards the end of the eleventh century, brought by the crusaders from Syria and Palestine. The large yellow *pamplemousse*, inedible except when sweetened as jam, appeared at about the same time, and the last to make its appearance was the Vietnamese tangerine, or mandarin, the year of its arrival in Europe being given as 1828. In fact the grapefruit, or *pomelo*, appears to be the only citrus fruit not to have an Asian background, its home being the West Indies, probably the island of Jamaica. It is not a success on the Riviera: is it perhaps the nurseries' fault for not having propagated the right varieties?

All are agreed on the poor quality of the orange on the coast; Comerford-Casey goes so far as to find them fit only for blacking his boots, and indeed is not joking for he even includes the instructions. You simply cut the orange in two, blacken it on a sooty kettle and apply it. Afterwards a polish with a soft brush, and the toughest leather will shine beautifully!

Before the United States stepped into the picture the citrus fruit market was an important part of the economy of the Riviera, particularly lemons, which were centred on Menton. The fruit growers of Florida and California are now responsible for something like two million boxes of oranges a year, which has changed the balance of things considerably. Menton, however, still proudly styles herself '*le pays des citrons*' and each year gives a fête celebrating her orchards. The Jardin Biovès, or central square, opposite the casino, is entirely given over to display during the fête and is laid out in a series of parterres patterned with lemons. Pyramids of the fruit are piled high each side of the gravel paths while processional cars tour the town smothered in gleaming citrus yellow, their spokes revolving wheels of lemons; a costly display that must use several tons of fruit. Before the 1914–18 war, entire cargoes of lemons used to be loaded onto freighters anchored in Nice harbour, and it is no exaggeration to say that the whole of Europe drew its supply from Menton, the best of the fruit being sent to America. Now lemons come largely from Israel, Spain, Italy and North Africa, and Menton's plantations can count about ten per cent of the production. The disastrous frost of 1971 had a lot to do with this drop in the market. The young growers, starting out in business, were quite understandably nervous about sinking funds in a crop involving so much risk. Lemons are not an easy crop, and very time-consuming. The highest altitude at which they can grow is roughly 1500 feet and they are killed immediately by a slight variation of temperature, four degrees below freezing being the maximum cold they can stand. Added to this, constant spraying is necessary, and further to complicate matters the pests to which they are prone appear to be on the increase; the two most usual being the Argentine ant, another the red spider, both imported. The lemon is also a tree that demands steady watering – sixty gallons every two weeks in dry weather. The summer of 1970 was particularly dry, and the frost the following year, during the two days that it lasted, wiped out the entire crop. It will be seen then that Menton, as the papers put it, 'may well cease to be the lemon-growing region', and already the colouring of last year's fête had changed from bright yellow to a panache in which oranges played an important role.

Reading this might give a false impression to the ordinary gardener, for so long as they are not grown as a commercial enterprise, lemons are a very rewarding tree. It is only when cultivated in large quantities that risk is involved. Providing one has a sheltered spot in the garden, with a southern exposure, there should be no problem. It is the only tree that I can think of that bears its fruit and its blossoms all the year round thus offering a constant supply to the kitchen. As to oranges, they are a much tougher tree and can stand several degrees more of frost. Like most fruit-bearing trees, they have only one crop a year, and unlike the lemon – which should only be picked when the fruit has turned really yellow – their colour is no indication as to their ripeness. They start turning red in December, can be picked for shipping in January, but are not really sweet before April, or even May. Some will tell you that they can be left on the tree for eighteen months, or two years and, according to one informant, are very much improved by the process. In this case they dry out in May and June when the hot weather begins and regain their sweetness again in October, after the rains, when apparently they are at their best. It is rare that the gardener can wait this long, since invariably some mighty gust sends them tumbling to the ground.

Another point to be remembered by the Riviera gardener is the fact that the citrus family are by far the most rewarding and supply the only fruit that will grow satisfactorily down by the sea. Apples, pears, cherries, peaches and almonds seem to thrive much better at an elevation of about two thousand feet; in fact, they don't appreciate the mild winter climate of the shore regions.

Gardens on the Riviera

So much then for the botanists. What of the first gardeners? Bennet was a good botanist but not much is known about his garden. At Cannes, following Lord Brougham, came Thomas Robinson Woolfield, a rich, much travelled Englishman with a mania for building. He first bought the Château St Georges, built by Sir Hubert Taylor, a friend of Brougham's. Tiring of it, Woolfield went ahead with the plans for a Gothic fantasy which he named the Château des Tours. This he sold to the Duc de Vallombrosa who added still more crenellations. His most successful venture proved the Villa Victoria, the house in which he died and which still stands more or less as he designed it; a charming Tudor pastiche with Victorian pitched roofs framed in elaborate barge-boarding. Woolfield's real pride, however, was its garden. A serious horticulturist, he was the first to start experimenting with plants from other countries. The Royal Botanic Gardens in Sydney sent him seeds of the *Eucalyptus globulus*, and in 1862 he managed to rear two magnificent specimens of the *Acacia dealbata* (or silver-leafed mimosa). The pretty blue and white woolly flower of the *Salvia eriocalyx* was another of his importations, the ordinary gooseberry yet another, also sweet potatoes from Jamaica. Originally the property, like Brougham's, his neighbour, ran right down to the sea, until the Marseilles to Nice railway appropriated a strip, paying Woolfield a pittance in compensation, 'not even enough to defray the expense of the bridge I had to build to secure access to the shore'.[1] It was on this land that Woolfield laid out the well-known croquet ground '. . . the source of so much pleasure and amusement to such numberless people', so many that later their host felt obliged to set aside one day a week for royalty.

Incidentally, while laying out the grounds of Villa Victoria an immense quantity of human remains were found, buried simply amongst the dunes down by the shore. Upwards of some hundred skeletons were

collected 'and only some four or five buried in coffins'. It transpired that
they were conscripts

> who had been ordered to the front by the first Napoleon, to replenish
> his army after the heavy losses sustained at the Battle of Marengo.
> They had marched from Toulon in the great heat, and, on arrival at
> Cannes, were crowded into the parish church as a hospital, too
> exhausted to continue their journey. A fever broke out amongst
> them, and they were hastily buried in the sands!

Woolfield must also have been the first gardener on the Riviera to
contribute regularly to serious horticultural magazines. He would note
the list of shrubs in flower during the winter months; many of them
considered rare plants in England and grown with difficulty in a hothouse. The subscribers' mouths must have watered at his descriptions
of creepers trained over 'pyramid forms to the height of fifteen feet'.
There were tea roses 'with blooms measuring from five to six and even
seven inches in diameter, and as double as a Camellia'. He was also
noted for his splendid bougainvilia.

Woolfield appears to have been a man of indefatigable energy.
We next hear of him developing his waste land. Dividing it up into
saleable lots, he laid out 'a series of gardens and made each one so
attractive, purchasers soon came forward, and the beautiful houses we
all know so well were speedily built, forming a most desirable coterie of
neighbours and friends'.

There are descriptions of the Duchess of Luynes's garden with not a
leaf out of place, and in contrast to this the Château Leader, part
jasmin farm, part semi-wild – a rambling redolent garden 'of a truly
Provençal neglect'. Vallombrosa appears to have worked on his garden
as well as on the crenellations of Woolfield's original house. Miss
Dempster, the author of *Vera*, a popular Victorian novel of the eighties,
is most impressed with her visits. She has trouble deciding which aspect
of the garden pleases the most – 'its gorgeous flower-beds on a May
morning, or its appearance by lamplight'. She describes palms thrown
in fantastic shadows on the lawns, fountains lifting in the moonlight and
roses flinging themselves from tree to tree. Dancing among the ropes of
flowers she imagines 'elves of some *Midsummer Night's Dream*'. On the
outskirts of Cannes, at La Californie, comes the Camille Dognin garden
and Baron Haussmann's terraces overhanging the Villefranche road.
Above Nice are the terraced gardens of the Villa Arson where Talleyrand

stayed and where Lord Lytton wrote one of his books, but the gardens don't appear to have been particularly interesting. Miss Brewster describes them as they were in the mid-nineteenth century. The villa at the time belonged to a Doctor Arnulfi, a homeopathic doctor who had married one of his rich and titled patients, and the gardens sound typically Italian – long walks lined with statues, grottoes and stair-cases. What intrigued people were the blue camellias; 'one of the fashion-able sights of the fashionable world of Nice', but Miss Brewster, a sensible Scot, is not impressed: 'probably fed with iron', she scoffs. She is also disapproving of the chained eagle she found 'under the vine walk – an incongruous abode'.[2]

There must have been several gardens after the style of Villa Arson, but this is not exactly one's interest here: rather one wants to con-centrate on the men responsible for the coast's exotic character, a character heightened by the importation of foreign plants, the different species of palms, *Agaves* and *Opuntias*, or prickly pears which have acclimatised so well as to appear indigenous, and escaping from the gardens lend the landscape an air of belonging elsewhere. The good nurseries were Charles Huber at Hyères and Narbonnard at Golf Juan, while the interesting citrus fruits – species like the bergamot – came from M. Sahuts at Montpellier. The most influential of these horti-culturists to succeed Woolfield was, undoubtedly, the diplomat-botanist Gustave Thuret. Buying an extensive acreage in the centre of the Cap d'Antibes, he built himself a house and round it laid out what George Sand describes as the most beautiful garden she had ever seen in her life. She wrote this in 1868, and her visit occurred twelve years after Thuret had started landscaping his arboretum. The site is perfect, the land sloping gently towards Golf Juan. In the foreground, furnish-ing the sea, comes the Iles de Lérins, and, beyond, the Esterel. Seen on a fine winter's morning, the mountains stand an opalescent, ragged outline on the horizon, and glimpsed through the fronds of Mr Thuret's exotic importations one might almost imagine oneself to be on some island in the Pacific. In George Sand's day, the villa one sees now did not exist. The house was small and 'hidden under a thicket of begonias and jasmine'. Enchanted by the atmosphere, she is nevertheless apprehensive about the future. What will happen, she asks, when the palms, the acacias and eucalyptus are fully grown? In a few years she visualises them hiding the sea and, later, the Alps. And yet, if one cuts too drastically to free the horizon, the trees will lose their '*divins hazards de mouvement'* and the place will become just a handsome botanical garden. Her intuitions were quite right, of course, at least about that part of the property that has been allowed to attain its maturity. At Thuret's death his sister-in-law left the estate to the nation with an endowment for its upkeep, and it has now become the Recherche Agronomique de Provence, its laboratories doing very useful work in various branches of horticulture, including the study of semi-tropical shrubs and trees with a view to furthering their propagation.

Wandering round the original garden is a nostalgic experience; one relives a period as old as the trees. There are sixty species of eucalyptus and amongst them descendants of those grown in the greenhouses at Malmaison and brought back by Ramel, its director, from Melbourne in 1856. Thrown against these giants with their peeling bark are the glaucous fronds of the *Juboea spectabilis*, a majestic Chilean palm displaying a smooth trunk, the ash-grey of an elephant. The collection is surprisingly varied and includes the *Brahea dulcis* from Mexico and several varieties of *Callistemon*, the Australian bottle brush, also from the Antipodes the *Livistona australis*, a new palm in Thuret's day and sent to him by the Jardin des Plantes in Paris. But the most exotic, if only for its associations, is the *Quillaja*, or soap bark tree, again from Chile. As its name suggests, the inner skin produces a fine lather which was discovered to be a splendid detergent for delicate fabrics. No doubt it was first employed by the Indians, and is now much in demand by archaeologists who use it when treating the more fragile of Peru's woven mummy wrappings.

La Mortola, the other famous garden down here, is just over the border on the Italian side of the Riviera. This does not stop it, however, from being included in this book for it belongs, quite legitimately, to the history of Côte d'Azur gardening. It was founded in 1867 by Sir Thomas Hanbury, a successful tea merchant from Shanghai. Sir Thomas had always dreamed of making a garden in a southern climate, and it was while on long leave in Menton that he discovered the promontory of La Mortola, a small peninsula almost astride the Franco-Italian frontier. The property had belonged to the Orengos, an old family from Genoa, and consisted of a dilapidated palazzo and about a hundred acres of land. The situation was ideal, fronted by sea and spreading gently upwards to a height of three hundred feet. Originally Sir Thomas had wanted to settle on Cap Martin, at that time almost completely uninhabited, but it hadn't the climatic appeal of the rocky, sea-washed point at La Mortola. When first acquired no garden to speak of existed – a few tilting terraces reached by crumbling stairs leading to nothing, and, away from the house, dark thickets of myrtle to which La Punta della Mortola probably owes its name, *mirto* or *mortella* being the Italian for myrtle. Sir Thomas was in his early forties when he started in earnest on the garden, and with him as partner came Daniel, his younger brother, who played an important part in the plant collecting. Daniel Hanbury knew the country well already, had made several sketching expeditions in the district, and was a serious scientific researcher in botany. Medicinal plants were his main interest and these formed the nucleus of the original collection, later to be added to by a wealth of exotic trees and shrubs. Augustus Hare, in his *The Rivieras*,[3] refers to La Mortola as the most important private garden in Europe and finds it 'more beautiful than anything out of the *Arabian Nights*', and indeed, at their height the gardens must have been a remarkable sight. They still are worth a visit, but no garden is ever quite the same when the person who planned it is no longer there to watch over it. A creative gardener might take risks that a well-trained horticulturist would never dare. Tidiness takes the place of an ordered muddle and the result is not at all the same. Sir Thomas died in 1907 and in the interim various members of the family have had a hand in running the property. One useful thing accomplished was the publication of an alphabetical catalogue naming all the plants. Lady Hanbury wrote the introduction, and Mr Berger, one of the curators, supplied the preface. Reading *Hortus Mortolensis* one realises that hardly a moment passed when La Mortola gardens were not in flower. September was the dullest month, and spring a crescendo, the flowering beginning and continuing on an ever-increasing scale until the middle of April, or the first part of May. Berger mentions the lovely single Banksian rose, the deep yellow variety, and the blue spikes of the Canarian *Echium*; *Pittosporum toberia* floods the place with its sweet-scented blossoms: all three plants common enough nowadays but for which Sir Thomas was, no doubt, originally responsible. La Mortola happens to have a small deposit of sandy soil and in it grow certain of South Africa's handsome *Proteaceae*. I have never seen them anywhere else on this coast and quite a few people I know have tried to grow them, but never with any success. In May the *Mesembryanthemums*, another Cape importation, begin to flower, also the *Opuntias* or prickly pears introduced from the Americas along with the *Agaves* during the sixteenth century. Closely related to the *Agaves* is the *Fourcroya longaeva* which, according to the Mexicans, flowers only once in four hundred years. Strasburger mentions it among the plants he found growing in the Mortola Gardens, but I have to admit I haven't as yet been able to track it down. The ordinary glaucous, or variegated Agave grow in great clumps all over the property and these, as we all know, take about ten to fifteen years to flower, and after a superhuman effort of producing what looks like a miniature fir-tree, crumples up and dies. Norman Douglas had a special affection for these spiky vegetable giants, and with considerable agitation describes a greyish-green, almost blue 'wonder' that he found growing on the hillside near his hotel. Drawn as if by a magnet, he returns day after day 'to drink deep draughts of contentment from its exquisite lines'. He finds it 'a prodigy of good style, more pleasing to the eye than all that generated tropicality of Mr Hanbury's Mortola paradise'. I see the attraction but personally find the writhing, metallic leaves barbed with merciless spines a trifle sinister. The botanist responsible for first recording them in the New World must have had much the same reaction. Witness the name – Agave, after the Theban Agave who, in orgiastic frenzy, tore to pieces her own son.

When visiting these early gardens, it is well to remember the change of habit regarding the seasons. When La Mortola was laid out, the idea of spending July and August on the Riviera was quite out of the question. Spring and autumn were the popular seasons, preferably spring. Like all the English, the Hanburys spent their summers in England and the gardens, along with the house, were put away, disappeared as it were under dust sheets. Heavy and clayey, the soil hardened and cracked, lawns were dug up and neat little circular trenches were hoed round each tree in preparation for the droughts. Into these, half-naked gardeners would spill the water, splashing it from zinc cans that had been filled from a tank. Even the gravel paths vanished, were scraped to one side ready for autumn when again one would be awakened by the soothing noise of a rake busy effacing any possible footprint. Today the opposite is almost the case, and it is during the long winter months that the Riviera gardens are apt to take on an abandoned air, waiting the spring before they are fed, pruned and clipped in preparation for the gaudy months of midsummer heat. As it happens, these changes do not really affect either the Villa Thuret or the La Mortola gardens: both are sufficiently stocked with rare specimens to warrant a visit at any time of the year. It is reasonable to suppose that what is left of the Villa Thuret garden will be carefully tended, while La Mortola was purchased from the Hanburys by the Italian state in 1969 and is being gradually restocked. But whatever their fate, these gardens have played an important role in helping other horticulturists along the coast. As for Sir Robert, he is remembered as an exceptionally altruistic man. In gratitude for his years at La Mortola, he founded the Botanical Institute at the University of Genoa, inaugurated in 1892, and what must appeal in a more personal way to all garden lovers is the fact that he is responsible for two of the best natural history books to have been published on this part of the world; one Comerford-Casey's *Riviera Nature Notes*, which Sir Thomas subsidised, and the other Edward Strasburger's *Rambles on the Riviera* which Sir Thomas suggested the Caseys translate from the German. I have quoted frequently from both of these works, and they have added considerably to my own enjoyment of the country they so ably describe.

The other important botanical garden on the Riviera is M. Marnier-Lapostolle's Villa les Cèdres at St Jean Cap-Ferrat. The villa is a large block of a house built in the usual Italianate style popular at the end of the nineteenth century. It belonged originally to King Leopold I of the Belgians, and sits on about fifteen hectares of land. Seen from the road, one would be apt to shrug it away as just another of those white elephants in which the coast abounds. One would be wrong, however, for in its wandering, park-like grounds is to be found the most complete collection of *Bromeliads* in the world, while its assembly of cacti, massed together in slatted, semi-open or glassed-in houses, is probably without peer in Europe and infinitely richer in species than the Jardin Exotique in Monaco. The garden hasn't the romantic turn of the century appeal of La Mortola, but is more rewarding, as far as concerns the variety of plants. Arranged in rock-strewn beds are to be found most of the different *Sempervivums* and an infinite variety of *Mesembryanthemums*, whole forests of bamboo and, of course, an almost exhaustive massing of *Acacia*. Les Cèdres is certainly the only garden down here to produce a night blooming *Cereus*, that rare South American succulent that few people have had the luck to catch at the moment of blooming. High growing with elongated, columnar stems, the chalice-like flowers burst open in fragrant splendour, but only under the moon. Another unexpected sight are the massive clumps of *Nelumbo indica*, or lotus, and, glimpsed through these, riding the mirror-like surface of an extensive pool, come the saucer-like leaves of the great *Victoria amazonica* – that giant water-lily which was first made to flower this side of the Atlantic in the greenhouse at Chatsworth. Paxton, the architect of the Crystal Palace, was at the time the bachelor Duke of Devonshire's head gardener, and he coaxed the lily to flower by the addition of a small wheel which churned up the water. The plant had not responded in a still pond and Paxton, wishing to approximate the flow of the Amazon, had thought of the wheel. The trick worked, but at what point, one wonders, did the capricious plant acclimatise to a sluggish habitat, for there is no question these days of churning water.

M. Marnier-Lapostolle employs twenty-seven gardeners at Les Cèdres, and René Hebding, its curator, has shown me around the grounds on several occasions, and each time I come away feeling I have travelled thousands of miles.

There are two distinct kinds of garden on the Riviera: the purely botanical, and the horticultural, and amongst the horticultural there are not as many as one might suppose, considering the climate and the opportunities.

Mrs Warre's Villa Roquebrune at Cap Martin must come high on the list as far as concerns the variety of plants. Like La Mortola, its near neighbour, it slopes up from the sea and faces due south and enjoys an almost total immunity from the prevailing winds. In the spring it is a mass of colour, and of late has been cleverly photographed in colour for the Royal Horticultural Society's journal. Accompanying the plates is an article written by Mr Basil Leng, himself an excellent Riviera gardener. La Serre de la Madone in the Gorbio valley behind Menton used to be another of the South of France's show places, and I am purposely using the past tense, for since Mr Johnson's death it has never been the same. Hidcote, in England, was another of his creations and those familiar with the gardens will readily understand the charm La Serre might have had. Another fascinating garden is the Baronne van der Elst's Haut de St Julien above the village of Biot. A spur of the Alps descends here towards the sea and on the very top the Baroness has laid out her massed groupings. The house was originally surrounded by a fine stand of cork trees, but these were largely destroyed about four years ago by one of the fires which are the bane of the country. The whole topography was changed, and taking advantage of the sweeping views thus opened up the Baroness completely altered the character of the garden. Plants are kept low and subtle swirls of colour lap the whitish-grey rocks. Drifts of white and pink cistus and whole rivers of wild thyme are incorporated with sophisticated plants ordered from the English nurseries. The result is most impressive and very pleasing.

Perhaps the ideal garden down here is the Vicomte de Noaille's Villa Noailles at Grasse. I can think of no other that can compare with it in taste and ability of planning. Not only does the Vicomte have impeccable taste, but he is blessed also with an exceptionally developed visual memory. There are few gardens he hasn't seen and as vice-president of the Royal Horticultural Society is always being asked to organise visits to gardens his fellows are not familiar with. Notebook in hand, he has wandered over most of Europe, America and the Far East. The eye is lively and not without a certain puckish humour. One year his Christmas card carried a coloured print of the sinister *Mandragora officinarum*, or screaming mandrake, which he had carefully nurtured, cringing amongst some rocks.

The Grasse garden is a series of surprises; round the house one is closed in by clipped box hedges forming a dark background for lichenous statues; everywhere there are pools and fountains, for M. de Noailles is lucky enough to have springs on the property. Water gurgles and splashes from moss-encrusted spouts in a wall, or then pours, in serpentine fashion, down a column placed at the end of a bed massed with tree peonies and framed in a wall-like hedge of yew. One terrace further up a pergola formed by Judas trees shades a long walk carpeted with the marbleised leaves of dwarf cyclamen. The bloom of the Judas tree has the habit of appearing before the leaves and clusters on the bare branches, particularly effective in this case since they have been planted in patches of colour, one white to every three red, making a delicious candy-striped effect.

Following the contours of the hill on which the property stands, one is led away from the house. Steps connect with the terraces, and each terrace marks a change. Away at the bottom, in the spring, foams a pale watery-pink collection of double flowering cherries, and in amongst them flash a family of homing budgerigars.

Madame Champin's garden, the Chèvre d'Or at Biot, is another attractive garden, and last but not least comes M. Arpad Plesch's La Léonina at Beaulieu. It belongs by rights in the botanical category of gardens and specialises in tropical fruits which are served on a brimming platter at the end of a meal – an exotic surfeit, for without any doubt the Plesches can claim to far the best cuisine of any private house on the Riviera. The property sits in what is locally known as *la petite Afrique*, a narrow strip of land running parallel to the shore and backed by a high limestone wall of mountain. The close proximity of stone catching the sun gives the extra warmth, making it easy to grow things that would be impossible anywhere else along the coast. Amongst a plethora of the different avocado Mr Plesch can produce soft fleshed custard apples, small finger bananas, and I even think he has managed to ripen a papaya. But the real glory of La Léonina is not so much the plants but Mr Plesch's collection of coloured-plate books, one of the most complete botanical libraries of rare editions to be found anywhere in the world.

Another aspect of horticulture on the Riviera is the cut-flower industry. The Alpes Maritimes and the Var between them make a turnover of three hundred and eighty million francs a year, roughly thirty-eight million pounds sterling – an impressive figure. The bulk of this is largely export trade, Germany and Great Britain being the most important buyers. The growers, however, complain that the market could be far better exploited, particularly when it comes to home consumption. The figures on this are surprisingly low, statistics showing that only thirty per cent of the general public can be relied on to buy flowers every month, and not necessarily in any great quantity. True that many have gardens, but even so, one would have thought that the flower markets, piled high with carnations, bunched in every conceivable colour, would have had a more magnetic attraction. We know that the French have relegated the chrysanthemum to their cemeteries, but surely the carnation is free of taint? Apparently not: they, too, appear to have some superstition attached to them. They mustn't be brought into the house and it's preferred that they should not grace one's table in a restaurant. How can one explain such absurd beliefs? Whatever the reason, enough are still in demand and the industry is important enough to command special transport. Planes take off daily for Paris, their hulls crammed with nothing but tightly packed boxes, while the railway runs what are known as the 'flower trains'. Car after car clatters through the night with their scented cargoes destined for the major ports, and places like Lille, Brussels and Strasbourg. Interesting also is the fact that carnations are by no means an especially new trade to the coast. Smollett mentions them way back in the seventeen-sixties and tells us that they were sent as far afield as London 'packed up in wooden boxes without any sort of preparation, one pressed upon another'. On reception they were steeped in water laced with vinegar and were good, so Smollett claims, for the best part of a month. —

Smollett was fairly accurate in his information, and it is possible that there were those who dealt in this form of exportation; it could not, however, have been a very important part of the country's commerce, for the first thing that struck Alphonse Karr, the nineteenth-century boulevardier journalist, on his arriving in Nice, was its lack of flowers. Fashionable, semi-retired from the writing world, Karr set about to remedy the situation, and hiring himself a garden in the *quartier St Philippe*, ordered a quantity of plants and seeds, concentrating on roses and carnations. A year later he opened a shop in the public gardens under his name, styling himself 'gardener' *tout court*. He became quite a figure, wore his hair *en brosse* with a moustache and pointed beard, and was always impeccably dressed – black velvet during the winter and nankeen for the warm weather. On fine mornings he would be met strolling down the *Promenade des Anglais* accompanied by his black labrador, Frieschutz. Behind him at a respectable distance trailed his mulatto servant, dressed in bright red. When receiving at night he did so garbed as a Turk – not really one's idea of someone seriously tilling the soil! —

Coming from the bustle of Paris, Karr settled quite happily in Nice. In the end it got too noisy for him and in 1864, leaving his black-draped flat with violet glass in the Rue Vivienne, he moved to St Raphaël. 'Come plant your walking stick in my garden,' he writes to a friend in Paris, 'the next day when you awake you will find that it has sprouted roses.' The house he named Maison Close, a hint, one presumes, for prospective callers.

Another aspect of the country that interested Karr were the scent factories of Grasse. When describing the coast, he makes a comparison: 'Other regions demand that the earth should satisfy the common appetite for food; but here the concern is for flowers and perfumes'. He is quite right, and it is impossible when writing about gardens not to include 'the city of perfumes'; the whole countryside is planted with smells that will be distilled by the factories. Drive up to Grasse in May and the air is heady with the scent of jasmin. There are fields and hedges of roses, the old-fashioned musk rose grown for its attar. Cutting across these heady smells comes the stringent, bitter-sweet fragrance of the *bigaradiers*, one of the bitter oranges. The scent factories prefer the bitter orange to the edible one; the extract from their blossoms is stronger and when distilled appears as an oily substance known to the trade as *néroli*, incidentally named after a *settecento* Italian duchess – Flavia Orsini, Princess of Néroli. This *néroli* is the basic ingredient of ordinary eau de cologne, and Grasse exports it by the ton to the Rhine.

Several flower scents are important to the manufacture of perfume, the first on the list to bloom being the single white hyacinth. Violets are another, and are planted in shade, very often under the orange trees. Yellow jonquil are also used, tuberoses and lavender, several varieties of it. Walking through the streets of the town is like being immersed in an enormous bowl of pot-pourri: the whole place is steeped in the fragrance that comes in wafts from the different factories, an amalgam of smells that stays with one for an hour or so after leaving the place. It comes as no surprise to learn that the pickers, when working among the oranges, are often made sick by the overpowering force of the smell.

While walking round the scent factories, they show you the different processes of extraction, the most interesting being what they call *enfleurage*. Purified animal fat is spread in thin layers on glass trays and onto this, their petals well opened by practised hands, the flowers are laid. The extraction is a question of time, fresh flowers replacing the exhausted ones. When saturation point is reached the fat is changed, and so it goes on through the flowering season. As can be imagined the pure concentrated pomade is worth a fortune. Should one be curious one can discover all kinds of things stored away in thin plywood boxes, or crammed into glass-topped jars: powdered orris root and the yellow, dried leaf of an East Indian grass known as *vetivert*, patchouli from Malaya and rhizomes of ginger, seeds of bitter almond, bark of cinnamon and cassia, cloves, ylang-ylang and the different resedas. The animal ingredients used in mixing scent are almost as numerous as the vegetable ones; glandular secretions from civet cats and musk from Himalayan deer, the best quality coming from Tibet. Ambergris is another intriguing product, an unlikely touchstone for lively imaginations. Grey-black and fatty, it is a biliary concretion sicked up by the sperm whale and is generally found floating at sea in the middle of nowhere or then washed up on some beach, the lucky finder being guided to its whereabouts by its peculiar, sweet, earthy odour, not particularly pleasant until diluted in one of the blends in which it is to be used. The largest piece ever found weighed 248 lbs, and was valued at £13,000. The role it plays in the olfactory world is a strange one: it not only adds an exotic flavour to scent but in some subtle way also intensifies and refines the bouquet, acting at the same time as a fixative. Patou has a scent called *Joy* which until recently they advertised as the most expensive scent in the world. Now it has been superseded by another distillation from the same house, which is even more expensive and appropriately known as *1000*. Not only is it way beyond most people's price range, but has the added cachet of being all but unobtainable – no advertising is involved and it is sold only by order! Needless to say, both scents have an unusually high ambergris content.

Grasse's history as the centre of the perfume trade goes back to the sixteenth century, and the first traceable name of importance would appear to be that of the king's physician and *parfumeur de la Reine*: Doria dei Roberti from Florence. For years one of its great specialities were its perfumed gloves, as famous in their day as Cordova's stamped leather. Langier, perfumer to Louis XVI, was also a resident of Grasse and lived in a house which is now the Hôtel de la Poste. Dating from about the same period, the second half of the eighteenth century, comes eau de cologne, and although, as its name suggests, not actually distilled in Grasse, most of the ingredients came from there. *Eau de la Reine de Hongrie*, or Hungarian Water, was the popular toilet product in use up until about 1750 when Johan Maria Farina, an Italian from Santa Maria Maggiore, near Domodossola, came forward with the new eau de cologne, a formula using *néroli* to which rosemary oil and a trace of peppermint had been added. The Seven Years War was in progress at the time, and the French held the Rhine provinces and it was they, it would seem, who were chiefly instrumental in making it so popular.

❧20

Lord Brougham's Cannes

Some way back we left Lord Brougham in Cannes, in the grounds of the future Villa Eleanor Louise. Finished in 1838, he spent the first sad winter of '39, after his daughter's death, moving in, and for the next thirty years few letters or diaries describing this part of the world are without mention of England's eccentric minister. Brougham was a curiosity, almost as well known in Paris as he was in London. Many of his contemporaries thought him a little deranged; a few, including the Duke of Wellington, admired him extravagantly, the Princess Lieven, going to the other extreme, pronounced him 'perfectly mad' but at the same time admitted his 'extraordinary mind'. His friends found him kind, warm-hearted even, while others are put off by his appearance. Augustus Hare, known for his acrimonious pen, found him 'repulsive and excessively dirty in his habits' and repeats the well-known story about the Prince Regent roaring at him at the Beefsteak Club, ordering him to go and wash his hands. The story is probably true, for Princess Lieven writing from Paris in 1850 complains that 'Lord Brougham spent two nights in the city, was clean and so calm that it quite upset me. I miss the old Brougham'. Reading all the accounts, one gets a picture of a gaunt, ungainly figure, stooping already by the time he started spending his winters in Cannes. Old fashioned in appearance, he invariably wore plaid trousers, with a high stock: in fact, was so fond of his checks that he had bought enough of the material to last him a lifetime. Hare remembers him cursing at his poor sister-in-law 'in the most horrible language before all his guests', and adds that 'if annoyed with people at table he would throw his napkin in their faces'. Prosper Mérimée, also wintering in Cannes, leaves us a picture of Brougham as being in 'an extraordinary state of preservation for a young man of 84', but a few months later finds him terribly changed. His memory had gone 'and being very deaf he can't even hear his own voice shouting and then whispering so that one could hear nothing'. He also had a habit of dispensing with his false teeth which could not have helped matters.

But these are memories of Brougham as an old man. Miss Brewster gives us quite a different impression after her visit in 1856, and reading her one feels that one would have liked this strange character. The villa, anyhow, sounds charming, light and airy 'with its graceful pillars and balustrades, and vases of bright flowers'. 'Strangers', she adds, 'still have considerable facility of access to the library, but not so much as formerly, owing to the books having been carelessly used.'[1] One mustn't forget that, when first attracted to Cannes, Brougham was barely past his middle age and still very energetic. As proof that he had not yet lost his extraordinary grip of things, his first act on taking up residence in the villa was to petition the king for a grant of money to help improve the port of the town. On intimate terms with Louis-Philippe, he could cut through the red tape and address him directly, pointing out the advantages of such a move. All the produce, not only of Cannes but also the far more considerable exports from Grasse, were consigned by carts and wagons to Marseille. No merchant vessel, however small its tonnage, could load or discharge at Cannes – there was not even a jetty. Brougham's proposition was perfectly straightforward: the west side of the small bay on which the town is situated ended in a reef, and it was these rocks that he suggested be incorporated into a wall. Not only would it provide a protected anchorage, but at the same time supply convenient access. It was admitted that the lie of the land favoured Brougham's argument and forthwith engineers were ordered south to report to the government. The result was a vote of two million francs and a marked improvement in the position Cannes could command on the coast. Within two years it had become the third most important centre of trade in the Mediterranean, Marseille and Sète alone superseding her. Brougham was entirely responsible, and in gratitude, after the overthrow of Louis-Philippe, the new government approached Brougham suggesting he should stand as deputy for the *département* of the Var. Delighted, Brougham immediately applied for French citizenship but withdrew the demand on learning that he would be obliged to renounce his British nationality to obtain it.

The Villa Eleanor Louise stood on the heights of the Croix de Garde, a little out of Cannes, and Brougham, writing home, describes the delights of the climate to his friends shivering in England. The skies are clear, 'there are refreshing breezes' and before them 'stretches the deep blue waters of the Mediterranean'. Orange groves and cassia plantations perfume the air 'and the forests behind, crowded with pines and ever-green oaks' reach right up to the Alps; a wall of 'eternal granite' which protects them from the cold north winds, 'but tempers the heat which often, even in March, becomes oppressive'.[2]

When Brougham first settled in the villa, wolves would come down and carry off his poultry, but this was not a condition that lasted for long. Within a few years the hills around were sprinkled with villas which Miss Gordon likened to 'pretty, fairy-tale castles' and Prosper Mérimée compares to 'tawdry paper flowers in a parterre'. The English, he feels, should be punished for importing such dreadful architecture. George Sand, writing at about the same time, also complains of the amount of building that is going on and is even harsher on the poor English. For her they have simply ruined the country with their 'odious follies'. How times have changed! One can hardly agree with her about the houses today: in fact, they should really be photographed before what is left of them disappears altogether. Autoroutes now march through their once extensive grounds, isolating their Gothicised lodges in an incongruous stream of traffic. For the most part the houses have been turned into flats and obviously don't have long to wait before the bulldozers crash into their solidly built walls. 'They are not economic' is the cry, and to tell the truth, the despoiling has gone so far that it seems rather pointless to worry about what happens to them any more.

I do, however, sympathise with George Sand about the social life; one is suffocated by it. What would her reactions be today? At least her 'oiseaux exotiques', as she calls them had style. Edward Lear, an habitué, mentions a few in one of his letters and the list is reassuring: Lord Londesborough and Lady Oxford, the Duke of Buccleuch, Lord and Lady Scott, Lord Mt Edgcumbe, Lady Houghton, Bradford, Limerick, Dalhousie, etc. Even more reassuring, if one has a mind for this kind of snobbery, was the arrival of no less than twenty-five Eton boys, a group that had formed for the holidays.

Lear was still in his twenties when he left England, a self-imposed exile brought about by his health which was never robust. The first years were spent in Rome, where he earned a good living as a drawing master. Short visits to England were to follow, interspersed with protracted stays in Nice, Malta, Egypt and Cannes. While in Nice he rented a ground floor flat on the Promenade des Anglais which he shared with his faithful Greek servant, Giorgio Kokali. In a typically whimsical letter to Fortescue, the future Lord Carlingford, he likens the place to St Leonards. 'The sea', he adds, 'is rather deadly stupid, and there is no opposite coast nor islands, nor ships nor nothing.' Menton also comes in for some ribbing: he finds it pretty but 'too shut in and befizzled a place for me'. The Via Longa depressed him. Hyères and St Tropez both are 'bosh'. At Cannes, at least, he has some success with his painting. Fortescue, writing to him during his Cannes period, complains of the faintness of the ink in his letters and Lear excuses it, putting it down to the dryness. 'When little children cry, they cry dust and not tears.' Clouds billow out behind every carriage, and Lear with his poor eyesight is much bothered by it, also 'the glare of white, hot roads and houses, and a sun of Bengal heat, though the air is bitterly cold in the shade'. He goes to church, though not often 'on account of the crush of carriages'. In another letter he tells of the lack of amusements, 'people who come to Cannes must live absolutely to themselves, a real country life and make excursions to the beautiful places about'. But in spite of the excursions, the place soon palls on him and in a letter dated July 1870 to Lady Waldegrave, he announces his renunciation of the coast. He finally leaves Cannes 'and the pigeon-shooting, swell community thereof' for San Remo, living first in his beloved Villa Emily and later moving to Villa Tennyson because they had ruined his view by building in front of him. He was seventy-six when he died, and going through his papers afterwards they found over ten thousand water-colours, sketches, on which he had noted additional details meaning one day to work them up into finished pictures – sketches, incidentally, which nowadays fetch anything from four to eight hundred pounds.

Miss Brewster's letters are another source of amusement and give pleasant glimpses of life on the coast during the latter part of the nineteenth century. When in Cannes, she stayed not far from Château de la Bocca, belonging to a Mr Sym, an English clergyman and a prominent figure in the social scene. She describes her villa as being the last house before the Esterel, and reminds her readers of the dangers inherent in these red and green porphyry mountains. Even in her day 'travellers were recommended not to cross them after dark'. But as far as Miss Brewster is concerned, she writes 'that they have excellent protection close at hand', a station of coastguards patrolling in front of the villa windows. She then explains how she felt like 'the little child that was crying for fear one night and was told by its nurse not to be so afraid, that its guardian angel was quite near. "Oh but", it sobbed, "it's my guardian angel that I'm so frightened of" '. In the end Miss Brewster's angels 'muffled in blue great coats and shouldering their *carabines* seemed rather nice sort of people, and lived in picturesque little huts on the rocks close to our gate'.

If one is to believe Miss Brewster, George Sand's scathing criticism of the English is somewhat exaggerated: the coast had not been entirely ruined. Miss Brewster finds plenty of local colour and describes the washerwomen 'kneeling by the hundreds wherever there are tanks, or little ponds, or fresh water rivulets running into the sea'. Next to them are baskets of washing and all around things spread out in the fields to dry. One gets a fleeting impression of gay petticoats and yellow and crimson kerchiefs tied over black hair, shading 'the dark, dreamy eyes of the south'. Miss Brewster is good at evoking things and one visualises the fishing boats with their white, yellow and burnt-umber sails manned by red-capped, red-scarved fishermen. *Feluccas* glide past over the glassy waters, a slight breeze bellying their long-curved Mediterranean sails. In her day Cannes was known for its sand-baths, particularly beneficial during the hot summer months. People would lie buried up to their necks in the burning noonday heat with white umbrellas over their heads. After an hour of baking, they were wrapped in blankets and exposed to a further grilling. The cure was said to be an effective one for all forms of rheumatism and especially beneficial for spinal complaints. Quite obviously Miss Brewster is writing from hearsay, for no one in her world had dared, as yet, brave the summer. On one occasion, Miss Brewster and a friend set out in an open carriage for Le Cannet and with them as guide went Annette, Miss Brewster's maid. Annette was not exactly loquacious, and on reaching their destination informed her mistress that the place was renowned for its wax. Wax for sealing letters her mistress erroneously supposed, but Annette 'looked quite horrified at the supposition. *"Non! non! pour faire les petits hommes comme ça"*, pointing to the length of her elbow. We were not a bit the wiser – but at last we found out that we had lighted on a manufacture of wax images for the churches'; not a sight that would have endeared itself to Miss Brewster, for she had strong prejudices about certain aspects of Catholicism, in particular its love of theatrical display and felt that Rome might make so many more converts were the churches affiliated to her a trifle less tawdry – 'had fewer wax dolls and less tinsel and did away with its artificial flowers and cotton lace'. There are many who will agree with her on this particular point; but Miss Brewster's feelings ran considerably deeper, aggravated, one supposes, though she makes no mention of it, by the troubles the English had experienced in Cannes regarding Protestant worship. Woolfield deals with it in detail in his book, and apparently an unfortunate Frenchman, a Huguenot priest who had been persuaded to officiate at some services held in private houses, had been expelled for his troubles. The local clergy, it seems, worried about the number of foreigners, were convinced that Cannes was about to become a Protestant enclave and in alarm had made protestations to the government who, in turn, had given orders to extradite M. Charbonny, the Frenchman in question. On another occasion, the commissaire of police, in full uniform, accompanied by two gendarmes, had put a stop to a service being held in a rented apartment. The English then referred the matter to Draguignan and after constant delays and much greasing of palms, finally obtained permission to build a small chapel while the plans for a church were put under way.

Usually so cheerful, a sinister note creeps into Miss Brewster's diary when on the subject of police: 'they move about in pairs, mounted on well-trained horses, and wherever you see their odious cocked hats, you may be sure that beside them is a large cart filled with chained prisoners'.

France had just occupied Algeria, and at the time of Miss Brewster's writing was busy clearing up pockets of resistance that had retreated into the Sahara. Any prisoners taken during these operations were automatically shipped back to Toulon, from where they were transferred to the seventeenth-century fortress built by Richelieu on the island of Ste Marguerite, the largest of the two Iles de Lérins opposite Cannes. By chance, Miss Brewster saw one of these bedouins at close quarters. 'I can scarcely tell you the strange repellent feeling that I had at the sight of him; there might have been several in the cart, but he was the only one I noticed.' She describes a wild figure wrapped in a hooded burnous, crouching with knees drawn up to his chin. 'It was a face I shall never forget, brown skinned with black ferocious eyes and in them a proud look of utter despair.'

We come now, inevitably, to Ste Marguerite's famous prisoner: the Man in the Iron Mask. Both Voltaire and Dumas have written on him at length, and various other theories as to the prisoner's true identity exist; but neither one nor the other have ever been definitely proven. The ingredients of the story are certainly intriguing; this distinguished figure in a velvet covered mask who spent more than half his life in different prisons, and always, in whichever prison he happened to be, being waited on with every mark of respect. Voltaire, who wrote about him in his *Age of Louis XIV*, first published in 1751, was responsible for the popularity of the story, and asserts, without a shadow of doubt, that the prisoner was the son of Cardinal Mazarin and Anne of Austria, the mother of Louis XIV, thus making the Iron Mask the King's half-brother. Richelieu, in his memoirs, goes even further, and claims the child as Louis XIV's twin, but does not intimate that Mazarin was the father. It had been predicted that if Anne of Austria had twins, it would be fatal for France. Louis XIV's birth took place at twelve in the morning on 5 September 1638, and on that same day in the evening, while the King was at dinner, Madame Perronett, the royal midwife, announced the probability of a second birth. Highly superstitious, the King sent for Richelieu who advised that if it happened, it should be carefully concealed. Those attending the Queen were sworn to secrecy, and the child was brought up by the midwife who passed him off as the illegit-imate son of a person of rank who had paid her handsomely for adopting him. When in his teens, the boy was sent off to Burgundy, and with the years grew more and more to resemble Louis XIV. Strange as it might appear, no one in his entourage had remarked on the resemblance, and it was the boy himself who discovered the likeness while looking at an engraving of the King. Unwisely he mentioned the fact to the governor of the château in which he was staying, and the man reported the incident to the court. Immediately orders came back for the boy's imprisonment, with a provision that he should wear a permanent mask, instant death following any attempt to uncover.

There are various theories about the mask, the most usually accepted, as the prisoner's assumed name would suggest, is that it was made out of iron and so contrived that the bottom part of the jaw was set on springs, thus allowing the wearer to partake of his meals. Considering the skill with which the smithies of the period worked, it would seem more than likely that the mask was cast out of steel rather than iron. It could then have been beaten to eggshell thinness and probably covered in velvet.

When first arrested, the Iron Mask was sent to Pinerolo and after a few years moved to Ste Marguerite where he remained until 1691, subsequently being confined to the Bastille where he died, a white-haired man of sixty-five. His death was very sudden and registered under a false name. Later, during the revolution, it was found that even this pseudonym had been removed from the registers.

Since the mysterious prisoner's death his prison on Ste Marguerite has been entirely transformed, after plans by Vauban. His particular cell, however, with its double door and barred window still remains, also the small chapel where he worshipped. They will even show you an old gilded chair in which he was supposed to have sat. Voltaire describes the prisoner 'of a stature above the ordinary, young and with features or rare nobility and beauty'. The features Voltaire must have invented to suit the image; however, judging from the testament of a doctor who often attended the Iron Mask at the Bastille, he must have had a certain allure. Although he had examined his tongue and the rest of his body, he had never seen his face, but the skin, though swarthy, was remarkably smooth and altogether he was admirably made, spoke in a deep, impressive voice and always courteously. It is hard to believe, but he is supposed never to have complained. As to his birth, there can be little doubt that he was someone of major importance. All accounts agree that he was treated as if of the blood-royal, waited upon by the governors of the different prisons, treated with respect and clothed in the finest linen, even served upon silver. Thus the story of the fisherman and the plate. According to Voltaire, the prisoner scratched something one day on his plate and threw it out of the window, towards a boat moored in a shallow skirting of sand at the foot of the tower. The fisherman to whom the boat belonged saw the thing flash as it fell, and picking it up carried it to the governor, who, surprised, questioned the man. Had he read the scratched message or had anyone else seen the plate? The fisherman was illiterate and answered that he had not had time to show anyone anything. Tesfed to prove the truth of his statement, he was then dismissed, puzzled perhaps by the governor's last words to him which could have left no doubt as to his fate had he not been able to prove himself unable to read.

The *Guide Michelin* proposes various alternatives to the story related above, one that the *Masque de Fer* was an Italian nobleman: Count Hercules Mattioli, Minister of State to the Duke Charles IV of Mantua. Apparently Mattioli had tried to doublecross Louis XIV in a complicated affair of state, and had been secretly abducted by the King. Another, newer, theory has it that the prisoner was none other than the son of Louis XIII's doctor. It would appear that the doctor had died leaving definite proof of the King's impotence, thus casting doubt on the Sun King's legitimate glory. The doctor had proved discreet, but the son, inheriting his father's papers, had not shown himself equally discriminating. Both theories would appear improbable since neither the doctor's son nor the Italian appear to merit the care and the mystery which attended the Iron Mask's imprisonment. On the other hand, one's romantic leanings are somewhat shaken when one learns that Prosper Mérimée tended rather to support the Mattioli theory. As Inspector-General of historic monuments, and an erudite historian in his own right, Mérimée would certainly have had access to any important papers, many of them, no doubt, containing material accumulated subsequent to the publication of Voltaire's history. There are further arguments that can be produced which render the story we have all been brought up on highly suspect, but I for one would rather keep my illusions; besides, nothing can be proved definitely either way.

Before passing on to the Marechal Bazaine, the other prisoner of note on the island, one last romantic tale should be told concerning the Iron Mask – the fact that the young Prince is said to have married. There was an attractive young girl in the fortress of Ste Marguerite, the daughter of one of the officials – her name was Julie de Bonpart. The prisoner had spied her from his window and had fallen in love with her. Somehow the couple managed some form of correspondence, and the young girl, seduced by the prisoner's ardour and by his reputed elegance, returned his sentiments. Touched by this idyll, the father persuaded the governor to allow a union, and the couple were married at an altar erected in the dungeon. Later Julie was to produce two sons who were secretly sent to Corsica under their maternal name of Bonpart, and from them sprung the Bonapartes who are therefore Bourbons![3]

Count de Las Cases in the journals he kept on St Helena[4] mentions having questioned Napoleon on this story, and the Emperor admitted to having heard it, commenting that 'such was the love of the marvellous, that it would have been easy to have substantiated something of the kind for the credulous multitude'.

Maréchal Bazaine's imprisonment and his eventual escape from the island Ste Marguerite makes quite different reading. He is an unsympathetic character and a real traitor to boot. Accused of betrayal by the French at the battle of Metz, he was court-martialled and condemned to be shot, the death sentence subsequently being commuted to imprisonment for twenty-five years. Under guard he arrived at the fortress of Ste Marguerite in December 1872 and by August the following year he had disappeared from off the face of the earth. His career makes singularly irritating reading, and one wonders how Napoleon III could possibly have given him the command of one of his armies, especially after his undistinguished record in Mexico, where he had been sent to bolster up the Emperor Maximilian's tumbling throne.

Of middle-class family from Versailles, trained to the life of a tradesman, he enlisted instead in the army as a private. Promoted to a lieutenancy in Algeria, he became a captain of the Foreign Legion and a general in the Crimean War. A coarse, pudgy-looking creature, he somehow managed to find himself a rich Creole wife when attending Maximilian in Mexico. The Empress Carlotta, watching him dance the *habanera* with his fiancée at one of her receptions, remarked that 'he reminds one of a huge, lazy fly'. She could not stand the man and from the very beginning shared her husband's mistrust of him. On his return from Mexico, a man without scruples and inordinately ambitious, he successfully manoeuvred himself into the command of the Imperial Guard. He was fifty-nine at the time of the war with Prussia and feeling prematurely aged should have refused the responsibility offered him by Napoleon. Not feeling capable of the job, he avoided any decisive action, retreated when he should have advanced, and in the end negotiated with Bismarck, surrendering Metz with fifteen thousand men. Not a very distinguished career.

In any case, arriving at Ste Marguerite, Bazaine was well lodged with three rooms and a terrace partially covered by an awning on which he arranged a kind of garden – one presumes a collection of pots. One day while watering his plants he came across a choked-up gutter. It pierced the wall, and working secretly over the next week or so he managed to get it cleared. It proved wider than might be imagined, wide enough even for the corpulent Bazaine to squeeze through. Informing his wife, who was allowed to visit him, they worked out a plan. First she procured a rope which he hid in the gutter, and then the rest of the operation was up to Madame la Maréchale. Going to Genoa, she chartered a large steam yacht, the *Baron Ricasoli*, announcing that she intended to cruise the ports of the Riviera on the pretext of looking for a villa. Reaching Golf Juan she anchored, and waiting for a dark night lowered a small boat. With her she had her nephew, Don Alvarez de Rull, and together they steered for the island. It was a long haul and during the trajectory a strong wind started to blow. The couple persisted nevertheless, and arrived at the appointed place. Meanwhile the Maréchal, having managed to negotiate the gutter, let himself down the rope. From the rocks to the water there was a further drop, and risking a possible bruising, the fat man rolled himself into the sea. The swim had not been part of the plan, but the waves had prevented his rescuers from approaching any nearer. Hauled into the boat they all set to with the oars and hurried back to the yacht, where, the Maréchal no sooner bundled up the companionway, orders were given for full steam ahead. Reports have it that they steered for the coast of Spain and from thence to total oblivion. ___

Returning to Cannes we must leave the heights of the Croix de Garde and wander further afield. I remember some thirty years ago being taken up to Le Cannet to see the Villa Sardou where Rachel, the great classical tragedienne, died. The house has been pulled down since, but I remember certain vague details. The main bedroom was decorated with a large bas-relief. It covered the whole wall above the bed and represented a nymph, on tiptoes, arms extended, holding up voluminous draperies that spread out across the plaster in a kind of tent. One could see them also as wings, pleated like those of a bat. Rachel, a thin, diminutive figure scarcely five feet tall, worn out by the intensity of her emotions, dying already at the age of thirty-eight, had been ordered by her doctor to take a complete rest and on arriving at Le Cannet and being shown to her room was appalled at the idea of sleeping under what, she must have felt, looked suspiciously like winding sheets. So disturbed was she that she insisted on having her bed made up next door, and there, too weak to move again, she died. Matthew Arnold wrote a poem about her death and he mentions the stucco and the 'stately room, where fell the shadow of a marble muse of yore'. It is a great pity that no museum attempted to preserve the room, for I remember it being rather remarkable of its kind.

Rachel died in 1858 about a year after Prosper Mérimée first started spending his winters in Cannes, also on account of his health. As Inspector-General of historical monuments, he had already visited the Riviera in 1834, the same year, as it happens, that Brougham discovered Cannes.

For twenty years Mérimée had struggled to save his country's architectural treasures, and Provence owes a great deal to this gifted man. It was through Mérimée's intervention that the palace of the popes at Avignon was evacuated. He was responsible also for clearing the amphitheatres at both Arles and Nîmes, also the theatre at Orange, all three, as mentioned already, choked up with encumbrances. Vienne and Maison-la-Romaine also benefited from his attention, and turning once again to Avignon he had to battle against the building of a railway which would have wrecked both the ramparts and the famous bridge. The fortress monastery of St Honorat is yet another building that he saved. Great integrity and an endless amount of travelling had been involved in Mérimée's career of Inspector-General, and now worn out by constant attacks of bronchial asthma he had decided to retire to the south and spend what remained to him of his winters in the sun. After two weeks in Nice, he moved to the Auberge de la Poste on the front at Cannes, and from here wrote to the Comtesse de Montigo, Empress Eugénie's mother, that he had a *passion complète* for the place. 'Where else in the world do they cultivate jasmine by the acre. I get up early and go to bed at nine . . . I live like a lizard, basking in the sun. Nice amuses me but there are too many people, too many English, too many Russians . . .' The Imperial court had recently adopted Nice as their winter quarters and the place must have been crowded, but the English, one would have thought, were far more numerous in Cannes; besides, judging from Mérimée's correspondence, he seems to have been inordinately fond of them. His letters are full of perceptive jottings; his description, for example, of the amiable Richard Cobden who had made a fortune in printed cottons and who, in spite of his background, was interested in travelling and museums. Lady Cunningham, George IV's ex-mistress, is another. 'She lives in Cannes in a baroque castle with her son, Lord Londesborough; she is eighty-four and looks sixty.' Mérimée finds her *'fort grande dame'* and is also enchanted with her daughter-in-law, 'a typical English beauty with the fragility of porcelain'.

When Mérimée took an apartment at number 6 rue du Bivouac Napoléon (now 3 Square Mérimée), Fanny and Emma Lagden, two elderly English ladies, came down to supervise the running of his household. Their parents had been friends of Mérimée's mother. Not much is known of them and they remain shadowy figures in the background of most of Mérimée's life. Fanny, the older of the sisters, was probably Mérimée's first mistress, and when he died he left her the bulk of his considerable fortune. This supposed relationship probably explains why they are buried together in the Protestant cemetery of the Grand-Jas at Cannes. It could possibly have been Fanny's wish – a last self-sought reward for a lifetime's devotion.

One gets charming glimpses of Mérimée's life, days spent visiting the surroundings, 'painting, chatting with friends, drinking tea, cultivating a praying mantis as a pet'.[5] Gradually as his illness gained on him, he saw fewer and fewer people, becoming automatically more dependent on the devotion of the Lagdens. Madame Juliette Adam, a young writer, leaves a touching description of Mérimée. He is president of the Cannes archery club, and in this capacity she catches a glimpse of him accompanied by 'his old English women friends in light-coloured dresses, one carrying a quiver and the other a large bag . . .' Mérimée held the bow and was fed the arrows, which he aimed at ripe fir cones for his fire. A successful shot was followed by exclamations and a scramble for the fallen target which, with retriever-like devotion, was popped into the bag.

Mérimée, alas, was witness to the fall of the empire at Sedan. His beloved Empress took flight for England and he himself boarded his last train for the south. He arrived at Cannes station 'mad with grief'. His doctor, who met the bent figure, took his arm. Mérimée was crying. 'France is dying,' he mumbled, 'I want to die with her'. He had his wish, and on the night of 23 September 1870 passed away quietly in his sleep.

21

The Railway Age

Nice has changed considerably in the intervening years since we last explored its streets. The railway age had turned the Riviera into a popular resort and Nice, already a city, was the first to feel the full effect. The so-called Voie Impériale from Paris to Marseilles, opened up by Napoleon III and his Empress, had slowly extended along the coast towards Italy. By April 1863, it had reached Cagnes and the following year Nice. The Paris–Lyons–Mediterranean railway brought out a special poster to commemorate the event: a brightly coloured coastline with a pretty Niçoise in her national costume smiling in the foreground. It was not yet known as the Côte d'Azur and had to wait a further twenty-three years before the author-poet, Stéphen Liégeard, coined the phrase by using it as the title of one of his books, a flowery historical evocation that wanders, long-windedly, from Ventimille to St Tropez.

The lines once laid, the *trains de luxe* were quick to arrive; the *Riviera Express*, and later the richly inlaid, velvet upholstered carriages of the famous *Train Bleu*. Another line served the Russian Imperial court. Wrapped in their furs, the snow melting on their trunks, they embark on the long line of carriages that drew them slowly out of St Petersburgh and clattered from Vienna to Nice. The Emperor and the Empress always arrived by ship, a flotilla of the Russian Navy being delegated to transport them and their suite safely to Villefranche.

Again we have recourse to Mérimée's amusing letters, this time touching on the Russians. 'Among the beauties who grace the Imperial court at Nice, is a certain Countess Araxine who tries to cultivate a dashing image. She wears wide-brimmed hats, smokes a cigar and feeds a pet goat on her sofa.' Among her other eccentricities she suddenly took it into her head to dress like a man and ordered a tailor to come round for her measures. A God-fearing Scot, the little man was seized with horror and 'refused to work for such a gorgon!'.

In 1865 the Czarevitch Nicholas-Alexandrovitch died in a rented villa up behind Nice in the St Philippe district, and Hare gives an account of the Grand Duke's death. Taking the hand of his affianced bride, the Princess Dagmar of Denmark, he placed it in that of his brother, Alexander, saying 'Marry him; he is as true as crystal, and I wish it'. He was obeyed and as Marie Feodorovna she became Empress of Russia. Afterwards, in typical grandiose slavonic fashion, Villa Oscar-Bermond was bought and pulled down and an orthodox Russian cathedral built in its place with adjoining it a chapel commemorating the Prince Imperial.

At this point Marie Bashkirtseff could well appear on the scene. She was Russian and although not belonging to the Imperial court, certainly belongs to Nice. But remarkable though this spoilt young lady proved to be – she wrote endless diaries, eighty-four volumes of which are housed in the Bibliothèque Nationale in Paris – she should by rights take second place, and wait in the wings to attend on more noteworthy individuals: one the tempestuous, wildly romantic composer of the *Symphonie Fantastique* – Hector Berlioz. He came to Nice on several occasions, the first time in 1831 when he was twenty-eight years old. He had just won the *Prix de Rome* with *Sardanapole* and was halfway through his *King Lear*. Courbet's portrait in the Louvre shows him in his middle age, and from this one can imagine him young: the same unruly black hair, sombre eyes and hollow cheeks, a large nose and thin lips; the determined, haunted face of someone given to great passions. At twenty-eight he was just recovering from an unsuccessful love affair with a Miss Harriet Smithson, the leading actress in Kemble's Shakespearian company, and on the rebound had become engaged to Camille Moke, a young pianist. His mood on his first visit to Nice is restless, but his letters show high spirits and an amused cynicism in respect to himself. He lodges in rooms on the Ponchettes. It is May and he is swimming and sleeping under the broom by the side of the road on the way to Villefranche. 'I live alone, I write, I sing. I believe in God . . . That's how I spent at Nice the most beautiful days of my life . . .' He then describes the amusing story of his arrest. Seeing the young composer all alone, wandering along the sea road, the police became suspicious and arrested him. The interview is described in one of his letters.

'What exactly are you doing here?' they ask him.

'I am recovering from a painful illness' (he refers to his unrequited love for Miss Smithson). 'I compose, I dream and thank God for the beautiful sunshine, the mountains – the sea.'

'You are a painter I take it?'

'No, Sir.'

'And yet we see you everywhere with a notebook making sketches. Would they, by any chance, be plans you are drawing?'

'Yes, I am roughing out the overture for King Lear; working on the instrumentation.'

'King Lear? And who may he be?'

'The unfortunate old man was King of England.'

'England!' Then Berlioz, taking pity on his interlocutors, explained that Lear was a figment of Shakespeare's imagination. The police, completely at sea, drop the subject and revert to an earlier part of the conversation.

'Let's leave the King. Explain to us what you meant just now by the word instrumentation?'

'It's a musical term,' Berlioz answered.

'Always this pretext! We know perfectly well, Sir, that one does not just compose like that without a piano, wandering along the shore with a pad and pencil.' Angrily they call the meeting to order.

'We will give you back your passport providing you leave Nice immediately. We insist also on your telling us where you intend to go.'

Berlioz answered that he would go to Rome. Then smiling and with a hint of a bow as he turned to leave, 'And with your permission go on composing without a piano.'

Returning to Nice in 1844 he is again alone. His engagement to Camille Moke had been broken off, the young pianist having abandoned Berlioz for a M. Pleyel. Frustrated, he had turned his attentions once more to Miss Smithson; only this time determined that she should succumb, he had staged a suicide scene and appeared in her rooms clutching a phial of laudanum, at the same time having taken the precaution of arming himself with an emetic. Berlioz himself describes the scene: 'Fearful shrieks from Harriet – sublime despair – mocking laughter from me – desire to live once more on hearing frantic avowals of love – emetic – result which lasted for ten hours'. The suicide scene succeeded but the marriage failed, and the two separated in 1840. Nice, however, still held the same attraction for the impressionable composer. 'I could not contain my emotion on seeing once more those places which had been my haunt thirteen years earlier.' The rooms he had worked in were occupied by an English family and he lodged elsewhere. More plunges in the sea, more excursions and then the return to Paris where he lost himself to the orgies of sound that were to be the new opera – *The Damnation of Faust.*

It is in the narrow streets behind Les Ponchettes where Berlioz stayed that one meets with another tormented spirit: the great Paganini! For days he agonised in a little room on the third floor of a simple house in the rue de la Préfecture. A very rich man, he could well have afforded more commodious lodgings, but it would seem that an innate parsimony stopped him from spending more money than was strictly necessary.* The house had been lent him by Count Spitalieri de Cessole, president of the senate of Nice, an important property holder and Paganini's fervent admirer – his only admirer as the difficult days ahead were to prove him to be.

The great virtuoso's death has about it the macabre quality of an Edgar Allan Poe story, and indeed even his life seems to have been haunted. Strange rumours had circulated about him; this gaunt figure all in black, his angular gestures and the great hand manipulating his precious violin. Like great white spiders they flayed the strings, wringing from the fragile instrument a quality of sound that had never been equalled. Italy, central Europe, France, England, the crowds sat enthralled. Since the age of twelve his virtuosity had astonished the master violinists. Both Rolla and Paër, to whom he had been sent for instruction, were dumbfounded by the ease and assurance with which he handled his playing. Rolla, after hearing him execute a particularly intricate passage, a piece he had difficulty himself in interpreting, told the boy that, quite frankly, there was nothing further he could teach him. Even when young Paganini had had the power to attract, men

---

* This makes the helping hand that he extended to Berlioz all the more impressive. It was April 1838 and Berlioz had just had a conspicuous failure with his opera *Benvenuto Cellini*. Feigning indifference to the critics, he followed up the much booed performance by a recital of *Handel en Italie* which he conducted himself at the *Conservatoire*. The concert over, he turned to walk through the orchestra when a sinister looking figure in black made his way across the stage, and taking Berlioz by the hand turned him towards the audience and on bended knees announced in a voice hardly above a whisper that '*Vous êtes allé plus loin que Beethoven*'. A cry went through the hall. It was Paganini! Praise indeed from the greatest virtuoso to have ever played on the violin. It was the following day that Achillino, Paganini's twelve-year-old illegitimate son by an Italian dancer, appeared with a letter from his father in which he again expressed his admiration enclosing a cheque of over two thousand pounds to be drawn on Baron de Rothschild's bank in Paris.

were fascinated and the women a little frightened, repelled and yet completely subjugated, like a bird watching a snake. The cold eyes held one, the nervous sensitivity of the man became almost tangible, and always those hands with their long bony fingers that had acquired a flexibility that was almost deformed. The way he stood when playing, his weight on one hip, the torso bent right over and the left arm held straight out from the shoulder. Alas, no instrument existed in those days that could register sound, but enough witnesses have left their impressions. One wrote that his music was 'inspired by the flesh, not the spirit', the music was *'sensuelle, voluptueuse, diabolique'*. People not only admired but were a little in awe of his performances. It was a romantic age and they were only too willing to imagine the most extravagant things. Paganini's own compositions helped in this respect, also his name which, spelt out in the language of his birth, stood for 'pagan' in the diminutive form of the word. There was nothing ritualistic about his playing, quite the opposite; it smacked, some people said, of the devil, and it needed very little effort of will to see the cadaverous performer with his sharp bones as a figure escaped from Hoffman – a Lucifer in sombre clothes. There were people also who crossed themselves after his performances, while the more bigoted, we are told, hurried to the nearest church to be absolved.

This then gives one a little of the background of the extraordinary man who lay fighting death in the rue de la Préfecture. He was fifty-six and for several years his health had been failing. Doctors had diagnosed a variety of complaints, one nervous prostration, another a syphilitic infection that had lodged in the marrow of his spine. What he was actually suffering from were bouts of severe rheumatism and, in the end, consumption of the throat which for months rendered him all but speechless. To begin with, different watering places and cures of mud baths helped alleviate the pain in his legs, and then gradually his throat condition took over. Refusing to admit the possibility of dying, he moved from Montpellier to Marseilles and from Marseilles to his home town. 'Here I am in Genoa,' he writes, 'iller than I was at Marseilles. I have decided to spend the winter in Nice.' Not able to give concerts, hardly able to leave his room, he was not ill enough, however, to forget about money and started a profitable trade in violins of which he had a fine collection, not counting, of course, his valued Guarnerius which he bequeathed to the municipality of Genoa, who preserve it as one of their dearest possessions.

The Nice correspondent of the *Gazette Musicale* reports having seen him nearly every day. 'He still has a good deal of strength and I sometimes hear him playing all alone.' One fine sunny day, tucking his violin under his arm, he descended the dark stairs on some unknown mission. Out in the streets he suddenly meets a barrel organ, and in a fury curses the man to silence and, as if to purify the air of the dreadful cacophony, opens his case and starts playing. A few magical chords hang in the garlic-scented air attracting a band of urchins who laugh at the grotesque silhouette as it vanishes round the corner.

By February he can no longer hold a pen: 'Convulsions, dizzy spells and coughing fits, rack my body, day and night.' He died 27 May 1840, and unable to speak had made signs to open the shutters. It was full moon with not a cloud in the sky.

And now, unfortunately for Nice, there follows a whole chapter of regretful incidents. In his will, Paganini left definite instructions. He wanted a quiet burial and specifically asked that no requiem be composed for his benefit. Apart from this, all arrangements were to be left to his son, Achille or Achillino. What actually took place scarcely reflects well on the Church. Monseigneur Galvano, the Bishop of Nice, and Dom Caffarelli showed themselves hopelessly dogmatic, as hysterical almost as the stupid women who filed past the defunct's corpse, and because of these men and their superstitious narrow-mindedness, it was to take Achillino exactly thirty-six years of constant struggle to procure a Christian burial for his father. The truth is that Paganini died without a confession, without communion, and without extreme unction – like the damned if one is to take the Catholic Church's point of view. Caffarelli claimed to have called twenty-five times on the dying man, and the dying man perfectly conscious but refusing to face the possibility of death, had turned the priest away. Achillino, anyway, refutes Caffarelli's statement and admits to only four visits. As to communion, the doctor attested to the fact that his illness prevented him from swallowing anything. Jean Baptiste Barla, the Niçois naturalist, has a more detailed account of Caffarelli's last visit. Was he actually there? One doesn't know. But as a man of science, one can probably trust him: his version, anyhow, has a ring of truth about it. Impatient at never gaining admittance, Caffarelli is said to have forced his way into the great man's room and finding him completely inert, his eyes closed, burst out excitedly in Patois: '*Ah! Ah! Moussie Paganini ahura es plus l'oura de souna lu zon-zon!*' ('Ah! Ah! Mr Paganini, it is no longer the time to scrape on that old violin!'). Rightly incensed at this inappropriate outburst, the maestro suddenly looked up and with a feeble gesture of his hand pointed to the door, through which Caffarelli fled.

There exists a lithograph of Paganini on his deathbed, and it shows him with his eyes open, his lips slightly parted, and a benign expression on his face. Was the lithograph taken from a contemporary drawing? One would hardly think so judging from the reaction of the crowds that filed past his bed. '*Vision horrifiante*' one reads in the papers. Guttering candles threw sinister shadows, accentuating the beak-like nose and exaggerating the deep lines furrowing the cheeks. There are moments when the stretched skin glows almost green. Women shrieked, another fainted, and all without exception hurried from the mortuary chamber to the church. What was it about this man that engendered such morbid fascination? It seems that even dead, people were frightened of him, and fearing him they filed past in even greater numbers. For two days Paganini's body lay to be gaped at, and then came the shocking news that Monseigneur Galvano had forbidden a Christian burial. Unprecedented procedure for anyone so famous. People now hurried past the house in the rue de la Préfecture crossing themselves, and the Church published a ban on '*cette exhibition immorale*' and hurried the body to the general hospital where it was stowed away in an old vat in the basement. Those living in the neighbourhood of the hospital started hearing strange noises, and there was even talk of burning his body. Achillino, desperate, appealed to Cessole, but Cessole, though sympathetic, was powerless to help. The family lawyer sent a petition to Monseigneur Tadini, the Cardinal-Bishop of Genoa and Achillino, while waiting for an answer implored Galvano to have a mass said for the *repos éternel de l'âme de son père*. The request was refused on the grounds that if celebrated it would be admitting Paganini to being a true Christian. No answer came from Genoa, and in the meantime a circus director, proffering the supreme insult, offered three thousand pounds for the body, proposing to exhibit the maestro's remains in England. When word arrived from Genoa, it was, as might have been expected, a flat refusal to interfere. Tadini felt obliged to uphold his counterpart's ruling in Nice. In the interim, Achillino had even petitioned the king who, quite understandably dared not intercede.

Paganini had died in 1840 and in August 1841 Achillino left for Rome, asking for an audience with the pope. Gregory XVI received him and ordered a special commission to review the case, the commission being headed by the Bishop of Turin. It was a job fraught with difficulties and one imagines that the Vatican was unwilling to press it.

Back in Nice, and much to his credit, Cessole was the person who made the next move. Not only president of the Assembly, he was also Magistrat de Santé, in other words guardian of the public health, and as such saw his chance of protecting the body from any possible abuse. The Assembly had shown itself unwilling to act, but as Magistrat de Santé, Cessole could declare the body unclean and insist on it being transported to the official morgue, the nearest being situated at Villefranche.

Embalmed shortly after death, the doctors had treated Paganini's remains to a further series of injections while lying in the hospital basement. And now dressed in a frock-coat with all his decorations, he was carried to a hearse. The move was made at night under military escort, and the papers report a moonless sky and total darkness, 'not even the men's drawn swords glinted as they rode by'. Reaching Villefranche and once safely under lock and key, Cessole put the mortuary in charge of a trusted subordinate by the name of Lenchantin. The transfer had been made with as little publicity as possible, but despite the precautions news leaked out and poor Lenchantin was offered enormous bribes by morbid individuals who wanted to see the body. Cessole, nervous that the moment would come when his henchmen could no longer resist the temptation of earning some extra pennies, decided that the keys would be safer in his own keeping. Lenchantin obediently turned them over.

Nearly a year had gone by since the move, and in the meantime the foreign press had got hold of the story and Cessole and Achillino between them, over-anxious about the dead man's safety, decided on a bold move: they were to steal the body and hide it – a remarkable decision on the part of Cessole considering his position in the senate and the firm injunction from the Church that the body was to remain within the precincts of Nice. Cessole owned plots of land on the Pointe St Hospice,* a small peninsula jutting out from Cap Ferrat, and it was here that Paganini was to be buried, in the hopes that a favourable solution would eventually be forthcoming from the Vatican.

Again the conspirators waited for a moonless night. There were a

* As far as can be ascertained, the headland where the body rested once formed part of the author's garden.

band of six, two of them representing the best families of Nice: Comte Garan de Coconnato and the Comte de Pierlas, and with them a sculptor, Alexis de Saint-Marc and a young romantic painter called Felix Ziem, who later was to become well known for his views of Venice. Achillino and Cessole, of course, made up the number. This time the secret was better guarded, and the *felucca* carrying the body crossed Villefranche bay without attracting notice.

A further two years Paganini lay on this deserted point under the ghost-like branches of wind-bent pines, and then much to everyone's amazement, in April 1844 Achillino received a message from the king, giving him official permission to bury his father in the grounds of the Paganini villa at Polcevera, outside Genoa. It was not consecrated ground, but at least Achillino felt that his father's remains had been respected. The Vatican, always careful, delayed twenty years before passing judgement and then, at a time when a majority of the prelates concerned in the affair were dead, at last gave consent for a Christian burial. Again Paganini was exhumed and his remains laid to rest in the cemetery of Parma. Yet another move was to follow, but not personal this time, rather a mass exodus for the hallowed when Parma decided on a new burial ground.

We appear to have stepped out of line as regards to dates, but it would have been impossible to leave Nice without mentioning Paganini. Nietzsche, the German philosopher, is another personality who often springs to mind, but at least his stays on the Riviera fall within the correct time cycle – that is to say, the second half of the nineteenth century. His great creative period lasted only nine years, between 1879 and 1888, and much of this time was spent in Nice. *Beyond Good and Evil* was composed while on walks round Eze, in particular the steep climb from the station on the shore, straight up an all but perpendicular path leading to the village above, perched on its rock. He writes that his muscles responded best when his mental faculties were at their most lucid. 'I have spent some unforgettable moments in the countryside of Nice and the memory of these hidden places and silent heights is sacred to me.'

A powerful writer and sensitive poet, he lived in constant pain, drugging and dieting and taking lonely walks. His illness was never diagnosed conclusively, but it is thought that he picked up a syphilitic infection when serving as a medical orderly in the Franco-Prussian war. He describes spells of almost total blindness and terrible migraine headaches, and one wonders how he was able to concentrate on his work at all. In 1889 he suffered a complete mental and physical breakdown, and one day was found weeping and embracing a horse. Carried home to Weimar, he died the following year.

Incidentally, it is on leaving Nice harbour by the lower corniche, on the way to Eze, that one notices a large pink building facing out across the bay at Mont Boron, known as the Château des Anglais. Its unfortunate crushed-raspberry colouring is a recent vandalism, but the building itself is interesting and dates from the last years of the 1850s. Its builder was a retired East India man called Smith, and his house was the first important edifice to appear west of Nice and was consequently regarded as something of a novelty. Smith is supposed to have based his plans on an existing folly known as La Martinière at Lucknow, the Anglo-Indian palace of a General Martin who made his fortune serving the Nawab of Oud. Having visited both places, I can vouch for a certain vague similarity. The Château, incidentally, has now been cut up into flats.

Another interesting building is the Villa Arson on a cypress-clad hill in the St Barthélemy district of Nice. Mention of it has already been made in a previous chapter on gardens. The house, now the Ecole des Arts Décoratifs, shows, like its gardens, remnants of its past grandeur, when it served as a country retreat for the Lascaris family. The place takes its name from a subsequent owner, a Count Arson who seems to have been something of an eccentric. Hare refers to him as an astrologer-necromancer and tells a strange story about him. 'He gave out that he was going to retire from the world for a year, and invited all his friends to a party before his seclusion.'[1] All the society of Nice came, found a banquet spread and an orchestra playing, but no host. The family excused the Count's absence explaining that important work must be keeping him. The crowd danced under the trees and left – still no Count. On the third day, the police forced his door open and found him stretched out dead. He had been dead three days.

Augustus Hare is indispensable for anyone interested in the Riviera. Not only did he produce excellent guides, but he was also well enough connected to be on nodding terms with most of its personalities. Lunching, for instance, with George Peabody, a rich merchant banker from Massachusetts – 'the dullest man in the world' – he met King Louis of Bavaria, 'then a dirty, dissipated old man . . .'[2] Again and again, he produces diverting snatches of gossip about people, and Hare himself is an interesting character. He came of a good but impoverished family of church people. His father was a rector, so also were two of his uncles, and further removed from him he could count at least three bishoprics in the family. A consumptive, Hare's father had gone to Rome, and dying there had left his widow all but destitute nursing the baby Augustus. Fortunately, her widowed sister-in-law, Augustus's god-mother, offered to take him off her hands. They sound a heartless lot. 'My dear Maria', Mrs Hare wrote, 'how very kind of you. Yes, certainly the baby shall be sent as soon as it is weaned, if anyone else would like one, would you kindly remember that we have others.' Maria Hare adopted her godson with the idea that he should take holy orders. A bright child, he was already reading German at the age of three, his evenings being spent with his adopted mother struggling to understand the Trinity. It must have been a miserable childhood. Twice a day he was given doses of rhubarb, a popular Victorian purgative 'because it was supposed to strengthen the stomach'. They talked of his favourite dishes, served them up and then would not let him eat them. Instead they were sent to the poor in the village, Augustus himself often being the messenger. He was badly bullied at Harrow and pursued by ill-health; finally he was taken away and subjected to a series of private tutors, followed by University College Oxford from where he graduated with a BA in 1857. He had seen enough of the world to know that he was thoroughly bored with the church, and revolting against a clerical career, followed his adopted mother to Europe. A semi-invalid, suffering from no special complaint, she had taken to wintering abroad and it suited her well to have her gifted ward in attendance. They were inveterate sightseers, Hare all the time making sketches. He was actually one of the best amateur water-colourists of the time, and judging from the stories that appear in his autobiography, he was also a first-rate raconteur. Another talent he discovered while travelling around with his adopted mother was his writing. When in London he was introduced to Murray, the publisher, who commissioned him to write on some of the English counties, and so began a long series of guides which were to make him a household word for at least two generations of travellers, his most popular being the books on France and Italy.

Hare was thirty-six when Maria died, and freed now from a constant attendance he became the hostesses' ideal – an extra man. He was invited everywhere, and it must have been about this time that he became well known as a raconteur of ghost stories. An acquaintance of his describes the way he would tell them, 'in rather a curious nasal voice' with much 'writhing' and 'twisting and wringing' of hands. Somerset Maugham, as a young man, stayed with Hare at Holmhurst, a small property he owned near Hastings, and in an essay he wrote for *Cornhill*[3] describes his host in some detail: a good forehead, prominent nose, black hair, piercing eyes and a moustache. Malcolm Barnes, who edited his long and rambling autobiography, tells us in his introduction[4] that gossips supposed that in middle age he wore a wig and painted his face.

One gets the impression, as Mr Barnes put it, 'of a dapper little man, a snob, genteel, somewhat old-maidish, a hob-nob of the landed nobility' but well travelled, deeply read, interested in history and with an insatiable curiosity, in fact the ideal person to take with one as a guide. His *South Eastern France* and *The Rivieras*, though published during the nineteenth century, are still books one should have on the shelves if one intends visiting this part of the world.

Hare's guide to the Rivieras first came out in 1897. Things have changed since then, they always do, and even in his own lifetime Hare was bitterly disappointed at what had happened on his beloved coast. Re-visiting Menton, he finds it quite spoilt by 'the building and the cutting of too many trees'. Other places had suffered similar fates. They were no longer 'characterful places where each member of the English community knew each other'. Cannes and Nice had grown out of all recognition, and it is precisely this Nice that we find so vividly described in Marie Bashkirtseff's diaries.

Bashkirtseff first started writing in 1873, aged fourteen, and from then on until she died in 1884 wrote in her diary every night, year after year. It needed great application, but this was not a quality Marie was lacking. Had it not been for her chronic laryngitis, she could have been a professional singer. Instead, she took up painting and in three months had already made enough progress to exhibit in the Paris Salon where she was given an honourable mention. She studied with Jules Bastien Lepage, who specialised in country scenes, and Marie, without moving so far afield, tended to emulate him in Paris producing competent but sad compositions of street waifs – murky nineteenth-century Murillos.

In 1882 at twenty-one she already knew she was dying. 'I shall not get better' she wrote in large capitals in her diary. There have been several editions of her diaries, and by the end of the century translations

had already been published in both London and New York. For a short
time this spoilt, introspective girl became a cult, even the eminent
Lord Gladstone reviewed her diatribe of words when published in
England. He found them admirable but not winning, and wrote that
'Mademoiselle Bashkirtseff attracts and repels alternatively, and
perhaps repels as much as she attracts'. However, as introspective and
aggravating as she could be when writing about herself, she showed a
delicate sensibility when describing places and atmospheres.

The family lived in a series of villas on the Promenade des Anglais,
and as a child we see her being drawn in a basket cart lined with white
bearskins harnessed to two matching ponies caparisoned with yellow
varnished trappings. It was a world of white lace veils, pale silks and
velvets, huge crinolines, and scarlet cashmere mantles. Ladies offered
her violet tea, and the weather seemed permanently fine. The sea
shimmered an intense blue, so intense that one would have said that a
brush, dipped into the water, would reproduce the exact colour of the
sky. Marie was pretty in a coarse kind of way, and in her teens seems to
have affected white, and lived in a roomcapitonned in *eau de nil* satin.
The shopkeepers and the fiacre drivers knew her as Mademoiselle Marie
and would call affectionately after her as she passed, hatless in the
streets, always accompanied by her dog. Nice for her was the Promenade
des Anglais. 'The real season in Nice is the month of May . . .' She
remembers the 'gentle waves that break rustling across the pebbles'.
In October we get her writing from Paris 'Here, morning and evening
are nothing: in the morning it's sweeping; in the evening I am irritated
by lamps everywhere . . .' and then she starts thinking longingly of
her Promenade. 'I get up with the dawn to watch the sunrise, over
to the left behind the mountain, clearly etoned against the blue sky –
a soft vaporous blue. The beauty makes me catch my breath.' Another
night she describes the moon cutting a great path in the sea, 'Like a
fish with diamond scales', and then a terrible *cri de coeur*: 'I'm home-
sick for Nice'. Back again in the south the following May she gives a
fête in the street, in the rue de France. Maypoles were a tradition
in Nice but according to Marie were becoming quite scarce since the
French occupation. There was singing and dancing, and her maypole
caused quite a stir. A popular song in Nice at that time was *Rossigno che
vola*. Marie has dated this entry 1876 and Carnaval* had started in
1873. She doesn't mention it, but Gustave-Adolphe Mossa, Alexis

* *Carnem-Vale*, goodbye meat, because it ends on the eve of Lent.

Mossa's (the Niçois painter's) son, designed the floats for this particular year; grotesques in papier-mâché straight from *la commedia dell'arte*. Another year Mossa, with his morbid and fertile imagination, chose *les ratapignata* as a theme: *ratapignata* in Niçois dialect meaning bats and, of course, baronial castles and vampires were very much part of the scene. Later Jules Chéret, revolutionising the poster art, imposes quite a different feeling at Carnaval time, creating an atmosphere of feminine gaiety with his flirtatious women, trailing paper flowers and masked in black velvet. The air is criss-crossed with multi-coloured streamers and whole sacks of confetti stipple the air. The English, when referring to Carnaval, generally did so with very mixed feelings. Included in the programme is a day set aside for the Battle of Flowers, a painful experience for many English lady gardeners who watched millions of spring blooms being trodden to death by the gaping mobs milling in the streets. A keen and greedy eye to trade, the ladies felt, was the motivating force, and the poor flowers, they complained, deserved a better fate.

✣22

Madame d'Angleterre ～

Queen Victoria visited the South of France nine times in all and came every year for the last five years of her life. The first visit in 1882 was spent at Menton, Cannes in 1887, Grasse in 1891, Hyères the following year, and from 1895 until 1899 Nice, or to be more precise, Cimiez, a little above the town. These trips abroad lasted exactly six weeks and were invariably timed to include Easter.

The Royal cavalcade numbered between sixty and a hundred, depending how many Princesses and their suites accompanied their mother. The Queen's personal attendants, apart from the household, consisted of a lady's maid and six dressers; a French chef and three cooks; a Scottish Gillie and Indian attendants, a coachman, an outrider, and a dozen grooms with the Queen's own carriages, horses and a donkey.[1]

The donkey, Jaquot, was a great favourite and had been bought by the Queen at Aix-les-Bains. Harnessed to a basket chair, its task was to draw its tubby mistress round the parks of the different places they stayed at. It would seem that whichever lady-in-waiting happened to be in attendance at the time was expected to trot behind this creaking contraption, but fortunately for all, Jaquot was a lazy beast, very obstinate, and refused to be hurried. ～

Marie Adeane, the future Lady Mallet, one of the Queen's ladies-in-waiting, describes the bustle attending one of these journeys. Arriving at Portsmouth, 'it took half an hour to unload the train and stow away the innumerable retainers both black and white'. The 'stowing' referred to took place on the royal yacht, the *Victoria and Albert*. 'The luggage', Miss Adeane continues, 'seemed unequally divided, the white having tons while the blacks carried all their worldly goods neatly tied up in a couple of pocket-handkerchiefs.' One presumes the elaborate liveries were packed up along with the household effects, a vast load which

included china and linen, certain pieces of furniture, mostly from
Osborne and Balmoral, and the Queen's mahogany bed. The blacks,
Miss Adeane refers to are, of course, the Indians.

As Mr Duff tells us, all journeys across the Channel were made in the
Victoria and Albert. Sailing from Portsmouth to Cherbourg, the Queen
spent the night on board and embarked on the train the following
morning. Torpedo boats escorted her across the Channel and directors
of the railway accompanied the train. Only one crossing, that of March
1898, seems to have been rough, and the Queen writes of it in her
journal. Not sick but having taken to her sitting-room, there is a
sudden lurch and the porthole bursts open, chairs are sent spinning and
the cabin is half flooded with water. 'The maids, stewards, and footmen
all rush in, in a great state . . . and I was taken in a rolling chair across
to my bedroom, where I got on the sofa, feeling much upset. Was very
thankful when we got into Cherbourg at last.' And then, somewhat
petulantly one feels, she adds 'that we had been quite misinformed
about the weather'.

The crowds gathered at Cherbourg were curious about this rotund
little figure in black. The court had gone into mourning after the
Prince Consort's death in 1861 and never came out of it. Thousands of
people lined the harbour and waited patiently for hours just for a sight
of this doll-like idol in a lace bonnet, garnished with edelweiss. They
generally cheered, for she was popular, and in Cannes, the year she
stayed there, they referred to her, perhaps not altogether respectfully
but with affection, as Madame d'Angleterre.

In photographs, Victoria always looks so discontented and only one,
I believe, was ever taken that caught her smiling. However, her
entourage found her cheerful. 'She enjoys everything', writes Miss
Adeane, 'as if she was seventeen instead of seventy-two.' Her energy,
in fact, was exhausting and on arrival at Grasse 'I need hardly tell you
the Queen was less tired than any of us, looked as fresh as a daisy and
beamed upon all the officials.' Another time, again at Grasse, a mistral
is raging. 'The hotel positively rocks with the violence of the gale.
Nevertheless out sallied the Queen for a two-hour drive in an open
carriage', the party returning, coated in dust, 'looking like millers.' At
Nice, with her Battenberg grandchildren, she insists on taking part in
the Battle of Flowers, showering the French officers in attendance with
constant attacks of carnations, a little game that went on for nearly
three hours.

The journey down from Cherbourg all sounds very splendid and here, described by Mr Duff, are some of the details. The royal train was made up of seven coaches, two of which were the Queen's private property; the drawing-room and sleeping-car. Built and furnished in Belgium, they were kept permanently at the station in Brussels. 'They had special springs and no brakes . . . the day car consisted of a small compartment for the Scottish servant who always travelled with the Queen', and then opening off this the drawing-room. 'A short corridor led to the sleeping-car which was divided into dressing-room, bedroom and a compartment for light luggage.' The maids slept with the luggage on sofas. As to the decoration, the drawing-room walls were pearl-grey, capitonned silk, the dado being picked out in blue. Woven into the material was a kind of pale yellow brocading representing Great Britain's national flowers: the shamrock, rose and thistle. 'The curtains were blue and white and a dark Indian carpet fully covered the floor.' Armchairs and sofa were upholstered in blue silk with yellow fringes and tassels, while the dressing-room was vaguely Chinese, the walls being lined with bamboo. Turning to the mechanics, 'the speed of the Royal train was limited to thirty-five miles an hour by day and twenty-five at night. It was halted between eight and nine in the morning so that the Queen could dress in comfort, and stops were made for her meals. Gentlemen requiring hot water for shaving sent word ahead and a jug awaited them at a convenient station'. Food was supplied in the same manner, and Miss Adeane gives one to understand that the entourage infinitely preferred the French cuisine, the alternative being Irish stew prepared at Windsor and kept tepid in red flannel cushions.

On her first visit to the Riviera the Queen stayed at Menton, or Mentone as it was still referred to in her day. She had taken a villa to the east of the town, called the Châlet de Rosiers. Lovely views of the sea were to be had from its terraces but unfortunately it was too exposed to its neighbours, and to give Victoria and her daughter, Princess Beatrice, the necessary freedom, Doctor Bennet put his eagle's nest of a garden at her disposal. Accompanied by the faithful John Brown in his kilt, the Queen would drive up to Bennet's place and spend the whole day. It was John Brown's last trip as bodyguard to his Queen, not an enjoyable one as far as he was concerned since he in no way shared his mistress's love of the French. Several attempts had been made on Victoria's life during her long reign, and rumours had it that a further attack had been prepared by agents in the pay of the

Irish. Already suspicious, John Brown regarded every chance encounter as being pregnant with danger and the people of Menton, not aware of the possible threat to the Queen, must have been somewhat taken aback by the aggressiveness of the square-faced bulldog in kilts. Already a conspicuous figure, he made himself even more so by refusing to budge without a toupee clamped firmly on his head. However, despite the tension the Queen seems to have enjoyed herself and taking advantage of the spring sunshine made daily excursions, including several visits to Hanbury's La Mortola garden where she did some sketching.

Nearly five years were to pass before Victoria returned to the coast. In 1884 Leopold, Duke of Albany, the Queen's youngest son, died in the Villa Nevada at Cannes, and perhaps drawn to the place on his account, or possibly influenced by its popularity with the English, the Queen passed some time at the Villa Edelweiss. It could not have been an outstanding success, for she never returned and the next visit, Easter of 1891, was spent at the Grand Hotel in Grasse. 'Grasse *à la royale*', writes Miss Adeane in a letter, 'is not a toothsome dish.' The gentlemen all complained bitterly of the dullness, but not the Queen, who sprang to the place's defence when attacked by the English press who reported the weather as bad, the food dangerous and the drainage far from sanitary. All completely untrue, of course. The hotel, though on the small side, was first-class. Furious telegrams were despatched and it was found that a medical paper called *The Lancet* was the culprit. The paper had vested interests in English seaside resorts and thus invariably undermined the Riviera when the occasion presented itself. Further variations are revealed by Miss Adeane who hints that the original information came from Cannes, 'whose envy reigns supreme owing to the Queen's preference for humble fare . . .'.

After Grasse came the Grand Hotel Costabelle at Hyères, and three years later, in 1895, Nice. Nice clearly was the favourite. Two consecutive years were spent at the Grand Hotel at Cimiez, to be followed by a protracted stay of three years at the neighbouring Excelsior-Regina; a shining, new colossus of stucco and marble that had sprung up right opposite the Grand, blocking its view. Cimiez was far from being the respectable middle-class *faubourg* it has now become. Our faithful Miss Adeane writing in March reports that everyone is in bright dresses and flowering hats. The place is smarter than Paris – 'and the assembly in the other portion of the hotel would, as regards clothes, put any Marlborough House Garden Party in the shade'. The Queen had more than half of the ground floor to herself. The rooms were enormous, with high ceilings and windows that gave out onto a terrace. One knows this kind of hotel only too well, and there is always something rather bleak about them: the floors creak and the rooms, due to their size, appear almost empty. The royal furniture must have helped in this respect and those of the apartments that had no extra embellishments were rendered more habitable by the use of screens and quantities of flowers. Meals were at set hours: breakfast at nine-thirty, lunch at two, tea at five-thirty, and dinner at half past eight. The Queen, a quick eater, resented dawdling and the principal meals of the day were timed to last half an hour. Fortunately for the court, the dining-room was so hot 'that all appetite faded away'. But one wonders about this, when confronted with a typical luncheon menu. They started with risotto and had two main courses consisting of grilled chops and chicken, then asparagus and two kinds of pudding, one of them tapioca.

The mornings were spent in work, much of it despatched in a tent set up in the grounds of a neighbouring villa lent to the Queen. She would receive ciphered telegrams dealing with important events. One year Balfour was acting as Foreign Secretary, Lord Salisbury having gone to La Bastide, his villa at Beaulieu, for his health – a house he was inordinately fond of since he had been responsible for its planning. It still stands on a hill above Beaulieu and one has to admit that his Lordship's architectural talents compare very poorly when measured against the skill he displayed in the Cabinet. It was while driving up to La Bastide one afternoon that the Queen met the bearded figure of Leopold II of the Belgians. He had arrived that morning on board his yacht and was taking a walk up the hill from Villefranche harbour. The King owned large tracts of land in the neighbourhood, as well as a major part of Cap Ferrat. Another time in the Villefranche district, one hears of Victoria distributing largesse to beggars, dipping into a bag full of francs which she kept clasped on her lap. In her own diary she tells of taking the salute of the garrison troops stationed at Nice. The Queen's carriage is drawn up near the pier* facing the Jardins Publiques. There are about two hundred men. 'It was a pretty sight and the marching very fast as is always the custom with the French . . . The day was splendid but the glare of the white road was very trying for the

---

* In need of scrap metal, it was dismembered by the Germans during the last war.

eyes.' A photograph exists of the Queen on this occasion, and, indeed, whole albums of faded prints commemorate the royal doings – posed groups of frock-coated figures and pinched feminine waists from which are draped the deflated remains of a bustle. Straw hats and parasols temper the bright light filtering down through the dusty leaves of the newly-planted eucalyptus. One sad, beautiful figure detaches itself from amongst these sepia ghosts: that of the Princess of Wales, the future Queen Alexandra, 'very restive', writes Miss Adeane, 'her one idea is to travel, she looks ill and dreads the possibility of raining'.

The photographs help animate the court, breathe life into it, even to the point where one feels that it is possible to listen in to their conversations. A certain Comtesse de la Grange, a doubtful figure, had a zoo up at Cimiez near the Regina, and wanting to please the Queen she sent her an ostrich egg with her name scrawled over the shell. 'Just as if she had laid it herself,' remarked the Queen.[2] Always inquisitive, Victoria had the egg carefully blown and the contents made into an omelette. She pronounced it delicious, and then reflectively, 'Why cannot we have ostrich eggs at Windsor? We have an ostrich'. 'Yes, Mama, a male one', was Princess Beatrice's unusually dry reply.

One day the Queen had a visit from M. Faure, the President. 'Bertie received him below, and brought him up and the Princesses with the ladies were at the top of the stairs.' The Queen stood at the doorway of the drawing-room. She found Faure courteous and amiable 'with a charming manner, so *grand seigneur*, and not at all parvenu'. He flattered the Queen and told her that she was loved by the people. It was no exaggeration; crowds always turned out to see her and every effort was made to make things agreeable, the authorities going so far as to suppress a tram service. A newly constructed line passed by the Villa Liserb where she worked and the passengers could see her over the wall. Learning of this, the service was immediately discontinued during the hours it inconvenienced her.

Even the celebrated Sarah Bernhardt, a fellow guest at the Regina, offered to perform for the Queen in her drawing-room. It was a short one-act play by Adrien Fleuriet called *Jean Marie*. The Queen found Bernhardt 'marvellous' and both monarch and actress were much affected.

An inveterate sightseer, there was usually some expedition arranged in the afternoon. 'We set off up the Valley of the Paillon', writes Miss Adeane, 'right into the country and I enjoyed the peace and absence of automobiles more than I can say, they make driving here a hideous nightmare, and kill at least three people a week.' Think what the gentle Miss Adeane's reaction would be if she were to return to the same scene today!

But of all the different expeditions, I think my favourite is the episode concerning the Queen and the gourds as told by M. Paoli, a detective who watched over Victoria and her outings. She was in the habit of attending fêtes, especially those which recalled the ancient customs of the country, and such an occasion was the *festin de cougourdons* held every Lady's Day up at Cimiez. It is the most important of the fêtes and very popular. Booths are set up in the square opposite the sixteenth-century Franciscan monastery, and here, under awnings, are to be found a display of artefacts, in particular the gourds or *cougourdes*, after which the fête is named. The gourds are cut into while still green, their smooth surfaces being netted over with different patterns under-lined with script, after which they are picked and hung up to dry. The natives of Peru have the same habit and use the gourds as carriers. The first year the Queen made several purchases, and on her second visit the following year was much surprised to see that most of the gourds were engraved with the royal coat of arms, under which was to be deciphered the usual 'by appointment'!

1899 was the last visit to France, and on May Day the Queen drove to Beaulieu. 'Had our tea at St Jean,' she wrote, 'where Lenchen and Beatrice joined us. Alas! my last charming drive in this paradise of nature, which I grieve to leave, as I get more attached to it every year. I shall mind returning to the sunless north, but I am so grateful for all I have enjoyed here.' Reading her diary, one might almost suppose that she knew she would never return.

❧23

Monte-Carlo

By March 1860 Nice had become French territory. Napoleon III had helped Italy in the war against Austria, and in return the newly created kingdom had ceded Nice and Savoy. Simultaneously Monaco, which had been under the protection of Sardinia since the Treaty in 1815, had a choice of either siding with Italy or then of going over to France, who guaranteed her independent sovereignty. She wisely chose France.

Little more than a sea-girthed rock with a coastline of something over three miles, and a width, at the broadest, of half this amount, no one really paid her much heed – least of all Nice who considered herself infinitely superior and in no way threatened in terms of position as a resort. Little did she realise that by the turn of the century she would be considered a cheap edition of her glamorous neighbour, that people would stay in Nice to economise, and travel over daily to Monte-Carlo to enjoy her newly-acquired splendours. The rapid metamorphosis makes an interesting story, but to understand it one must first sketch in a rough outline of Monaco's history. The beginning need not be gone into in detail: suffice it to say that the Grimaldis can legitimately lay claim to being the oldest reigning house in Europe. Of Genoese origin, they were created Lords of Monaco in the year 968 and shortly following this acquired more lands, the whole coast from St Tropez to Fréjus being conferred on them in reward for the part they played in helping William, Count of Provence, in expelling the Saracens. A Grimaldi raised the siege of Rome and delivered the Pope, Gregory VII, when attacked by the Emperor Henry IV. It was a Grimaldi whom Phillip of Valois sought out to fight the English when sorely pressed by Edward III. However, brave as Monaco's princes were to prove themselves, her position, and the nature of her holdings, forced her to play a comparatively subservient role, obliging her to seek the friendship of neighbours, to whom she more or less stood in the relation of vassal.

The Genoese, the Spaniards, the Sicilians and French have all in turn been either allies or foes, and, but for the Grimaldis' (despite their Italian origin) instinctive clinging to France, they would, long since, have disappeared. In 1529 the Principality became a Spanish protectorate and remained so for a little over a hundred years, until September 1641 when Honoré II, the reigning prince, conducted a secret treaty with Cardinal Richelieu at Péronne whereby France would garrison Monaco but at the same time respect her independence. By stealth, the Spanish troops were overcome and the Grimaldis raised to the rank of Prince, Louis XIII likewise conferring on them the titles of Duke of Valentinois and Marquis des Baux, with grants of land in Provence and in the Auvergne.* Today Prince Rainier III can lay claim to a whole string of titles, over nineteen in all, amongst them four dukedoms, two marquisates and several times over baron and count. With these honours, the family had acquired further land extending eastwards as far as Menton, and it was from these lands that they drew their revenues; a *rente* that was further augmented by the *droit de mer* which gave them a right to stop coastal shipping and exact a toll: an institution that smacked of piracy and which was enforced with great vigour by a flotilla of galleys.

Weathering eight long centuries and various vicissitudes, the House of Grimaldi managed its affairs with ability enough to remain undiminished until the catastrophic revolution of 1789, a torrent that not even the Bourbons could resist. In 1793, the National Convention dispossessed the reigning family, arrested Honoré III in Paris, and annexed Monaco to France, Monaco proper being renamed Fort Hercules. There was no bloodshed, but the palace was pillaged and later turned into a hospital for Napoleon's troops. Honoré III died in 1795 to be succeeded by his son Honoré IV. In the meantime, forming part of the French Republic, Monaco was attacked by the English and pillaged, and under the circumstances it is hardly surprising that, with the rise of the Empire, many Monégasques fought in the ranks of Napoleon's armies against the English. Generals de Bréa, Adhéman and Monléon all distinguished themselves, but none more so than Honoré-Gabriel, Honoré IV's eldest son. The young prince won so many laurels that Napoleon, to honour him, gave him the post of grand equerry to the

---

* The recompense might appear somewhat excessive, but it must be remembered that Monaco was an important stronghold and barred the only road of communication between Italy and Provence.

Empress Josephine. After the divorce the Emperor wished him to serve the new Empress, Marie-Louise, but the Prince refused, remaining faithfully attached to Josephine's household till the year 1814, the year of the Empress's death and the Treaty of Paris which restored the Grimaldis to their throne. Honoré IV never acceded, felt too old and infirm and instead delegated the responsibility to his son Honoré Gabriel. Honoré V had no children and was succeeded by his brother Florestan. Florestan died in 1856 and was succeeded by his son Charles III, and it is with Charles that the story of present-day Monte-Carlo really begins.

Already in 1789 there had been a question of Menton and Roquebrune demanding their independence, and during the second revolution of 1848 the rupture was made quite definite, and reluctantly Charles III relinquished his rights over them in return for an indemnity of £160,000 and the assurance that France would keep the road joining Monaco to the Grand Corniche in constant repair, and, as soon as possible, build a shore road from Nice to Monaco. There was a clause also in which the prince was to allow the railway from Nice to Genoa to pass through his territory; arteries of communication that were to prove all-important in the fairly new future, but that as clauses on paper were meagre fare as immediate recompense. It now meant that the Monégasques were shorn of their principal means of livelihood which up till this moment they had reaped from the olive groves and citrus orchards of their eastern shores, in particular Menton's famous lemons. Already Prince Florestan, Charles III's father, had been contemplating turning the Principality into a resort. Plans had been drawn up for a bathing establishment to be installed to the left of the Rock, down on the shoreline in an area known as the Condamine, while a casino for gambling was envisaged on the denuded plateau of the Spélugues, the headland opposite the palace. Bathing was still being indulged in as a therapeutic, but fashionable pastime, while Baden-Homburg, in Germany, provided the shining example of the fortunes to be made in casinos.

Homburg, the capital of Hess-Homburg, one of the many miniature states into which the Germany of the period was split up, was little more than an elegant village nestling at the gates of a palace before the Blancs had turned it into a fashionable resort. The Blancs, François and Louis, were twin brothers born at Courthezon, a small town to the north of Avignon. Clever, it might even be said cunning, they had amassed a fortune dealing in government bonds while living in

Bordeaux, afterwards deciding to invest their money in a gambling establishment. There was no question of starting a casino in France, since a law passed in 1838 had abolished gaming houses: so, looking around, they had picked on Homburg. Its landgrave had recently died leaving a rich widow, Princess Elizabeth, daughter of England's George III. The Princess, bored with Homburg, had retired to Hanover but before retiring had so arranged matters that the Principality was kept solvent with payments from her dowry. The landgrave's heir was hardly in a position of refusing anything and after a certain amount of haggling an agreement was concluded and a casino opened in 1843. Louis died and François carried on, making a spectacular success of the enterprise. Lord Brougham in a letter dealing with the Riviera, addressed to one of the English quarterlies, writes of meeting François Blanc when already installed in Monaco, and refers to him as one of the most capable financiers of France. At any rate, this was the Blanc who Prince Florestan and his capable wife, Princess Caroline, had their eyes on. The prosperity François had brought to Homburg might, with luck, be duplicated in Monaco. Attached to the Court Florestan had an astute lawyer, a certain Maître Eynaud who was as enthusiastic as were his masters in seeing Monaco launched on what they hoped would be its future career, and it was Eynaud who was sent as emissary to Homburg. François Blanc received him, listened to what he had to say and gave him an evasive answer. At least it wasn't a flat refusal. Blanc was interested but wasn't yet ready to invest in another venture, particularly one that involved sinking considerable capital. Monaco had no hotels, and furthermore was tucked away on a rocky shoreline that, at the time, was notoriously difficult of access.

In the meantime, disappointed in Blanc's lack of co-operation, the rulers of Monaco sought elsewhere for some other likely backer to launch a casino. It was a question of finding a lucrative employment for their subjects, without money they might be tempted to vote for union with France; a threatened merger that was frequently on the agenda of certain politicians. Anything to avoid this, and above all some way of improving the lot of the Monégasques. The Principality had an old motto:

> *Son Monaco sopra un scoglio*
> *Non semino e non raccoglio*
> *E pur mangiar voglio*

I am Monaco on a rock by the shore
I neither sow nor reap
But all the same I mean to eat

a saying that must have appeared only too apt during the years
following the loss of Menton and Roquebrune. At last, in 1856, two
men came forward who were ready to risk investing in a casino, a
venture the Prince insisted on calling 'La Société des Bains de Monaco'.
Contracts were signed, and exactly two months later Florestan I died,
to be succeeded by Charles III, an even more enthusiastic backer of his
father's project. In the contract it was stipulated that twenty-five
per cent of the earnings should go to the Principality, in addition to
which it was understood that the backers, Langlois and Aubert,
would undertake the opening of bathing facilities, also build a hotel and
villas in the neighbourhood of the casino to be situated on the
Spélugues. There were various other clauses and certain privileges for
the investors. Langlois and Aubert went so far as to buy a hundred
thousand square metres on the Spélugues; but when it came to actually
building, backed down protesting that they couldn't meet the expenses.
Instead a casino was opened in what they were pleased to call the
'Palais de la Condamine'. No mention was made of the bathing
establishment. The casino, badly managed, failed to pay and in 1858 a
General Assembly annulled the contract, another being drawn up
almost immediately, this time in the favour of Monsieur Daval.
Foundations were laid for the casino on the Spélugues, the first stone
being cemented by the royal family. But Daval, alas, was to prove himself even less able than Langlois and Aubert – was, in fact, nothing but
a simple adventurer. In 1860 yet another attempt was made, this time
headed by M. François le Febvre.

It could be said that Prince Charles showed poor judgement in his
backers, or rather that he was unlucky in the men who presented
themselves. He showed considerable flair, however, when it came to a
question of real estate. He accepted vague promises from these
speculators, but in one thing remained firmly resolute – the casino,
when finally finished, should stand on the Spélugues. He very rightly
saw his Principality as two quite separate entities: the Rock with its
fortified palace and town, and opposite, crowning the promontory of
waste land, a shining new enterprise. Daval's temporary casino had
been installed in a private house looking onto the Palace square, and

le Febvre, having pledged to finish the building started by his predecessor, also chose a makeshift site in what was known as La Maison du Général close to the palace.

The backers or backer of each new venture started off confident of success, and each time lack of capital proved their undoing. It needed a considerable sum of money to turn the stony, olive-clad slope of the Spélugues into a luxurious resort that would attract a rich, cosmopolitan crowd; the other great drawback, of course, being the question of transport. There were only two ways of getting to Monaco and both were bad: one by the Grande Corniche from Nice to La Turbie, and the other by sea in a little vessel of eighteen tons called the *Palmaria*. The *Palmaria* made people sick and could only sail in fine weather, while the corniche, though only twenty-three miles to Nice, involved a great deal of climbing and took a good three to four hours. It was expensive hiring a carriage, and when reaching La Turbie one was obliged to go on to Menton by road and then double back, or failing this, hire a horse and ride down the mountain-side; both ventures were time-consuming, the ride down taking a good hour – not exactly an auspicious beginning for someone whose main object was gambling.

Le Febvre proved as inexperienced as the other directors, but at least he managed to finish the building started by Daval before deciding to throw in his hand. It consisted of an ante-room, a salon where the gambling tables were installed, and a little concert hall which was far too small. Architecturally speaking, it hardly existed and is now entirely engulfed in Garnier's splendid gingerbread. However, le Febvre had done well enough to attract attention; sufficient people came to make it clear that, if properly managed, the casino could be turned into a paying concern. Le Febvre would probably have stayed had he possessed sufficient capital, but the high gamblers who were starting to patronise the place frightened him off. One big win and le Febvre would have been cleaned out. Wisely, he let it be known that if sufficiently reimbursed, he would be willing to relinquish his concession, and Blanc, who had been keeping an eye on the scamperings of Monaco, was the man to tug at the bait. Homburg had been pressing lately for larger shares of the profits, besides which Blanc, a man of intuition, felt that things were about to change in Germany. Here was his chance to get out before it was too late. Blanc met le Febvre in Paris and agreed to take over the concession, a reunion being arranged in Monaco to finalise the deed. Blanc arrived in time for breakfast and by evening, before the departure of the *Palmaria*, everything had been settled. On 1 April 1863 Blanc registered the famous SBM,* a contract that was to hold for fifty years, with a capital of fifteen million francs. The shares were issued at five hundred francs a share and, strange to relate, amongst the first buyers appeared Cardinal Pecci, later Pope Leo XIII.

François Blanc was fifty-seven when named the director of SBM, a small rotund figure with a prematurely white moustache. On catching the boat on the evening of 1 April, he had already left orders for the enlarging of the casino and the building of a first-class hotel to be accompanied by several elegant villas, the whole to be embellished by extensive gardens clumped with various species of palm. From this moment on all went well for Monaco. The Monégasques had heard tell of the splendours of Homburg and regarded the little M. Blanc as a man in whose hands everything turned to gold. Their faith proved well founded. Not only had they the one man who would really help them, but they were also blessed by the most fortunate sequence of events. Prussia's victories in the 1866 war against Austria unified Germany, the state of Hess-Homburg ceased to exist, and following shortly on its dissolution came the order to abolish all gaming houses. Monaco now ruled supreme as a place of 'perdition', was, in point of fact, the only authorised gaming establishment in the entire western world. To further help matters, in 1868 came the opening of the Nice to Monaco railway, the coast road being completed two years later.

For some time now, even before the advent of M. Blanc, those interested in the gambling concession had been casting around for a name by which to dignify the supposed development on the promontory facing the Rock. Various suggestions had been made; Charlesville, or Albertsville after the heir, even Elysée Alberto, but the Prince had refused, not having confidence enough in the supposed success of the venture. But with Blanc his attitude changed, and in the summer of 1866 the once goat-grazed plateau des Spélugues was officially baptised Monte-Carlo, Mount Charles, a euphonic name and easy to pronounce.

Overnight almost the Monégasques had been given a living: more than that even – by 1869 the profits from the casino proved so satisfactory that the Prince was able to abolish all direct taxation. The Franco-Prussian war of 1870 cast a slight blight over the procedure, but with

---

* SBM, to be more precise, stands for *la Société Anonyme des Bains de Mer et Cercle des Etrangers à Monaco.*

the peace of 1871 visitors started to pour in again. By 1875 the crowds were considerable, and amongst them were the Prince and Princess of Wales. The great days of Monte-Carlo had begun.

François Blanc died in 1877 to be succeeded by his son Camille. Before dying François had made plans to build a grand theatre which was to be annexed to the casino. Astute man that he was, Blanc recognised that gambling alone would not guarantee permanent prosperity, and set out to make Monte-Carlo attractive for a class of rich people who were not necessarily drawn to the place by the wheel. There must be other lures, amongst them a theatre, and Charles Garnier was the architect chosen for the job. Not only had he built the new opera house in Paris, one of the most famous buildings of the century, but he was also under a heavy obligation to François Blanc. Started in 1861 the building of the opera house had been interrupted by the Franco-Prussian war, and after the war the government had no money left to complete it. It stood half finished until Blanc came to the rescue with a large loan.

Garnier's theatre in Monte-Carlo was opened with great éclat on 25 January 1879. Prince Charles III with his family sat in the royal box, while on the stage the renowned Sarah Bernhardt spoke the prologue, her golden voice carrying in ringing tones across the stalls to the Prince who sat with closed eyes in his box. He had been blind for close on thirty years.

The theatre is wonderfully baroque; four white-fleshed muses, draped in gold, hold aloft palms at the corners over the stage, and on the side walls heavy swags link marble cartouches inscribed with the names of the great composers. Centred at the back of the theatre, cantilevered out over the stalls, sits the royal box hung in gold-embossed velvet and heavily crowned, looking strangely like some maharajah's howdah on an elephant. From the ceiling hangs an enormous crystal and bronze chandelier, and the ceiling itself is strewn with poppies from the brush of Gustave Boulanger, a popular academician of the time.

From outside Garnier's new addition has a character peculiarly its own and takes masterful command. His dome, posed at a reasonable height, is flanked by square towers from which flutter bright red and white flags: the Grimaldi colours. To the right, just across the road, Jacobi's Hôtel de Paris reflects the master's confection in muted tones. At the back of Garnier's building are to be found flanking niches in which gesticulate two outsized muses: 'Dance' by Gustave Doré, and 'Song', much to most people's surprise, by the 'divine' Sarah. Looking at 'Song' now (and she is fairly carefully hidden), one feels that Garnier might possibly have been browbeaten into the commission. Rodin had no patience with Bernhardt in any other capacity than that of an actress and with contempt bans her work to the attic as 'old-fashioned tripe'. Contemporary critics were not much kinder; the winged song-stress, they wrote, was too robust, and the fingers striking the harp were those of a peasant. Her timid expression and half-open mouth, they agreed, accorded ill with her frame. A woman of that stature would be better employed belting out martial refrains. One reads that in 1882 Sarah's impresario arranged an exhibition of her painting and sculpture at the Grosvenor Gallery in London and that one of her paintings, *Après la Tempête*, fetched four hundred pounds. Perhaps it is just as well that the great actress was not allowed with her brushes inside the casino. She did quite enough harm at the roulette table. An obsessive player, she never won a franc in her life, and according to Paul de Ketchiva, a professional croupier, she was so possessed by the game that she had a wheel of her own which she carried with her wherever she went. 'One night', he tells us, 'she came into the *salle privée*, a tense and determined look on her face.' By the end of the evening she had lost a million francs. 'Clasping and unclasping her hands in a way that was characteristic of her, she rose from the table and left the casino returning to her hotel.' Two hours later there was a rumour that she had taken her life. Gradually details leaked out and it was learned that on regaining her suite she had tried to take poison. Just as she was about to swallow the fatal dose, an old admirer, the Vicomte de —— 'entered the room and prevented her'[1] and offered gallantly to pay her debt.

The theatre was not to be the only addition; in quick succession sumptuous gaming rooms spread out to the left of Garnier's columned atrium, the last to be built dating from 1910. Again the wonderfully elaborate decorations: marbleised columns capped with heavy gold capitals, and round the walls paintings depicting a never-never-land of naked ladies bathing in azure pools, or then, diaphanously clad, wandering under the olives, their veils and their scantily disguised charms stained like shot-silk by the flushings of a sunset. In the foreground trail overblown roses, scenting the blue air. Above them, up on the ceiling, their sisters, equally nude, lie in abandoned and ex-

hausted poses and those hovering over the bar of the Salle Schmit –
better known as the 'kitchen' – are shown puffing away at cigars, a
state of emancipation, the painter is reputed to have told Blanc,
indicating that his nymphs were not all that they should be. The Salle
Schmit, or 'the kitchen', is the largest of the gambling rooms and,
according to tradition, picked up its somewhat bizarre name after some
grand English visitors had seen their servants playing roulette there.
Quite the opposite is the Salle Privée, an inner holy-of-holies where the
very rich gather to play. Before the 1914 war, gold coins were used and
the tables would glitter with piles of pinkish *louis*. It was usual to see
players win or lose the equivalent of forty thousand pounds and 'now',
as General Polovtsoff tells one, 'about two thousand or three thousand
is enough to set people's tongues wagging'.[2]

Fortunately the SBM have had the wit to restore the rooms so that
they now shine out in all their original splendour. Great chandeliers
glitter, reflected in countless mirrors, and as the poet Stéphen Liégeard
puts it: 'It's a place of enchantment, where night descends in a robe of
light.'[3] 'Indeed, the sun had never been known to penetrate these stuffy
rooms; its dancing motes might possibly disturb the tense, neurotic
atmosphere. Daylight is a cleansing medium. Gambling belongs
essentially to the ways that are dark, and it is in their hushed, smoke-
filled interiors that one must envisage the gay cosmopolitan crowds;
emperors, kings and cocottes, grand dukes, barons, countesses – even
the monarchs' wives. The kaiser would visit Monte-Carlo in his yacht,
and the Prince of Monaco was often seen in the casino, but had very
decided views on gambling, his heir harbouring even stricter ones.
According to Sir Osbert Sitwell, he hardly recognised the existence of
the gaming rooms and when forced to do so by some guest up at the
palace, indicated them with a vague nod in their direction, *'en face la'*.[4]
The tzarina was a regular player and when she played was phenomenally
lucky. Queen Margherita of Italy was another who invariably won and
when she appeared always wore a wonderful tiara of rubies, one turn of
her head flashing great pools of fire under the blaze of lights. Among the
women, Eleonara Duse was frequently seen at the table, until one day a
beautiful Italian girl took poison while sitting next to her. She never
played again. But all this information is in de Ketchiva's book, also the
story of the Baroness Groner, a dark attractive woman, related by
marriage to the Hohenzollern family. Twice in one evening she broke
the bank. Two *commissaires de jeux* were sent to fetch more money,

and the table was draped in black crêpe to acknowledge the fact that the bank had been broken. In the old days when this happened, play was suspended while a fresh stack of money was obtained. Nowadays the money at each table is replenished whenever it reaches a certain minimum. There is a dramatic denouement to the Baroness and her winnings, but too long to tell here.

Another feature of the gaming rooms were the endless cranks who appeared with foolproof systems of how to get the best of the casino. The kaiser paid through the nose for a system devised by a professor of Heidelberg University, and Camille Blanc offered forty thousand pounds to anyone who could prove that an infallible system existed, but none has ever been found.

Of the countless dramas told relating to famous figures is the incident touching on Mata Hari, the German agent. Half Chinese, half Javanese, she had an exotic appeal, and on this particular evening caught the fancy of a bearded Russian officer. She had been playing heavily and watching her, the officer had found her languorous opulence irresistible. Driven wild, he had come up to her, and encircling her hourglass waist had kissed her full on the lips. Mata Hari kept a small revolver in the bosom of her dress, and using it shot the Russian through the chest. The bullet did no real harm, but that same night the dancer was advised to leave the Principality, and in her great white Hispano-Suiza, she headed towards Spain – at that time her headquarters as an enemy agent.

Belonging to this same world are the *demi-mondes*, beautifully turned out by Worth and Doucet. La Belle Otero had the reputation of being the most brilliant and beautiful of the casino's habituées. The tzar and the kaiser had both been her lovers, also Edward vii. The Duke d'Aumale and King Léopold of the Belgians, two of the older specialists of female beauty, were also her fervent admirers, and Vanderbilt gave her her famous pearls, each pearl having been hidden in the oysters she was made to eat whenever she dined with him. Her collection of jewels were known the world over, and amongst them her famous black velvet jacket sewn back and front with diamonds – great blue-white stones that caught the light with each movement. Strange, that in her photographs she looks coarse and heavy-featured, with unattractively pudgy hands. Far more beautiful, to my mind, was Liane de Pougy. I can imagine her appearing on the steps of the Hôtel de Paris, a gloved hand resting lightly on the arm of her escort. A pause, and then slowly she would walk to the casino, a slight hesitation lent to her movements by the elaborations of her dress.

Les grandes horizontales these ladies were sometimes referred to, and in connection with them I remember an episode involving Sir Cecil Beaton. He was staying with me at the time and had been commissioned to photograph Cléo de Mérode, who aged ninety was still living in Nice. He had made an appointment with 'Mademoiselle' in her lodgings. She received him in a silk crocheted skull-cap that hid any possible thinning of hair, and Beaton explained how she instinctively took up poses: hand under the chin and an arched look in the still lustrous eyes, the kind of pose that would have been fashionable in the days when she reigned. Beaton found it a very moving experience.

There was, of course, a sad side to all this glare of light – paradise to some, for others, the moralists, it was the plague spot of the Riviera. More often than not one finds Monte-Carlo depicted in far from flattering terms, one writer likening it to a candle drawing moths to its flame. Nor was there any hiding of its suicides: the dark secrets of its scented gardens were read aloud at countless breakfast tables. De Ketchiva, not given to exaggeration, writes of 'women with bodies as beautiful as a tropic dawn'. He watches them throw their last franc away 'and then with a tightening of the lips and an ugly glitter in their eyes too terrible and heartbreaking for description, walk out of the hothouse atmosphere of the gaming rooms and under the star-powdered sky, blow their brains out, or take a feverish gulp of the contents of a phial and drop, their limbs convulsed to the ground and die'. There was also the question of crime, of vice rubbing shoulders with virtue, and the casino has its *brigade de jeux*, or private detectives. No casino has a more watchful corps, but even so it is impossible to guarantee the inmates' complete security. There are the pickpockets and unavoidable petty thieves who will try and claim other people's winnings. Heavy winners were watched and enticed into rooms in hotels while special gangs patrolled the trains. The train was new enough to be smart: there were few cars and the distances were tedious by carriage. Henrick Sienkiewicz, author of *Quo Vadis*, gives us a charming description of passengers: the men, their buttonholes flowered with violets or a gardenia, the women heavily perfumed with iris or heliotrope, veiled under hats loaded with muslin blooms. There is much lace and velvet, eyebrows are heavily blacked, and lips a trifle too red. The train plunges into a tunnel, a burst of sunlight and then another tunnel; splendid views, bunches of palms, *'les villas dressées à l'ombre des oliviers où dans la blancheur les amandiers fleurissent'*.[5] Quick stops at the various stations and then the tingling excitement as Monte-Carlo approaches. De Ketchiva warns that should you have occasion to catch a late train out of Monte-Carlo, 'you would do well to restrain yourself from falling asleep, especially if you have had a run of luck at the tables'. Robberies were a nightly occurrence and the Monte-Carlo to Nice *rapide* was covered by a certain gang composed of five women, all *demi-mondaines*, under the leadership of a ruffianly Greek. Small wonder that writers like Miss Dempster, the author of *Vera*, a popular novel of the time, gets so over-excited when dealing with Monte-Carlo. 'It is the casino that keeps up the palace, the army, the roads, the opera house and the Hôtel de Paris. It is the green table that keeps the gardens green and the violins in tune; that has brought three thousand residents and so many hundred prostitutes to the town; it gives work to a thousand servants.' Further on she explodes 'the subject is so hackneyed, and in some respects so repulsive, that I prefer to leave to other pens to describe'. Of course, she doesn't. 'Monte', in those days, had an almost morbid curiosity for those who professed to disapprove of it, and Miss Dempster was no exception. She tells us how the powers that be, the directors of the SBM, deal with any adverse criticism which, according to this English spinster, was rife on every side; an anti-Monaco meeting held in Nice was interrupted by howls while 'a respectable Parisian paper which told the truth, was forbidden to enter the territory'.[6] At intervals the French government made a show of wishing to suppress the gambling tables, but considering the Prince's position as an independent ruler, it might have posed a problem had the motion been pressed too anxiously.

It seem sincredible, but there were those who, when compelled to pass through the Principality, ostentatiously drew down the blinds of their railway carriage 'lest they should ever see that wicked place'. Queen Victoria had a horror of Monte-Carlo and rather unkindly, when staying at Menton, drove over and stumped around the Rock like any ordinary tourist. The Prince, quite understandably, was furious. But this, one supposes, was dear Bertie's fault considering his fondness for the place.

Another unfortunate episode was the row between the Anglican Bishop of Gibraltar and, indirectly, Prince Charles III. The bishop, newly appointed in 1873, wanted to establish an English church in

Monte-Carlo, just at the time when the Prince hoped Monaco would become a separate Catholic diocese. In a roundabout way the pope had made it quite clear that this would not come about if the Prince permitted an Anglican church to be built. Although a tolerant man, as ruler of a Catholic state Charles had no alternative but to obey the pope's wishes. Messages were forwarded to the bishop, and no doubt, for diplomatic reasons, the text was somewhat vaguely worded. The bishop, refusing to read between the lines, flew into a rage, his riposte being a diatribe in the form of a letter to be read out from the pulpit by every English clergyman on the Riviera; a childishly vindictive condemnation inferring that Monte-Carlo was polluting the whole coast; in short, that the Riviera had become an evil influence and was no longer a fit place for habitation by decent, self-respecting people. The bishop cited one of Monte-Carlo's better known cases of suicide to give his rantings more punch. 'Is it right,' he stormed, 'for Christian men and women ever to enter a place where they are sure to rub shoulders with the swindler, the harlot and the thief, whose chambers are built with the wages of iniquity, and whose riches are the price of blood?' Nice, delighted, published the bishop's vitriolic address as an editorial, at the same time trying her level best to have the Monte-Carlo casino closed down, but all to no avail. It was, anyway, pure hypocrisy, for Nice had for some time established her own casino. Powerless, she was obliged to stand by and watch the élite crowd into her trains for Monte-Carlo; and, what was even worse, watch herself being completely ignored. Towards the end of 1873 Rome created Monaco an independent diocese and straight away building was started on a cathedral, a glaringly white affair designed by Charles Lenormand in a pseudo-byzantine, romanesque style. No longer beholden to the pope, Prince Charles gave his authority for the consecration of a Protestant church, and strange to relate, not very long afterwards an earthquake damaged every religious building in Monaco. It was quite a serious quake, but left the casino completely unscathed. 'So much for Divine Judgement!' scoffs the General Polovtsoff, employed by SBM as president of the Sporting Club. Interesting also is a detail which, for his peace of mind, one hopes, escaped the notice of the Reverend Lord Bishop Charles Waldegrave Sandford. It would seem that those of the English gamblers who attended services on Sunday showed a marked interest in the board announcing the hymns. If the numbers happened to fall below thirty-five, they would hotfoot it to the casino. Most gamblers are superstitious, and why shouldn't numbers announced in a church have certain prophetic connotations? The first to practise this nefarious deed happened to be an elderly, much respected peer of the realm. The number came up and before lunch-time a major part of the congregation had heard the story. The following Sunday the parson had never witnessed such a crowd, again one of the hymns happened to be a low number, and there was a concentrated rush to the roulette wheel. The Sunday after this the attendance was almost embarrassing. The parson, however, was no fool, and never again were hymns below the denominator of thirty-seven announced, to a disappointed and dwindling congregation.

Charles III died in 1889 to be succeeded by Albert I. In 1892 the Monte-Carlo Opera was founded under the direction of Raoul Gunsbourg. Wagner is produced for the first time outside of Bayreuth and amongst the guest singers appears the great Chaliapin. Prince Albert, a world-recognised oceanographer, spends much time on his yachts the *Alice* and the *Alice II*, both named after his second wife, the Duchess of Richelieu. It was on the fourteen hundred ton *Alice II* that the Prince brought back many of the specimens now displayed in his museum built after the designs by Mr Delafontie. Its architect chose the site well, posing its great rusticated walls flush with the rock that plunges some four hundred feet directly into the water below. The aquarium, in the basement, is one of the finest in Europe, and above follow a suite of great halls hung with vast seascapes and set with the skeletons of monster fish, including that of a whale. By 1910 the shareholders of the SBM could congratulate themselves on their choice of investments – the net profits in a year were over a million pounds. Camille Blanc used his block of the profits wisely, reinvesting the money in different ventures which he hoped would attract a still more diverse clientèle. In 1911 he inaugurated the Monte-Carlo Rally. Twenty-three competitors started, converging on Monaco from different points in Europe: Paris, Boulogne-sur-Mer for the English, Brussels, Berlin, Vienna and Geneva. The distances had to be covered at an average speed of ten kilometres an hour, which worked out roughly to eleven hundred kilometres in twenty-four hours. This scheme of Blanc's proved an immense help to motoring, and in the words of Charles Graves 'most of the development and improvements of the modern motor-car have been directly due to the influence of the Rally. Anti-skid devices, defrosters, fog-lamps, car heaters and better springing are only a few of the devices invented by

motor manufacturers to improve their entries' chance in the race'.[7]
Another of Blanc's ideas, and the most extravagant, was the golf
course at Mont Agel, above La Turbie. It cost the SBM two hundred and
fifty thousand pounds. It meant carting up tons of soil, planting grass,
and above all keeping it healthy, once sown. At the time it was made
there were only three courses on the Continent, one at Mandelieu, and
the others at Pau and Paris. Encouraged by the success of the motor
rally, Blanc financed the Schneider trophy, a similar scheme applying
to aeroplanes, the competitors taking to the air from different parts of
Europe. The 1912 race was won by Roland Garros: a prize of £1200 for
flying from Monaco to Paris in twelve hours seventeen minutes.

Previous to this, in 1911, the SBM had engaged Diaghilev and his
Ballets Russes, and one of the most marvellously creative eighteen
years of theatre ensued. Nijinsky dances in *Le Spectre de la Rose*,
Léon Bakst doing the set and costumes. Nijinsky's dancing had the
most extraordinary effect on people, and women fainted when he made
his last spectacular leap through the window. Diaghilev had this
extraordinary flair for assessing young talent and of experimenting
with it. When engaged by the SBM his company was made up almost
exclusively of young people. Alexandre Benois and Diaghilev himself
were its oldest members, and Diaghilev was scarcely past his middle
thirties. The names are legion: Nijinsky and Nijinska, the beautiful
Karsavina, Massine and Nemtchinova and Danilova – Lifar – Dolin.
The painters Diaghilev persuaded to work for him have, for the most
part, become the masters of this century: Picasso, Braque, Mirò and
Max Ernst. Marie Laurincin, not quite in the same class it must be
admitted, designed costumes for *Les Biches*, Juan Gris those for *The
Gods Go A-Begging*, while Chirico worked on *Le Bal*. Leaving the
recognised classical works aside, Prokofiev and Stravinsky were both
commissioned by Diaghilev to write ballets for him. Henry Sauguet
composed *La Chatte*, and Francis Poulenc his lyrical *Les Biches*, and
Georges Auric *Les Fâcheux*. Darius Milhaud produced *Train Bleu*,
Chanel dressing the beach scenes. The list is endless: amongst the
English Lord Berners composed *The Triumph of Neptune*, and Constant
Lambert *Romeo and Juliet*.

Now come the war years. By 1914 Monaco had become almost derelict,
the great rooms at the casino lay silent, deserted except for their ghosts.
But things pick up again and a year later the great doors are thrown

open and business resumed. Thousands were dying daily on the battle-fields of Europe, but there were the living and half-living to be amused and distracted. A great effort was made, but gambling remained desultory and the SBM got into financial difficulties. Eventually they succeeded in inducing the famous millionaire, Sir Basil Zaharoff, to take a controlling interest in the company; the deal concluded over breakfast at the Ritz Hotel in Paris while the one-time waif of Istanbul quietly munched his toast.* Albert I died in 1922 and was succeeded by Prince Louis II, the dynasty being assured by his daughter and grandson, the present reigning Prince – Rainier III.

With the peace, life seemed to return to normal, a somewhat frenzied normal. Diaghilev and his ballet reappeared at the opera house, and accompanying them, as it were, came the gamblers and a smattering of royalty, more often than not kings without their crowns. The tables probably lacked the éclat, but with the introduction of baccarat, formerly forbidden, the gambling became more interesting to watch. The centre table in the Salle Privée had no limits and became a kind of mecca for the curious. Zographos, head of the Greek syndicate, is reputed to have won anything from two to ten million pounds from the casino. He would sit with as much as thirty thousand pounds in front of him in casino plaques. Needless to say, the cards were not always with him and one evening, playing against M. Citroën and the old Agha Khan and Mr James Hennessy, he lost nearly three hundred thousand pounds. The players of those days are not yet people of a distant past, and their names still mean something to us; there was Gordon Selfridge and the Dolly sisters, the Duke of Westminster and Sacha Guitry with Yvonne Printemps, whose voice Melba found 'the most irresistible in the world'. Josephine Baker, heavily jewelled, could be seen charlestoning: 'the bosom of her décolleté frock bulging and rustling with bank-notes, diamond-studded heels clicking over the floor'.

In 1925 Zaharoff sold his interest in SBM to a rich banking corporation in Paris, and René Léon was made its director. Following the fashion of the time, Léon decided to create a summer season and Monte-Carlo beach was thought up. No beach was possible in Monaco, and by an amicable agreement with the government he poached on French territory, building an agreeable Provençal-looking hotel overlooking

* Zaharoff had a private box at the casino theatre, and his own suite at the Hôtel de Paris. The hotel kept a special dinner service for him and Vermeille knives and forks.

the small bay he had chosen to the west of the Principality. The only drawback to the bathing were the pebbles. To launch this new venture, Elsa Maxwell, with her vivacity and talent for mixing people, was appointed ambassador. She filled it with amusing people but balked at the pebbles. Suffering noisily, but with her usual enthusiasm, she did her best to cope with the situation. Huge sheets of crêpe rubber were obviously the solution – a rubber beach! It was only after the third manufacturer had told her that her project was out of the question that Miss Maxwell gave up. Instead the 'famous' were issued with espadrilles.

With the outbreak of World War II, Monaco should by rights have been treated as neutral territory, but Italy, when she declared war on France, paid not the slightest attention to these niceties and billeted her men in its hotels, and the English residents were sent to Sospel. Later, the Germans arrived; the Gestapo occupied the Hôtel de Paris, the Metropole being taken over by the headquarters staff of a complete German panzer division.

On 15 August 1944 came the Allied landings, the American seventh army under General Patch and seven divisions under Général Lattre de Tassigny. Moving from west to east, they disembarked on the islands of Hyères, Cap Nègre and the beaches of Pampelonne, La Nartelle, and Val d'Esquieres, opposite St Tropez, and Cap Dramont the far side of St Raphaël.

As I write this it seems just the other day, but counting the years one is appalled that already thirty years have slipped by and with them have appeared many changes, principally the frenzied spate of building that has been going on up and down the coast, and in particular in Monte-Carlo. I seldom go there but when I do I am invariably astonished at the rapidity with which the contractors work. Giant cranes swing against the sky piling up storey after storey; apartment blocks appear to grow with the facility of bamboos during the rains, and the density with which they have appeared has been the cause of much criticism. Old inhabitants who have known the place all their lives don't hesitate to pronounce on the subject. It is quite simple – 'they are ruining the place', 'they' referring presumably to Prince Rainier and his ministers. Even amongst the Monégasques themselves, opinions seem to be divided. Naturally one sees their point, but have those who are so fervently in favour of the old order of things really given the subject much thought? Have they asked themselves what might have prompted the initial

activity? I doubt it, and yet the arguments in favour of this contro-
versial venture in real estate are more than convincing – it is simply a
question of economic transformation. The takings of the casino, once
all important, now represent a comparatively low percentage of the
overall earnings of the country, and Prince Rainier, looking to the
future, felt that his people must have more solid ground on which to
base their economy. After all, tourism and gambling can be ephemeral
assets and at all times dependent on the fluctuations of world affairs.
Already the Italians, one of the SBM's most liberal spenders, are in
difficulty in obtaining permits to export capital, and no country, for
that matter, with the exception of the Middle East's oil producing
states, is in a position to encourage any form of extravagance. On the
face of it, it looks as if Rainier acted more than wisely to encourage the
building, and by so doing has augmented the population and automatically increased the supply and demand. The figures are impressive.
Some seven hundred firms are lodged in these towering apartments,
giving employment to 18,000 people. But the new Monte-Carlo has not
yet swamped the old and the resort crowd complain at the towers: 'Why
the skyscrapers?' they say. Why here of all places?' Precisely *here* is
the answer. As with New York, there is a valid reason for this particular
form of architecture – a question of space, Monaco being even more
constricted than Manhattan. The only possible criticism, as I see it, is
the question of planning. It seems a pity that a place built as an amphitheatre in a scoop of the mountains did not regulate the height of its
buildings to fit in with the landscape; in other words, push the skyscrapers to the back and diminish the height towards the shore-line.
But here again, the Principality is hardly in a position to be dominated
by a question of aesthetics which, in her case, would amount to an
extravagant waste.

No, all in all, I think it exciting, this new Manhattan by the Mediterranean, and viewed from afar, standing at night in the grounds of
Augustus's trophy, Monaco glitters and shines in the dark like a
riviere of diamonds.

Prince Rainier and Princess Grace are idealists and have worked hard
to achieve the respect now paid to them. It was not an easy task, to
live down first the musical comedy aspect of a small principality, and
secondly, the Princess's highly successful Hollywood career. She
accepted a challenge that unless handled with tact could very well have
smacked of burlesque. Slowly, with patience and a great deal of hard

work, heart, and much common sense, she has carved out a niche for herself amongst a people given to cynicism. There can be little doubt of the Monégasques' affection for their ruling couple after the accolade accorded to them recently when celebrating the twenty-fifth anniversary of the Prince's reign. Another important factor to be taken into consideration is the image the Principality herself now represents. She is still 'good old Monte', said with a twist of the moustache and a certain gleam in the eye, but dispelled for good are the old insinuations of disrepute: rather, thanks to the farsightedness of her sovereign, she would seem to present a small area of solvent calm in a troubled world beset by violence. ——

However, I do not mean to end on too serious a note. The Monte-Carlo of our parents is still intact for those who are in search of such a place. Standing at the top end of the gardens, close by the double stairs mounting to Barclays Bank, one is not conscious of any change. The flower beds, carefully planted, dip as they have always dipped, towards the façade of Garnier's casino, and pink pleated lampshades still light one through dinner, served on the terrace restaurant of the Hôtel de Paris – a soft glow, a real *couleur de rose* that matches the famous raspberry soufflé, a confection guaranteed to soothe the most troubled of spirits.

❦24

The Circle Completed

Several times, already, I have made mention of the move from the big house to the Clos. The references were fleeting and no explanation given, but now that the book is drawing to its close, the moment has come to be more coherent. This evocation of Provence and its coast begins in a personal vein, and to complete the circle should end the same way. In a sense, this book is the story of a house, and the interest must now switch from the big to the small – to my terraces in the sun – 'Terraces in the Sun' having been the original title of this book.

By 1961 my mother was spending more and more of her time in Kenya. She had been an East African *habituée*, since the Happy Valley days, and my parents' safaris – amongst the first to be properly organised – have passed into the lore of the country, my stepfather, Furness, being known to his porters as 'Champagny Lordy'. Widowed from Furness and remarried, and widowed again from Kenmare, my mother had taken up racing in Nairobi. It was not a new hobby, having once been the owner of what is now the National Stud in Somerset. My mother had extraordinary powers of concentration and whatever she undertook she did so wholeheartedly, and it was not long before she felt the lack of challenge evident in Nairobi's race course, and when her doctor advised her to move to a lower altitude she immediately jumped at the excuse to go property hunting in South Africa, and at the age of seventy-four, still extraordinarily beautiful, acquired Broadlands Stud, one of the first English farms to be settled in the Cape – a large property of several hundred acres which my sister, her own licenced trainer, now runs very successfully.

This digression is to help explain the sale of Fiorentina. Left on my own, I was obliged to rent the place during the summer months and by degrees came to feel it altogether too much of a responsibility. One extremely fortunate episode, however, came about through my rents:

I met, and now count amongst my friends, one of America's most remarkable women – Mrs Albert Lasker. She made Fiorentina a part of her annual schedule and by so doing gave, not only myself, but many distinguished guests a great deal of pleasure. Apart from her charm and warmth of character she has an extraordinary faculty for giving; is a real life enhancer, on a scale rarely met with. Not only does her presence ensure the enjoyment of things, she is also a public-spirited benefactor: witness the recent changes in Washington's landscaping and the flowers each spring that enliven New York's Park Avenue, and on an even higher altruistic scale, the millions each year for which she is responsible, seeing that they are delegated to the right quarter in the States programme of cancer research, an act of sheer force of character. As to the sale, there was another factor to be considered: my brother and his family lived in England, which meant that I was the only one to benefit from the place. Here I was hanging on to what amounted to a sizeable amount of the family capital, living on in a house I no longer could really afford. I had made Fiorentina and in a way it has become quite an institution, but how hampering to indulge in sentiments. Real estate on the Riviera in the late sixties was still at an enormous premium, and properties such as Fiorentina were able to command exaggerated prices. How long, one wondered, would the market hold? With these thoughts in mind, I suddenly one morning decided to sell, and within a matter of months was lucky enough to find the ideal purchasers – Mr and Mrs Harding Lawrence. Harding, a good-looking Texan in his early fifties, is chairman of Braniff International Airlines, and Mary his wife better known as Mary Wells, a vital and alive woman, is president of Wells, Rich and Green, one of the world's leading advertising agencies. They saw the house and fell in love with it for all the right reasons, and the takeover went through in a wonderfully painless fashion. I took to the Lawrences immediately, and to make things even easier their decorator, William Baldwin, is one of my oldest friends, an enchanting person, blessed with infinite tact. It could have been a difficult situation for Baldwin with myself sitting, as it were, at the gates, but he handled it all with great discretion and on each visit made from New York stayed with me at the Clos.

This brings us, then, to myself. I have already explained how we lived in the Clos while rebuilding Fiorentina, which makes the move just a reversal of time. As to the house, it dates from the end of the eighteenth century and is the oldest house on Cap Ferrat, or more exactly the Pointe St Hospice. It has no pretensions to architecture, but in its simplicity can lay claim to a good deal of charm, and is typical of the country: has red tiled floors and white marble stairs, a Roman tiled roof, green shutters, and pinkish-ochre walls. Directly outside the front door stands the old covered-in well, once the house's only water supply. Constructionally the alterations were few. The rooms were on the small side, which meant knocking down walls and adding the extra accommodation needed; an improved kitchen, servants' hall and pantry being scooped out of the rock at the back of the house, while the underside of the terrace, heavily reinforced, became a garage.

As to the refurbishing, it has been kept fairly plain. Limited in space, I purposely chose simple colours, concentrating on variations of yellow and green. The stairs and corridors are chalk-white, with white cotton curtains, the curtains being always kept drawn for the sake of the drawings; a collection of delicate sepia washes of India by the Daniells, a Chinnery of Canton, and some Lear water-colours of Egypt. In the drawing-room I was obliged to block out two windows in order to obtain space for the paintings and to compensate for the loss of light painted the room a pale yellow, matching the curtains to the walls, the floor being laid with old terra-cotta tiles. It makes a deliciously cool room in the summer, and the luminosity acts as a foil for the leather-bound books and the glint of gilded bronze on the Louis XVI tulipwood furniture, signed pieces from the big house but which in spite of their quality look well in a reduced space. Other notes in the room are the yellowish-whites of two Elizabethan portraits, and an extra-large sofa of dusty blue colour which mixes well with the pale limes of the Kashmir carpet, one of a pair especially worked for Fiorentina. Opening off this, through a swing door made to simulate a part of the book-case, is the small winter dining-room divided up into panels and lozenges of false marble, purposely naïve in their rendering, the work of the same old man who painted the hall at Fiorentina and, as with the hall, the ceiling simulates a cloud-driven sky, a common practice down here in the older houses. Both these ground-floor rooms give onto the terrace overlooking Beaulieu Bay and the mainland; a vine shaded area which acts as an outside drawing-room during the hot summer months.

As regards to the terrace and swimming-pool furniture, I have purposely avoided bright colours. Living in the sun, I find one tends to avoid them, and this, I feel, applies to any of the Mediterranean countries – something to do with the sharpness and quality of the light.

This question of muted tones is also carried through to the garden, and wherever possible I have kept to a mixture of greens laid out in casual formality. Not actually occupying the house until recently, I have had years to plan the layout. As basic elements, I had the side of a hill buttressed with terraces leading down to the sea, also the stones from the ruin of an early-seventeenth-century fort to carry on with if any further construction was needed. The fort, as depicted in early drawings, looked a massive affair and was erected by Charles-Emanuel I as a protection against piratical raids from North Africa. Judged a useless encumbrance by later generations, it was blown up in 1706 by one of Louis XIV's generals, and took two months of concentrated mining to tumble, the walls still bearing the marks where the powder blackened the stones. Along with the terraces, we also inherited some twenty magnificent olives which, judging from their size, must be at least six hundred years old. As is usual in this form of cultivation, the olives are planted in rows and are on the same level as the house, centred in a terrace about eight feet wide along which I have clumped great cushions of grey-green echium, a handsome contrast to the grey of the olives when they burst out with their blue candle-like flowers in the spring. Another feature of the garden is a walk of mandarin trees with their trunks daubed in whitewash. Under them, confined by a low border of box hedging, I have planted double rows of arums and it looks very effective when the lilies are out, their white chalices catching the light filtered through the mandarins' pointed leaves. In one place, copying the Italians, I have massed a bed of aspidistra and on the terraces to the left of the house, where the rocks begin to obtrude and the soil is thin, I have naturalised broad drifts of the wild tulips from Greece and Turkey, also a collection of dwarf narcissi, a native of stony reaches in the Alpille. The steep banks behind are anchored with a solid flank of judas trees with, under them, blue drifts of *anenome blanda* alternating with clumps of the pale *iris stylosa*.

A garden is a fascinatingly mobile way of expressing oneself, and all the time new ways of presenting things occur to one. The idea, for instance, for the topiary work behind the house came to me while on a flight to Cape Town, the whole terrace, quite broad in this instance, being divided up with squares of box and in the centre of each square a tapering cone of the same plant – nothing spectacularly original but just the right accent, to my mind, at this particular point of the garden. From here stairs railed in a Chinese Chippendale design mount to a further terrace backed by cypress with an underplanting of agapanthus.

The terracing, of course, has played a major role in dictating the character of the garden. It has imposed a strict architectural setting, a frame into which I have tried to work a mixture of loose and tight plants. By varying from light to dark and changing from narrow to broad, I have been able to create an illusion of space, the garden appearing much larger than it actually is.

So much then for the move – how about the setting? It is no use pretending that life on the coast hasn't changed. Those of us who have known it over the years tend to lead more restricted lives, accept fewer invitations and import our friends who, for their part, seem always to accept with the same alacrity. After all, the beauty of the country is indestructible. Often I am asked if I miss Fiorentina, and the answer is that regrets are a waste of time. The house has been entirely re-furnished, Baldwin having been given instructions to duplicate the atmosphere wherever possible, and so, although entirely redone, it has become a slightly more contemporary blueprint of the way I left it. Sometimes when going to see the Lawrences, walking up the steps, I have a strange sensation, so different and yet the same. Of course, I miss the big room; the light in the morning when coming downstairs in the winter; the great heavy clots of warm sunshine lying in panels across the floor, striping the furniture; and in the evening the dancing motes as the sun sinks in a searchlight of intensity through the great doors. No, otherwise I feel entirely at home at the Clos, and have not the slightest impression of living at the gates. Fiorentina, as far as concerns my life, is miles away, the Clos being altogether another idiom, small and intimate, surrounded by its hidden gardens.

The other afternoon, when at the top of the house in what is known as the Anglo-Indian room – the study in which I work – Emilienne came through on the house phone: the admirable Emilienne who has been running things for us for the last thirty-five years. I must come down, there was an old lady of ninety-one who wanted to see the garden. Emilienne has an infallible judgement about people, and wouldn't have called had the visitor not passed muster. So down I went, and there at the door stood Madame Delor accompanied by three friends. Impul-sively she held out both hands – 'I was born here, grew up in this house, and it is only now I have dared to come back'. She apologised for intruding, and her eyes were misted with tears. Equally moved, I took her arm and we walked off down under the pergola. Excitedly she exclaimed on this and that, and turning into the spring garden she showed me where the family used to play *boulles*: 'and you know, we would get so worked up that we struck a candle on the *couchonnet* and went on playing in the dark'. She carried her years well and there was no faltering or fumbling for words. 'You still have that palm, I see. You know the coastguards were always after my father about cutting it down. They claimed that it made a landmark for the smugglers.' Again the tears of joy behind the glasses: 'And that Madonna up there' – she was referring to a twenty-foot Virgin and Child cast in copper which stands next to the King of Sardinia's mortuary chapel capping the head of the point. 'The sculptor was a friend of my father's and he used my hands as his model.' The Madonna is not actually in the garden, but looms over the wall and was originally intended for the tower – all that remains of the original fort. Her role was to be that of guardian angel to the fishermen, but somehow she never quite made her supposed elevation and now dwarfs her surroundings, a miniature Statue of Liberty, an ecclesiastical landmark cradling the Christ Child instead of holding aloft a lamp of liberty.

Before leaving, I asked Madame Delor to sign the visitors' book: the date is 20 May 1974, and without hesitation she wrote out her piece, ending with a well-turned phrase, thanking me – 'Who has given me today, at the age of ninety-one, the opportunity of reliving my early years'. ―

I close these pages with apologies to the reader for the numerous omissions of which, alas! there are many. I regret, for instance, my total silence on the subject of the Félibres, a group of nineteenth-century poets brought together by Joseph Roumanille, a schoolteacher of St Rémy. There seems to be some doubt about the origin of the word *félibres* but more than likely it comes from the Greek *philabros*, 'he who loves the beautiful'. The Félibres were fiercely proud of their birthright and their aim was the glorification of Provence and its ways. Their poetry, written in *langue d'oc*, the language of the country, concentrated mainly on traditional love songs woven around descriptions of local life, scenery, customs and legends: it was an echo of the troubadours and their melodies. Frederique Mistral, with his epic poem *Mireille*, was the most powerful personality of the group. In 1856, when still a young man, Dumas *père* took him to visit Lamartine in Paris, who was captivated by his beauty. He was twenty-six at the

time and always kept his looks. Mary Darmesteter, who saw a lot of the
Mistrals, describes him as strikingly handsome when he was three times
that age. She was also enthralled by his voice, and writes that he so
resembled 'Buffalo Bill' in appearance that one day, when the two
celebrities met by accident in a Parisian café, it gave them quite a
shock. Bewildered they stared at each other, and then, rising, advanced
and shook hands! Mistral's house at Maillane is exactly as he left it
when he died, so also is the Museon Arlaten with its exhibits of folk art.
The Museon fills several floors of a large sixteenth-century town house
at Arles, and was installed by the poet himself with money he gained
when awarded the Nobel Prize. 'My countrymen,' Mistral stormed on
meeting Sir Theodore Cook, 'are not slaves like the men of Nice and
Cannes who sell their soil to foreigners and to syndicates from Paris.' He
points to the fact that his people have kept their liberty and local
character. 'Fools prefer similitudes . . . the wiser man loves difference;
difference in dress, in speech, in life', and this Museon of his is a remarkable memorial to the poet's point of view. It covers every facet of
provincial life, even down to the country people's superstitions – a
string necklace of thirteen knots against strangulation, and peach
stones for happiness, and most of the exhibits bear carefully noted
labels written in faded ink, in Mistral's own hand. The Museon must
have taken him years to instal. On the top floor are drawings by Leo
Lelee who made a detailed study of the Arlésienne women. Strangely
enough, he is not in the Bénézet dictionary; an omission, for he has
done for Arles what Pancho Fierro, the Peruvian painter, did for the
women of Lima, those cyclopean creatures known as *tapadas* who
enveloped themselves in long petticoats, even covering the head,
leaving just one provocative eye with which to view the world. Lelee's
Arlésiennes are equally absorbing, and one feels that he must always
have had a notebook to hand. He draws them kneeling in church,
holding their skirts to cross the streets. One sees them marketing,
fanning themselves against the heat; and always he catches their
dignity, their straight backs and the proud turn of their heads. He has
also stylised them, painted them dancing in friezes across the litho-
graphed surface of posters; books carry their black silhouettes; he has
even marshalled their figures in profile on the border of plates.

This now brings us to the museums of the coast, most of them of
fairly recent origin, and for this reason, I feel, should be included before
taking leave of the reader. Of all the museums, the least often visited is

Les Collettes, Renoir's modest little villa at Cagnes-sur-Mer, which he built himself in his declining years when he was crippled with rheumatoid arthritis. He chose the site well. It sits on the heights opposite the village surrounded by old olives, and it is here that he would sit and paint, slipping his brush in between the fingers of his poor deformed hand. The rooms are simply arranged with a few pieces of the original furniture; some, even, are empty, and in the studio one can see his wheelchair and his palette. There are photographs, a few pieces of sculpture, but no paintings to speak of; yet despite this it is not a sad house. It is bathed in light, and there is a feeling of peace about the place. Renoir loved Les Collettes – 'In this wonderful country it seems that unhappiness cannot touch you; the atmosphere protects, like cotton wool.'[1] He painted without respite, flowers, fruit, his serving maids in the nude. His last words were about his work – '*J'ai fait encore du progrès*',* he murmured just before dying, referring, no doubt, to the unfinished canvas lying on his easel.

Amongst my own personal preferences, I would single out the Picasso museum at Antibes, and in particular the fascinating collection of plates beautifully exhibited in transparent cases invisibly attached to the rough cast walls of the castle. The collection comprises some forty-odd pieces and represents Picasso's early experiments with ceramics baked by him personally in Madura's kilns at Vallauris. They are wonderfully fresh and vigorous and, indeed, the museum is an experience not to be missed. Once a Grimaldi stronghold, the building sits flush with the ramparts of the old town, and immediately after the war its curator had the fortunate idea of lending Picasso the great empty rooms to work in. They are awash with refracted light from the sea, and Picasso with his bull-like energy started on a series of paintings depicting mythological creatures from the past, populating the airy whiteness with centaurs, nymphs and fauns; evocations of Antibes past. Canvas was not yet available, and he painted on great hardboard panels in light washes of blue, grey and almond-green, and on the back inscribed each one with the word *Antipolis*. The main hall of the museum, bare except for Picasso's panels and its colourless Venetian chandeliers, its windows opening onto the Mediterranean, is one of the most exciting museum rooms I know. It was a happy time in Picasso's life: he was with Françoise Gilot, his new love, and the place reflects his mood.

* 'I have progressed even further.'

It is not my intention to enumerate all the museums; Cocteau's frescoes in Villefranche's Chapelle St Pierre are a joke, and in still worse taste are his daubings in Menton's town hall. One's spirits lift again, however, when confronted with Matisse's beautiful stained-glass windows in Vence's Chapelle de St Marie du Rosaire, but how one wishes that they had pierced all the walls. Inspired also are the vestments, not usually shown unless a special permit is forthcoming from the mother superior. The paper cut-outs for these and the windows, worked on by Matisse when confined to his bed, are to be seen along with some fine drawings in the Matisse Museum at Cimiez; the whole collection a handsome gift to the town of Nice from the family. Two artists, Léger and Chagall, have the distinction of an individual museum in the region, the former at Biot and the latter newly opened at Cimiez. I have mixed feelings about the Maeght Foundation, disapprove of the José-Louis Serte building material and the somewhat fussy layout of the garden. There are, however, fine things to be seen in the permanent collection; for one, Calder's great black mobile under the pines, also Giacometti's gaunt figures striding across the inner courtyard: but if only they would leave them alone and not keep moving them. Another thing not to be missed is Braque's amethyst-coloured window in the little chapel, easily overlooked unless one knows where to find it. But, above all, as a parting gesture, I would again urge the visitor to pay a visit to the museum at Antibes: it will help eradicate the unfortunate impression left, for those who have seen it, of Picasso's posthumous exhibition of his last paintings – a bewildering array that remained up far too long in the great echoing halls of the palace of the popes at Avignon.

Notes

1 THE SOUTH OF FRANCE, A BIRD'S EYE VIEW

1 J.A.R. Pimlott, *The Englishman's Holiday*, Faber & Faber, London 1947.
2 J. Henry Bennet, MD, *Winter in the South of Europe*, John Churchill & Sons, London 1866.
3 William Scott, *The Riviera*, A. & C. Black, London 1907.
4 Doris Langley Moore, *Marie and the Duke of H*, Cassell, London 1966.
5 Paul de Ketchiva, *The Devil's Playground*, Sampson Low, London.
6 Calvin Tomkins, *Living Well is the Best Revenge*, Viking Press, New York 1971.

3 THE SURROUNDINGS

1 J. Henry Bennet, *Winter in the South of Europe*.
2 George Sand, 'Lettres d'un voyageur', written for the *Revue des Deux Mondes*.

4 THE CIRCLE WIDENS

1 A.N. Brangham, *The Naturalists' Riviera*, Phoenix House, London 1932.
2 O. Comerford-Casey, *Riviera Nature Notes*, Quaritch, London 1903.
3 I. and H. Chamberlain, *Common Objects of the Riviera*, London 1913.
4 E.B. Page and P.W. Kingsford, *The Master Chefs*, Edward Arnold, London 1971.
5 Ibid.

5 TO PEOPLE THE LANDSCAPE

1 Taken from Madame Balsan's memoirs as being more accurate than I can remember: *The Glitter and the Gold*, William Heinemann, London 1953.

6 MENTON MAN, LIGURIAN TRIBESMEN AND THE GREEKS

1 Norman Douglas, *Alone*, Chapman Hall, London 1921.
2 Charles Lenthéric, *The Riviera Ancient and Modern*, Fisher & Unwin, London 1895.
3 W.H. Bullock Hall, *The Romans on the Riviera*, Macmillan, London 1898.

7 MARIUS AND THE BATTLE OF POURRIÈRES

1 Sir Theodore Cook, *Old Provence*, two volumes, Rivingtons, London 1905.

8 THE COAST AND PROVENCE UNDER THE EMPIRE

1 W.H. Bullock Hall, *The Romans on the Riviera*.
2 Mary Darmesteter, 'Impressions of Provence', *Contemporary Review*, London 1892.
3 Charles Lenthéric, *La Grèce et l'Orient en Provence*, Paris 1878.

9 ST HONORAT

1 F.R. Hoare, translator, *The Western Fathers*, London 1954.
2 Guizot, *Histoire de la Civilization de France*, volume I, Paris.

10 SARACENS, CRUSADES AND THE MIDDLE AGES

1 Arnold Fleming, *The Troubadours of Provence*, Maclellan, Glasgow 1952.
2 J. A. Symonds, *The Renaissance in Italy*, Smith Elder and Co., London 1880.
3 William Dudley Foulke, translator, *Some Love Songs of Petrarch*, Oxford University Press 1915.
4 Abbé de Sade, *Mémoirs pour la vie de François Petrarch*, 1764.

11 THE PALACE OF THE POPES

1 Mary Darmesteter, 'Impressions of Provence', *Contemporary Review*, London 1892.
2 Charles Lenthéric, *Le Rhône Histoire d'un Fleuve*, Plon, Paris 1892.

3 Prosper Mérimée, *Notes d'un Voyage dans le Midi de la France*, Paris 1835.
4 Robert Doré, *L'Art en Provence*, Les Beaux Arts, Paris 1921.

14 THE EIGHTEENTH CENTURY

1 J.A.R. Pimlott, *The Englishman's Holiday*, Faber & Faber, London 1947.
2 The Rev. Hugh Macmillan, *The Riviera*, London 1885.
3 The Countess of Blessington, *The Idler in Italy*, Galignani, Paris 1839.
4 Sir Theodore Cook, *Old Provence*, volume II.
5 Constantia Maxwell, *The English Travellers in France 1698–1815*, Routledge, London 1932.
6 W. Cobbett, *Rural Rides*, London 1832.
7 Lieutenant-Colonel Pinkney, *Travels through the South of France in the Years 1807 and 1808*, London 1814.
8 Philip Thicknesse, *Observations on the Customs and Manners of the French Nation*, London 1766.
9 Augustus J.C. Hare, *The Rivieras*, London 1898.

16 A GROWING COLONY

1 Saqui (Directeur des Musées de la Ville de Nice, L'Eclaireur de Nice), editor, *Les Anglais dans le Comté de Nice et en Provence*, Nice 1934.
2 F. Bénézet, *Dictionnaire des Peintres, Sculpteurs, Dessinateurs et Graveurs*, Librairie Gründ, Paris 1950.
3 Sir Archibald Alison, *Travels in France*, London 1816.

17 THE INVALIDS

1 Thomas Robinson Woolfield, *Life at Cannes*, London 1890.
2 Pliny, Book V, in a letter.
3 J. Henry Bennet, *Winter in the South of Europe*.
4 William Chambers, *Wintering in Menton*, London 1870.
5 Edmond Strasburger, *Rambles on the Riviera*, translated from the German by Comerford-Casey, Fisher Unwin, London 1906.

18 THE NATURALISTS

1   O. Comerford-Casey, *Riviera Nature Notes.*
2   Edward Strasburger, *Rambles on the Riviera.*
3   Robert Standish, *The First of Trees*, Phoenix House, London 1960.

19   GARDENS ON THE RIVIERA

1   Thomas Robinson Woolfield, *Life at Cannes*, London 1890.
2   Margaret Maria Brewster, *Letters from Cannes and Nice*, London
    1857. Miss Brewster was the daughter of the famous 'natural
    philosopher', Sir David Brewster.
3   Augustus J.C. Hare, *The Rivieras.*

20 LORD BROUGHAM'S CANNES

1   Margaret Maria Brewster, *Letters from Cannes and Nice.*
2   Lord Brougham and Vaux, *Statesmen of the Time of George III*,
    volume III, London 1849.
3   Accounts from *Les Prisons de l'Etat dans le Midi de la France.*
4   *Journals of the Private Life and Conversations of the Emperor
    Napoleon at St Helena.*
5   A. W. Raitt, *Prosper Mérimée*, Eyre & Spottiswoode, London 1970.

21 THE RAILWAY AGE

1   Augustus J.C. Hare, *The Rivieras*, George Allen, London 1897.
2   Augustus J.C. Hare, *The Story of My Life*, London 1896.
3   W. Somerset Maugham, 'Augustus', *Cornhill*, winter 1949–50.
4   Malcolm Barnes, editor, *In My Solitary Life*, George Allen & Unwin,
    London 1953.

22   MADAME D'ANGLETERRE

1   David Duff, *Victoria Travels*, Frederick Muller, London 1970.
2   V. Mallet, editor, *Life with Queen Victoria: Letters from Court,
    1887–1901*, John Murray, London 1968.

23 MONTE-CARLO

1 Paul de Ketchiva, *The Devil's Playground*, Sampson Low, London 1934.
2 General Pierre Polovtsoff, *Monte-Carlo Casino*, Stanley Paul, London 1937. The figures date from the publication of the book, but are roughly applicable to the present time. For years General Polovtsoff was the president of the International Sporting Club.
3 Stéphen Liégeard, *La Côte d'Azur*, Librairies Imprimeries Réunies, Paris 1894.
4 Sir Osbert Sitwell, *The Scarlet Tree*, Macmillan, London 1946.
5 Henrick Sienkiewicz, *Sur la Côte d'Azur*, Librarie Universelle, Paris 1905.
6 Miss C.L.H. Dempster, *The Maritime Alps*, Longmans Green, London 1885.
7 Charles Graves, *Royal Riviera*, Heinemann, London 1957.

24 THE CIRCLE COMPLETED

1 Georges Rivière, *Renoir et ses Amis*, H. Floury, Paris 1921.

Index